COLLEGE
LAW
FOR BUSINESS

SIXTH EDITION

By

A. ALDO CHARLES, LL.B., D.Ed.
VIRGINIA BAR
PROFESSOR OF BUSINESS LAW
UNIVERSITY OF GEORGIA

Published by

**SOUTH-WESTERN
PUBLISHING
COMPANY**

CINCINNATI
CHICAGO
BURLINGAME, CALIF.
DALLAS
NEW ROCHELLE, N. Y.

L88

Copyright, © 1963

by

SOUTH-WESTERN PUBLISHING COMPANY

CINCINNATI, OHIO

All Rights Reserved

The text of this publication, or any
part thereof, may not be reproduced
in any manner whatsoever without permission in writing from the publisher.

Library of Congress Catalog Card Number: 63-11998

H668

Printed in the United States of America

PREFACE

The law is relatively stable. Changes in the law, either by legislative enactment or by judicial decision, are slow and gradual. For that reason, a revision of a textbook on business law need not be revolutionary. The primary need is to bring it up to date in the light of the changes that have been made. But writing a good textbook is like painting a good picture. The job is never complete. There is always the need to add a touch here and there to bring it as near as possible to perfection.

Many students in the field of business education tend to place a utilitarian value upon all knowledge. This tendency can be carried to extremes; but if one's goal is to achieve professional competency, case illustrations, case problems, and the instructor's lectures that clearly contribute to the students' professional growth add zest and interest to the course. A special effort has been made in this Sixth Edition to make the instructor's task easier. If a course arouses the students' interest and enthusiasm, the instructor receives and deserves the credit. The text can be only a tool. It is hoped this Sixth Edition will prove to be an even more efficient tool than the preceding editions.

The specific improvements in the Sixth Edition include a thoroughgoing revision of text material involving addition of legal concepts and principles heretofore not included, revision of illustrative cases, revision of end-of-chapter materials, introduction of preview questions and cases for each part of the book, expansion of the glossary, and revision of the supplementary materials—study reports, tests, and instructor's manual.

The significant development of the Uniform Commercial Code has been taken into account in the preparation of this edition of COLLEGE LAW FOR BUSINESS. Since so many states have adopted the Code, it becomes imperative for one to be familiar with the major provisions of the Code even though the state in which he resides has not adopted the Code, for he may find that he will be involved in business relations with those who live in states operating under the Code. In the text wherever the Code materially changes the present law, the change is discussed along with the old law.

The basic structure of the text remains the same as in the previous edition, but the topic "Termination of Contracts" has been expanded into two chapters. Likewise, the topic "Bills of Exchange" has been expanded into two chapters so that the subject of checks could be treated separately and more thoroughly.

Many of the questions at the end of each chapter have been revised. There has been an extensive revision of the case problems, approximately 50 percent of them being new. Similarly, there has been an extensive revision of the summary cases that are designed for review of the basic legal concepts in each part of the text.

A new feature of the Sixth Edition is an introduction to each part of the text through the vehicle of Preview Questions for Part 1 and Preview Cases for the other nine parts of the text. The questions and cases are designed to whet the appetite of the student, to challenge him, and to provide a general idea of the nature of the legal principles and problems he will be concerned with in his study of each part.

The glossary of legal terms has been expanded and revised. The terms that are included in the glossary have been selected because of their helpfulness to the beginning student. The glossary supplements terms that are defined and explained in the text.

The supplementary items for COLLEGE LAW FOR BUSINESS have been thoroughly revised and strengthened in order to provide student and instructor with even more helpful study and teaching devices.

The author acknowledges a debt of gratitude to those instructors who continue to share with him their experiences and helpful teaching aids. Their suggestions and comments are always welcomed. They make possible a quickened pace toward an ideal text.

The author also wishes to express his indebtedness to Arthur C. Stephens, formerly of the Detroit Business Institute, for his careful reading of the manuscript and for his helpful suggestions. The author also wishes to express appreciation to Charles H. Johnson, attorney at law, Madison, Wisconsin, formerly instructor of business law at Madison Business College, for his suggestions for improvement of the Sixth Edition.

A. A. C.

TABLE OF CONTENTS

Part 1. LAW AND ITS ENFORCEMENT

Part 2. CONTRACTS

Part 3. SALES

Part 4. BAILMENTS

Part 5. NEGOTIABLE INSTRUMENTS

PART 1

LAW AND ITS ENFORCEMENT

Preview Questions for Part 1: Law and Its Enforcement

What is law?

What is business law?

What is the common law?

What is equity law?

What is law by judicial decision?

What is constitutional law?

What is administrative law?

What is criminal law?

What is the function of a court?

What is the jurisdiction of a court?

What are the federal courts?

What are the state courts?

What are the functions of court officers?

What is the procedure for filing suit?

What is the basic procedure for trial?

How may an appeal be made from a decision?

These are some of the basic questions that are answered in the chapters constituting Part 1. For an introduction to Parts 2 to 10, you will be given a number of interesting preview cases. Preview questions and cases are designed to set the stage for your study of the many important areas of the law.

CHAPTER 1

INTRODUCTION TO LAW

DEFINITION OF LAW

Nothing so complex as law could be completely described in one short definition. Many authors have tried to define it, but none have excelled Blackstone's famous definition: *"Law* is a rule of civil conduct, commanding what is right and prohibiting what is wrong." There are many rules of civil conduct and there are many admonitions commanding what is right and condemning what is wrong, but rules and admonitions are not necessarily laws. Only when a sovereign state issues rules prescribing what is right and what is wrong can a rule be called a law. Even then rules would not be laws unless sanctions are applied when the rules are broken.

Religious teachings, the mores of society, habit, group pressures to conform—all contribute to social control of conduct, but only the rules of law are all-pervasive, applying with equal force to every member of society. A breach of some of these rules is a crime, and the sanction is a fine, a jail sentence, or both. The sanctions for the breach of the other rules of law are for the most part damages. Every deviation from prescribed rules of conduct has an appropriate penalty. *Business law* is concerned primarily with those rules of conduct prescribed by government for the performance of business transactions.

Law is an evolutionary process. The vast number of laws governing business transactions in America did not come into existence overnight. They are the result of man's changing concepts of what is right and what is wrong. For example, for several centuries in England and America one who owned land owned the soil and minerals below the topsoil and the air above the land "all the way to heaven." The law prohibited trespassing on one's land or in one's

3

air. A telephone company that wanted to string a telephone wire through one's air had to buy a right of way. When airplanes were invented, this law became a millstone about society's neck. By judicial decree the courts modified the rule or else a transcontinental airline would have to buy a right of way through the air of every property owner from New York to San Francisco. Our present laws are the result of man's reactions to changed circumstances. Law promotes stability, but it does not stagnate progress.

THE COMMON LAW

Every student of law must have some concept of the common law, its origin and development. In all nations having some form of representative democracy, the legislative department of the government is separate and distinct from the judicial department. It is fundamentally the function of the legislative department to enact the laws and the function of the judicial department to enforce the laws. *Common law* is in reality law as pronounced in court decisions. If we go back to the eleventh century in England, there were simply no statutory laws prescribing the proper rule of conduct in hundreds of business situations. If there were no statutory law governing the situation when a dispute was brought before the judge, the court prescribed a rule of its own. Over a period of several centuries, judge-made laws constituted the larger percentage of the law. The American Colonists brought judge-made laws to America. After America became a sovereign nation, most of these common laws were either enacted as statutory laws or continued as judge-made laws. Thus the common law is the source of much of our business law today.

EQUITY LAW

Equity law evolved somewhat in the same manner as the common law. In England by 1200 A.D. many common-law rules had been formulated. These rules were gradually formed into categories to which judges could refer to guide them in their decisions in particular cases. Uniformity in the common law spread throughout England because judges tended to decide cases the same way other judges had decided them in the past when the facts were similar. Emphasis developed upon the form of action so that after a few centuries, the form became more important than the law itself. The common law in its beginning was very flexible, too flexible to be called a law, but by the year 1500 A.D. it had gone to the other extreme and had become extremely rigid and inflexible.

In all social institutions man must strive to harmonize two conflicting desires—the desire for stability and the desire for liberty. Law must encourage the fulfillment of both desires. If stability is overemphasized, laws become so rigid and inflexible that many wrongs can exist for which there are no remedies. If law is so flexible that each judge is free to formulate his own law in each case, unbound by any rule except his own conscience, liberty is precarious. It is essential to both stability and liberty that the laws governing our social conduct be recorded, either in statutes or in judicial precedents that are honored by judges.

Some flexibility must be maintained so that when justice and equity demand it, the judge may decide a particular case, not by some rigid rule of law, but by what his conscience tells him ought to be done. This was the function of equity law in its beginning. The equity judges were the keepers of the king's conscience. In America today this is still the concept of equity law even though some rigidity has crept into it. The decision in each equity case is recorded and becomes a precedent in future cases of a similar nature. Lawyers cite these decisions in order to persuade an equity judge to render a similar decision in the case that is presently before the court.

Only a few states maintain separate equity or, as they are frequently called, Chancery Courts. The same judge hears both law and equity cases. If the law provides an adequate remedy for a dispute between two individuals, the case will be tried as a law case and in most instances as a jury trial. If the law does not provide an adequate remedy, the judge, sitting as an equity judge, will hear the case and decide it according to the rules of equity. A jury is seldom impaneled in equity cases.

LAW BY JUDICIAL DECISION

Along with the development of both the common law and equity law, many statutory laws were passed. In England as Parliament gained supremacy over the king, statutory law became the chief source of law. In America, most of our laws have been statutory laws from the beginning. Interpretation is an essential part of statutory law, common law, and equity law.

By its very nature, a statute has to be somewhat general. In their interpretations of the statutes, judges particularize statutes to individual cases. Interpretations by the various supreme courts become precedents and under the *doctrine of stare decisis* (stand by the decision) are binding upon all state courts below the supreme court of the state. Any state supreme court or the Supreme Court of the United States can reverse a decision of a lower court. If the law is to promote stability so that we can know what our rights are before we undertake a business transaction, the courts must adhere to the judicial precedents set by earlier decisions.

Law by judicial decision has not evolved in the same way the common law and equity law evolved. Law by judicial decision is the interpretation of an existing statute or common law; it is not the enunciation of a law itself out of the whole cloth. The interpretation, however, may be as important as the law itself. For example, the Sherman Antitrust Act is a statutory law passed by Congress. Its purpose was to promote competition in business by controlling the mergers of business firms designed to eliminate competing businesses. In interpreting the Act, the Supreme Court of the United States broadened it to cover primarily the formation of labor unions. The Clayton Act was then passed by Congress in an attempt to compel the Supreme Court to apply the Sherman Antitrust Act to combinations of business firms only, not to labor unions. This is one of the ways a law by judicial decision can be repealed. If the interpretation involves a section of the constitution, only an amendment of the constitution can repeal the law. The third way by which a law by judicial decision may be repealed is for the Supreme Court to reverse the decision in a later case.

CONSTITUTIONAL LAW

In a sense a constitution is not a law. A constitution lays down boundaries beyond which no law may go. No lawmaking body may pass a statutory law that is in conflict with the constitution. The United States Constitution is often called the supreme law of the land because the state constitutions as well as statutory law must not conflict with it. The Supreme Court of the United States is the final arbiter in disputes involving the constitutionality of any state or federal law. This court is also the final authority on whether or not any state constitution, or any part of a constitution, is in conflict with the federal Constitution.

ADMINISTRATIVE LAW

Many of our governmental functions today are carried on by means of administrative agencies set up by our legislative bodies. Because of the complex nature of our economic order, these boards and commissions must be given wide latitude in setting up rules of procedure. They are semi-judicial bodies even though they are an arm of the executive branch of the government. They issue orders and decrees that have the force of law.

STATUTES

Within the limitations fixed by the Constitution, lawmaking bodies may pass any law they deem desirable. These *statutes* constitute the most important source of law. Constitutions are difficult to amend and, for this reason, are not so responsive to the changing demands of the people. Statutory laws may be enacted, repealed, or amended at any regular or special session of the lawmaking body.

The three chief lawmaking bodies in the United States are the federal Congress, the state legislatures, and the city councils. The laws of the city councils are called *ordinances,* but an ordinance is properly called a statutory law. In the United States, if any law, whether federal or state, is in conflict with the federal Constitution, it is unconstitutional. If there is a conflict between a state law and a law of the United States passed by the United States Congress in accordance with the federal Constitution, the latter prevails.

In the field of business law the most important statutes are the uniform laws, such as the Uniform Sales Act and the Uniform Negotiable Instruments Law. The Uniform Commercial Code incorporates many of the uniform acts into one law or code.*

CRIMINAL LAW

Criminal law is that branch of the law which has to do with crimes and the punishment of wrongdoers. A *crime* is an offense of a serious nature that tends to injure society as a whole. Business law has to do with crimes only incidentally. There are, however, certain criminal offenses, such as arson, forgery, fraudulent conveyances, embezzlement, and the like, that are closely related to business activities.

---

* As of September, 1968, the Code had been adopted in every state except Louisiana. The Code has also been adopted in the Virgin Islands and for the District of Columbia.

Crimes are usually classified according to the nature of the punishment as felonies and misdemeanors. Generally speaking, *felonies* are the more serious crimes and are usually punishable by death or by imprisonment in a penitentiary. *Misdemeanors* are offenses of a less serious character, which are punishable by a fine, or by imprisonment in a county or local jail, or by both fine and imprisonment. Committing a forgery is a felony, but driving an automobile in excess of the prescribed speed limits is a misdemeanor. The criminal statutes define acts that are felonies and those that are misdemeanors.

QUESTIONS

1. What is meant by the *doctrine of stare decisis*?
2. What is a judge-made law?
3. Are judges as free today to decide cases according to their ideas of what is right as they were 100 years ago?
4. Why are we justified in classifying law by judicial decision as a source of law?
5. If a common law and a statutory law are in conflict, which one prevails?
6. Define equity law and show wherein it differs from common law.
7. If one party announces an intention to perform some act that will unlawfully deny another party his legal rights, what remedy does the innocent party have if he wishes to prevent the injury?
8. What is the legal effect of an order issued by an administrative agency?
9. Classify the following crimes into felonies and misdemeanors: murder, theft of 10 cents, drunkenness, robbery, overtime parking, and forgery.
10. What is business law?

CHAPTER 2

COURTS AND COURT PROCEDURE

FUNCTIONS OF THE COURTS

The function of a court is to declare and apply the common law and to enforce the laws passed by the legislative arm of the government. This is not the whole story, however. Constitutions by their very nature must be couched in generalities. The statutes passed by the lawmaking bodies are less general than constitutions but still must be made specific to apply to a particular court case. It is one of the chief functions of the courts to interpret and apply the law of whatever source in a given situation. For example, the federal Constitution gives the federal Congress power to regulate commerce among the several states. In conformity with this constitutional provision Congress passes a law to regulate interstate commerce.

A specific case involves the regulation of wage rates in a sawmill located in a rural section of the country. The court must decide whether or not this sawmill owner is engaged in interstate commerce. The court's decision may become a judicial precedent that will be followed in the future until the court changes its decision in a subsequent case.

JURISDICTION OF COURTS

A corporation's officials consist of a president, a vice-president, and many subordinate officials. Each individual has very definite authority in his limited field, with the authority broadening as one goes from the foreman up the scale to the president. To a certain extent courts follow a pattern, starting with justice-of-the-peace courts and extending up to the Supreme Court of the United States.

The power or authority which each court has to hear cases is called its *jurisdiction.* This jurisdiction may involve the subject matter of the case before the court. If the claim is for damages due to an automobile accident, a probate court will not have jurisdiction since this court deals with wills and the distribution of property of deceased persons to the heirs. A court may have jurisdiction over the subject matter but not over the person. If a resident of Buchanan County is charged with trespassing on his neighbor's property in the same county, the judge in adjoining Tazewell County does not have jurisdiction over the person of the accused. Nor does the judge in Buchanan County have jurisdiction over the person of the accused if the accused has not been properly served with notice of the trial. Before any court can try a case, it must first be established that it has jurisdiction over both the subject matter and the person in the case at issue.

CLASSIFICATION OF COURTS

Courts are classified for the purpose of determining their jurisdiction. This classification can be made in a variety of ways. One classification can be made according to the governmental unit setting up the court. In this sense they are classified as (1) federal courts, (2) state courts, and (3) municipal courts. The same courts may be classified according to the method of hearing cases. In this sense they are called trial courts and appellate courts. The *trial courts* conduct the original trial of the cases and render their decisions. The *appellate courts* review the cases appealed from the decisions of these trial courts.

The federal government and the states have a separate court structure, and this structure is best understood by classifying first the federal courts and second, the state courts.

FEDERAL COURTS

The federal courts are classified as:

1. Federal district courts
2. Federal courts of appeals
3. United States Supreme Court
4. Special federal courts

(1) Federal District Courts. By far the largest class of federal courts consists of the district courts. These courts are strictly trial courts in which are tried all criminal cases involving a violation of the federal law. The federal courts also have jurisdiction of civil suits which are brought (a) by the United States; (b) by citizens of the same state where the amount in controversy is $10,000 or more and arises under the Constitution, federal laws, and treaties; (c) between citizens of different states; and (d) between citizens of one state and a foreign nation or one of its citizens or subjects.

Also bankruptcy, IRS, Postal, copyright, patent, maritime, Nat Bank Assoc.

(2) Federal Courts of Appeals. The federal courts of appeals hear only appeals from a federal district court or from a state supreme court decision if the case involves a federal constitutional question. If one is convicted in a state court for "unlawfully distributing pamphlets," he may appeal to the state supreme court. If he loses in the state supreme court, he may next appeal to the federal court of appeals since the federal Constitution guarantees freedom of speech. If only the state constitution is involved, no right of appeal to a federal court exists.

(3) United States Supreme Court. For the most part, the United States Supreme Court hears only appealed cases from the federal courts of appeals. Under certain circumstances a decision of a federal district court may be appealed directly to the Supreme Court. The Supreme Court is the highest tribunal in the land, and its decision is final until the Court reverses its own decision or until the Congress changes the effect of a given decision by a constitutional amendment or by a legislative enactment. A decision of a federal court of appeals is binding upon all lower courts within the jurisdiction of that circuit court unless the Supreme Court reverses that decision. *Also hears Ambassadors, public ministers and case where the state is a Party.*

(4) Special Federal Courts. The special federal courts are limited in their jurisdiction by the laws of Congress creating them. For example, the Customs Court hears only cases involving the rates of duty on various classes of imported goods, the collection of the revenues, and similar controversies. The decisions of the Customs Court may be appealed to the Court of Customs Appeals. There is also a Claims Court to hear cases involving claims against the United States government. The government, being supreme, cannot be sued without its consent, but this consent is seldom withheld.

CONTROL OF APPEAL COURTS OVER LOWER COURTS

All federal courts derive their authority from the people, either through the Constitution or the Congress, but the appellate courts exercise considerable authority over the courts under them. A judicial trial calls for a verdict; and the basis for this verdict in all cases is the trial court's authority as set out by the Congress and the appellate courts. Rules for the admissibility of evidence, trial procedure, the manner of selecting the jury, and many other important matters are determined by the appellate courts. The district court must adhere strictly to these rules as well as those laid down by the Congress. Furthermore, the district court, which is the trial court, is bound by the decisions of the federal courts of appeals and the Supreme Court in cases where the facts are substantially the same.

One can say that the Constitution gave the Supreme Court authority to exercise authority over any inferior courts which Congress might establish and that the Supreme Court gave the federal courts of appeals the power to exercise authority over the federal district courts, subject to review by the Supreme Court.

CLASSIFICATION OF STATE COURTS

State courts can best be classified into the following groups:

1. Inferior courts
2. Courts of original general jurisdiction
3. State supreme courts
4. Special courts

(1) **Inferior Courts.** The inferior courts of the states hear only minor disputes between citizens and minor criminal offenses. In the counties and smaller towns the most common inferior court is the justice-of-the-peace court. A justice of the peace hears all claims between citizens up to the maximum fixed by the state, usually $500 or less. In addition, he may try all criminal cases involving misdemeanors. In the cities the function of the justice of the peace may be performed by the mayor, small claims courts, and police courts. The loser in any of these courts may appeal to the court of original general jurisdiction.

(2) **Courts of Original General Jurisdiction.** Courts of original general jurisdiction are for the average citizen the most important

courts of the state. These courts have broad general jurisdiction involving disputes between two or more parties as well as criminal offenses against the state. They are called *courts of original jurisdiction* because it is in them that the case is first instituted. They hear appeals from inferior courts, but this does not make them appellate courts since the trial is conducted *de novo*, that is, as though it had never been instituted in the inferior courts. An official, permanent record is kept of the trial showing the testimony, evidence, statements of counsel and the judge, the judgment, and the findings of the court. For this reason these courts are often referred to as trial courts and courts of record. The official name of such a court in most states is Circuit Court.

Circuit court, then, is the official name given to a court of record, a trial court, or a court of original general jurisdiction.

If the defendant in a criminal case, or both parties in a civil suit, are satisfied that the decision of the trial court is in accordance with the law and the evidence, the controversy ends here.

(3) State Supreme Courts. In all states provision is made for an appeal to an appellate court by the party dissatisfied with the final judgment of the trial court, or any of its rulings and instructions. Only a court which hears appeals from a trial court is an appellate court. Usually the name of such a court is State Supreme Court.

(4) Special Courts. Many states have special courts, such as *probate courts* to probate wills; *juvenile courts* to try cases when children, usually under fourteen years of age, are charged with a crime; and *domestic relations courts* to hear cases involving disputes between husbands and wives. These are not courts of general jurisdiction, but of special jurisdiction. In many states these courts are of the same level as the trial courts. When this is the case, they, too, are properly called trial courts and courts of record. In other states they are on the same level as the inferior courts and are not courts of record.

If a case that is tried in a trial court involves a federal constitutional issue, then it may, after reaching the state supreme court, be appealed to a federal court of appeals. It may in turn be further appealed to the United States Supreme Court. For example, if a man is tried and convicted in a circuit court for illegally distributing printed leaflets, he may appeal to the state supreme court on the ground that this violates his freedom of speech as guaranteed by the federal Constitution. If the state supreme court rejects his appeal, he is then permitted to take an appeal to a federal court of appeals, and finally to the United States Supreme Court. If only a state law or the state constitution is involved, however, he cannot appeal to a federal court.

COURT OFFICERS

The chief officer of an inferior court is the *justice of the peace*, trial justice, or similar officer; while the executive officer is the *constable*. In a state court of record the chief officer is the *judge*, the executive officer is the *sheriff*, and the recorder is the *clerk of the court*. This is also true of the federal courts except that the executive officer is called a *marshal*.

Persons who are educated in the profession of the law and who are legally qualified to practice law are known as *lawyers* or *attorneys*. They are officers of the court and are subject to punishment for a breach of duty. Lawyers ordinarily represent the parties in a civil or a criminal action, although many states permit the parties to a case to conduct their own trial. The practice of conducting one's own trial, however, is usually not advisable.

PROCEDURE IN FILING SUIT

Courts with but few exceptions are powerless to settle disputes between individuals unless one of the parties petitions the court. This petition or complaint is the beginning of a civil suit. The one who institutes the action is called the *plaintiff*, and the one against whom action is brought is called the *defendant*. The order of events in bringing an action is generally as follows:

(1) The complaint or petition is filed with the clerk of the court. This petition sets forth the nature of the claim and the remedy sought.

(2) As soon as the petition is filed, the clerk issues a *summons* or, as it is sometimes called, a *process*. This merely summons the defendant to appear in court and file his answer to the petition. The complaint and the answer constitute the first pleadings or attempts to join issue. Before the case can be placed before a jury, the issue or issues of the suit must be clearly specified through these preliminary pleadings, answers, and motions.

(3) The jury is impaneled and the trial opens.

TRIAL PROCEDURE

The trial proceeds in the following order:

(1) The attorney for the plaintiff makes an opening statement to the jury indicating the nature of the action and what he expects to prove. This is usually followed by the opening statement of the defendant's attorney.

(2) The plaintiff presents his evidence in the form of witnesses and documents. This is followed by the defendant's evidence.

(3) The attorney for each side summarizes the evidence and argues his points in an attempt to win the jury to his version of the case.

(4) The judge instructs the jury as to the points of law which govern the case. The judge has the sole power to determine the points of law, and the jury decides what weight is to be given to each point of evidence except that it cannot disregard undisputed evidence.

(5) The jury adjourns to the jury room and in secret arrives at its *verdict*. This verdict may be set aside by the court if it is contrary to the law and the evidence. Unless this is done, the judge renders judgment in accordance with the verdict.

APPEALS

If either the plaintiff or the defendant is dissatisfied with the jury's verdict and the court's judgment, he may appeal to the state supreme court. When an appeal is taken, a complete transcript of the trial is printed and the state supreme court reviews the entire proceedings. The attorney for each side files a brief setting forth the reasons which warrant the supreme court in either affirming or reversing the judgment of the lower court. If this action is the first time that the legal issue involved has been passed upon by the supreme court, the decision of this court becomes a *judicial precedent* and is binding upon all lower courts in the state. The supreme court may, however, reverse itself in a future case. This is seldom done unless the personnel of the court changes, and even then, reversals seldom occur.

QUESTIONS

1. What is the function of a court?
2. Which is the most specific—a constitution, a statutory law, or a court decision?

3. A corporation located in Alabama commits an act in Alabama that is illegal in Georgia. Does a Georgia court have jurisdiction over the Alabama corporation?

4. (a) Name the largest class of federal courts.
   (b) Name two special federal courts.

5. If the Supreme Court of the United States declares a law unconstitutional, how may that decision be changed?

6. Is a decision of a state supreme court binding upon all the lower courts in that state?

7. Name the court in which the following disputes would be settled: (a) a dispute over the interpretation of a will; (b) a claim for an unpaid bill of $10; (c) the claim of a wife that her husband refuses to support her; (d) a damage suit for $2,500; (e) an appeal from the decision in the preceding suit; and (f) a claim against the federal government.

8. Who are the officers of a court?

9. (a) What is the first step in bringing a civil suit?
   (b) What is the first step in a civil suit after the jury is impaneled and the trial opens?

10. Smith sues Jones for $5,000, and the jury renders a verdict for $3,000. May either or both of these parties appeal this decision?

PART 2

CONTRACTS

Preview Cases for Part 2: Contracts

- Dewey was employed by Harmon to work as a carpenter on Harmon's house for $16 for one day's work. On each of the following four days, Dewey worked at Harmon's house, but Harmon made no effort to stop him. Must Harmon pay Dewey for the additional four days of work?

- Hall and Karl were rowing in a boat. The boat overturned. Hall could not swim. He called to Karl, "I will give you my sports car if you will save me." Karl risked his life to save Hall. Later Hall refused to give Karl the car. Is he obligated to do so?

- Hoover offered by letter to sell Harrell a new car for $209. Harrell accepted by letter immediately. The true price was $2,009, but the typist erred in writing up the offer. Could Harrell hold Hoover to the offer?

- Harold purchased a used car from Jarvis. He gave a check for $300 in payment. The check was a bad check, and Jarvis threatened to prosecute Harold. Later he said to Harold, "If you will buy a new car for $2,200 cash, I will refrain from prosecuting you." Harold accepted the offer but later wished to avoid the contract. Does he have the right to do so?

- Sanders, a minor, owned and operated a service station. In this capacity he purchased gasoline, tires, and other merchandise amounting to $3,000. He was sued for this amount, and his station was sold to satisfy the debt. There still remained a balance of $350 unpaid after the proceeds of the sheriff's sale were applied on the debt. Must Sanders pay the balance of $350?

- Arnold and Goodnoe form a contract with Alwine agreeing to sell Goodnoe 10,000 shares of stock one month from date at $42 a share. They do not intend actually to buy and sell the stock, but they do agree to settle for the difference between $42 a share and the closing price on the date fixed in the contract. Is the contract valid?

- McClellan orally promised Henrietta to deed his home to her if she would marry him. After the marriage, McClellan refused to deed the property to Henrietta. Is McClellan legally obligated to do so?

These preview cases are designed to serve as a springboard for the study of this part. As you read through each chapter in this part, you will find the actual decisions for all these preview cases. Of course, there are many more such illustrative problems as well as case problems for decision at the end of each chapter. And there are also a number of even more challenging cases for review at the end of the part.

CHAPTER 3

CONTRACTS—NATURE
AND CLASSES

DEFINITION OF A CONTRACT

A *contract* can be defined as an agreement between two or more persons that is enforceable at law. At first glance this seems like a very simple definition. In reality Chapters 4-9 are devoted exclusively to explaining and clarifying this definition. Making contracts is such an everyday occurrence that we are often inclined to overlook their importance, except when they are of substantial nature. When one buys a cup of coffee during a "coffee break," he has made a contract. When the purchaser agrees to pay ten cents for the coffee, the seller agrees not only to supply one cup of coffee but also agrees by implication of law that it is safe to drink. If the coffee contains a harmful substance that makes the purchaser ill, there has been a breach of contract that may call for the payment of damages.

Business transactions are the result of agreements. Every time a person makes a purchase, buys a theater ticket, or boards a bus, an agreement is made. Each party to the agreement obtains certain rights and assumes certain duties and obligations. When such an agreement meets all the legal requirements of a contract, the law recognizes it as binding upon all parties. If one of the parties to the contract breaches it by failing or refusing to perform, the law allows the other party an appropriate action for obtaining damages or enforcing performance by the party breaching the contract. It is evident, then, that contracts form the very foundation upon which all modern business rests.

Business consists almost entirely of the making and performing of contracts. Business is conducted for profit, and valid, enforceable contracts are the source of this profit. Good contracts are made by people who understand the law of contracts.

CONTRACTS CONTRASTED WITH AGREEMENTS

A contract must be an agreement, but an agreement is not necessarily a contract. Whenever two or more persons' minds meet upon any subject, no matter how trivial, there is an agreement. It is only when the parties intend to be obligated by the terms of the agreement that a contract comes into existence. In addition, the subject matter of the contract must involve a business transaction as distinguished from a social transaction.

- Mary and John promise to meet at a certain place at six o'clock and have dinner together. This is an agreement, not a contract, since neither is legally bound to carry out the terms of the agreement.

  If John says to Mary, "I will pay you $10 to type this manuscript for me," and Mary replies, "I will accept your offer," the agreement results in a contract. Mary is legally obligated to type the manuscript, and John is legally bound to pay the $10.

CLASSIFICATION OF CONTRACTS

Contracts are often referred to by many names or terms. Unless these terms are understood, the law cannot be understood. For example, the law may state that executory contracts made on Sunday are void. This law cannot be understood unless one clearly understands the words "executory" and "void." For this reason one must study classification of contracts before he studies contracts. Every contract may be placed in one or more of the following classifications:

1. Express and implied contracts
2. Valid, void, and voidable contracts
3. Formal and informal contracts
4. Executory and executed contracts
5. Unilateral and bilateral contracts

(1) **Express and Implied Contracts.** When contracts are classified according to the manner of their formation, they fall into two groups—express and implied contracts. An *express contract* is one in which the parties express their intentions definitely, whether in writing or orally, at the time they make the agreement. Both their intention to contract and the terms of the agreement are expressly stated.

- Kemp by letter offers to purchase a particular typewriter for $300, and Sampson by letter accepts Kemp's offer. This is an express contract. An analysis of the contract, however, shows that many essential parts have been omitted. Is this a cash sale or a credit sale?

When is delivery to be made? Since nothing is said about credit, it is implied that Kemp will pay cash. The seller implied he would deliver the typewriter within a reasonable time. That which is customary need not be expressed in an express contract.

An *implied contract* is one in which the duties and the obligations which the parties assume are not expressed but are implied by their acts or conduct. The adage "A man's actions speak louder than his words" very appropriately describes this class of contract. The parties may indicate so clearly by their conduct what they intend to do that there is no need to express the agreement by words to make it binding.

- Dewey was expressly employed by Harmon to work as a carpenter on Harmon's house for $16 for one day's work. The next day Dewey reported for work again. He worked for four days after the first day and Harmon made no effort to stop him. Harmon must pay Dewey for five days of work at $16 a day. They had an express contract for the first day Since essentially the same relationship continued for four more days, each party implied by his actions that the terms of the express contract would apply to the four days for which they had no express contract.

(2) **Valid, Void, and Voidable Contracts.** If one wishes to classify contracts according to their enforceability, then all contracts would be valid, void, or voidable.

A *valid contract* is one that will be enforced by the courts upon a plea by one of the parties. In order to be enforceable, that is, valid, a contract must fulfill the following definite requirements:

(a) It must be based upon a mutual agreement by the parties to do or not to do a specific thing.

(b) It must be made by parties who are, according to law, able and competent to enter into a contract that will be enforceable against both parties.

(c) It must include consideration (such as the payment of money, the delivery of goods, or the promise to do or refrain from doing some lawful future act) given by each party to the contract.

(d) It must be for a lawful purpose; that is, the purpose of the contract must not be illegal, such as the unauthorized buying and selling of narcotics.

(e) It must, if it falls into a class of contracts required by law to be in a special form, meet the requirements of the law as to that form.

These five requirements are the criteria by which one may test the validity of any contract. If the agreement fails to meet one or more of these requirements, the contract may be void or voidable but never valid. A layman can, in most instances, analyze all business transactions in the light of these five requirements to ascertain their enforceability.

A contract that is of no legal effect is a *void contract*. Since there is no contract in the first place, the agreement is not enforceable in a court of law and thus does not come within the definition of a contract. The term "void contract," however, is widely used by the legal profession and must be understood. A void contract must be distinguished from an *unenforceable contract*. If the law requires a certain contract to be in a particular form, such as a deed, and it is not in that form, it is merely unenforceable, not void; but it can be made enforceable by changing the form to meet the requirements of the law. An agreement between two parties involving an illegal act is a void contract. Nothing the parties can do will make it enforceable.

A *voidable contract* is one that may be set aside by at least one of the parties. Basically, a voidable contract is an enforceable agreement; but, because of circumstances or the capacity of one party, it may be set aside by one of the parties. The test of a voidable contract is the existence of a choice by one party to abide by or to reject the contract. A contract made by an adult with a person not of lawful age (legally known as a minor or infant) is often voidable so far as the minor is concerned. It is enforceable against the adult but not against the minor. If both parties to an agreement are minors, either one may avoid the agreement. Until the party having the choice to avoid the contract exercises his right to set the contract aside, the contract remains in full force and effect.

(3) Formal and Simple Contracts. A contract under seal is a *formal contract*. In olden days when very few men could write, contracts were signed by means of an impression in wax. As time passed, a small wafer pasted on the contract replaced the use of wax. The wafer seal was in addition to the written signature. This practice is still used occasionally, but the more common practice is to sign formal contracts in one of these ways:

John Doe (Seal); John Doe [L. S.]; John Doe **(SEAL)**

In jurisdictions where the use of the seal has not been abolished, the seal implies consideration and gives validity to the contract. However, in most states today only a few types of contracts require the use of the seal, the most common being corporate contracts and deeds.

Today many contracts are made formal by the parties to them even though their enforceability does not depend upon their being formal. Bonds and deeds are virtually the only contracts required by most states to be formal. But in many states if any contract is made formal, even though the law does not require it to be formal, some added significance is attached to it. In Virginia a note under seal has a longer life than a note not under seal. A person has five years from the date of the note in which to sue for its collection if the note is not under seal. Some states make no distinction between contracts under seal and other written contracts.

All contracts other than formal contracts are informal and are called *simple contracts*. A few of these, such as an agreement to sell land or to be responsible for the debt of another, must be in writing in order to be enforceable; otherwise they need not be prepared in any particular form. Generally speaking, informal or simple contracts may be in writing, may be oral, or may be implied from the conduct of the parties.

A *written contract* is one in which the terms are set forth in writing rather than expressed orally. The law requires some contracts not only to be in writing but also to be in a particular form. Among important contracts of this nature are negotiable instruments discussed in Chapter 20.) Some writers classify these as formal contracts because of their required form. The more common practice is to restrict the definition of formal contracts to those contracts that are in writing and under seal.

An *oral contract* is one in which the terms are stated in spoken, not written, words. Such a contract is usually enforceable, but it is not so satisfactory as a written contract. When a contract is oral, disputes may arise between the parties as to the terms of the agreement. No such disputes need arise about the terms of a written contract if the wording is clear, explicit, and complete. For this reason most businessmen avoid making oral contracts involving matters of considerable consequence.

(4) Executory and Executed Contracts. Contracts are classified to indicate the stage of performance as executory contracts and executed contracts. An *executory contract* is one the terms of which have not been fully carried out by all parties. If a man agrees to work for another for one year in return for a salary of $300 a month, the contract is executory from its inception until the twelve months expire. Even if the employer should prepay the salary, it would still be an executory contract because the other party has not yet worked the entire year, that is, executed his part of the contract.

An *executed contract* is one that has been fully performed by all parties to the contract. The Collegiate Shop sells and delivers a suit to Benson for $60, and Benson pays the purchase price at the time of the sale. This is an executed contract because nothing remains to be done on either side, that is, each party has completed performance of his part of the contract.

(5) Unilateral and Bilateral Contracts. A contract that contains a promise in consideration for an act is a *unilateral contract*. If Smith loans Johnson $1,000 and Johnson promises to repay the loan in 90 days, this would be a unilateral contract. It is unilateral in the promise made. Johnson promises to pay Smith for his act of loaning him $1,000. A *bilateral contract* consists solely of a mutual exchange of promises to perform some future acts—one promise is the consideration for the other promise. If Brown promises to sell a truck to Adams for $500 and Adams agrees to pay $500, then the parties have exchanged a promise for a promise—a bilateral contract.

QUESTIONS

1. Name the five requirements of a valid contract.
2. Would it be possible to conduct a business of any size if it were not for the law of contracts?
3. Would property have much value without the law of contracts?
4. May a contract be partly implied?
5. Relative to the enforceability of contracts, name the three groups into which they are classified. Define and give an example of each group.
6. Define:
   (a) a unilateral contract
   (b) a bilateral contract
7. (a) Illustrate three ways by which one may indicate that a contract is under seal.
   (b) Does a seal add anything of importance to a contract?
8. Is an oral contract usually just as valid as a written contract?
9. If one has ten witnesses to an oral contract, can he enforce it if the contract is required by law to be in writing to be enforceable?
10. (a) Define an executory contract.
    (b) If one party to a contract has executed his part but the other party has not, is the contract properly termed an executory contract?

CASE PROBLEMS

1. John and Henry agree to go on a hunting trip, starting the next day at 6 a.m. John purchased a gun, some shells, and a hunting outfit. The following day Henry called John and told him he had changed his mind and would not go hunting. Does this agreement have all the elements of a valid contract?

2. Gentry owned a home in Augusta. Hall promised to build Gentry a fallout shelter under his house for $700. Gentry agreed to pay $100 before the work started and to pay the balance upon completion of the shelter. Hall agreed to have the job completed within two weeks.

    (a) Is this an express contract or an implied contract?
    (b) Is it void, voidable, or valid?
    (c) Is it executed or executory?
    (d) Is it formal or informal?
    (e) Is it unilateral or bilateral?

3. In a certain state all executory contracts made on Sunday are void. Bell purchased a pair of shoes from Reese on Sunday, had them wrapped, and paid for them but asked Reese to hold them until Tuesday for him. On Tuesday he refused to take the shoes and demanded a return of his money. To determine the rights of the parties it was necessary to classify this contract. Was it an executed contract or an executory contract?

4. Harper was a real estate broker. He entered into a contract with Cohen to sell Cohen's house for $22,500. Harper was to pay Cohen a commission of 5 percent "when the sale is consummated." The law required all contracts for the sale of land to be formal. Must this contract be formal to be enforceable?

5. Morehead, a minor, purchased a suit from Jensen for $75. Jensen, as a part of the sales price, agreed to alter the suit to fit. When the suit was ready, Morehead refused to take it and pay for it. (a) Since a minor is liable only on his executed contracts for necessaries, was he within his legal right in refusing to purchase it? (b) If your answer to the question above was yes, state how Jensen might have made this a valid contract at the time the agreement was made.

6. Isabella was invited to a formal dance. Her mother engaged Mrs. Schwartz to make an evening dress for Isabella for $150. After the dress was finished but before it was delivered, Isabella's boy friend canceled the invitation. Her mother then refused to accept and pay for the dress, claiming the transaction was a social obligation, not a business transaction. Do you agree with this interpretation?

CHAPTER 4

OFFER AND
ACCEPTANCE

MUTUAL AGREEMENTS

Usually there can be no valid contract unless the minds of the contracting parties are in complete accord. This accord is achieved by means of an acceptable offer and an unqualified acceptance of this offer. In other words, there must be a meeting of minds before a contract can come into existence.

The parties may expressly state, either orally or in writing, what they agree to do, or they may indicate their intentions by their actions. The innermost thoughts of a person's mind can be known only to himself. If his conduct reasonably leads another person to believe that the party intends to enter into a binding contract, then that party is bound as effectively as if he had expressed his intentions. In business, seldom does one indicate his full intentions solely by his acts. In most cases he expressly states a part of the contract and implies the other part.

Furthermore, one may have a contract imposed on him by law. This will be done only when a failure to do so would result in an unjust enrichment of one person at the expense of another. For example, suppose a tenant is obligated to pay rent of $50 a month but by mistake hands the landlord $100. The law requires the landlord to return the overpayment of $50 on the basis of a quasi-contract obligation, that is, the law creates an agreement for repayment even though no agreement exists. For the landlord to keep the money would mean that he would be unjustly enriched at the expense of the tenant.

Two essential elements of a contract are: (1) an offer, either expressed or implied; and (2) an acceptance, either expressed or implied.

THE OFFER

The beginning of a contract is the offer made by the offeror to the offeree. The *offeror* is the person who makes the offer; the *offeree* is the person to whom the offer is made. An *offer* expresses the willingness of the offeror to enter into a contractual agreement. There are three tests of an offer:

1. The offer must be definite
2. It must be seriously intended
3. It must be communicated to the offeree

(1) **The Offer Must Be Definite.** A contract will not be enforced unless the court can ascertain the intentions of the parties. The offeror's intentions are ascertained from the offer, and this cannot be done unless the offer is definite.

> ▪ Harold wrote to Davis as follows: "I will lease your building at 564 Main Street, alterations and floor layout to be mutually agreed upon." Davis accepted the offer, but Harold changed his mind and refused to lease the building. There was no contract because the expression "to be mutually agreed upon" is too indefinite. Harold would not be bound even though Davis agreed to make any alterations Harold wanted. The offer must be specific from the beginning.

The Uniform Commercial Code modifies this strict rule somewhat for sales contracts. It is not always practical for a businessman to make an offer for the sale of merchandise that is definite as to price. The offer may call for the price to fluctuate or to be fixed by a third party. This would be considered a definite offer. Furthermore, an offer to sell is an acceptable offer under the Uniform Commercial Code even if the offeror states no price. In this case, the court would fix a reasonable price.

(2) **The Offer Must Be Seriously Intended.** One may make an offer in jest, banter, fear, or extreme anger; and if this fact is known or should be known by the offeree because of the surrounding circumstances, no contract is formed. A business transaction is ordinarily not entered into in jest or because of extreme fear or anger, and the offeree has no right to think that the offer is seriously intended when it is made under these circumstances. There are times, however, when the offer is not seriously intended, but the offeree has no way of knowing this. In that event such an offer may be accepted. This is the exception, however, not the general rule. In the two examples that follow these points are illustrated:

- Hall and Karl were rowing in a boat. The boat overturned. Hall could not swim. He called to Karl, "I will give you my sports car if you will save me." Karl risked his own life to save Hall. Hall refused to give Karl the sports car. He was within his rights. An offer made under extreme emotional circumstances is not an acceptable offer.

As previously noted, the innermost thoughts of the parties are not the controlling factors. If the offeree with reason thinks that the offer is made in earnest and accepts it, a binding contract will result even though the offer is made in jest.

- Hendler in a serious manner offered Knapp a painting worth $250 for $10. Knapp, being a poor judge of the value of paintings, accepted the offer. Hendler contended that he had made the offer just as a prank to see if Knapp appreciated the value of the painting. Since there was no circumstance or act on Hendler's part to indicate that the offer was made in jest, Knapp was reasonable in believing that the offer was seriously made.

(3) The Offer Must Be Communicated to the Offeree. Even if the offer is definite and is seriously intended, it is still not an acceptable offer until it has been communicated to the offeree. If one writes out an offer and the offer falls into the hands of the offeree without the knowledge or consent of the offeror, it cannot be accepted. Furthermore, an oral offer directed to a specific individual or firm cannot be accepted by anyone else. This is true because one has a right to choose the people with whom he deals.

- Henderson wrote Miller offering to sell him his stock in an oil company. Before Henderson mailed the letter, he heard on the radio that the company had struck oil. Miller also heard the news. Miller called Henderson on the phone and orally accepted the offer, since he had learned of the unmailed letter from Henderson's secretary. There was no contract since the offer was never communicated to the offeree.

INVITATIONS TO MAKE OFFERS

In business many apparent offers are not true offers. They are instead treated as invitations to the public to make offers at certain terms and prices. If the invitation is accepted by a member of the public and an offer is submitted embodying all the terms set out in the invitation, the offer may be rejected. The most common types of general invitations are advertisements, window displays, catalogs, price lists, and circular sales letters. If a merchant displays in his store window a suit for $65, he is not bound to sell at this price. Most businessmen consider this a very poor business policy, but it is nevertheless the law.

- The Denny Shoe Store placed a pair of shoes with a price tag of $8.95 in the store window. Stephen saw the shoes and offered to purchase them at that price. Denny claimed the price was in error. It should have been $18.95. There was no contract since the window display was a mere invitation to Stephen to make an offer.

The general rule is that a circular sales letter is not an offer but an invitation to the recipient to make an offer. It is often difficult, however, to distinguish between a general sales letter and a personal sales letter. The fact that the letter is addressed to a particular individual does not make it a personal sales letter. One may extend an invitation to make an offer even in a personal sales letter. If the wording is such as to indicate that the writer is merely trying to evoke an offer on certain terms, this is not an offer but an invitation to the other party to make such an offer.

- Landis wrote Hall: "If I were offered $20,000 for my house, I would be delighted to sell." Hall wrote immediately accepting the offer. There was no contract. Hall's acceptance was an acceptance of the invitation to make an offer.

Under special circumstances advertisements may also be offers. This is primarily true with advertisements that offer rewards.

- Foster placed the following ad in the newspaper: "I will pay $1,000 to anyone giving information leading to the arrest and conviction of the person who set fire to my property." Brewer saw the ad and set out to find the guilty party. As a result of Brewer's information, Dunnaway was arrested and tried. There was strong circumstantial evidence of his guilt, but the jury acquitted him. Brewer demanded his $1,000. Foster did not have to pay because his ad laid down two conditions, namely, that the guilty party be "arrested" and "convicted." Since Dunnaway was not convicted, Foster did not have to pay.

DURATION OF THE OFFER

When an offer is once sent out, a large number of laws come into play. Ignorance of any one of them may seriously affect one's rights. Here is a summary of the more important ones:

(1) The offeror may revoke an offer any time prior to its acceptance.

(2) Some offers contain what is known as an *option* to hold the offer open for a specified period of time. If this option is gratuitous, then it is not binding on the offeror, and he may revoke the offer before the expiration of the time specified. If the offeree, however, gives something of value, called a *consideration*, to the offeror for the option, then the offeror does not have the right to revoke the offer until the time allowed expires.

(3) A revocation of an offer must be communicated to the offeree prior to the acceptance. Mere intention to revoke is not sufficient.

- Davis wrote the Towns Tire Company offering to lease them a building for five years for $400 a month. He gave thirty days to accept or reject the offer. Ten days later Davis leased the building to the Bell Tire Company and the Towns Tire Company learned of this lease. This revoked the offer to the Towns Tire Company as it is irrelevant how the revocation is communicated to the offeree.

(4) An offer is revoked by the lapse of a reasonable length of time before the acceptance. What is a reasonable length of time varies with each case depending on the circumstances. It may be ten minutes in one case and sixty days in another.

- A New Orleans cotton broker wrote the Gulf Textile Company as follows: "Because of the unstable world conditions, I am anxious to dispose of my stock of cotton. I will take $165 a bale f.o.b. New Orleans." The Gulf Textile Company waited 25 days and then accepted. The offer had lapsed since its wording clearly indicated that the offeror wanted an immediate reply.

(5) Death or insanity of the offeror automatically revokes the offer by operation of law. This is true even though the offeree is not aware of the death or the insanity of the offeror at the time he accepts. Both parties must be competent to contract at the moment the acceptance is properly communicated to the offeror or his agent.

- Dean wrote Denny offering to sell Denny 1,000 shares of stock for $18,000. A few days later Dean was fatally injured in an automobile accident. Denny, unaware of Dean's death, accepted the offer. There was no contract because Dean's death revoked the offer.

(6) A few states retain the common-law rule that an offer made under seal for a specified period of time could not be revoked until the time specified elapsed. New York goes further and includes any written option offer on the theory that the writing or the seal is a consideration. Most states hold that the consideration must be either money or something having monetary value.

(7) Rejection of an offer or counteroffer terminates the offer.

THE ACCEPTANCE

When an offer has been properly communicated to the party for whom it is intended, and that party, or someone authorized to act for him, accepts, a binding contract is formed. The minds of the parties have met. No formal procedure is required for this acceptance. The acceptance may be made by words, oral or written, or by some act which clearly shows an intention to accept. Silence does not, except in rare cases, constitute an acceptance; nor is a mental intention to accept sufficient. The acceptance must be made in the manner, at the place, and within the time limit stipulated in the offer.

COUNTEROFFERS

An offer must be accepted without any deviation in the terms of the offer. If the intended acceptance varies or qualifies the offer, this is a *counteroffer* and is a rejection of the original offer. This counteroffer may be accepted or rejected by the original offeror.

- Dale wrote Williams as follows: "I will sell you my insurance agency for $15,000." Williams replied by letter: "I accept your offer with the understanding you will agree not to enter the insurance business again in this town for two years." This was a counteroffer and thus a rejection of the original offer.

INQUIRIES NOT CONSTITUTING REJECTION

The offeree may make an inquiry without rejecting the offer. For example, if the offer is for 1,000 shares of stock for $10,000 cash, the offeree may inquire as follows: "Would you be willing to wait thirty days for $5,000 and hold the stock as collateral security?" This is a mere inquiry and is not a rejection of the offer. If the inquiry is answered in the negative, the original offer may still be accepted, provided it has not been revoked in the meantime. This is not true of counteroffers.

If the general price level is either rising or falling rapidly, or if the price of the particular item is subject to a rapid fluctuation in price, the lapse of a relatively short period of time before an offer is accepted may constitute a rejection of the offer. A good example of this is found in the sale of stocks. An offer to sell U. S. Steel common stock today at a certain price does not imply that the offer will be good tomorrow. Not much time is allowed for inquiries or investigations in situations of this kind.

OFFERS AND ACCEPTANCES BY CORRESPONDENCE

When a person makes an offer by mail, he may, if he wishes, state that the acceptance will not be valid until it is actually received. In that case the agreement is not completed until the acceptance is actually delivered to the offeror. If, however, a person sends an offer by mail but does not specify that the acceptance is not to be valid until it is received, he is considered to have authorized the acceptance to be sent in any manner the offeree chooses. If the acceptance is sent by the same means as the offer, the contract is formed the minute the acceptance is sent. If the acceptance is sent by some other means of communication, the contract is not formed until the acceptance is received. The rule that a properly mailed acceptance takes effect at the time it is mailed is applied strictly. The rule applies even though the acceptance is never received by the offeror. In any court case involving such a situation, it becomes a question of fact, not a question of law, as to whether or not there was an acceptance.

It must not be presumed, however, that if the offeree adopts an unauthorized method of sending the acceptance, he has rejected the offer. If an offeree who receives an offer through the mail sends his acceptance in the form of a telegram or a personally delivered message, the agreement is completed when the acceptance is delivered to the offeror.

Similarly, when an offer is received in a telegram, the delivery of an acceptance to the telegraph company completes the agreement. If in such a case the acceptance is sent by mail, the agreement is not completed until the acceptance is received by the offeror.

Because of the hazards involved, careful and prudent persons can avoid most of these difficulties by stipulating in the offer how it must be accepted and when the acceptance is to become effective. If this stipulation is ignored, the offeror is not bound. For example, the offer may state, "The acceptance must be sent by wire and be received by me in Chicago by 12 noon on June 15 before the contract is complete." If the acceptance is mailed, the offeror is not bound. The acceptance is not effective unless it is by wire and is actually received by the offeror and by the time specified in Chicago. The offeror may, however, elect to be bound if acceptance is received later or by other means.

- Taul owned a negotiable option to purchase 500 shares of stock in a uranium company at $12 a share. He wrote ten letters to ten different people offering to sell the option for $1,000. Three of these parties immediately accepted. Taul could be sued by two of them for breach of contract because he can sell to only one. He should have included a protective clause in the offer such as, "contract not to become effective until acceptance acknowledged by me."

QUESTIONS

1. What is a quasi contract?
2. If one receives an offer by letter and he wishes to accept the offer before the offeror revokes it, which would be better—to accept by letter or by telegram?
3. How would it be possible for one to be bound on a contract and not be aware of it for quite some time?
4. If John has only one hi-fi set but writes five letters to five different people offering to sell it for $300, could he find himself in considerable difficulty if he were ignorant of the law regarding offer and acceptance?
5. Under what conditions may one accept an offer that is made in the form of a newspaper advertisement?
6. (a) When may an offer be revoked?
   (b) What is the effect of death or insanity of the offeror on an offer?
7. What is the effect of a counteroffer?
8. How may an offer by mail be accepted?
9. When one makes an offer by correspondence, how is it possible that he can be bound on a contract and not be aware of it?
10. If an offer is made by telegram and the acceptance is sent by letter, when is the contract formed?

CASE PROBLEMS

1. The Hargrove Milling Company wrote an offer to the A & B Bakery as follows: "We will sell you flour at $20 a hundred, terms 2/10, n/30." The Bakery replied, "I accept your offer for 1,000 barrels if we can get terms 2/10, n/60." The A & B Bakery waited 20 days and did not hear from the offeror. A new acceptance was then mailed ordering 1,000 barrels with terms as originally quoted. Was a contract ever formed?

2. The S & C Bank ran this advertisement in the local paper: "We will pay $500 for information leading to identification of the person who robbed this bank." Davis had written down the getaway car's license. He supplied this information, and the robber was apprehended. Is he entitled to collect the $500?

3. Dawson, the sales manager for the Builders Supply Company, offered to sell Dobbs Brothers 500 gallons of paint at $4 per gallon. On October 1 Dobbs Brothers accepted by letter with a stipulation that the paint was to be delivered 50 gallons a week. No reply was ever made to this acceptance. Was there a contract?

4. Carrol was arrested by the police and put in jail for an attempted robbery. Samuel saw a picture of Carrol in the local paper and recognized him as a suspect wanted for robbery in a distant city. There was a reward of $5,000 for "arrest and conviction." Samuel called the police department in the distant city and informed them that Carrol was in a local jail. He demanded the reward of $5,000. Was he entitled to it?

5. Uncle John promised Fred a new car if Fred passed the bar exam. After he took the exam, he was exultant over how easy it was. He assured his uncle he had passed, so Uncle John gave him the car. A few days later the results of the bar exam were announced, but Fred's name was not among those who passed. Uncle John demanded a return of the car. Fred claims there was no contract binding him to return the car. Do you agree?

6. A local corporation formed for the purpose of drilling for oil was defunct. The stock was considered by all the townspeople to be absolutely worthless. Hipps, the owner of 1,000 shares of this stock, offered to sell them to Hurley for 10 cents a share. Hurley accepted. A few minutes later a radio report stated that oil had been discovered on a tract of land adjoining the property of the defunct corporation. Hipps refused to sell Hurley the stock, claiming that the offer was made in jest. Was there a contract?

7. Joel wrote Broadnax a letter, offering to sell him a tract of real estate owned by Joel. Twenty-four hours later Joel sold the land to Ledbetter without waiting to hear from Broadnax. As soon as Broadnax received Joel's offer, he accepted. Joel contended that his selling the land to Ledbetter was a revocation of his offer to Broadnax. Do you agree?

8. At 9 a.m. Potts wired Lemly as follows: "I will sell you 1,000 bales of cotton 1-inch middling at 35 cents a pound." At 3 p.m. Lemly sent an acceptance in writing by a messenger boy. Before the boy reached Potts' office, Lemly received a telephone call from Potts stating the offer was revoked. While Potts was talking to Lemly on the phone, the messenger boy delivered the acceptance. Was a contract formed?

CHAPTER 5

DEFECTIVE AGREEMENTS

MISTAKES THAT MAKE AGREEMENTS DEFECTIVE

As a general rule, a mistake made by one party without the knowledge of the other has no effect on the validity of the contract. There are, however, certain mistakes that make agreements defective:

1. Mistakes as to the nature of the transaction
2. Mistakes as to the identity of the party
3. Mutual mistakes as to the identity of the subject matter
4. Mutual mistakes as to the existence of the subject matter

(1) **Mistakes as to the Nature of the Transaction.** A mistake as to the nature of the transaction renders the contract void. If, through trickery, a man is induced to sign a deed under the impression it is a note, he is not bound by his signature. But to avoid the contract on the ground of mistake, he must not have been negligent. Thus, one unable to read will not be excused on the ground of mistake if he fails to have some disinterested party read the contract to him.

- Godfrey owned two ships, one named the Empress, and one named the Emporia. The Empress was worth only half as much as the Emporia. He sold the Emporia to Kaiser for $60,000. The contract was in writing. When Kaiser read it, he agreed to all its terms. While his attention was diverted, another contract was placed before him exactly like the first. The Empress was substituted for the Emporia. Kaiser signed it without reading it a second time. There was no contract because of this trickery.

(2) **Mistakes as to the Identity of the Party.** Freedom of contract includes among other things the freedom to choose the parties with whom one contracts. With but rare exceptions, the law does not

compel one to contract with a person who is objectionable to him for any reason. If one is mistaken as to the identity of the party with whom he is contracting, then the contract is void. Naturally such a contract would have to be negotiated by mail, telegram, or telephone.

If a person contracts with another in a face-to-face relationship, he is presumed to have intended to contract with this particular individual even though he thought it was someone else. Even if the other party said, "I am Charles Greene," when in fact he was Francis Barlow, the contract would be valid if the party was mistaken only as to the man's name, not his real identity. If he deals with him at a distance, however, and the other party falsely represents himself to be someone who he is not, the contract is void. Under these circumstances he has no way of ascertaining through reasonable diligence that he was mistaken.

If the mistake as to the identity of the party involves an executory contract, then the remedy consists merely of refusing to perform the contract. If it is executed, then the innocent party may rescind the contract by returning anything of value which he received and demanding that the other party do likewise. As far as possible, the law provides that both parties be restored to their prior positions.

- Holden had once been defrauded by a salesman for the Handy Book Company. A salesman for the Handy Book Company called on Holden to sell him a set of encyclopedias. The salesman knew of Holden's extreme distaste for the Handy Book Company. For this reason, he told Holden the encyclopedias were published by the United Book Company. Holden agreed to buy the books. When they arrived he learned the identity of the true publisher. He rescinded the contract, and demanded a return of his money. He was within his rights.

(3) Mutual Mistakes as to the Identity of the Subject Matter.

Unlike the mistakes described in the two preceding sections, mistakes as to the identity of the subject matter of a contract must be mutual. If both parties do not have in mind the same subject matter, their minds can never meet; and thus there can be no contract. For example, if A offers to sell and B agrees to buy "all the pulpwood on my Barnett Shoals Road farm" and A has two farms on that road, the parties may not have the same farm in mind. This cannot become a binding contract until the farm described in the offer is clearly identified.

Often the parties correctly identify the subject matter of the contract but are mistaken about some other aspect of the transaction. For example, John has two stacks of lumber. One is high grade and the other is low grade. John, pointing to the high-grade lumber, says, "I will sell you this lumber for $5,000." Henry, the offeree, accepts. They both thought the particular stack of lumber identified was the low-quality lumber. The contract is valid, however, since the offeror pointed to, that is, identified, one particular stack of lumber. They were not mistaken as to which stack was meant.

> ▪ Biddle was the purchasing agent for a steel mill. He called on the Loef Brothers Scrap Iron Company to purchase scrap iron. There were two piles of several hundred tons each, one valued at 4 cents a pound and the other at 6 cents. The seller pointed directly at the 6 cents scrap and said, "This is the 4 cents pile of scrap iron." Biddle purchased it. Later the seller learned of his error in identifying the cheaper pile of scrap. It was too late. Since there was no mistake as to the pile to which he pointed, the contract was binding.

(4) Mutual Mistakes as to the Existence of the Subject Matter.

If two parties enter into a contract relative to a specific subject matter, but at the moment of the contract this specific subject matter does not exist, the contract is void. Again the mistake must be a mutual mistake, not a unilateral one. Such a mistake most often arises when the subject matter of the contract has been destroyed by flood, fire, tornado, or other means, but its destruction is unknown to either party when the contract is formed.

> ▪ Smith sold the Missouri Pacific Railroad 5,000 railroad ties for $1.50 each. Prior to the contract but unknown to either party, the ties had been destroyed by a forest fire. The contract was void since the mistake involved 5,000 specific railroads ties, not just any ties of a designated grade.

It is evident from these four classes of mistakes that it is not the function of the law to save us from the consequences of all mistakes. These four classes of mistakes cover a very small percentage of those made in business transactions. Knowledge and diligence, not law, are the chief bulwarks against losses due to mistakes.

MISTAKES THAT DO NOT MAKE AGREEMENTS DEFECTIVE

Some of the most common mistakes in business transactions do not affect the validity of the contract. Two of these classes of mistakes need special emphasis.

1. Mistakes as to value, quality, or price
2. Mistakes as to the terms of the contract

(1) Mistakes as to Value, Quality, or Price. When two parties deal face to face, the law will not intervene to protect either of them simply because one was mistaken as to the value, quality, or price of the subject matter of the contract. If the buyer does not trust his judgment, he has the right to demand of the seller a warranty as to the quality, quantity, or the value of the article he is buying. His ability to contract wisely is his chief protection against a bad bargain. If Snead sells Robinson a television set for $350, Robinson cannot rescind the contract merely because the set proved to be worth only $150. This is a mistake as to value and quality. He should obtain as a part of the contract an express warranty as to the set's quality. Conversely, if the seller parts with a jewel for $50, thinking it is a cheap stone, he cannot later complain if the jewel proves to be worth $2,500.

Mistakes as to value, quality, and sometimes quantity are mistakes, as a rule, of judgment. Mistakes as to price, however, may be the result of errors in typing or in misunderstanding of an oral quotation of the price. But again the wheels of commerce could not run smoothly if either party could avoid the contract merely because he was mistaken as to price. If the E & S Tire Company offers by letter to sell 1,000 tires at $14 each, it cannot avoid the contract on the basis that the secretary incorrectly typed the price $14 instead of $16, the price dictated. The seller is bound on the contract for $14.

- McGregor dictated an offer to the Instant Typing Service and quoted a price for a certain grade of typing paper at 90 cents a ream. Mary, his secretary, by error typed the offer at 80 cents a ream. McGregor did not catch the error in signing his letters because he sold many grades. The Instant Typing Service immediately accepted the offer and ordered 1,000 reams. It was then that the error was discovered. The contract was valid.

Mistakes of quantity may also be mistakes as to price or value. If both parties are mistaken as to the quantity, there is no meeting of the minds and there is no contract.

- The Elite Jewelry Store sold Dennis a box of knives and forks for $160. The box was marked to indicate it contained eight knives and eight forks. There were actually six of each. The buyer relied on the notations on the box, unaware that there were only six knives and forks. This was a mistake of fact as to quantity and value, not a mistake as to value; therefore, there was no contract.

It is the purpose of the law to promote equity, not inequity. If these laws as to value, quality, and price were enforced to the letter, the result would often be very inequitable. For that reason, we find one basic exception to these rules. This exception is that one cannot knowingly take advantage of another's mistake as to value, quality, or price.

The mistake must be one of fact, not mere opinion. If A buys a painting from B for $10 that is actually worth $5,000, and A knows B is mistaken as to its value, there is a valid contract. B's opinion as to its value is erroneous. He is not mistaken as to a fact as illustrated in the two cases below.

- Hoover offered by letter to sell Harrell a new Plymouth automobile for $209. Harrell accepted by letter immediately. The true price was $2,009, but the typist erred in writing up the offer. The error was so gross and apparent to Harrell that he could not in good conscience hold Hoover to the offer.

- The Vaugh Lumber Company sold the Hope Construction Company 10,925 feet of lumber at $187.75 per thousand board feet. The bookkeeper, because of his lack of knowledge of business arithmetic, prepared an invoice showing the total price to be $205.11. The correct amount was $2,051.17. After the purchaser had paid the $205.11, he received a bill for an additional $1,846.06. He must pay it because here there was no error in the unit price of $187.75. The error in calculation on the invoice should have been evident to the purchaser. There was, in fact, no error in the contract price.

(2) Mistakes as to the Terms of the Contract. One of the most common mistakes relates to the terms of the contract. Such a mistake is usually the result of a failure to read the contract if it is written or a failure to understand its meaning or significance. If the contract is oral, either of the parties may be mistaken as to the terms of the contract without the other party's being aware of it. Such mistakes in both written and oral contracts do not affect their validity; otherwise anyone could avoid his contract merely by claiming that he was mistaken as to its terms.

Frequently contracts are entered into orally and then reduced to writing. If through an error in typing the written form does not conform to the oral form, then the parties may not be bound by the written form if the error is such that its detection could not be ascertained by a casual reading of the written contract.

- The Welch Auto Supply Company orally agreed to purchase some tires of a certain grade and size for $12.50 per tire. When the sales agreement was drawn up, the price was erroneously typed $14.50. Under these conditions the seller could not enforce the $14.50 price.

FRAUD

One who induces another to enter into a contract as a result of a false statement of a material fact, is guilty of *fraud*. A contract so induced is voidable, not void, since the party defrauded intended to make the contract but was induced to do so through fraud.

Fraud may be perpetrated by:

1. Express misrepresentation
2. Concealment of material facts
3. Silence when it is one's duty to speak

(1) Express Misrepresentation. Fraud, as a result of express misrepresentation, consists of four elements, each one of which must be present to constitute fraud:

(a) A false statement of a material fact must be made.

(b) The false statement must be made by one who knew it to be false, or by one who made it in reckless disregard of its truth or falsity.

(c) There must be an intent to induce the innocent party to act by reason of the false statement.

(d) The false statement must be relied upon by the innocent party.

If these four elements are present, the injured party may, at his option, rescind the contract. If he has been damaged by reason of the fraud, he may, in addition to rescinding the contract, sue for damages.

- Simpson falsified his financial statements to induce a bank to make him a loan of $5,000 for ninety days. After the loan was made and the discounted value of the note was deposited to his account, the bank learned of the fraud. The bank was entitled to rescind the contract and demand immediate repayment. Had the bank acted to its detriment, it could have also sued for damages.

Statements of opinion, as contrasted with statements of fact, do not, as a rule, constitute fraud. The dividing line between fact and opinion is often obscure, but close analysis will usually enable even a layman to distinguish between the two.

Such expressions as "This is the best buy in town," "The price of this stock will double in the next twelve months," "This business will net you $15,000 a year" are all statements of opinion, not statements of fact. If one says, "This business has netted the owner $15,000," this is not an opinion or a prophesy, but an historical fact.

(2) Concealment of Material Facts. If one actively conceals material facts for the purpose of preventing the other contracting party from discovering them, such concealment is fraud even though there are no false statements.

Merely refraining from disclosing pertinent facts unknown to the other party is not fraud as a rule. There must be an active concealment to constitute fraud.

- A coal company had been prospecting for coal on A's land and found none. Later A filled up the excavations to keep B, a prospective purchaser, from discovering the failure to find coal. This active concealment was fraud if B, to the knowledge of A, thought there was coal on the land.

(3) Silence When It Is One's Duty to Speak. If one's relationship with another is that of trust and confidence, then silence may constitute fraud. Such a relationship exists between partners in a business firm, an agent and his principal, a lawyer and his client, a guardian and his ward, a physician and his patient, and in many other trust relationships.

Silence, when one has no moral duty to speak, is not fraud. If Lawrence offers to sell Marconi, a diamond merchant, a gem for $500 that is actually worth $15,000, Marconi's superior knowledge of value alone does not impose upon him the duty to speak. If Lawrence's error is the result of misreading the price tag, and Marconi is aware of this error, Marconi cannot remain silent.

DURESS

For a contract to be valid, all parties must enter into it of their free will. *Duress* is a means of destroying another's free will by obtaining his consent to a contract by means of a threat to do him, or members of his family, some harm. The threat may relate to one's property or to his earning power. Regardless of the nature of the threat, it is duress if it is serious enough to destroy one's free will.

- Harold purchased a used car from Jarvis. He gave a check for $300 in payment. The check was a bad check, and Jarvis threatened to prosecute Harold. Later he said to Harold, "If you will buy a new car for $2,200 cash, I will refrain from prosecuting you." Harold accepted the offer but later wished to avoid the contract. He could do so because the contract was voidable on his part because of duress. His guilt was irrelevant. The threat destroyed his free will to contract.

UNDUE INFLUENCE

Undue influence may destroy one's free will even though there is no duress. If a party in a confidential or fiduciary relationship to another induces him against his free will to enter into a contract, the agreement is voidable because of *undue influence*. If, under any relationship, one is in a position to take undue advantage of another, undue influence may render the contract voidable. Undue influence may result also from sickness, infirmity, or serious distress. Examples of such relationships are family relationships, a guardian and his ward, an attorney and his client, and physician and his patient, and any other relationship where confidence reposed on one side results in domination by the other.

In undue influence there is never any use of threats to harm the person, property, or relations of the other party as in duress. Usually the party exerting undue influence upon another is suave and friendly rather than gruff and threatening as in duress. But suavity per se is not undue influence. The relationship of the two parties must be such that one yields because his will cannot hold out against the superior position, intelligence, or personality of the other party.

- John's father was ill and totally dependent upon John for his support and comfort. John offered to buy his father's home at less than its true value. John made no threats, but his father was afraid to antagonize John for fear he would not care for him. This fear destroyed his free will to contract. The sale was voidable.

REMEDIES FOR BREACH OF CONTRACT BECAUSE OF FRAUD, DURESS, OR UNDUE INFLUENCE

Since fraud, duress, and undue influence render contracts voidable, not void, one must know what to do when he is a victim of one of these acts. If he does nothing, the contract is ratified. The contract may also be ratified by some act or word indicating an intention to be bound. After the contract is affirmed or ratified, one is as fully bound on it as if there had been no fraud, duress, or undue influence. But still the innocent party may sue for whatever damages he has sustained.

If instead of affirming the contract, one elects to rescind it, he must first return or offer to return any consideration he received under the contract. After this is done, he is in a position to take one of three actions depending upon the circumstances:

(1) He may sue to recover any money, goods, or other things of value he has parted with, plus damages.

(2) If the contract is executory on the part of the innocent party, he can refuse to perform. If the other party sues, he can then interpose fraud, duress, or undue influence as a complete defense.

(3) He may bring a suit in equity to have the suit judicially declared void and ask for damages.

- Darter, a shoe merchant, was induced through fraud to purchase some shoes for $6,500. The shoes were purchased on 90 days' credit. Darter's best remedy in this case probably is to affirm the contract but to refrain from paying for the shoes. When the seller sues him, he can set up the fraud as a counterclaim. If he could prove that he was damaged to the extent of $3,000 by reason of the fraud, then he would pay the balance of the account, or $3,500.

QUESTIONS

1. How is a contract affected by a mistake as to the nature of the transaction?
2. What is the effect of negligence on the part of a person who attempts to avoid a contract on the ground of mistake as to the nature of the transaction?
3. (a) If one is mistaken as to the identity of the party with whom he contracts, may he avoid a contract in which the dealings were face to face?
   (b) Can the minds of the parties be in mutual agreement when they are honestly mistaken as to the identity of the subject matter of the contract?
4. If the subject matter of the contract did not exist at the time the contract was formed and both parties were unaware of this fact, is the contract valid or void?
5. (a) May either party avoid the contract on the grounds of a mistake as to quality by both parties?
   (b) May one party who knows the true value of an article take advantage of the other party's ignorance of the value of it?
6. If an oral contract is typed incorrectly but the error cannot be detected by a casual reading of the contract, is the contract valid?
7. If A buys a ring set with a zircon thinking it is a diamond, is he bound if the seller did nothing to mislead him?
8. Is a contract induced by fraud void or voidable?
9. Define duress.
10. If one does not rely on a misrepresentation, may he plead fraud as a defense when sued on the contract?

CASE PROBLEMS

1. Mary Jones was a secretary in the Hope Furniture Company's office. Gowen wished to purchase $10,000 worth of furniture. He inquired of Miss Jones, since her employer was out, what were the terms of sale. She replied, "2 percent discount for cash." Thereupon Gowen bought the merchandise and paid cash for it. The invoice read "$10,000, less 2% discount, or $8,000." Later the Hope Furniture Company learned of the error and attempted to collect the difference between the $2,000 discount given by Miss Jones and the correct discount of $200. Could it collect?

2. The Lapp Jewelry Company had a diamond necklace for sale. The price was $7,500. McLean, a prospective purchaser, inquired of the salesman as to the price. The salesman looked up the price and said "$750," thinking that was the price shown on the price list. Neither the salesman nor the buyer knew the true value of the necklace. McLean agreed to purchase it. Was the Lapp Jewelry Company bound on this contract?

3. Harris Bibb was office manager for the Griffin Wholesale Company. In this capacity he signed a contract with the Atlanta Collecting Agency to collect $50,000 of delinquent accounts receivable. The written contract with the agency contained this clause: "The Griffin Wholesale Company agrees to pay the Atlanta Collecting Agency 25% of the aggregate listing as its collection fee." Bibb thought this meant that for each $1,000 collected, the agency would take $250 and remit $750 to the Griffin Wholesale Company. The true meaning was that the agency kept the first $12,500 collected and remitted all over that. Was the Griffin Wholesale Company bound on this contract?

4. Pearson owned a deep sea fishing boat. He agreed to sell it to Huntley for $10,000, delivery to be made as soon as the boat returned to port. At the time the contract was made, the boat had sunk during a storm. This fact was unknown by both buyer and seller. Was there a valid contract?

5. The Sailors Antique Shop displayed several old-style beds. Hargrove purchased one for $2,700, thinking it was a very valuable Louis XIV make. The seller knew Hargrove was mistaken about the antiquity of the bed but said nothing to enlighten him about his ignorance. The bed was of fairly recent make and actually worth only $150. When Hargrove learned of this fact, he attempted to rescind the contract. May he do so?

6. Barry, in an effort to sell Mr. and Mrs. Andrews a house, stated, "In my opinion this house could not be built today for $25,000." Barry, a building expert, knew the house could be built for less than $20,000. In a suit for fraud, Barry attempted to prove he had expressed only an opinion, not a fact. Was this a false representation?

7. Henrietta was secretary to the president of the Coulter Corporation. She had an invalid mother to support, and their only source of income was Henrietta's salary. Her employer by means of persuasive salesmanship sold her 500 shares of stock in the corporation and had her assign 50 percent of her weekly salary in payment. She now wishes to disaffirm this contract. May she do it?

CHAPTER 6

COMPETENCY OF
PARTIES

CAPACITY TO CONTRACT

In order that an agreement may be enforceable at law, all parties must have the legal and mental capacity to contract. The general rule is that all parties are presumed to have this capacity. Some parties, however, in the eyes of the law, lack such capacity because of age, physical condition, or public policy. Among those whom the law considers to be incompetent to some degree are minors, insane persons, intoxicated persons, convicts, married women, and aliens.

MINORS

The common-law rule that persons under twenty-one years of age are *minors* has been retained by most of the states. In nine states laws have been passed making girls competent to contract at eighteen years of age. In a few other states all minors who are married are fully competent to contract. In still other states minors who are in business for themselves are bound on all their business contracts.

Contracts of Minors. A minor may make contracts freely, and many of these contracts are fully as valid and enforceable as those of an adult. A few of his contracts are void, but most of them are merely voidable at the minor's option. If a minor wishes to treat a contract made with an adult as valid, the adult is bound by it.

Business firms that carry on business transactions in all the states must know the law dealing with minors in each of the fifty states. Mail order houses and correspondence schools are particularly susceptible to losses when dealing with minors. The significance of the law is that, with but few exceptions, one deals with a minor at his own risk. The purpose of the law is to protect minors from unscrupulous adults, but in general the law affords the other party no more rights in scrupulous contracts than in unscrupulous ones. The minor is the sole judge as to whether or not he wishes to be bound on a voidable contract.

Contracts of Minors for Necessaries. A minor is fully liable for the reasonable value of necessaries actually supplied to him. There are a large number of court cases in all states defining necessaries. The dividing line between necessaries and luxuries is often a fine one; but, for the most part, there exists a well-defined group of goods and services which can be classed as *necessaries.* These are food, clothes, and shelter; necessary medical services, including surgery, dental work, and medicine; education through high school or trade school, and in a few states through college; working tools for his trade; and other goods which are luxuries to some people but necessaries to others because of peculiar circumstances.

Technically, it is not correct to say that a minor is liable on his contracts. He is liable for the reasonable value of necessaries furnished to him—not already provided him by his parent or guardian; and his liability is quasi-contractual in nature. If a minor contracts to purchase a suit for $75, a necessary, he incurs no obligations until the suit is delivered. A quasi-contractual liability is one imposed by law to prevent unjust enrichment. The minor is not unjustly enriched unless the suit is delivered to him and he fails to pay for it. Even though it is a necessary, he incurs no obligation until the suit is delivered. Even then he is not liable for the contract price. The court will impose on him a liability for a reasonable price, which may or may not be $75.

> ▪ Harold, a minor, purchased a suit for $80 from Hope Tailors. All
> necessary alterations were to be made without extra charge. After
> the alterations were made, Harold refused to take the suit and pay
> for it. Even though the suit be a necessary, Harold would not be held
> liable because delivery of the suit had not taken place.

Disaffirmance. The term *disaffirmance* means the repudiation of a contract, that is, the election to avoid it. A minor has the legal right to disaffirm a voidable contract at any time during his minority or within a reasonable time after becoming of age. An adult does not, however, have the right to avoid a contract because the other party is a minor.

If the contract is wholly executory, a disaffirmance completely nullifies the contract.

If the contract is executed by one of the parties but not by the other party, it is still classed as an executory contract. Here, however, the minor, upon electing to disaffirm the contract, must return whatever he may have received under the contract, provided he is still in possession of it. The fact that the minor is not in possession of the property, however, regardless of the reason, does not prevent him from exercising his right to disaffirm the contract. The same rule generally applies if the contract is wholly executed.

- Bowen, a minor, purchased a watch for $75 from the Brush Jewelry Company. About one month later the watch was stolen. Bowen disaffirmed the contract and demanded a return of his $75. He may do so. The fact that he cannot return the watch does not bar his right to disaffirmance.

If a minor elects to disaffirm a contract and demands not a return of the goods but their value, the disaffirmance cannot be made retroactive. In most states he is entitled only to the value of the goods on the day he disaffirms.

- Landry, a minor, sold 500 shares of United States Steel stock to Hinton for $20,000. Six months later, when the stock had declined in value to $17,500, Landry demanded not only a return of the stock but $2,500 in cash as well. The court held he was not entitled to this as the disaffirmance could not be made retroactive to the sale.

If a minor purchases real estate, many serious legal problems arise. Even if a minor is married, the purchase of a home is not a contract for a necessary. He cannot disaffirm his real estate contracts until he reaches his majority. If the minor abandons the property before he becomes of age, the adult cannot repossess it and get good title to it.

- Kilgore, a minor eighteen years old, purchased a house from Stone for $20,000. A windstorm blew the roof off, and Kilgore attempted to disaffirm the contract. Stone returned his money, then repaired the house, and rented it for $125. Eighteen months later Kilgore attained his majority and then demanded a return of his house and tendered a return of the purchase price. He also demanded the eighteen months' rent and refused to reimburse Stone for repairing the house. He was within his rights since an adult contracts with a minor at his own risk.

If an adult purchases an asset from a minor, the adult has only a voidable title to the property. If he sells the property to an innocent third party before the minor disaffirms the contract, the innocent third party obtains good title to the property. If the minor disaffirms the contract, he cannot get a return of the property, but he can demand that the adult give him the entire amount which the third party paid.

- Granville, a minor, sold Halleck a car for $1,000. Halleck spent $200 repairing the car and then sold it to Johnson for $1,500. Granville then disaffirmed the contract and demanded the $1,500. Since Johnson was an innocent third party and had good title to the car, Granville was entitled to collect the $1,500 from Halleck.

Ratification. A minor may ratify a voidable contract only after he has attained his majority. By *ratification* is meant a restatement of one's willingness to be bound by his promises made during minority. It is in substance a new promise and may be oral, written, or merely implied by his conduct. He cannot ratify a part and disaffirm a part; he must ratify all or none of it. Ratification must be made within a reasonable time after majority.

It should be noted that there is a difference between a minor's executed contracts and his executory contracts. After he reaches majority, his silence ratifies an executed contract, while it disaffirms an executory contract.

- Clarke purchased 100 shares of stock in the Gulf Oil Company and paid cash for them. One week after reaching 21, he received a dividend check. He cashed the check and spent the money. Soon thereafter he attempted to disaffirm the contract. He could not do so. When a minor ratifies a contract by some act, as in this case, he cannot later disaffirm it.

Minor's Business Contracts. Many states, by special statutory provision, have made a minor's contract relative to the business in which he is engaged fully binding on him. The minor's liability is limited to the assets of the business that he is operating.

- Sanders, a minor, owned and operated a filling station. In this capacity he purchased gasoline, tires, and other merchandise amounting to $3,000. He was sued on this account, and his filling station was sold to satisfy the debt. There still remained a balance of $350 after the proceeds of the sheriff's sale were applied on the debt. He is not obligated to pay this $350 since his liability is limited to the net worth of the business which he owns and operates.

How One May Contract Safely with Minors. Since in general one deals with minors at his own risk, every businessman must know how to protect himself when contracting with minors. The safest way is to have an adult guarantee in writing that the minor will abide by the terms of the contract. This does not bind the minor, but it does give the other party the right to sue the adult who guaranteed the contract. In addition, the adult should, if in doubt, ask the other party if he is twenty-one, or eighteen, as the case may be. If he answers "Yes," in a majority of the states this is a tort if false and will either bind him on the contract or subject him to a suit for damages. Thirdly, a merchant must run some risks when dealing with minors. If he sells to a minor, the contract may be avoided by the minor years later and a refund of the purchase price demanded. Since few minors exercise the right, it is more profitable for a businessman to run this risk than to seek absolute protection against loss. The loss in profits in lost sales would exceed the refunds.

Minors' Torts. A *tort* is a legal wrong, such as negligently or willfully damaging another person's property. As a general rule, a minor is liable for his torts as fully as an adult. If a minor misrepresents his age and the adult relies upon this misrepresentation to his detriment, this is a tort. The law is not uniform throughout the United States as to whether or not a minor is bound on a contract induced by misrepresenting his age. If it is a face-to-face contract and the minor appears to be of age, most courts will hold him bound on his contracts when he expressly states he is of age.

INSANE PERSONS

In determining an insane person's capacity, the status of his insanity must be fixed. If he has been examined according to law and been formally adjudicated insane and a guardian has been appointed, then in most states his contracts are void. Whether or not the subject matter of the contract is a necessary or whether undue advantage was taken of him are wholly irrelevant questions. He is considered incapable of making a valid acceptance of an offer no matter how fair the offer is. If he is merely insane but has not been officially adjudicated insane, then his contracts are voidable, not void. Like a minor, he is liable for the reasonable value of necessaries that have been supplied to him. He may elect to avoid all other contracts. Upon disaffirmance, he must return anything of value received under the contract provided it is still in his possession.

In many types of insanity, a person has lucid or sane intervals. During these intervals he is as fully competent to contract as any adult except in those states where his contracts are void if he has been judicially declared insane. His guardian must be discharged before he regains full competency to contract. After one has regained sanity, he may affirm or disaffirm his voidable contracts. In general, the same rules governing affirmance and disaffirmance of minors' contracts apply to the contracts of insane persons. Most of the laws governing the contracts of insane persons are the result of state statutes. Although these laws are reasonably uniform, there are but few general statements that hold true in every state.

> ▪ Robert Stacey was judicially declared insane. A guardian was appointed for him. Later Stacey sold his car for $500, a fair price. His guardian sued for a return of the car. The court held that the buyer had to return the car because Stacey's contract was void. Stacey had to return any money which had not been lost or spent.

INTOXICATED PERSONS

Contracts made by a person who has become so intoxicated that he cannot understand the meaning of his acts are voidable. Upon becoming sober, he may affirm or disaffirm his contracts made while he was drunk. Disaffirmance is contingent upon there being no innocent third party who would be injured thereby. In this sense, the drunkard's contracts differ from those of minors and insane persons. If one delays unreasonably in disaffirming a contract made while intoxicated, he may lose the right to have the contract set aside.

CONVICTS

Laws of the various states differ with regard to the capacity of a convict (one convicted of a major criminal offense, a felony, or treason) to contract. In some states, for example, he may not make a valid transfer of his property. Some states place a partial disability on capacity to contract; others, a total disability. In any event, however, the disability lasts only so long as the person is imprisoned.

MARRIED WOMEN

Common law held that a married woman could not make a binding contract and considered her contracts to be void. Even though living apart from her husband, she was still held to be under the common-law disability. In most states, however, the common-law disability has been removed by statute with but a few restrictions on the right of a married woman to contract. For example, in some states a married woman may not contract with her husband; in some states she may not contract to act as surety for her husband.

ALIENS

An *alien* is a citizen or subject of a foreign country residing in this country. Originally subject to disabilities to contract, an alien is in most instances able to make binding contracts. As a rule, an *enemy alien*—subject or citizen of a country with which we are at war—may not make binding contracts or sue on an existing contract. But an enemy alien may defend himself when sued on an existing contract.

QUESTIONS

1. Whom does the law consider to be incompetent in some degree to contract?
2. Why is it important for business firms to know the law dealing with minors in their own and other states?
3. If a minor wishes to treat a contract with an adult as binding, may the adult avoid it because the other party is a minor?
4. Name some necessaries for which a minor may be held liable for payments.
5. When may a minor disaffirm his contracts?
6. When a minor disaffirms a contract, must he return any benefit which he received from the contract?
7. When may a minor ratify a voidable contract?
8. (a) If a minor purchases two articles by the same contract, may he disaffirm the contract for one of the items and ratify it for the other one?
   (b) How may a businessman protect himself when dealing with minors?
9. If a minor disaffirms a contract, may he make it retroactive if he demands only a return of value?
10. Are the contracts of an insane person void or voidable if he has been judicially declared insane?
11. If John purchases a car from Henry, a minor, and then sells it to Watson, may Henry demand that Watson return the car to him?
12. If a minor lies about his age, is he guilty of a tort?
13. Are enemy aliens permitted to make valid contracts?
14. Are the contracts of married women generally governed by the common law?

CASE PROBLEMS

1. Holcomb, 18 years of age, was a cripple and was working his way through college with a paper route necessitating a car. He purchased one from A & H Motors for $900. Holcomb would not agree to buy the car unless A & H Motors would agree to repair a dented fender. They finally agreed that Holcomb was to have the car for $895 and that he would then pay the A & H Motors $5 for repairing the fender. Before the car was delivered, Holcomb attempted to disaffirm. May he do so?

2. Graff, a married minor, 18 years of age, purchased a house from Ivan for $18,000. He lived in the house until he was almost 21 and then sold it for $13,000. The large depreciation in value was due entirely to a new highway having been built near the house since Graff bought it. As soon as he reached 21, he disaffirmed the contract and demanded that Ivan pay him the $5,000 he lost on the sale of the house. May he do so?

No

3. Burson, a minor, owned and operated the Red and Black Cleaners. He incurred about $5,000 in debts for rent, equipment, and cleaning materials. He failed to pay any of them, and his creditors brought suit to foreclose on the business and his home in order to collect payment. Burson claimed that since he was a minor, he was not liable for these debts. Is this contention sound?

No minors are bound to pay necessaries debt

4. Towns purchased 500 shares of stock from Fain, a minor, for $3,000, a fair price. Towns held the stock for 15 months and then sold it to Dillard for $4,200. Fain had just passed his twenty-first birthday by one week. He disaffirmed the contract and brought suit against both Towns and Dillard to get a return of his stock. Discuss the rights of all the parties.

5. Frank Clark, aged 20 years and 10 months, became engaged and bought his fiancee an engagement ring costing $200. He paid $25 down and agreed to pay $2 a week on the balance. About three months after he reached his majority, his fiancee broke the engagement and returned his ring. Having no other prospects, he offered to return the ring to the jeweler and demanded the return of the $69 which he had paid and a cancellation of the balance of the debt.

(a) Did he have a legal right to do so? Discuss fully.

(b) Would your conclusion be different if he had paid cash in full at the time of the purchase and had demanded a return of his money within ten days after attaining his majority?

6. Howard was found by the judge of the superior court to be insane, and the judge appointed Sailors as his guardian. A few days later Howard purchased a suit on credit, but the guardian refused to pay for the suit. Was this a valid contract?

No

7. Paris, a boy 17 years old, left his home and rented a room in town for $50 a month. After one month, he refused to pay, claiming a room was not a necessary for him since he could have stayed at home. Is his contention correct?

CHAPTER 7

CONSIDERATION

NATURE OF CONSIDERATION

Courts will compel compliance with an agreement only when it is supported by consideration. Consideration distinguishes mere agreements from legally enforceable obligations. *Consideration* may be something of value to the promisor, or something detrimental to the one who gives it. Consideration also may be another promise. It need not be money or money's worth, but it must be something which, in the eyes of the law, has value.

A common form of consideration is an exchange of promises. Not every promise for a promise, however, constitutes a consideration. The subject matter of the promise must be a business transaction rather than a mere social obligation. Furthermore, the two promises must be concurrent in time to constitute a consideration. The promise of one party must induce the other party to make his promise.

For an exchange of promises to constitute consideration, the promises must create mutual obligations. If a merchant promises to order all the carbon paper he will need in the future in exchange for the seller's promise to supply all the carbon paper he may order at a given price, this is not a contract. It imposes upon the merchant no obligation to order any carbon paper; therefore, there is no mutuality of obligation. There is no certainty the merchant will need any carbon paper. He may discontinue the line or even go out of business. Such an agreement as this one is frequently called *illusory*.

- The Plaza Hotel signed a contract with the Dillard Coal Company in which the key promise was, "The Dillard Coal Company agrees to supply all coal that the Plaza Hotel may order for the next twelve months in consideration of the Plaza Hotel's promise to pay $17 per ton for all coal delivered." The hotel switched from heating coal to gas and notified Dillard Coal Company it would not order any coal. There was no contract because the Plaza Hotel was under no obligation to order any coal, but the Dillard Coal Company was obligated to supply the coal if ordered. This is a unilateral, not a mutual or bilateral obligation.

Sometimes it is difficult to see the detriment to the promisor. If one promises to forego smoking or drinking, is this a detriment to the promisor? The courts hold that it is because the law assumes that any legal right has value. Since one has the legal right to smoke or to drink, one's promise to forbear from these acts is a valuable consideration. Giving up a legal right is a detriment.

ADEQUACY OF CONSIDERATION

As a general rule, the adequacy of the consideration is irrelevant. The law does not prohibit bargains. In many contracts where the consideration consists of an exchange of promises, it is often impossible to fix an exact monetary value on each promise. The law merely requires that each promise have a monetary value. Justice need not be blind, however. If the consideration given by one party is grossly inadequate, this is a relevant fact in proving fraud, undue influence, or mistake. Then, too, the inadequacy of the consideration may be a factor in a court of equity where the equity judge is not bound by strict rules of law but is free to decide the case according to what is right.

If Smith knows that uranium has been discovered on Hall's farm and he enters into a contract to purchase it at one tenth of its true value, a court of equity would not compel Hall to sell. The inadequacy of the consideration is so great, it would not be fair and equitable for Smith to take advantage of Hall's ignorance. If, however, the contract has been fully executed before Hall learns of the true value, then his only remedy is to sue in a law court for damages. Law courts, as distinguished from equity courts, are bound by the strict rule of law that the adequacy of the consideration, in the absence of fraud, is irrelevant.

PART PAYMENT

A partial payment of a past-due debt is not sufficient consideration to support the creditor's promise to cancel the balance of the debt. The promise of a creditor to accept $800 in full settlement of a

$1,000 debt which is past due is a new independent promise which is to be distinguished from his original promise for which the debtor agreed to pay the $1,000. This new promise must have a consideration entirely apart from the original promise. Although the payment of $800 alone will not cancel the debt of $1,000, yet this payment plus the delivery of a calculator will cancel the debt, if the calculator was bargained for and intended by the creditor as consideration for his promise to discharge the debt. The calculator is the consideration to support the new contract. There are several exceptions to this rule:

(1) If the amount of the debt is in dispute, the acceptance in full settlement of a lesser sum than that claimed will cancel the debt.

- The Georgia Supreme Court, based on similar cases in other states, held that a check marked "In full of account," but for an amount less than the payee claimed, discharged the debt if the check was accepted and deposited. If the payee, before depositing the check, marks out the words "In full of account," this does not change the rule. The theory here is that making the check out for an amount less than that claimed by the payee is evidence that the amount owed is in dispute.

(2) If there are several creditors, and each one agrees to accept in full settlement of his claim a percentage of the amount due, all creditors receiving the same percentage, this agreement will cancel the debts owed to these creditors. This is known as a *composition of creditors.*

(3) If the debt is evidenced by a note or other written evidence, cancellation and return of the written evidence cancels the debt.

(4) If the payment of the lesser sum is accompanied by a receipt in full and some indication that a gift is made of the balance, the debt may be canceled.

(5) If a secured note in a lesser amount is given and accepted in settlement of an unsecured debt, the entire unsecured debt is discharged. The security is the consideration to support the contract to settle for a lesser sum.

INSUFFICIENT OR INVALID CONSIDERATION

Many apparent considerations lack the full force and effect necessary to make enforceable agreements. Sometimes the distinction is very narrow, and close scrutiny is required to determine whether or not the consideration is valuable. Consideration of the following classes is either insufficient or invalid:

1. Performing or promising to perform what one is already obligated to do

2. Refraining from doing or promising to refrain from doing what one has no right to do

3. Moral obligation

4. Past performance

(1) Performing or Promising to Perform What One Is Already Obligated to Do. If the consideration in an agreement consists merely of a promise to do what one is already legally obligated to do anyway, there is no valid contract. Such a consideration is said to be invalid; and if the consideration is invalid, the contract is invalid. Such invalid promises usually consist of promising to do what the law requires one to do anyway, or promising to do what one is already obligated to do under a previous contract.

Parties to a contract may at any time mutually agree to cancel an old contract and replace it with a new one. For this new contract to be enforceable, there must be some added features that benefit both parties though not necessarily to an equal extent. If a contractor agrees to build a house of certain specifications for $20,000, a contract of the homeowner to pay an additional $1,000 is not binding unless the contractor concurrently agrees as a consideration for the $1,000 to do something the original contract did not bind him to do. The value of the additional act by the contractor need not be $1,000. It merely must have a monetary value. If unforeseen difficulties arise that make it impossible for the contractor to complete the house for $20,000, these unforeseen difficulties may in rare cases be a consideration. Strikes, bad weather, a change in prices are foreseeable difficulties, not unforeseeable. War with price controls and rationing, underground rock formations, a change in the law relative to the building codes and zoning laws are examples of unforeseen difficulties. The homeowner does not have to agree to pay more because of these unforeseen difficulties; but if he does do so, they will constitute a consideration even though the contractor does not agree to do anything additional. Also, the homeowner is not bound to agree to pay more merely because of unforeseen difficulties. The law merely says that if he does do so, he cannot raise the question later that the consideration was invalid.

(2) Refraining from Doing or Promising to Refrain from Doing What One Has No Right to Do. When one promises to refrain from doing something, such an act is called *forbearance*. If the promisor had a right to do the act, forbearance is a valid consideration. When the forbearance consists of a promise to refrain from doing something which one has no right to do, however, such a promise is an invalid consideration. This is particularly true where one promises to refrain from unlawful conduct.

Often the forbearance consists of promising to refrain from instituting a legal claim against the other party. Promising to refrain from suing another for slander in the amount of $5,000 is a good consideration if one has a reasonable right to demand damages for slander and intends to file such a suit. If there is a basis for a suit for slander, but there is evidence that the promisor had no intention of filing such a suit, then a promise to refrain from suing is an invalid consideration.

> ▪ Morgan, a newspaper columnist, wrote and published articles highly critical of Senator Borgman. The article impugned the character of Senator Borgman and contained much innuendo that Senator Borgman was accepting bribes to vote for certain bills. Senator Borgman told several people he could sue Morgan for libel but that he was not going to do so because he probably could not collect anyway. Later he threatened to sue Morgan for libel unless Morgan promised to donate $5,000 to his campaign fund for re-election. Morgan promised to do this but subsequently refused to make payment. He was within his rights. Promising to refrain from doing what one has no intention of doing is not a consideration.

(3) **Moral Obligation.** Theoretically, a moral obligation ought to be the highest type of consideration, but the difficulty lies with defining it. One may feel strongly that a child has a moral obligation to support his aged parents; but in the absence of a statute so requiring, the courts will not hold that such an obligation exists. If a groceryman supplies John's invalid and penniless mother with $100 worth of groceries, John has no legal obligation to pay the groceryman even though he could easily do so without financial embarrassment. Many of the agreements involving the question of moral consideration concern promises to make gifts to churches or charitable organizations. These promises for the most part are mere gratuities supported only by a moral obligation to comply. There is one fairly well-defined exception to this rule. It is called the *theory of justifiable reliance.* If the donee charitable institution relies upon a promise of the donor to give money, and as a direct result of that promise makes commitments that cannot be performed unless the gift is made, then the promise is enforceable. The donee must have altered its position to its injury as a result of the promise.

- Kelly, along with many other communicants, subscribed to a building fund for the First Methodist Church. The finance committee of the church let a contract for the construction of the church, the cost to be met from the subscriptions. Kelly attempted to revoke his subscription after the church was half finished because he did not like the architecture. He is legally bound on his promise because the church has altered its position to its injury by reason of the promise by Kelly.

(4) **Past Performance.** As a rule, an act performed prior to the promise does not constitute a detriment to the promisee. If a carpenter gratuitously helps a neighbor build his house with no promise of pay, he cannot enforce a promise to pay that is made after the house is completed. The promise to pay must induce the carpenter to do the work, and this cannot be done if the promise is made after the work is completed. There is no new benefit to the promisor (neighbor) or detriment to the promisee (carpenter).

- Barnes, a groceryman, supplied David with groceries on credit while David was unemployed. Later Thomas, a friend of David, promised Barnes he would pay the bill if David did not. This promise was unenforceable since it was past consideration.

A debt that is discharged by bankruptcy may be revived under certain circumstances, usually by the debtor's agreeing in writing to pay it. Such promises are enforceable even though the creditor, the promisee, gives no new consideration to support the promise. The debtor is said to have waived his defense of past consideration under such circumstances. This is an exception to the general rule that past performance will not support a present promise.

QUESTIONS

1. (a) What is consideration?
   (b) Must every contract have consideration to make it valid?
2. How may the consideration in contracts be expressed?
3. (a) If two parties enter into a contract, the consideration of which is an exchange of promises, why must each of these promises have value?
   (b) If a promise does not impose a legal obligation upon the promisor, can such a promise constitute a consideration?
4. If a boy promises his father that he will not own and operate an automobile until he is eighteen in exchange for his father's promise to pay him $2,000, is this a valid contract? What is the value of the boy's promise?

5. If one owes a note for $1,000 and the holder agrees to mark it "Paid in full" if the maker will pay $800 even though the note is past due, will such a payment cancel the note? Explain.

6. During Halloween night, two young men promised not to damage Day's car if Day would agree to pay them $50. Is this contract enforceable?

7. Give two illustrations of when the inadequacy of the consideration would be relevant.

8. Give an illustration of when the court will impute a consideration even if none is present.

9. If Davis owes Dennis $10,000 and Dennis offers to settle for $7,000, what must Davis do to make the contract binding?

10. Is a moral obligation ever an adequate and valid consideration?

CASE PROBLEMS

1. Brodie owed the Lanier National Bank $5,000. The note was past due, and the bank was on the verge of suing Brodie. Mrs. Brodie executed a $5,000 first mortgage on the home that was in her name to secure the Brodie note. She did this to induce the bank not to sue her husband. Four years later the bank brought suit against Mrs. Brodie to foreclose on the mortgage since Brodie's note was still unpaid. Mrs. Brodie denied liability on the grounds of no consideration. Is this defense good?

2. Henry and Doris lived in a house owned by Henry's father. They paid a monthly rental of about 50 per cent of its true rental value. Over a period of five years Henry spent $3,200 on the house and greatly improved its value. Henry's father, before he died, stated in writing that Henry should be reimbursed out of his estate for this $3,200. The administrator refused to pay it. Can Henry compel him to do so?

3. Branch was the bookkeeper for the Brown Lumber Company. His duties were not only to keep the books but also to prepare and file all tax returns. One year his employer felt that the company had paid too much excess profits tax and asked Branch to seek a refund. He promised to give Branch 50 percent of any refunds received. Branch worked many hours overtime preparing the application for a refund and finally received $24,000. He demanded his share of $12,000, and the Brown Lumber Company refused to pay. Must it do so?

4. The Brooks Construction Company had a contract with Kirby to build a 40-unit motel according to a certain blueprint for $500,000, "the building to be completed within a reasonable time from date." For several reasons progress in completing the motel was slow, and Kirby said to Brooks, "If you will make a special effort to complete the motel in 30 days, I will pay an extra $5,000." He modified Kirby's offer to include a neon sign not included in the original blueprints. Kirby refused to pay the $5,000. Is the Brooks Construction Company entitled to collect since it finished the building in 30 days and included the neon sign?

5. Fleeman employed the Banner Home Supply Company to furnish the labor and materials to modernize his kitchen. The total cost was to be $1,100. Fleeman was not satisfied with the work. He called at the office and tendered his check to the secretary if she would accept $800 "in full of account." He left a check for $800 on which was written "in full of account" and asked the secretary to discuss it with her employer when he returned. By error she deposited this check along with other receipts. What was the effect of her depositing the check?

6. Harmon contracted to build a house for Lewis for $21,000. The house was to have a full basement. In excavating for the basement, Harmon struck a solid rock so that the basement would have been a hole in the rock. Harmon refused to proceed unless Lewis promised to pay him an additional $2,000. Lewis did this but later refused. Can Harmon enforce this promise?

7. Baldwin agreed to help Murphy, his brother-in-law, who was unemployed, build a house with the understanding that Baldwin was to receive no pay. After the house was completed, Murphy said to Baldwin, "When I go back to work, I am going to pay you $400 for the work you did for me." Later Baldwin attempted to enforce this agreement. Was Murphy liable for the $400?

8. Diamond was unemployed and had no place to live. His aunt, feeling sorry for him, allowed him to live with her until he could find work. Diamond lived with his aunt for four months and then obtained employment with an excellent salary. His aunt demanded that he pay a reasonable board bill for the four months, and Diamond refused. Was the aunt entitled to collect?

CHAPTER 8

ILLEGAL AGREEMENTS

ILLEGALITY

A contract, to be valid and enforceable, must among other things be for a lawful purpose, and this purpose must be achieved in a lawful manner. If this were not true, the court might be placed in the absurd position of compelling one party to a contract to commit a crime. Any act the commission of which would be a crime cannot be the subject of a contract. If the act itself is legal, but the proposed manner of committing the act is illegal, the contract is void.

A contract that is void because of illegality does not necessarily mean the commission of the act is a crime—it may consist merely of a private wrong. If A sells his car at an auction, it is a private wrong against the bidders for A to have B, a friend, bid on the car just to raise the price. The successful bidder, when he learns of this, has no liability under the contract. Furthermore, if B's bid is the highest bid and he decides to keep the car, A has no recourse.

If the contract is entire and cannot be performed except as an entity, then illegality in one part renders the whole contract invalid. If the contract is divisible so that the legal parts can be performed separately, the contract is enforceable for these parts. For example, when one purchases several articles, each priced separately, and the sale of one or two of these articles is illegal for some reason, the whole contract will not fall because of these one or two articles.

- The Varsity Sports Center employed Fain as an accountant at $100 a week. He was to do all the accounting and, in addition, to handle all wagers on each week's football games. The latter act is illegal. Since it was not stated how much of Fain's salary was for his duties as an accountant and how much was for taking the wagers, the whole contract was void because of illegality. The legal part cannot be separated from the illegal part. Fain could not collect any salary.

CONTRACTS PROHIBITED BY STATUTE

Any act specifically prohibited by statute cannot constitute the subject matter of a valid contract. The number of such acts is legion, but some of them are of such general interest that they need to be given special emphasis.

These acts may be classified under the following six headings:

1. Gambling contracts
2. Sunday contracts
3. Usurious contracts
4. Contracts of an unlicensed operator
5. Contracts for the sale of articles that cannot be the subject matter of an ordinary sale
6. Contracts in unreasonable restraint of trade

(1) Gambling Contracts. A *gambling contract* is a transaction wherein the parties stand to win or to lose based on pure chance. What one gains, the other must lose. There is no exchange of values as with legitimate business transactions. Under the early common law wagering contracts were enforceable, but they are now generally prohibited in all states by statute. In recent years certain classes of gambling contracts, such as pari-mutuel systems of betting on horse races and dog races, have been legalized in some states.

In general the courts will leave the parties to a gambling contract where it finds them even though one of the parties gains an unfair advantage. If two parties to a gambling contract pay over money to a stakeholder with instructions to pay the money over to the winner, the law varies with each stage of the transaction. The law encourages repentance. Consequently, if one of the parties to a gambling contract repents before the outcome of the gambling event is known, he can demand a return of his money. If the stakeholder pays the money over to the winner, then the loser may sue either the winner or the stakeholder for reimbursement. Some states permit the one who repents the right to demand a return of his deposit even after the outcome of the event is known. This is the minority view. No state will permit the stakeholder to keep the money, for he is considered to be merely a trustee of funds. The court in this event requires the stakeholder to return each wagerer's deposit.

Closely akin to gambling debts are loans made to enable one to gamble. If A loans B $100 and then wins it back in a poker game, is this a gambling debt? Most courts hold that it is not, but some hold otherwise. If *A* and *B* bet $100 on a football game and *B* wins, and if *A* pays *B* by giving him a 90-day note for the $100, this is clearly a gambling debt and is null and void.

Trading on the stock exchange or the grain market represents legitimate business transactions. But the distinction between such trading and gambling contracts is sometimes very fine. These two sets of facts illustrate the distinction:

- Alewine and Goodnoe form a contract whereby Alewine agrees to sell Goodnoe 10,000 shares of stock one month from date at $42 a share. They do not intend actually to buy and sell the stock, but they do agree to settle for the difference between $42 a share and the closing price on the date fixed in the contract. This is a gambling contract.

- Arnold agrees to sell Bolde 10,000 bushels of wheat to be delivered six months later at $1.70 a bushel. Arnold does not own any wheat, but he expects to buy it for delivery. At the end of the six-month period, the seller may not actually deliver the wheat; but if the price of wheat has gone up, the seller may pay the buyer the difference between the current price and the contract, or if the price of wheat has gone down, the buyer may pay the seller the difference. Nevertheless the contract is legal because the intention was to deliver.

The primary difference between the two situations is in the intention to deliver. In the second case Arnold intended at the time of the contract to deliver the wheat and Bolde intended to accept it. In the first case no such intention to deliver existed.

(2) **Sunday Contracts.** The laws pertaining to Sunday contracts are the result of statutory legislation and judicial interpretation. These laws and interpretations vary considerably from state to state. Some of these laws prohibit all Sunday labor except works of necessity and charity. In others both labor and transactions of business on Sunday are prohibited. If only labor is prohibited, a contract though made on Sunday is valid if it does not provide for labor on Sunday. Conversely, if the contract is made on a weekday but calls for labor on Sunday, it is void. If business transactions on Sunday are prohibited, a contract made on Sunday is void because that is classed as a business transaction.

The performance of an act on Sunday which is prohibited by law is a misdemeanor, but seldom are the violators prosecuted. For this reason the types of transactions one observes being carried on on Sunday are not good guides to the restrictions in these laws.

(3) Usurious Contracts. Nearly every state has enacted a law to limit the rate of interest which may be charged for the use of money. Frequently there are two rates, the contract rate and the legal rate. The *contract rate* is the maximum rate which may be charged; any rate above that is *usurious*. The *legal rate*, which is a rate somewhat lower than the contract rate, applies to all situations in which interest may be charged but in which the parties were silent as to the rate. If merchandise is sold on thirty days' credit, the seller may collect interest from the time the thirty days expire till the debt is paid. Since no rate is ordinarily agreed upon in a situation of this kind, the legal rate may be charged.

One cannot accomplish by subterfuge what is prohibited by statute. *Subterfuge* is an attempt to charge a higher rate of interest than is permitted by law, that is, the contract rate. The following are some of the subterfuges that have been held to be usurious:

(a) Requiring the borrower to execute a note for an amount in excess of the actual loan

(b) Requiring the borrower to antedate the note so as to charge interest for a longer period than that agreed on

(c) Requiring the borrower to perform some service or labor for the lender without charge

(d) Charging a brokerage fee for lending one's own money when no broker was used

(e) Requiring the borrower to purchase some article from the lender at an exorbitant price

(f) Requiring the borrower to sell the lender some property he owns at a price considerably below its market value

The penalty for usury varies from state to state. In most states the only penalty is to prohibit the lender from collecting the excess interest. In other states the entire contract is void, and in still others the borrower need not pay any interest but must repay the principal. If the borrower has already paid the usurious interest, the court will require the lender to refund to the borrower any money collected in excess of the statute.

In all states there are special statutes governing loans by pawnbrokers, small loan companies, and finance companies. In some states these firms may charge as much as 42 percent a year. Any rate above that fixed by statute is usurious. On installment loans, the rate may actually be much higher than the legal rate without being considered usurious.

- Solomon borrowed $300 from the City Finance Company, agreeing to repay it in 12 equal monthly payments. The maximum rate of interest is 16 percent. The City Finance Company added the $48 interest to the $300 loan and had Solomon sign a noninterest-bearing note for 12 months at $29 a month. Since he paid interest on all this loan for 12 months but had the use of only one payment for 12 months, the rate of interest was greatly in excess of 16 percent, but it was not usurious. The same law can apply to any installment loan.

- Dupree loaned North $1,000 at 8 percent, the contract rate of interest. They agreed to antedate the loan 90 days. This is a subterfuge to evade the usury law.

(4) Contracts of an Unlicensed Operator. Laws make it illegal to operate certain types of businesses or professions without a license. Most of these laws are made to protect the public from incompetent operators. The most common types of professional persons who must be licensed to operate are doctors, lawyers, certified and licensed public accountants, dentists, insurance salesmen, and real estate salesmen. If anyone performs these services without license, he not only cannot sue to collect for his services but he may also be guilty of a crime. A licensing law may be designed solely as a revenue measure by requiring payment of a fee for a license. If a person operates in one of the fields or businesses covered by such a law, his contracts are held valid even though he does not have a valid license.

(5) Contracts for Sale of Prohibited Articles. If a druggist sells morphine or a similar drug to one who does not have a prescription, he cannot sue to collect the price. One who sells cigarettes or alcoholic beverages to a minor when such sale is prohibited cannot sue on the contract. The court will leave the parties where it finds them.

(6) Contracts in Unreasonable Restraint of Trade. It is the policy of our government to encourage competition. Any contract, therefore, intended to restrain trade unreasonably is null and void. The dividing line between reasonable and unreasonable restraint of trade is often dim, but certain acts have by judicial decision become well established as being in unreasonable restraint of trade. The most common acts in this class are:

(a) Contracts not to compete
(b) Contracts to form a monopoly
(c) Contracts to fix the resale price
(d) Unfair trade practices

(a) **Contracts Not to Compete.** When one purchases a going business, he purchases not only the physical assets but also the goodwill, which is often the most valuable asset of the firm. If the seller should attempt to regain any of the physical assets without paying for them, he could be prosecuted for larceny, robbery, or burglary depending on the method used to regain them. In the absence of a contract prohibiting his attempt to retake the asset "goodwill," he may do so. It is customary and highly desirable when purchasing a business to include in the contract a provision prohibiting the seller from entering the same business again in the trade territory for a specified length of time. Such a contract not to compete is legal if the restriction is reasonable as to both time and space.

The time varies with the type of business, but five years is too long for most types of business. The court decides what is a reasonable time in each individual case, but three years tends to be the maximum safe limit. This gives the buyer time to establish his own goodwill.

The restriction as to territory should not go beyond the trade area of the business. For many types of businesses, such as hardware stores, grocery stores, shoe stores, and similar types of retail outlets, the trade area can be established with reasonable accuracy. But for such firms as motels, barbecue stands, and filling stations the area may be very indefinite. The law simply states the restriction must be reasonable.

- The M and N Cafeteria was owned by Mooney. He sold all equipment and the goodwill to Cohen and agreed not to enter the restaurant business again in the state for two years. The time was reasonable, but the restriction as to territory was too large, making the provision null and void.

Closely allied to this type of contract is one whereby an employee, as a part of his employment contract, agrees not to work for a competing firm for a certain period of time after terminating his employment. These contracts must be reasonable as to time and space. What is a competing firm is not always definite but must be determined in each case by the circumstances.

(b) **Contracts to Form a Monopoly.** Contracts among businessmen to fix prices, divide up the trade territory, limit production so as to reduce the supply, or otherwise limit competition are void. Such contracts which affect interstate commerce and which are therefore subject to regulation by the federal government are specifically declared illegal by the Sherman Antitrust Act and the Clayton Act. Most of the states have similar laws applicable to intrastate commerce.

(c) Contracts to Fix the Resale Price. Under the Federal Sherman Act of 1890 it is illegal for a manufacturer to attempt to control the resale price of its manufactured goods unless the individual manufacturer has his own retail outlets. Several of the states passed legislation permitting resale price maintenance to apply to intrastate trade. In 1937, Congress passed the Miller-Tydings Act, which is in substance a modification of the Sherman Act of 1890 in that it permits manufacturers in one state to make contracts with merchants in other states having resale price maintenance laws without being guilty of restraint of trade. If a state does not have a resale price maintenance law, the Miller-Tydings Act does not permit resale price maintenance. The McGuire Act, passed in 1952, provides that fair-trade agreements are lawful in those states that have fair-trade statutes and that such agreements are binding on nonsigners as well as on signers. Thus an agreement between a manufacturer and a single merchant in a state that legalizes fair-trade agreements becomes binding on all other sellers handling the same merchandise.

(d) Unfair Trade Practices. The Robinson-Patman Act attempted to eliminate certain unfair trade practices in interstate commerce. Under this act it is unlawful to discriminate in price between large and small buyers if the goods are of like grade and quality. Most states have passed similar laws for intrastate commerce. These state laws as a rule go further and prevent the resale of goods at a loss to attract customers. The purpose of these laws is to encourage competition and to prevent monopolies.

Contracts Contrary to Public Policy. Many contracts are unenforceable because they are contrary to public policy. Many acts have been declared by statute to fall within this category; but, as a rule, the courts must determine from the very nature of the act whether or not it is contrary to public policy.

One court, in attempting to classify contracts contrary to public policy, defined them thus: "Whatever tends to injustice, restraint of liberty, restraint of a legal right, whatever tends to the obstruction of justice, a violation of a statute, or the obstruction or perversion of the administration of the law as to executive, legislative, or other official action, whenever embodied in and made the subject of a contract, the contract is against public policy and therefore void and not susceptible to enforcement." (*Brooks* v. *Cooper,* 50 N. J. Eq. 761, 26 A. 978.)

The most common types of contracts that are invalid because they are contrary to public policy are:

1. Contracts limiting the freedom of marriage
2. Contracts obstructing the administration of justice
3. Contracts injuring the public service

(1) Contracts Limiting the Freedom of Marriage. It is contrary to public policy to enter into any contract the effect of which is to limit freedom of marriage, and such contracts are void. The following provisions in contracts have been held to render the contract a nullity: (a) an agreement whereby one party promises never to marry; (b) an agreement to refrain from marrying for a definite period of time (an agreement not to marry during minority, however, is valid); (c) an agreement not to marry certain named individuals; (d) an agreement to seek a divorce for a consideration.

(2) Contracts Obstructing the Administration of Justice. The impartial administration of justice is the cornerstone of democracy. Any contract that may obstruct our legal processes is null and void. It is not necessary that justice actually be obstructed. If the contract has the tendency to do so, the courts will not enforce it.

The following provisions have been held to render contracts void: (a) an agreement to pay a witness a larger fee than that allowed by law, provided the promisor wins the case; (b) an agreement by a candidate for sheriff that he will appoint a certain individual deputy sheriff in return for his aid in bringing about the promisor's election; (c) an agreement to pay a prospective witness a sum of money to leave the state until the trial is over; (d) an agreement not to prosecute a thief if he will return the stolen goods.

(3) Contracts Injuring the Public Service. Any contract that may, from its very nature, injure public service is void. A person may contract as an attorney to appear before any public authority to obtain or oppose the passage of any bill. But a contract to use improper influence to obtain the desired result is void. Also, an agreement to supplement a legislator's salary has been held to be void because it tends to injure public service.

Contracts to use one's influence in obtaining a public contract usually let to the lowest competent bidder, to obtain pardons and paroles, and to pay a public official more or less than the statutory salary are also void.

QUESTIONS

1. May a contract for a lawful purpose be enforced if it calls for performance by illegal methods? Explain.
2. What is the effect of a contract a part of which is illegal?
3. What are some of the types of contracts that are illegal?
4. What is the test of a gambling transaction?
5. What is the distinction between gambling and trading on the stock or grain exchanges?
6. If a law prohibits acts of labor on Sunday, what effect does it have on a contract?
7. What is the difference between the contract rate of interest and the legal rate of interest?
8. Give three illustrations of subterfuges to avoid the usury laws.
9. If a real estate agent who is not licensed sells a house, is the owner bound to pay the commission?
10. If John loans Henry $100 so that they can have a poker game, is this a gambling debt?
11. If John purchases the Trenton Shoe Store from Mitchell, may he include an enforceable clause in the contract binding Mitchell not to enter the shoe business again in the United States?
12. Donald promises to pay Henry $1,000 if he will leave the state so that he cannot be called as a witness against Donald. Is this a valid contract?
13. Give an illustration of a contract restricting the freedom of marriage.

CASE PROBLEMS

1. Hall entered into a contract with the Dale Plumbing Company to install an extra bathroom in his home. All the terms of this contract were agreed upon and signed on Sunday. The Dale Plumbing Company installed the fixtures in a very haphazard manner so that the fixtures were unusable without expensive repairs. This condition was not discovered until after Hall had paid the contract price.

   (a) If the law merely prohibits labor on Sunday, may Hall recover damages from the Dale Plumbing Company for breach of contract?
   (b) If the law prohibits both labor and business transactions on Sunday, would your answer be different?

2. Andrews entered into a contract with the Chapman Construction Company to build a garage for $60,000. The construction price included all labor, materials, and architectural services, the architectural designs having been prepared by an employee of the Chapman Construction Company. Neither the employee nor anyone connected with the firm was a licensed architect. After the Chapman Construction Company had done about $5,000 worth of work, Andrews ordered him to stop and refused to pay for any work already done. Is Andrews liable? If the contract had called for the

labor and materials to be $58,000 and the architectural fees to be $2,000, would your answer be different?

3. Frances, 30, was engaged to marry Leonard. Dr. Hoag, the grandfather of Frances, disapproved strongly of Leonard. He paid Frances $15,000 upon her promise "to break the engagement and never to marry Leonard." About six months later she and Leonard were married, and Dr. Hoag sued for a return of the $15,000. Must Frances repay it?

4. Lund was store manager for the Downtown Sporting Goods, Inc. Boland wished to purchase an expensive pistol the store had for sale. A state law made it illegal to sell pistols to anyone who did not have a police permit to carry one. Lund did not know of this law and sold the pistol to Boland on credit. Boland never paid for it, and the seller sued. Must Boland pay for it?

5. The Akin Trucking Company was in desperate need of a loan of $10,000 but could not obtain one without collateral as security. It had no acceptable collateral. The bookkeeper owned $10,000 worth of industrial bonds. He offered to loan these to the firm to use as collateral if the firm would pay him 10 percent a year for their use. The offer was accepted. Was this contract usurious?

6. Harrell was desperately in need of money. Fortson was willing to loan him some money if some way could be devised to enable him to charge more than 8 percent interest, the contract rate. Harrell suggested that he give a note for the loan but antedate it 6 months. Fortson accepted this offer and loaned him $500 for 6 months, but the note was made to read 12 months. Was this contract usurious?

7. Hunt contracted with the Blank Manufacturing Company to use his influence with the proper government officials to obtain a $10,000,000 government contract for the Blank Company. Hunt was to receive 5 percent of any contract he obtained, nothing if he was unsuccessful. His contract bound him to use all methods "fair or foul" to obtain the contract. Through bribery he obtained a $6,000,000 contract and then demanded a fee of $300,000. Was he entitled to collect?

8. Pearl Klug purchased and paid for a dress on Sunday in a state where executory contracts on Sunday were void. She asked the seller to hold the dress a few days, and said she would call for it later. Two days later she took the dress home. A week later Pearl returned the dress and demanded the return of her money. Was she entitled to its return?

9. Adams owned a hardware store in a town of about 10,000 population. Many of his customers were farmers who lived in the surrounding territory. The street on which the store was located was a state highway. Therefore, he did a small amount of business with tourists and travelers. Adams sold the business, including the goodwill, to Baker. As a part of the selling price, Adams agreed not to engage in the hardware business in that particular county for five years. Three years later Adams again entered the hardware business in that county, and Baker brought suit to prevent his doing this. Discuss the legal rights of the parties, and state your conclusion.

CHAPTER 9

FORM OF CONTRACTS

REASONS FOR WRITTEN CONTRACTS

All contracts of importance ought to be in writing, but only a few must be written in order to be enforceable. An oral contract, if its meaning can be ascertained, is just as effective and enforceable as a written contract unless it is one of the few types specifically required by statute to be in writing.

A written contract has several advantages over an oral contract, provided it includes all the terms and provisions of the agreement. In the first place, the existence of a contract cannot be denied if it is in writing. If there were no witnesses when an oral contract was formed, one of the parties might successfully deny that any contract was formed. The party suing on a contract must establish the existence of that contract together with its contents by a preponderance of the evidence. In the second place, one of the parties may die or become insane. The administrator or executor of an estate in case of death, or the committee or guardian in case of insanity, is tremendously handicapped in enforcing an oral agreement made previously by the deceased or insane person. Even when there are witnesses present at the time an oral contract is formed, the testimony may vary considerably as to the actual terms of the contract. Written evidence, composed in clear and unambiguous language, is always better than oral evidence.

For these reasons most businessmen prefer to have contracts pertaining to matters of considerable importance reduced to writing even when this precaution is not required by law.

PAROL EVIDENCE RULE

There would be little reason to reduce a contract to writing if its terms could be altered by *parol evidence,* that is, oral testimony. The law presumes that a written contract contains all the provisions agreed to by the parties during their preliminary negotiations culminating in an offer and an acceptance. This written document is now the sole evidence of the contract. The law presumes that each of the contracting parties read the contract before he signed it and further that he would not have signed it had the written form deviated from the terms of the oral contract. The parol evidence rule applies only (1) when the writing indicates a complete contract, and (2) when the contract is not defective in any manner. Below are listed some conditions where either one or both of these criteria are not met:

(a) If the written document contains only an offer, oral testimony may be introduced to establish an oral acceptance of that offer. Here the writing is clearly not a complete contract.

(b) If the contract was obtained by fraud, duress, undue influence, or a rectifiable mistake, oral testimony may be introduced to establish these facts. It was never a completely valid contract.

(c) If there is clearly a typing error, or if there is some contradictory term, oral testimony may be called upon to clarify these items so as to determine the true contract, not to alter it.

(d) If a written contract is delivered upon an oral agreement that it was not to become effective until the happening of some named event.

(e) If some important terms of the contract are not stated, this may be due to custom. For example, if nothing is said about whether a sale is for cash or credit, one party can prove by oral testimony that the custom is always cash if nothing is said about credit terms. The custom must be uniform and widespread in the particular business or locality.

(f) The parties to a written contract may orally agree at a subsequent date to substitute a new oral contract for the written one. Parol evidence can be used to establish the substitution.

(g) If there is any ambiguity or apparent alteration in the written contract, oral testimony may be introduced for establishing ambiguity or alteration.

STATUTE OF FRAUDS

In the year 1677 the English Parliament enacted a statute, one of the chief provisions of which was an attempt to prevent fraud and perjuries. This act was known as the *Statute of Frauds*. The statute listed certain classes of contracts which could not be enforced unless their terms were reduced to writing and unless they were signed by the parties to be bound. The fourth and the seventeenth sections of the Statute of Frauds contained a list of these contracts. Most of our states have adopted these two sections with but slight variations.

It is well to remember that in our country it is not the English Statute of Frauds but its American adaptation that determines which contracts must be in writing. The general provisions of the fourth section are given below, while those in the seventeenth section will be discussed in Chapter 14.

The Statute of Frauds applies only to executory contracts. If two parties enter into an oral contract, which in order to be valid must be in writing, and both parties have fully performed according to its terms, neither party can challenge the validity of the contract. The purpose of the Statute of Frauds is to bar oral testimony and to establish the terms of certain contracts, not to prevent the performance of contracts that are valid in all particulars except that they are not in writing.

FOURTH SECTION OF THE STATUTE OF FRAUDS

The fourth section of the Statute of Frauds provides that the following types of agreements must be in writing:

1. An agreement of an executor or administrator to pay debts of the estate from his personal funds

2. An agreement to become responsible for the debts, default, or miscarriage of another

3. An agreement in which the promise of one person is made in consideration of marriage

4. An agreement to sell, or a sale of, land or any interest in or concerning land

5. An agreement the terms of which do not call for performance within one year from the time it is made

(1) An Agreement of an Executor or Administrator to Pay the Debts of the Estate. When a person dies, his executor (if he left a will), or his administrator (if he left no will), takes over all his assets and from these assets pays all the debts of the deceased before distributing the remainder to the heirs. The executor or the administrator is not expected to pay the debts of the deceased out of his personal funds. He may wish to do so under certain circumstances, however, in order to protect the estate. For this reason, his promise to pay the debts of the estate from his personal funds is in reality a contract to become responsible for the debts of another and must be in writing to be enforceable.

The Statute does not apply when the administrator or the executor enters into an original contract relative to the estate. For example, an agreement to cover burial arrangements for the deceased does not come within the statute.

(2) An Agreement to Become Responsible for the Debts, Default, or Miscarriage of Another. The term "debt" here refers to an obligation to pay money; "default" refers to a breach of contractual obligations other than money, such as a contract to build a house; and a "miscarriage" refers to duties and obligations not based on a contract, such as a sheriff's obligation to perform the duties of his office in a creditable manner.

A man may obligate himself to pay the debts of another if he cares to do so even though he receives no benefit from it. To be enforceable, such a contract must be in writing. Contracts of this nature are generally referred to as "guaranty" and "suretyship," topics which are discussed in Chapter 42. It is important to note carefully the wording of a guaranty. One must actually stand for the debt of another. Taking upon oneself an original obligation, even though another receives the benefit, need not be in writing.

> ▪ John, nineteen and married, needed a house. He contracted with Johnson to purchase a house for $16,000. Johnson, knowing the risk of contracting with minors for real estate, required John to have his Uncle Henry guarantee performance by John. He wrote out a guarantee as follows: "I hereby guarantee John will perform on this contract as agreed. If he does not, I obligate myself to do so." This was signed by Henry. This is the precaution the law requires if one wishes to avoid the risk of loss in contracting with minors.

This rule does not hold if the main purpose of the guaranty is to gain some advantage for the guarantor. This provision of the Statute of Frauds was designed especially for those situations where one guarantees the debt of another person purely as an accommodation to that person. There are situations where one person guarantees the debt or default of another because it is to the guarantor's personal financial interest to do so. When the guaranty is not gratuitous but is a calculated business proposition, the contract of guaranty need not be in writing.

- Ward owned and operated a farm. Robinson worked the crops on a share-crop basis. Ward said to a merchant, "Let my tenant, Robinson, have credit up to $50 a month during the crop season; and if he does not pay you in the fall, I will." This wording makes this a contract of guaranty, but it need not be in writing. The main purpose was to gain some advantage for Ward himself.

This provision does not apply if one party promises the debtor directly that he will pay his debt. For this provision to apply there must be three parties and two contracts. The two contracts consist of (1) one between the principal, that is the creditor, and the debtor and (2) one between the creditor and the guarantor. If one promises the debtor directly to pay his debt, then there is no contract between the creditor and the alleged guarantor.

- Durwood sold Kenney an air conditioner for $400 and gave him 90 days to pay for it. Kenney became ill and his Uncle Glen said to him, "Don't worry; when it falls due, I will pay it." Durwood learned of this promise and attempted to compel Glen to pay it. Durwood cannot do so since the promise was not made to him.

(3) An Agreement in Which the Promise of One Person Is Made in Consideration of Marriage. Mutual promises to marry constitute an enforceable contract in most states. The consideration of each party is the promise of the other party, and the contract need not be written. An agreement that is based upon marriage as the consideration for a promise to pay money to another or to settle property upon another must be in writing.

- McClellan orally promised Henrietta to deed her his home if she would marry him. After the marriage, McClellan refused to execute the deed. He was not bound to do so since the promise was made orally.

(4) An Agreement to Sell, or a Sale of Land, or Any Interest in or Concerning Land. In a sale of land generally two contracts are involved. The first is a contract to sell. This contract should include all the terms agreed upon by the parties. At a later date, another contract is executed and title to the land is conveyed. There must be written evidence of both of these contracts to make them binding. The contract conveying real estate, called a *deed*, must not only be in writing but also must be notarized.

One may wish to sell, not the land itself, but only an interest in the land. The evidence of this contract also must be in writing. These sales usually involve rights of way, joint use of driveways, mineral rights, timber, and any other interest in land. A lease for more than one year must also be in writing.

- Truman orally agreed to permit Smith to build a driveway across his lot. The price was to be $500. Truman later refused to go through with the agreement. He is within his rights because such agreements must be in writing to be valid.

Frequently, oral contracts relative to land are performed before any question of their validity is raised. For example, one leases a building by oral contract for two years. He occupies the building for that period and then refuses to pay the rent, alleging that the contract is invalid because it is oral. The law will compel him to pay the rent. If one has paid money or performed a service under an oral contract, he may recover the money or the value of the service even though he cannot enforce the executory part of the contract.

(5) An Agreement the Terms of Which Do Not Call for Performance Within One Year from the Time It Is Made. The terms of a contract that cannot be performed in one year are likely to be forgotten. To minimize the need to resort to the courts to determine one's right, the law requires all contracts that cannot be performed within one year to be in writing.

This provision of the Statute of Frauds has led to endless litigation because there are so many different interpretations put upon it. Properly interpreted, it means that if the terms of the contract are such that by their nature they cannot be performed within one year from the date of the contract, then the contract must be in writing. The contract can be so worded that it may not be completed for fifty years, yet if it is physically possible to complete it within one year, it need not be in writing. If John agrees in consideration of $5,000 to care for Smith for "as long as he (Smith) lives," this contract need not be in writing because there is no certainty Smith will live one year.

NOTE OR MEMORANDUM

The laws dealing with written contracts are concerned primarily with requiring written evidence of the contract rather than requiring the contract itself to be in writing. In the sale of land, the contract itself, that is the deed, must be in writing. In other cases the law is complied with if some written note or memorandum setting forth all the relevant facts is present. The memorandum must contain the names of the parties, the subject matter of the contract, the basic terms of the contract, including the price and the manner of delivery, and it must be signed by the one to be charged.

A written contract must be signed by both parties. This is not true of the note or memorandum. If suit is instituted on a contract that is evidenced by a memorandum, clearly one of the parties wishes to be bound. He need not sign it since he will abide by its terms anyway. If he sues, the other one is the party that is charged. If this party has signed the memorandum, the contract is enforceable against him.

The law states that the memorandum must contain all the essential terms of the contract; yet it differs materially from a written contract. Probably the chief difference is that one may introduce oral testimony to explain or complete the memorandum. Under the parol evidence rule, this is not true of a contract. The court held the following receipt was an adequate memorandum: "Received of Sholowitz twenty-five dollars to bind the bargain for the sale of Noorigan's brick store and land at 46 Blackstone Street to Sholowitz. Balance due $1,975." The size of the lot, the type of deed, and other essentials could be established by oral evidence.

The memorandum need not be made at the time of the contract. It need be in existence only at the time suit is brought. The one who signs the memorandum need not sign with the intention of binding himself. If Jones writes Smith, "Since my agreement to buy your Buick for $1,200 was oral, I am not bound by it," this is a sufficient memorandum and makes the contract binding on Jones.

OTHER WRITTEN CONTRACTS

The five classes of contracts that are listed by the Statute of Frauds are not the only contracts required by law to be in writing in order to be enforceable. Every state has a few additional requirements. The more common ones are insurance contracts, contracts reviving a debt that has been extinguished by bankruptcy or by a Statute of Limitations, and agreements that are not to be performed during the lifetime of the promisor, but only after his death.

QUESTIONS

1. As a general rule, an oral contract is just as enforceable as a written contract. Why, then, should all important contracts be in writing?
2. What is the parol evidence rule?

3. Give an example of oral testimony that may be introduced to explain the terms of a written contract.

4. Which contracts of an administrator or an executor need not be in writing?

5. Under what circumstances would an administrator promise to pay the debts of the estate from his personal funds?

6. (a) If one takes upon himself an original obligation, even though the benefits go to another party, must the contract be in writing to be enforceable?

(b) If one contracts to be responsible for the debt of another in order to obtain some advantage for himself, must this contract be in writing?

7. What is the difference between a "contract of sale" of land and one "to sell"?

8. Must a memorandum be made at the same time the contract is made?

9. Is a memorandum binding on the one signing it even though he never intended it to be a memorandum?

10. If the main purpose of entering into a contract of guaranty is to gain some advantage for the guarantor, must the contract be in writing?

11. Was the Statute of Frauds passed to prevent fraud?

12. Name some types of contracts that must be in writing.

CASE PROBLEMS

1. By means of an oral contract Holcomb was appointed an agent for the Burlington Life Insurance Company for five years and was to be paid a commission of 12½ percent of premium on the first five years' premiums. The insurance company refused to pay any commissions after the first year, claiming no liability on the oral contract. Are they bound?

2. Kemp was a combination cashier and bookkeeper for the Kerns Brick Company. Since he handled all the money for the firm, he was required to furnish a $10,000 bond. Kemp's father-in-law, DuPont, orally agreed to be personally liable for any shortages that might be found in the company's funds. Kemp could not get a bond from a commercial bonding company and would have lost his job if DuPont had not supplied the bond. Kemp owed DuPont $3,000; DuPont was afraid Kemp could not pay him if he lost his job. The auditor discovered a $2,000 shortage in the company's accounts, and the shortage was traced directly to Kemp. Can DuPont be held liable on his oral promise?

3. The Cofer Office Equipment Company entered into a written contract with the Hunt Insurance Company to keep all the insurance company's equipment repaired for the next three years for a monthly fee of $100. This written contract was signed, and each party retained a copy. It was orally agreed that the contract was not to become effective unless Congress passed

a new accelerated depreciation law. This law was never passed. The Cofer Office Equipment sued for breach of contract. The Hunt Insurance Company attempted to prove by parol evidence the existence of this oral side agreement. May it do so?

4. Casey was employed by a written contract to serve as bookkeeper for the Standard Block Company at a salary of $400 a month. The contract was to run for one year. After Casey went to work, he learned that he was expected to work 48 hours a week. He had expected to work only 40 hours. Casey attempted to prove by oral testimony that it is customary for bookkeepers in that community to work only 40 hours a week. May he do so?

5. John rented a house by oral contract for two years at $125 a month. He soon became dissatisfied with the deal since he learned he could rent a better house for $100 a month. He did not learn that this oral contract was not binding on him until after two years. He then demanded that the landlord reimburse him $25 a month for two years. May he do so?

6. The Reed Paper Company had for some time been negotiating with Downs on a business deal of the utmost importance to the company. The parties finally reached an agreement. Paul Chapman, secretary to the president of the Reed Paper Company, made a written memorandum of the contract, and Downs signed it. Chapman filed the memorandum. Later Downs refused to conform to his agreement. The memorandum could not be found since Chapman could not remember how or where he had filed it. The contract involved the sale of several thousand acres of pulpwood and the processing of the wood into paper over a period of three years. Could this contract be enforced if the memorandum was not found?

7. Mosely was employed by the Crawford Company at $350 a month. A competing firm in a nearby city offered Mosely $400 a month. The contract was made on May 10 with the work to start on July 1 and was to last for at least twelve months from July. All the arrangements were made orally. Mosely resigned his position with the Crawford Company, sold his home, and had his furniture packed and ready to move when he was notified that the position was not available. What recourse did Mosely have?

8. John Barner was sales manager for the Patterson Motor Company. Billy Seabolt, a minor, agreed to purchase a secondhand car for $1,400. As a part of the contract Barner stipulated that an adult must "stand good" for the payment. Steedman, an uncle of Seabolt, said, "Let him have the car; and if he does not keep up the payments, I will." This was an oral promise. Barner interpreted this wording to meet the test of a contract of guaranty; consequently he did not require it to be in writing. Seabolt wrecked the car and then demanded a refund. Could Barner look to Steedman for the selling price?

9. Pat Snow owned and operated the Snow Barber Shop. He orally contracted with Buddy Broadnax to give Broadnax, a druggist, and his three boys all the haircuts and shaves they needed for the next two years for $300 cash. Broadnax was to pay the money the next day, but he changed his mind and refused to pay it. Snow wrote Broadnax a letter and demanded that "you pay me the $550 as you promised." Broadnax immediately replied by letter, "I never agreed to pay $550. It was $300. Anyway it is an oral contract, so try to collect it." Snow claimed this constituted a sufficient memorandum. Do you agree?

10. Beverly Hick and Myrna Mathis were secretaries. On October 8 they rented an efficiency apartment where they could prepare their meals. To tidy up the apartment, they repapered it, painted all woodwork, and made various other improvements. The total cost of the improvements amounted to $180. Their oral lease was to run to December 31, the following year. Three months later the landlord raised the rent $25 a month. Could he compel them to pay it?

11. Darlington purchased a piano from Davey, Incorporated, for $560. A sales ticket was made out and signed by Darlington. The sales ticket contained a statement that delivery was to be made December 5, and payment was to be made on delivery. When the truck drivers brought the piano, Darlington refused to receive and pay for it. Davey, Incorporated, sued him for breach of contract. Was he liable?

12. John and Mary Dennis entered into an oral agreement with George Carpenter, a contractor, to build a house for them. Many proposals and counterproposals were made. When the parties finally agreed to all the terms, they decided to reduce the terms to writing. Carpenter agreed to write the contract. When John and Mary Dennis read it, they contended that the price agreed upon included a terrace not shown on the blueprint. Carpenter then agreed to include the terrace, but he suggested that they sign the contract as it had been prepared. They signed the contract. When he built the house, Carpenter refused to include the terrace, and John and Mary Dennis withheld $100 from the final payment. Carpenter sued for the $100. Who was entitled to win? Why?

CHAPTER 10

ASSIGNMENT OF

CONTRACTS

RIGHTS AND OBLIGATIONS

A contract grants both rights and obligations. Originally, one who is not a party to the contract has no right to the benefits to be derived from the contract, nor has he any of the duties or obligations. Third parties, however, may acquire these rights or assume these duties.

If a contract is executory, that is, if it has not been performed by either party or both parties, one of them may wish to transfer his rights or to delegate his duties under the contract, or to do both. If one party assigns the contract in its entirety, this is referred to as an assignment while in reality it is "an assignment and a delegation." The term "delegation" is, however, used only to describe a contract whereby one transfers to another his duties or obligations under a contract but retains his rights. Whether or not he may legally do so depends upon the nature and content of the contract.

- Johnson made a contract with DeFoe whereby DeFoe was to wire Johnson's house. For this service Johnson agreed to pay DeFoe $325. DeFoe delegated the job to Harris who agreed to do the work in payment of his note to DeFoe. This is a valid delegation of duties without assigning the right to receive $325 upon the completion of the work.

ASSIGNMENT OF RIGHTS

As a general rule, the rights under a contract may be assigned, but the duties and obligations under a contract may not be assigned. One's rights under a contract may be transferred almost as freely as his property rights. Such a transfer is referred to in law as an assignment. An *assignment* may, therefore, be defined as the means whereby one party conveys his rights or interest in a contract to another who is not a party to the original undertaking. The party making the assignment is known as the *assignor*; the one to whom the right is transferred is the *assignee*.

RESTRICTIONS ON ONE'S RIGHT TO ASSIGN

Since an assignment is a voluntary act, it is not the purpose of the law to impose many restrictions upon one's liberty to assign his rights under contracts. About the only legal restriction of any significance is a law prohibiting the assignment of future pay by soldiers, sailors, and marines. This is based on the theory that it is contrary to public policy. Many states and cities also prohibit the assignment of the pay of public officials. Employees on public works are in many states prohibited by law from assigning a certain minimum percentage of their wages. This is to protect the wage earner and his family from hard-pressing creditors.

Often one's right under a contract is to receive the services of the other party, such as a bookkeeper, salesman, or other employee who contracts to work for a stipulated period of time. The right to this party's personal services cannot be assigned, but such a restriction is not the result of a statutory law. Courts merely refuse to honor and enforce the attempted assignment. This limitation applies to all employees. The law will not compel you to work for a man or firm against your will.

An assignment of a right is voidable if it imposes new conditions upon the party to the contract, whether the new conditions are favorable or unfavorable. For example, if you have the right under a contract to have 50,000 bricks delivered at a stipulated price to a certain town, you cannot assign that right to another person and have the bricks delivered to a different town even though it is nearer to the seller's place of business. If the assignment imposes a new condition that is material upon the other party, he is not bound to honor the assignment. This in reality constitutes a material alteration of the contract.

The parties to a contract may include a provision that prohibits the other party from assigning his rights. A limitation to this rule is that if the only right under the contract is to receive money, this right cannot be prohibited by contract.

DELEGATION OF DUTIES

A party to a contract cannot delegate his duties under the contract with the same enforceability as he can assign his rights. If Allen retains Bentley, an attorney, to obtain a divorce for him for a fee of $250, Bentley can assign his right to receive the $250 to anyone and Allen must pay. He may not, however, delegate his duty to represent Allen in the divorce proceeding. In those contracts that involve trust and confidence, one may not delegate his duties. If one employs the Local Wonder Band to play for a dance, the contract cannot be assigned even to a nationally known band. Taste, confidence, and trust cannot be scientifically measured. But if one hires Horne to paint his house for $300, whether or not the house has been painted right can easily be determined by a painting expert.

Only when the performance is standardized or nontechnical may one delegate its performance to another. In the construction industry, for example, there are many instances of delegation of duties because the correct performance can be easily ascertained. Contracts calling for unskilled work or labor may in most instances be delegated.

In all cases of delegation the delegating party remains fully liable under the contract. He may be sued for any breach of contract even though another party actually performed. In such an event he may in turn sue the party who performed inadequately.

ASSIGNMENT OF FUTURE CONTRACTS

As a general rule one may not assign a contract not yet in existence even though one may make a valid contract "to assign" when the contract does come into existence. If A has a contract to sell B his house for $20,000 and to take a $15,000 mortgage as security for the unpaid purchase price, A may not assign this mortgage to C until he actually gets it. He can, however, contract for a future assignment. The contract for future assignment must have a reasonable certainty of coming into existence. If Ashby assigns his wages to Campbell, there must be some wages due at the time of assignment. Ashby may not on Friday assign next week's wages but after he begins work Monday morning, he may assign all that week's wages. The laws in this regard vary widely from state to state, but the general rule is that only rights actually or potentially held under contracts may be assigned. Contingent rights and expectations may not be assigned by law. Equity courts are not bound by strict rules of law; they may approve an assignment of a mere contingent right if justice will be served.

EFFECT OF AN ASSIGNMENT

The nonassigning party retains all his rights and defenses as though there had never been an assignment. For example, if the nonassigning party was incompetent to contract, or entered into the contract under duress, undue influence, fraud, or misrepresentation, he may offer these defenses against the assignee as effectively as he could have done against the assignor.

The assignee must take the contract as it exists at the time of the assignment. The effect of the assignment upon the assignor is not uniform throughout the various states. If Smith leases a house for two years from Hart, and then assigns the lease to Sebba, Smith, in most states, remains liable for the rent. He may avoid this liability by obtaining a release from Hart.

Most assignments involve claims for money. The Fair Deal Grocery Company assigned $10,000 worth of its accounts receivable to the First National Bank. The assignor warranted that the accounts were genuine. If a customer, therefore, refused to pay the bank because he did not owe the account, the grocery company would be liable. If he failed to pay merely because he was insolvent, most courts would hold that the assignor was not liable.

WARRANTIES OF THE ASSIGNOR

When one assigns his rights under a contract to an assignee for a consideration, he makes three implied warranties:

(1) That he is the true owner of the right

(2) That the right is valid and subsisting at the time the assignment is made

(3) That there are no unrevealed defenses available to the debtor

As in all contracts, if there is a breach of warranty by the assignor, the assignee may seek to recover his loss from the assignor. There is one important implied warranty, however, that the assignor does not make, namely that the debtor is solvent.

■ The Harbottle Distributing Company owed the Norfolk Brewery $10,000. In payment Harbottle assigned $10,000 of its accounts receivable to the Norfolk Brewery. The assignee was able to collect only $7,000 of these accounts because the debtors were insolvent. The brewery has no recourse to Harbottle. Had the $3,000 been uncollectible because the debtors had valid defenses to the claims, then the Harbottle Distributing Company would have had to make good the loss.

In the case above the Norfolk Brewery Company erred by taking these accounts receivable by assignment. In this case Harbottle Distributing Company paid its debt, not with cash, but by a transfer of title of its accounts receivables. From the brewery company's standpoint the same result could have been obtained, not by taking title to these accounts, but by taking them merely as collateral security for their debt with a provision that the brewery was to collect the accounts and apply the proceeds on the $10,000. Under this arrangement, the brewery could have looked to the assignor for the balance of $3,000.

FORM OF THE ASSIGNMENT

An assignment may be made either by operation of law or by the act of the parties. In the event of death, the rights and duties (except for personal services) of the deceased are assigned by law to the administrator of the estate. In the event of bankruptcy, the rights and duties of the bankrupt are assigned by operation of law to the trustee in bankruptcy. These two types of assignments are automatic. The assignment is effective without any intervening act of the parties.

When the assignment is made by act of the parties, it may be either written or oral. If the original contract is one which must be in writing, the assignment must be in writing; otherwise, it may be made orally. It is always preferable to make the assignment in writing. This may be done in the case of written contracts by writing the terms of the assignment on the original contract. Oral contracts may be assigned by executing an informal written assignment. The following written assignment is adequate in most cases:

> In consideration of the Local Finance Company's canceling my debt of $500 to it, I hereby assign to the Local Finance Company $500 owed to me by the Dale Sand and Gravel Company.
>
> Signed at noon, Friday, December 16, 1963, at Benson, Iowa.
>
> (Signed) Harold Locke

NOTICE OF AN ASSIGNMENT

As a general rule, no notice of an assignment need be given. Business prudence demands that the original promisor be notified. The promisor has a right to assume that the claim has not been assigned unless otherwise notified. For example, F. Dodd promised to pay Hodges $500 in thirty days. When the account came due, Dodd, since he had no notice of assignment, was safe in paying Hodges. But if Hodges had assigned the account to Wilson and Wilson had not given Dodd notice, then Wilson would not have been able to collect from Dodd. If Hodges were inclined to be dishonest, he could sell the account to several persons. The assignee who first notified Dodd of the assignment would have the first claim. A few states hold that the first assignee gets preference.

In the event the assignor assigns a larger sum than the debtor owes, there is no obligation on the debtor to pay the entire assignment. If there are several assignments, the sum of which exceeds the amount owed, then the debtor must exercise due caution in determining which ones to honor. Two problems generally arise. The first one arises when all assignees notify the debtor before he pays anyone. Here he must pay according to the law of his state. Some state laws stipulate that the assignee who first notifies the debtor gets paid first. Because of this law, prudence demands that a memorandum of the notice should be made, fixing the day, the hour, and even the minute notice was received. Other state laws stipulate that the assignments must be honored in the order in which they are made. This is always difficult if the assignment is oral. Even written assignments seldom show the hour of day the assignment was made. Regardless of the difficulty, the debtor is held responsible for fixing the priority.

The second problem arises when the debtor has paid the assignee and then receives another notice of assignment from one having priority, the case in those states in which the first assignment has priority. Most states permit the assignee who was paid first to keep the money. A few states still follow the common-law rule barring the creditor from splitting up the assignment. Most states now permit the creditor to do this.

- Aderholt was head of the Payroll Department of the Frost Tire Company. One of the employees assigned $150 in wages in three separate assignments, but the company owed him only $90. Aderholt paid them in the order of the date of the assignment. The law in his state required him to pay them in the order the notices were received. The Frost Tire Company was required to pay the assignee who first gave notice even though it did not owe the employee any additional wages.

NOVATION

Novation is the substitution of a new obligation for an old one, which is thereby extinguished. In the assignment of duties and obligations, the assignor is not relieved of his duties. He becomes fully responsible for the proper performance of the duties by the assignee. It is very important, therefore, to distinguish between an assignment and a novation.

If Goff owes Ratcliff $500, Goff cannot shift this obligation to Lester without Ratcliff's consent. Ratcliff, however, can consent to the release of Goff and the substitution of Lester. In this event there is not an assignment, but a novation; that is, a new contract is formed. Goff is fully discharged. An obligation may be shifted in this manner only with the consent of all the parties.

THIRD PARTY BENEFICIARY CONTRACTS

At common law only the parties to a contract could sue upon it or seek to enforce it. It was held that strangers to a contract had no interest and thus no rights under a contract. But courts began to make exceptions to the rule when it seemed evident that the contracting parties intended to benefit a third person, called a *third party beneficiary*.

The rule today is that a third person who is expressly benefited by the performance of the contract may enforce it against the promisor if benefit to the third party was intended by the contracting parties. The third person may be either a creditor beneficiary or a donee beneficiary. A *creditor beneficiary* is a creditor of the person whose obligation will be discharged to the extent that the promisor performs his promise. A *donee beneficiary* is one to whom no legal duty was owed by the promisee but to whom performance is a gift. A common example of a donee beneficiary is the beneficiary named in a life insurance contract.

Not everyone who benefits by the performance of a contract between others is properly considered a third party beneficiary with rights under the contract. If a person is merely incidentally benefited by the performance of a contract, he is not entitled to sue for breach or to sue for performance. For example, if a town contracts with a contractor for the paving of a certain street and the contractor fails to perform, the property owners whose property would have been improved by the paving are not entitled to sue for damages for nonperformance because they were to be only incidentally benefited. The contract for the paving of the street was designed essentially to further the public interest; it was not designed to benefit certain property owners.

JOINT, SEVERAL, AND JOINT AND SEVERAL CONTRACTS

When two or more persons enter into a contract with one or more other persons, the contract may be joint, several, or joint and several.

Joint Contracts. A *joint contract* is one in which two or more persons jointly promise to carry out an obligation or one in which two or more persons are jointly entitled to the performance of another party or parties. If Sands and Cole sign a contract stating "we jointly promise . . . ," the obligation is the joint obligation of Sands and Cole. Unless otherwise expressed, a promise by two or more persons is generally presumed to be joint and not several.

Several Contracts. A *several contract* arises when two or more persons individually agree to perform the same obligation even though the individual agreements are contained in the same document. If Sands and Cole sign a contract stating "we severally promise" or "each of us promises" to do a particular thing, the two signers are individually bound to perform.

Joint and Several Contracts. A *joint and several contract* is one in which two or more persons are bound both jointly and severally. If Sands and Cole sign a contract stating "we, and each of us, promise" or "I promise" to perform a particular act, they are jointly and severally obligated. The other party to the contract may treat the obligation as either a joint obligation or as a group of individual obligations, and he may bring suit against all or against one at a time. By statute in some states, a joint contract is interpreted to be a joint and several contract.

QUESTIONS

1. What is an assignment?
2. Name and identify the parties to an assignment.
3. In what ways may an assignment be made?
4. Why may rights to personal services not be assigned?
5. If one delegates his duties under a contract, what is his liability under the contract?
6. What is the effect of an assignment upon each party involved?
7. Whom should the assignee notify of the assignment?

8. Give an illustration of a serious loss that might occur if a bookkeeper failed to make a record of the day, hour, and minute when he received notice of an assignment.

9. If one becomes dissatisfied with a contract, may he get rid of it by assigning it to someone else?

10. What is the difference between a third party beneficiary and an incidental beneficiary?

11. Explain the meaning of joint, several, and joint and several contracts.

CASE PROBLEMS

1. The Commerce Building Supply Company purchased $5,000 worth of saw logs from Brown. Brown assigned his right to this $5,000. Davis was the assignee for $4,000, Dorsey for $3,000, and Martin for $2,000. Each of the assignees notified the Commerce Building Supply Company of the assignment, but the secretary failed to make a record of the day and the hour each notice was received. If the law requires the assignments to be paid in the order the notices were received, how can the Commerce Building Supply Company determine whom to pay?

2. Hamblen Lumber Company made all its employees sign a contract agreeing not to make any assignment of their wages. In spite of this, Stover, an employee, assigned $80 of his wages to the Ferguson Company. This company immediately notified Donahue, the bookkeeper of the Hamblen Lumber Company, of the assignment. Donahue refused to honor it and paid Stover the full amount due him. The Ferguson Company sued the Hamblen Lumber Company for the $80 since Stover never paid the account. Was the lumber company liable?

3. Eugene Black was credit manager for a furniture store. Stine purchased some furniture and in payment assigned to the furniture store $800 which was owed to him by the Clarke Engineering Corporation. Since the $800 was not due until ten days after the date of the assignment, Black held it until that date and presented it for payment. Payment was refused because Stine had offered the Clarke Engineering Corporation a 10 percent discount if they would pay him before the account was due. This they did. Must the corporation also pay the furniture store?

4. The Holcomb Filling Station sold a lot of gasoline on credit to local business firms. One of these firms, The Apex Bakery, was in debt to the station for $450. The owner of the bakery offered to turn over to the station $500 of its accounts receivable if the station would not sue the bakery. The offer was accepted. The filling station was able to collect only $100 on the accounts receivable because the debtors were insolvent. The station sued the bakery later for $400, the uncollectible balance of the accounts receivable. Was it entitled to collect?

5. Delaney, who owned and operated the M & N Cafeteria, sold it to Harper for $30,000, with $10,000 cash and the balance paid by note. Some-

time later Harper sold the cafeteria to Mitchell; and Mitchell, as a part of the purchase price, agreed to assume Harper's obligation to pay Delaney the $20,000. Mitchell operated the cafeteria profitably for several months during which time his net profits were $18,000, but he made no payment on the notes. He became ill and the business declined rapidly. Delaney demanded that Harper pay the balance due on the original selling price. Was Harper obligated to pay this?

6. Miss Harder contracted with the Dixie Red Coat Band to play at a party she was giving. The charge was $800. At the time the party was to start, Sherman's Blue Coat Band appeared and presented a written assignment to play from the Dixie Red Coat Band. Must Miss Harder honor this assignment?

7. The Marbut Office Supply Company had a contract with the Second National Bank to keep all its office machines repaired for $100 a month. The Marbut Company sold its business in bulk to the McGregor Corporation and assigned this repair contract to this company. The bank refused to honor the assignment. Must it do so?

8. Elson and Ransom entered into a written agreement by which Elson promised to name his son after Ransom in exchange for Ransom's promise to pay Elson's son $5,000. Elson performs his part of the agreement. His son then brings action to enforce payment by Ransom. Is he entitled to do so?

CHAPTER 11

TERMINATION OF CONTRACTS

METHODS BY WHICH CONTRACTS ARE TERMINATED

The preceding chapters have dealt with the law relative to the formation of contracts. It is equally important to know the law dealing with the termination of contracts. Some contracts, like marriage, are easy to enter into but often are difficult to terminate. There are five common methods by which contracts may be terminated. These are (a) performance of the contract, (b) discharge by operation of law, (c) by voluntary agreement of the parties, (d) by impossibility of performance, and (e) by breach of contract. The first two methods are covered in this chapter; the others are treated in Chapter 12.

PERFORMANCE

When all the terms of a contract have been fulfilled, the contract is discharged by performance. Not all the parties, however, may be discharged simultaneously. Each party is discharged as soon as he has done all that he agreed to do. The other party or parties are not discharged if any material thing remains to be done.

It may seem to be a simple matter to determine when a contract has been discharged by performance. There are several factors to be considered, however. They are:

1. Substantial performance
2. Satisfactory performance
3. Tender of performance
4. Time of performance

(1) Substantial Performance. Under the early common law, each party to a contract had to perform to the last letter of the contract before he was entitled to demand his rights under the contract. Such a rule was often extremely inequitable. If a contractor builds a $50 million office building, it is almost impossible to avoid some slight deviation from the contract. It would be grossly unfair to say that he could collect none of the $50 million because of this slight breach.

The law today can be stated as follows: If a contract is substantially performed, then the party performing may demand the full price under his contract. The other party then is entitled to file a counterclaim for the deficiency. In the case of the office building, if the cost of completing the building according to contract would be $3,000, the contractor could collect $50 million minus the $3,000. Suppose, however, that the contractor completed the excavation and then quit. He would be entitled to collect nothing. Just how far he must proceed toward full performance before he has substantially performed is often difficult to determine. The performance must be almost complete.

- Hartwell contracted with The Herald Press to run ten quarter-page ads on ten consecutive days at a cost of $4,000. On one day the ad was run upside down. Hartwell refused to pay any part of the $4,000. The court held The Herald Press had substantially performed and Hartwell must pay for nine ads.

(2) Satisfactory Performance. It frequently happens that contracts specifically state that the contract must be "satisfactory to" or "to the satisfaction of" a certain person. What constitutes satisfactory performance is frequently a disputed question. Certainly one should not be permitted to avoid a contract on an arbitrary standard of satisfaction impossible to attain. The courts generally have adopted the rule that if the contract is performed in a manner that would satisfy an ordinary, reasonable person, the terms of the contract have been met sufficiently to discharge it. There is one exception to this rule: If the performance involves the personal taste or fancy of one of the parties, he may arbitrarily reject it on the ground that it is not satistory to him.

- Mary employed Janet, an expert seamstress, to make her wedding gown. It was to be made "to your absolute satisfaction." The wedding was called off, and Mary refused to take the gown on the ground "it doesn't look exactly right on me." This was insufficient reason for refusing to pay for the gown.

(3) Tender of Performance. An offer to perform an obligation in satisfaction of the terms of a contract is called a *tender of performance*. If a contract calls for the performance of an act, a tender of performance will discharge the obligation of the one making the tender so long as the tender conforms to the agreement.

- Cook hired the Thomas Transfer Company to move his household furniture to Atlanta on Monday, June 6, at 8 a.m. On that day the Thomas Transfer Company sent a truck to Cook's residence to load the furniture. Cook told the driver he was not ready and asked him to return at 2 p.m. As far as the Thomas Transfer Company is concerned, the contract is terminated since it tendered performance at the time specified. The transfer company's rights are determined by the circumstances. If their truck was idle because of Cook's breach of contract, it can sue for damages, the profit it would have made. It is under no obligation to return at 2 p.m.

An offer to pay money in satisfaction of a debt or claim is a *tender of payment*. The debtor must offer the exact amount due, including interest, if any. He must also make an actual offer of the money. If he says, "I am now ready to pay you," he has not made a sufficient tender. He must pay or tender the creditor the amount due.

A tender in the form of a check is not a proper tender. The payment must be tendered in *legal tender*. With but few minor exceptions, this is any form of United States money. If a check is accepted, the contract is performed as soon as the check is cashed or deposited. Some courts have held that if a check is tendered in payment and payment is refused for some other reason, later proved invalid, the party cannot later claim the check was an improper tender. If a check is marked, "In full payment," the tender may be refused because the amount is not correct. If, in a suit, the debtor proves that the amount was correct, the other party cannot then for the first time raise the objection that the check was an improper tender. He must raise this objection at the time of the tender.

If the tender is refused, the debt is not discharged. Although a proper tender does not pay the debt if the tender is refused, it does stop the running of interest. In addition, if the creditor should bring suit, the person who has tendered the correct amount is not liable for court costs. The debtor must, however, hold himself in readiness to pay at any time. In other words, the debtor must keep his defense good.

(4) Time of Performance. If a contract does not specify the time when the contract is to be performed, it must be performed within a reasonable time. If a definite time is specified, then the question arises as to whether or not time is of the essence of the contract.

DISCHARGE BY OPERATION OF LAW

Under certain circumstances the law will effect a discharge of the contract, or at least the law will bar all right of action. The most common ways by which the law operates to discharge contracts are:

(1) Bankruptcy
(2) Statute of limitations
(3) Alteration of written contract

(1) Bankruptcy. It is not uncommon for individuals and business firms to be overwhelmed with financial obligations. The law permits these individuals and firms to petition the court for a decree of voluntary bankruptcy. Creditors may, under certain circumstances, force one into involuntary bankruptcy. (Bankruptcy is treated fully in Chapter 48.) In either event, all rights of action to enforce the contracts of the bankrupt are barred except for certain classes of debts, such as wages for the preceding three months, taxes, alimony, and court costs. However, a creditor's right of action is revived by the debtor's promise to pay made after his discharge in bankruptcy.

(2) Statute of Limitations. When one party to a contract breaches it, the other party has the right to sue for breach of contract, but he must exercise this right within the time fixed by a statute which is called the *Statute of Limitations*. This time varies from state to state and for different types of debts. For open accounts, called accounts receivable, the time varies from two to eight years, while for notes it varies from four to twenty years.

After a person has brought suit and obtained judgment, the judgment must be enforced by having the property of the debtor levied upon and sold. If this is not done, the statute of limitations operates even against judgments. The time varies from five to twenty-one years from date of judgment; one state, Connecticut, has no limit.

In some cases the time is calculated from the date of the account; in others from the due date; and in still others from the date of the last payment if the debt has been partially paid. In the case of accounts receivable involving several purchases, the time starts from the date of the last purchase. If the promisor leaves the state, the statute ceases to run while he is beyond the jurisdiction of the court.

▪ On July 1, 1950, Dover purchased a set of encyclopedias on the installment plan. The total price was $269.50. He was to pay $10 a month. The last payment he made was on September 1, 1951, leaving a balance of $129.50. The Statute of Limitations in his state was five years. In December, 1955, suit was brought to collect from Dover. He claimed the suit was barred by the Statute of Limitations. The court ruled the time ran from the date of the last payment. The five years had not expired.

A debt that has been outlawed by a statute of limitations may be revived. This is done in some states by a written acknowledgment of or a promise to pay the debt, in others by part payment after it has been outlawed, and in still others by the mere payment of the interest. After the debt is revived, it is a new obligation and runs the full period of the Statute of Limitations again.

(3) **Alteration of Written Contract.** Written contracts contain the provisions upon which the minds of the parties have met. If one of the parties alters one of these provisions, the old contract is discharged; and the minds have not met on the altered form of the contract. To discharge the contract, the alteration must be done intentionally and without the consent of the other party. In most states the alteration must also be material, although it need not injure the other party. If a note is noninterest-bearing and the holder adds the term "with 6% interest from date," the maker is discharged. (If the holder is an innocent purchaser, the maker is still liable for the principal of the note. This is set out more fully in Chapter 27.)

QUESTIONS

1. State the ways in which a contract may be terminated.
2. If one party does not perform every detail of a contract, is the other party released from his obligations under the contract?
3. If one party contracts to perform a contract "to your absolute satisfaction," may the other party avoid the contract merely by claiming that he is not completely satisfied?
4. If a debtor tenders payment of money but payment is refused, is the debt discharged?
5. If a check is accepted in payment, when is the contract performed?
6. Name two ways by which time may be ruled to be of the essence of the contract.
7. Does a proper tender that is refused stop the running of interest?
8. If a contract calls for an act, what is the effect of a refusal of a tender of performance?

CASE PROBLEMS

1. Mary Lou Collins was bookkeeper-secretary for the Dudley Wholesale Company. She received a check from a customer for $1,890 in the lower left-hand corner of which were these words: "In full of account." She checked the accounts receivable ledger and found that the balance of the account was $2,190. Consequently she marked out the words "In full of account" and deposited the check. What was the effect of this act?

2. Daniel tendered a certified check in payment of his account. Cohen refused the check "because the amount is incorrect." Later Cohen sued Daniel on the account. Daniel proved that he had tendered a certified check for $500 as the full amount due, and he offered before the trial started to pay this amount. Cohen refused to accept it, claiming $700. The jury awarded Cohen a judgment for $500. Who must pay the court costs? Did Cohen use his knowledge of law wisely in this case?

3. Harmon employed Darwin to paint his house inside and out for $800. Darwin finished the job but, through an oversight, failed to paint the eaves boards on one end. Harmon offered Darwin $750, claiming he was withholding $50 for damages. Darwin offered to return and complete the job, which would require about two hours' work. Harmon refused to let him complete the job, and Darwin sued for $800. Who, in your opinion, was entitled to win the case?

4. Harbin contracted with Campbell to wire Campbell's house for $300. One week later, Harbin with his two helpers called at Campbell's residence and reported ready to begin the wiring. Campbell refused to let them enter the house. Being unable to get anyone else to wire it for less than $350, Campbell called Harbin and told him to go ahead and wire the house. Harbin refused and Campbell sued him for breach of contract. Was Harbin liable for damages?

5. Jason entered into a written contract with the White Brewery Company to work as their bookkeeper for 12 months at a salary of $700 a month. Jason signed two copies of the contract and mailed them to the White Brewery Company for its signature and a return of one copy to Jason. When Jason's copy was returned, the figure 12 was crossed out and 6 written over it. This alteration was made without Jason's consent. Is Jason bound on this contract?

6. The Martin Construction Company contracted to build a house for Mason for $21,000. The specifications called for the use of yellow pine lumber throughout except the flooring. After the house was completed, it was discovered that the rafters were hemlock. Mason refused to pay any part of the $21,000, claiming the breach of contract released him. What is your opinion?

7. Hunter with three other men planned an extensive fishing trip starting at 5 a.m., June 4. He purchased a boat from the Lanier Boat Company. The seller agreed to deliver it by 5 p.m. on June 3. At 5:45 p.m., June 3, the boat had not arrived, so Hunter purchased one from Daniel. At 5:54 p.m. the first boat was delivered, but Hunter refused to accept it. Was he within his rights?

CHAPTER 12

TERMINATION OF

CONTRACTS (Continued)

VOLUNTARY AGREEMENT OF THE PARTIES

A contract is a mutual agreement. The parties are as free to change their minds by mutual agreement as they are to agree in the first place. Consequently, whenever the parties to a contract agree not to carry out its terms, the contract is discharged. The contract itself may recite the events or circumstances which will automatically terminate the agreement. The release of one party to the contract constitutes the consideration for the release of the other. If Walker agrees to build a house for Troelson, and Troelson agrees to pay Walker $20,000 upon completion of the house, they may at any time mutually agree to terminate the contract.

IMPOSSIBILITY OF PERFORMANCE

If the act called for in a contract is impossible of performance at the time the contract is made, no contract ever comes into existence. Frequently, impossibility of performance arises after a valid contract is formed. This type of impossibility discharges the contract under certain circumstances. If the impossibility can reasonably be anticipated, such as one due to a strike, a tornado, or any other common catastrophe, the promisor is not discharged unless the contract itself provides for its discharge upon the occurrence of such events. The most common causes of discharge by impossibility of performance occurring after the contract is made are:

1. Destruction of the subject matter
2. New laws making the contract illegal
3. Death or physical incapacity in personal service contracts

(1) Destruction of the Subject Matter. If the contract involves specific subject matter, the destruction of this specific subject matter discharges the contract because of impossibility of performance.

A similar situation often arises when the subject matter of a contract is to be manufactured and delivered. If the contract specifies that the goods are to be fabricated in a particular plant, the destruction of that plant renders the contract impossible to perform. If the contract does not specifically designate the plant in which the articles are to be fabricated, the implication is that if for any reason the seller cannot manufacture them in his plant, he will procure them elsewhere and deliver them regardless of the hardship. The destruction of the plant in which the seller intended to manufacture the goods does not under these circumstances render the contract impossible to perform.

- The Campbell Builders Supply Company had a contract to manufacture and deliver to the Dade Construction Company 100 aluminum windows of a certain size. Before the windows were made, the Campbell Builders' Supply Company's plant was destroyed by a tornado. This did not terminate the contract. Had the offer included a statement that the windows were to be made in the Dalton plant, then its destruction would have rendered the contract impossible to perform.

(2) New Laws Making the Contract Illegal. If an act is legal at the time of the contract but is subsequently made illegal, the contract is discharged. Under local option laws alcoholic beverages may be banned if a referendum approves such action. All executory contracts for the sale of alcoholic beverages in that locality are discharged when the ban becomes effective.

- The Gates Construction Company contracted with Segrest to build a filling station on Segrest's property. After the contract was entered into, but before work began, the city council passed a zoning ordinance restricting the site of the proposed filling station to residential purposes. The contract was discharged by this ordinance.

During a war or other emergency, government rationing may make it impossible for one party to a contract to perform because of inability to purchase supplies and materials to complete it.

- The City of Buffalo entered into a contract to have a water main laid to some new subdivisions. Because of the outbreak of the Korean War, the contractor could not purchase the materials needed to complete the work on the date fixed in the contract. The court held the contractor could not be sued for breach of contract because of a legal impossibility to perform on time.

(3) Death or Physical Incapacity. If the contract calls for personal services, death or physical incapacity of the promisor discharges the contract. The personal services must be such that they cannot readily be performed by another or by the personal representative of the promisor.

Such acts as the painting of a portrait, representing a client in a legal proceeding, and other services of a highly personal nature are discharged by death or incapacity. A contract, however, to build a dwelling would not be discharged because any competent construction man can build it according to the specifications.

- Gutherie entered into a contract with his father whereby Gutherie agreed to support his father as long as his father lived. Gutherie performed this contract for two years and then died while his father was still alive but mentally incompetent. The guardian for the father sued the administrator of Gutherie's estate to force him to continue supporting the father. The court held Gutherie was fully released by his death. This decision stressed the fact that in such a contract it is the intent of the parties that death of the promisor terminates it.

BREACH OF THE CONTRACT BY ONE OF THE PARTIES

When one of the parties fails or refuses to perform the obligations assumed under the contract, there is a breach of the contract.

If one party, prior to the time the other party is entitled to performance, announces his intention not to perform, there is an anticipatory breach of the contract. In either case the nonbreaching party is, if he so elects, discharged from his obligations. He then has three courses of action open to him:

1. Sue for damages
2. Rescind the contract
3. Sue for specific performance

(1) Sue for Damages. The usual remedy for breach of contract is to sue for damages. In a suit for damages there are really two suits in one. The first is to prove breach of contract. The second is to prove damages. The first suit may be easy to win, while the second often is difficult, if not impossible. Because of this, there are four kinds of damages: (a) nominal, (b) compensatory, (c) general and punitive, and (d) liquidated.

(a) Nominal Damages. If the plaintiff in a suit for damages because of a breach of contract is able to prove that the defendant

broke the contract but is unable to prove he sustained any loss because of the breach, then the court will award him *nominal damages,* generally one dollar. The reason for this is to throw the court cost on the loser, the defendant.

- Thoben Textile Company contracted with the Dale Warehouse to purchase 1,000 bales of cotton for $20,000. The Dale Warehouse failed to perform, and the Thoben Textile Company purchased 1,000 bales of cotton of the same grade elsewhere for $19,975. In a suit for breach of contract these were the undisputed facts. The court awarded the plaintiff nominal damages of $1 since it did partially win its case by proving a breach of contract, but it failed to prove it had sustained any loss. The defendant had to pay the court costs.

(b) Compensatory Damages. The theory of the law of damages is that an injured party is to be compensated for any loss he may sustain but should not be permitted to profit from the other party's wrongdoing. The law, when there is a breach of contract, entitles the injured party to compensation for the exact amount of his loss, but no more. Such damages are called *compensatory damages.* Sometimes the actual loss is easily determined, but at other times it is very difficult to determine. As a general rule, the amount of damages is a question to be decided by the jury.

(c) General and Punitive Damages. General damages are those damages that are the direct result of the breach of contract. The loss for which general damages are awarded must be the natural consequence of the defendant's breach of contract. In most instances the awarding of general damages fully meets the ends of justice. There are rare cases, however, where general or compensatory damages are not adequate. In these instances the law may permit the plaintiff to receive punitive damages. *Punitive damages* are similar to a fine, but the fine goes to the plaintiff rather than to the government. The purpose of punitive damages is to punish the defendant, not to compensate the plaintiff. If a tenant maliciously damages property he is occupying, the landlord may frequently recover as damages the actual cost of repairs plus double or triple damages as punitive damages.

(d) Liquidated Damages. Closely akin to punitive damages are liquidated damages. When two parties enter into a contract, they may include a provision fixing the amount of damages to be paid in the event one party breaches the contract. Such a provision is called *liquidated damages.* Theoretically, such a clause in the contract pre-

cludes a suit for damages if there is a breach of contract. If the amount of damages fixed by the contract is unreasonable and in effect the damages are punitive, then the court will not enforce this provision of the contract. Liquidated damages must be reasonable and should be provided only in those cases where actual damages are difficult or impossible to prove.

> ▪ O'Dell employed the Dade Construction Company to build a house for him for $20,000, to be completed by November 1. The contract stipulated that for every day the contractor was late in completing the house, $500 in damages should accrue. The house was not finished until November 11. O'Dell's only actual loss was that he had to pay one more month's rent. The $5,000 liquidated damages were thus unreasonable and unenforceable.

(2) Rescind the Contract. The aggrieved party, when a contract is breached, may elect to rescind the contract. He then is released from all obligations not performed by him. If he has executed his part of the contract, his remedy is to sue for recovery of what he parted with. He does not ask for damages when he elects to rescind.

(3) Sue for Specific Performance. Sometimes neither a suit for damages nor rescission will constitute an adequate remedy. The injured party's remedy under these circumstances is a suit in equity to compel *specific performance,* that is, the carrying out of the specific terms of the contract.

This remedy is available in most contracts for the sale of real estate or any interest in real estate and for the sale of rare articles of personal property, such as a painting or an heirloom, the value of which cannot readily be determined. There is no way to measure sentimental value attached to a relic. Under such circumstances mere money damages may be inadequate to compensate the injured party. The court may compel specific performance under such circumstances.

> ▪ The Small Art Museum contracted with McCloud to purchase a famous work of art for $40,000. Before McCloud delivered the painting to the buyer, another museum offered him $50,000 for it. McCloud failed to deliver the painting to the Small Art Museum. The Small Art Museum's remedy was to sue for specific performance.

As a general rule, contracts for the performance of personal services will not be specifically ordered, both because of the difficulty of supervision by the courts and because of the restriction of the Constitution prohibiting involuntary servitude except as a criminal punishment.

QUESTIONS

1. Is a contract to fly to the moon invalid because of impossibility of performance?

2. If one cannot perform a contract on time because of a strike in the trucking industry, is this a legal impossibility?

3. If a singer contracts to sing at a party, is he released if he develops laryngitis just before the party starts?

4. May one sue for specific performance in employment contracts?

5. Will the courts always enforce provisions in contracts for liquidated damages?

6. Give an illustration of when the courts may award punitive damages.

7. Under what conditions may one sue for specific performance of a contract rather than sue for damages?

8. A professional performer agreed to put on a program for a club for a $200 fee. Due to illness, he was unable to perform. Could he be sued for breach of contract?

9. What are compensatory damages?

10. What are nominal damages?

CASE PROBLEMS

1. Hanson entered into a contract with Holcomb to construct a filling station at the corner of Case and Mell Streets. Before Hanson could start construction on the project, the city passed a zoning ordinance prohibiting commercial properties in the area of the proposed filling station. Holcomb bought a lot in another section of the city and the whole project at the new location cost him $2,000 more than the cost at Case and Mell Streets. He sued Hanson for damages of $2,000. Can he collect?

2. The Brunswick Molasses Company contracted with the Candler Feed Company to deliver 100,000 gallons of molasses on or before April 1. Due to a strike at the Brunswick plant, the company was shut down for two months and could not fulfill its contract with the Candler Feed Company. When sued for damages, it set up the defense of impossibility of performance. Is this a good defense?

3. Holcomb leased a Gulf Oil Service Station for seven years. One year later the Gulf Oil Company, due to no fault of Holcomb, canceled Holcomb's franchise. Holcomb was unable to obtain a franchise from any other oil company, so he notified the lessor that he was no longer bound on the lease. Does the cancellation of the franchise terminate the lease?

4. Kerr, a noted singer and entertainer, was engaged by Flossie to sing at an annual dance at her dance studio. One day before Kerr was scheduled to sing, he was afflicted with a throat infection that left him temporarily speechless. Flossie had already paid him in advance one half of the price for his services. Flossie sued him for a return of this advance payment plus damages. Is Kerr liable for both damages and a return of the payment?

5. Hobbs entered into a written contract with Raub to sell Raub his house for $17,500, deed to be delivered within two weeks, at which time payment was to be made. When the time came to complete the sale, Hobbs refused to execute and deliver the deed since another buyer was willing to pay $18,500. What were Raub's rights?

6. The Carson Construction Company had a contract to erect a $2 million office building. It called for bids to supply the wire for the electrical wiring needs for the building. The invitation for bids stated that time was an extremely important factor. The Heller Copper Company submitted a bid. It wished to include a clause such as "Performance on the date specified is to be waived if performance cannot be made due to fire, flood, tornado, or other acts of God." The Heller Copper Company knew its nearest competitor would not include a similar clause in its bid. The Heller Company used this clause: "This wire to be fabricated in our plant located at Watkinsville." This plant was destroyed by a tornado before the wire was fabricated. Was the Heller Company released from its contract?

7. Four college boys rented a house from Duncan at $120 a month. The term was for ten months. There were several heated disputes between the boys and Duncan over whether or not the terms of the lease were being broken. The boys, to get even with Duncan, deliberately let the bathtub overflow, causing $700 water damage to the building. What are Duncan's rights?

8. The Vaughn Paper Company contracted with the Guest Printing Company to supply the printing paper for the Guest Printing Company for 12 months for $20,000. The paper was to be supplied in 12 equal shipments. A clause in the contract stipulated, "If any one shipment is late in arriving by 48 hours, the Vaughn Paper Company agrees to pay damages in the amount of $20,000." One shipment was four days late in arrival, but there was no evidence the Guest Printing Company was inconvenienced since it had ample stock on hand. It sued the Vaughn Paper Company for $20,000. How much damages is the Guest Printing Company entitled to receive?

9. The Hope Manufacturing Company entered into a contract with the Georgia Well and Supply Company to fabricate for the latter company certain sizes of well casings. A given quantity was to be delivered on the first of each month. Due to a heavy flood which seriously damaged the Hope Manufacturing Company plant, it was unable to fill its order for several months. The Georgia Well and Supply Company sued it for damages, alleging breach of contract. Was it entitled to damages?

10. The N & O Restaurant had a contract with the O'Kelley Dairy Farm to purchase ten gallons of raw milk a day for twelve months. About one month after this contract was signed, the city council passed an ordinance prohibiting the serving of raw milk in the city's public eating places. The N & O Restaurant stopped its purchases of milk from O'Kelley, and O'Kelley sued for breach of contract. Was he entitled to collect?

SUMMARY CASES

PART 2

1. Kershaw & Son wrote a letter to Moulton in which was this key section: "We are authorized to offer Michigan fine salt, in full carload lots of 80-95 barrels." Immediately upon receipt of this letter Moulton replied, "You may ship me 2,000 barrels Michigan fine salt as offered in your letter." Due to changed circumstances, Kershaw & Sons did not wish to be bound on their offer. They contended the letter was a mere sales letter inviting offers, not an offer itself. Was this an offer? (Moulton v. Kershaw, 59 Wis. 316, 18 N. W. 172)

2. Failing wrote Nelson, asking him, "Will you and your wife accept $49,000 for your property?" Six days later Nelson replied, "I will not sell for less than $56,000." One day after receiving this letter from Nelson, Failing wired Nelson, "Will accept your offer $56,000 net." Failing was acting in this transaction as Blakeslee's legally authorized agent. Did Nelson make an acceptable offer? (Blakeslee v. Nelson, 212 App. Div. 219, 207, N. Y. S. 676)

3. The defendant Rosenbusch owned a 1/160 interest in an oil lease on some land in Oklahoma. Rosenbusch was a resident of Washington, D. C., and was not familiar with conditions in Oklahoma. She had never received any income from the lease. Deardorf wrote to her offering to purchase her "nonproductive royalty interest" for $10. She accepted the offer but later learned that some very productive wells had been drilled near her lease and that it was now a very valuable lease, a fact known to Deardorf when he wrote her. She brought suit to set the deed aside. May Rosenbusch recover her lease? (Deardorf et al. v. Rosenbusch [Okla.], 206 P. 2d 996)

4. Shoenung, while a minor 19 years of age, purchased from the defendant an automobile for $300, trading in an old car with an allowance of $50 and giving a note for $250. Shoenung lived with his parents on a farm and worked in town, three miles distant. He returned the car two months later and demanded his old car back and the return of his $250 note. Was he entitled to disaffirm the contract? (Schoenung v. Gallet, 238 N. W. 852, 206 Wis. 52)

5. The Midtown Motors employed Wise as an expert automobile mechanic for three years at a salary of $4,500 the first year; $5,000, the second; and $5,500, the third. After eight months Wise was discharged without justifiable cause. He sued for damages and obtained a judgment. He went to work in the meantime for another auto firm. To collect his judgment Wise garnisheed the Midtown Motors' bank account. The owner of the Midtown Motors went to Wise's new place of employment and engaged in considerable verbal abuse of Wise. He threatened him with legal action for garnisheeing the bank account. Wise's present employer joined in the verbal abuse and told him he was "fired" unless he accepted the proffered $200 in full settlement and signed a release for the balance. While in a state of extreme mental confusion as to what to do, he signed the release. The next day he changed his mind and repudiated the release and demanded the full amount due him. May he repudiate the signed release? (Wise v. Midtown Motors, 231 Minn. 46, 42 N. W. 2d 404)

6. Jaffray owed Davis $7,714.37. The debt was past due. Davis offered to settle the $7,714.37 if Jaffray would give him three promissory notes totaling $3,462.24 secured by a chattel mortgage on the stock and fixtures and other property owned by Jaffray. Jaffray accepted the offer and in due course paid the three notes as they fell due. Davis then brought suit to collect the difference between the original debt of $7,714.37 and the sum of the three notes. Is he entitled to collect? (Jaffray et al. v. Davis et al., 124 N. Y. 164, 26 N. E. 351, 11 L. R. A. 710)

7. Parker sold his bakery business to Thomas. As a part of the sales agreement, this clause appeared: "together with goodwill and bakery machinery in said bakery." Another clause stipulated, "Parker agrees that he will not engage in the bakery business directly or indirectly for a period of seven years within a radius of seven miles of Boston." About one year later Parker began working as a baker for the Boston Syrian Baking Company. Thomas brought suit asking that Parker be enjoined from working for the Syrian Baking Company. Is he entitled to the injunction? (Thomas v. Parker, Mass. 98 N. E. 2d 640)

8. The Tile Company sold Drake some of its stock. An officer of the corporation in an effort to induce Drake to buy the stock stated that the corporation owned land that contained clay peculiarly adapted to the manufacture of clay tile. It later developed that this clay was not suitable for the making of clay tile. This fact was unknown to the officer of the corporation at the time he made the statement. Drake relied upon the statement and purchased the stock. Drake brought an action to rescind the contract, and the Tile Company raised the defense, not that the statement was true, but that the officer innocently made the misrepresentation. May Drake rescind? (Drake v. Fairmont Drain Tile and Brick Company, 129 Minn. 145, 151 N. W. 914)

9. Lee was a student at Yale University. He rented a room from Gregory for 40 weeks. He occupied the room for about three months and then gave it up without alleging any breach of contract on Gregory's part. Gregory brought suit to collect for the balance of the 40 weeks' rent. Is he entitled to collect? (Gregory v. Lee, 64 Conn. 407, 30 A. 53)

10. Rich owed a board bill contracted while he was attending college. As he was unable to pay the board bill, he persuaded Kilgore to pay the board bill for him and promised to reimburse Kilgore. Rich failed to reimburse Kilgore and was sued for the money. Rich pleaded minority as a defense, claiming that a loan of money was not a necessary. Was Rich's defense good in this case? (Kilgore v. Rich, 85 Me. 305, 22 A. 176)

11. Chevalier entered into an oral contract with Lane's, Inc. to work for the corporation for a period of 12 months, work to begin shortly after the contract was made. Chevalier began work and continued for a period of six months. According to his oral contract, Chevalier was to be paid a monthly salary plus a bonus of $1,500 at the end of six months. He was laid off without cause at the end of the first six months without receiving his $1,500 bonus, although his monthly salary had been paid. He brought suit for his $1,500 bonus plus his damages for having been discharged without cause. Is he entitled to either the $1,500 or damages? (Chevalier v. Lane's, Inc., 1948, 147 Tex. 106, 213 S. W. 2d 530)

12. Kelley entered into a contract with Hance whereby Kelley was to construct a sidewalk and curb in front of Hance's property. The price for the work was to be $3 a running foot, or $420 for the 140 feet. Kelley was to start work within one week and complete it before cold weather. Although the contract was entered into in September, Kelley did not begin work until December 4. He continued to work until he had removed dirt to a width of 12 feet. He then discontinued the work and never returned. In March the following year, Hance notified Kelley that the contract was canceled. Kelley then brought suit to recover for the value of the work he already had done at the time the contract was terminated by Hance. Is Kelley entitled to any compensation? (Kelley v. Hance, 108 Conn. 186, 142 A. 683)

13. Somerville held a charter to an ocean vessel, the Henry S. Little. Somerville assigned his charter to this vessel to Piaggio whereby Piaggio agreed to pay Somerville $1,500 upon the clearance of the vessel at Mobile. At that time Germany was carrying on unrestricted submarine warfare, and the owners of the vessel refused to clear it for fear it would be sunk by a German submarine. Since Piaggio was unable to get clearance for the vessel, he refused to pay the $1,500; and Somerville brought suit to collect. Is Piaggio's defense of impossibility of performance valid in this case? (Piaggio v. Somerville, 119 Miss. 6, 80 So. 342)

14. Potter purchased lumber from the Pacific Coast Lumber Company. A dispute arose as to the amount owed. Potter paid for the lumber, one lot by check and one by a draft. In both instances a voucher was attached in which appeared these words: "In full settlement of account stated below." The amount paid was less than the amount claimed. The Pacific Coast Lumber Company accepted the check and the draft as written. It then sued for the difference between the amount claimed and the amount paid. Was the lumber company entitled to collect? (Potter v. Pacific Coast Lumber Company, 37 Cal. 2d 592, 234 P. 2d 16)

15. Silverstein and Silverstein held a three-year written lease in space in Dohoney's property to be used for cigarette vending machines. The lease provided for the payment of rent by means of a commission on all cigarettes sold, but the amount of the commission was not stated. Prior to this lease the plaintiff had a machine in Dohoney's property and had paid him commissions on all sales of cigarettes. In a suit involving this contract, the key question was whether or not oral testimony could be introduced to prove the amount of commissions that were to be paid. Would oral testimony to this effect vary the terms of the written contract? (Silverstein v. Dohoney, N. J. Sup. Ct., 108 A. 2d 451)

PART 3

SALES

Preview Cases for Part 3: Sales

- Frost owned a house trailer that was parked in the Wee Acres Trailer Court. He had it fully covered with fire insurance for $7,500. He sold the trailer on June 7 to Green for $7,000 cash. Green was given the keys and told to "haul it away whenever you are ready." Two days after the contract was made, and before Green had insured the trailer, the trailer was completely destroyed by fire. Who must take the loss?

- Middlebrooks orally promised to sell the Watkinsville Bank a nonnegotiable note he owned as part payment of a loan he owed the bank. He later refused to make the transfer, and the bank sued for breach of contract. Middlebrooks claimed the contract was invalid under the Statute of Frauds because it was oral. Was the contract one that involved a sale?

- Tucker, a cabinet maker, contracted with Hill to make Hill a black walnut cabinet for $750, Tucker to supply the lumber. The contract was entirely oral. When the cabinet was finished, Hill refused to take it and pay for it. Was he obligated to do so?

- Green attended a livestock auction where several registered brood cows were being sold. Green made a deal with two other bidders whereby he would not bid against them if they in turn would not bid on the animals he wanted. When the owner of the livestock learns of the agreement, may he refuse to sell to any of the three bidders?

- Kirkpatrick sold Himler a color television set for $800. As part of the selling price Kirkpatrick agreed to have it repaired to remove a slight defect in the performance of the set. While the set was at the repair shop, it was stolen. Who must stand the loss?

- Webster bought his fiancee an engagement ring from a pawnshop because it was offered at a bargain price. Valerie, his fiancee, was very proud of it and showed it to many people. Ruth recognized it as her engagement ring that had been stolen. She demanded that Valerie return the ring. Who is entitled to the ring?

These preview cases are designed to serve as a springboard for the study of this part. As you read through each chapter in this part, you will find the actual decisions for all these preview cases. Of course, there are many more such illustrative problems as well as case problems for decision at the end of each chapter. And there are also a number of even more challenging cases for review at the end of the part.

CHAPTER 13

SALES OF PERSONAL PROPERTY

IMPORTANCE OF SALES CONTRACTS

In terms of the number of contracts as well as in the dollar volume, contracts for the sale of goods—tangible personal property—constitute the largest class of contracts in our economic system. Every time one purchases a package of cigarettes, he enters into a sales contract. If the cigarettes contained some harmful substance, the sale could be the basis of a suit for thousands of dollars in damages.

For a long time the law of sales varied considerably from state to state. Few laws applied to every state in the union. To overcome this weakness, the Uniform Sales Act was drawn up. Up to this time about two thirds of the states have adopted the Uniform Sales Act, and the other states have brought their laws dealing with sales more in line with the Uniform Sales Act.

The Uniform Sales Act has now been merged into the Uniform Commercial Code in all those states that have adopted this Code. The Uniform Commercial Code does not contain any revolutionary changes in the Uniform Sales Act, but it does modify several of its provisions. The major changes will be shown in this and the following chapters on sales.

SELL, ASSIGN, AND NEGOTIATE

In law there are slight differences in the meanings of the words "sell," "assign," and "negotiate." In Chapter 10 we studied the meaning of the word "assign." In Chapter 20 we will study the meaning of the word "negotiate." This chapter and the three that follow deal with contracts of sales, but even the law of sales does not apply to every sale of property. Property may be described in many ways, such as real and personal, tangible and intangible, choses in action and choses in being. *Real property* is land, interests in land, and things permanently attached to land. The law of sales does not apply to real estate sales. It does apply to sales of personal property. *Personal property* is any property or property right which is not classified as real property. Personal property includes movable physical property and notes, stocks, bonds, and all written evidences of debt. *Tangible personal property* consists of all physical items which are not real estate, such as merchandise, clothing, and furniture. *Intangible personal property* consists of evidences of ownership of personal property, such as contracts, copyrights, and stocks. Accounts receivable, notes receivable, and similar assets are *choses in action* or intangible personal property. Goods such as merchandise, equipment, and machinery are *choses in being.* The Uniform Commercial Code specifically limits the law of sales to choses in being, that is, tangible personal property.

Sales contracts must have all the essentials of any other contract, but they have some features that apply only to this type of contract. As the subject is developed in this and the following chapters, it will be seen that there are many rules pertaining to sales of personal property that would have no significance to any other type of contract, such as a contract of employment.

SALES AND CONTRACTS TO SELL

Under the Uniform Sales Act, a distinction is made between a sale and a contract to sell at a future date.

A *sale* of goods is an agreement whereby the seller transfers the title in goods to the buyer for a consideration called the price. It is a contract in which the ownership changes hands at the moment the bargain is made regardless of who has possession of the goods.

A *contract to sell* goods is a contract whereby the seller agrees to transfer the title in goods to the buyer for a consideration called the price. This is a contract in which one promises to buy or to sell in the future.

The important distinction between a sale and a contract to sell is that in the former the title, or the ownership of the subject matter, is transferred at once; in the latter it will be transferred at a later time. A contract to sell is not in the true sense of the word a sale; it is merely an agreement to sell.

Since in a sale title passes to the buyer immediately, and in a contract to sell, title passes at some future date, it is extremely important to distinguish between the two. Except in rare instances, title to personal property is held by someone at every moment of time. There can be no such thing as an intervening period during which time title rests with neither the seller nor the buyer. The risk of loss, with the exceptions set out later in this chapter, is borne by the owner. Also, any increase in the property belongs to the one who has the title. It is essential, therefore, to have certain definite rules to aid the courts in determining when title passes if the parties to the contract are silent as to when title passes. If the parties, themselves, agree as to when title passes, then the courts will enforce this agreement. When the parties are silent and the court must decide, the first task the court must perform is to determine whether the agreement is a sale or a contract to sell.

Many insurance problems arise when a sale is made. If one has fire insurance on his property, the coverage ceases the minute he gives up title. If the goods are destroyed before the buyer places insurance on them, no one can collect. If both the seller and the buyer carry full insurance coverage but in different companies, then it is important to know which company must pay. Often the key to fixing the liability of the insurer is whether the contract is one "to sell" or "of sale."

> ▪ Frost owned a house trailer that was parked in the Wee Acres Trailer Court. He had it fully covered with fire insurance for $7,500. He sold the trailer on June 7 to Green for $7,000 cash. Green was given the keys and told to "haul it away whenever you are ready." Two days after the contract was made, and before Green had placed insurance on the trailer, it was completely destroyed by fire. This was a contract of sale. Frost's policy had expired at the moment of sale. Frost's insurance company had no liability.

PRICE

The consideration in a sales contract is expressed in terms of money or money's worth and is known as the *price*. The actual payment may be made in property or services, but the value of these must be converted to a price in order for it to be a sale.

When the purchase price is paid with other personal property, it is often difficult to determine whether it is a barter or a sales contract. A *barter* is an exchange of personal property without the mention of price. The Uniform Commercial Code clarifies this point by specifically providing that if the price is to be paid in goods, then each party is a seller of the goods which he transfers.

- Martin entered into a contract with Case whereby Case was to receive 25 percent of the selling price of Martin's automatic vending machine. Martin licensed the manufacture and distribution of the machine to a manufacturer in Canada. Case demanded that he receive 25 percent of the license fees. The court held this was not a sale as defined by the Uniform Sales Act; therefore, he was not entitled to any portion of these fees.

Frequently the sales contract is an express contract, but some of its terms are implied. In a contract of sale, the price may be implied, in which case the courts will consider the market price a reasonable price. In this event, however, the seller and the buyer must both clearly imply by their conduct that they are willing to contract for a reasonable price. Unless the price can definitely be fixed, no contract results since their minds have not met. This situation would occur when the contract, or apparent contract, simply stipulates that the price is to be fixed at a later date. If it stipulates that the price is to be fixed later by a third party or by market quotations, then the price would be determinable and an enforceable contract would result.

In Chapter 4 it was stated that an offer must be definite and specific. An offer to sell goods must also meet this test; but because of the peculiar nature of sales contracts, the courts cannot be too arbitrary in applying this rule. The buyer and the seller might wish to enter into a contract for the sale of goods each week over a period of several weeks with a stipulation that the price is to fluctuate with each week's sales according to market conditions. There must be a certainty that the price can be determined.

- The Angus Textile Company entered into a contract with the Williams Cotton Merchant to purchase "all its needs of raw cotton for the next twelve months, the price to be that quoted on the New Orleans Cotton Market on the day of each delivery, or the last day the market was open prior to delivery if delivery is on Saturday or a holiday." This was a valid contract even though the offer does not state a definite price. The market price can be used when there is an established market.

GOODS NOT YET IN EXISTENCE

Goods that are not in existence at the time the contract to sell them is made may be classified as:

1. Future goods
2. Potential goods

(1) **Future Goods.** *Future goods* are goods which the seller does not now own. He expects to acquire them in the future by purchase or by manufacture. The Uniform Sales Act clearly stipulates that any contract purporting to sell future goods is a contract to sell and not a contract of sale. This law was not passed to hinder a man in making any type of contract he wishes, but it was necessary to enable the court to determine the rights of the parties under certain contingencies.

- Taylor, a shoe manufacturer, contracted to sell the Mitchell Shoe Store 2,000 pairs of shoes. At the time this contract was made, the shoes had not been manufactured. After they were manufactured but before they were shipped, Taylor's creditors levied upon the shoes. Taylor claimed they were not his shoes since he had sold them to the Mitchell Shoe Store. Since the shoes at the time of the contract were not in existence, they were future goods. Consequently, this was merely a contract to sell, not of sale. The title rested with Taylor until the shoes were shipped. Since the shoes belonged to Taylor, his creditors could levy on them and sell them for Taylor's debts.

(2) **Potential Goods.** Closely akin to future goods are potential goods which the seller owns at the time of the contract. They consist primarily of agricultural products that are to be produced in the future. Fish that are to be caught from one's own fish pond are potential goods, but fish to be caught from the ocean, for example, are future goods. To be *potential goods,* the seller must own the source from which they are to be produced or caught. The Uniform Sales Act makes no distinction between future goods and potential goods. Neither class can constitute the subject matter of a contract of sale, only to sell. Many of the states which have not adopted the Uniform Sales Act permit a contract of sale of potential goods, but no state recognizes a contract of sale for future goods.

BILL OF SALE

A *bill of sale* is written evidence of one's title to tangible personal property. It is not necessary to have evidence of title; but should one's title be questioned, such evidence is highly desirable. Most states specifically require all automobile owners to have a bill of sale. One should not purchase an automobile unless the seller can produce his bill of sale as proof that he has title to the car. If one buys a stock of merchandise in bulk, a house trailer, livestock, and many other relatively expensive items, such as jewelry and furs, he should demand that the seller give him a bill of sale. This serves two purposes: (1) If the buyer wishes to resell the goods and the prospective buyer demands proof of title, he can produce his bill of sale; (2) if any question arises as to whether or not he came into possession of the goods legally, he has his bill of sale as proof.

- Howard purchased a trailer from Henderson. A few months later he contracted to sell it to Tucker. Tucker would not pay Howard for the trailer unless he could produce a bill of sale showing he had title to it. This often is a wise precaution.

ILLEGAL SALES

Many difficulties arise over illegal sales, that is, the sale of goods prohibited by law, such as alcoholic beverages in a "dry" locality. If the sale is fully executed, the court will not intervene to aid either party. If an innocent party through fraud is induced to enter into an illegal sale, the court will compel a restoration of the goods he has transferred.

If the illegal sale is wholly executory, the transaction is a contract to sell and will not be enforced. If it is only partially executory, the courts will still leave the parties where it found them unless the one who has performed is an innocent victim of a fraud.

If the sale is divisible and a part is legal and a part illegal, the court will enforce the legal part. As a rule the nature of the contract, not the nature of the goods, determines its divisibility. If the sale involves several separate and independent items but is a lump-sum sale, then the sale is indivisible. If any part is illegal, the entire sale is illegal. If the individual items are separately priced, the sale is divisible.

- Jameson, a married minor, purchased $100 worth of groceries on credit from the Jackson Super Market. On two occasions the purchases included two bottles of wine. A state law prohibited the sale of wine to anyone under 21 years of age. The wine on the sales tickets was separately priced, so the illegal part could easily be separated from the legal part. Jameson had to pay for all groceries but not for the wine.

QUESTIONS

1. Why is the Uniform Sales Act important?
2. Distinguish clearly between a sale and a contract to sell.
3. Why is it important to make a distinction between a sale and a contract to sell?

4. What is the one feature that distinguishes a sales contract from a contract to barter?

5. If the price in a sales contract is not stated, what may the court consider to be a reasonable price?

6. (a) What are future goods?

(b) Can future goods ever constitute the subject matter of a contract of sale?

7. How do potential goods differ from future goods?

8. (a) What is a bill of sale?

(b) Is a bill of sale necessary to pass title?

9. Give three illustrations of choses in action.

10. What is the difference between a barter contract and a sales contract?

11. Is an offer to sell wheat at the Chicago Market price on June 7 an acceptable offer?

12. If one orders and is served a steak dinner in a restaurant, is this a sale?

CASE PROBLEMS

1. Barnett delivered 1,000 bushels of No. 1 wheat to the Temple Warehouse to be stored. Barnett was to get back, at Temple's option, either an equal quantity of wheat or the market price in cash. Barnett considered this a sale and consequently did not carry fire insurance on the wheat. It was destroyed by fire, and Temple refused to pay for it. Was this a sale?

2. The purchasing agent for the Stanley Wholesale Grocery Corporation agreed to purchase sugar from the Domino Refinery over a period of six months, the price not to exceed 3 cents a pound nor to fall below 2¾ cents a pound, the condition of the market to determine the price of each shipment between these two extremes. The question arose as to whether or not these terms violated the rule that an offer must be definite and specific to be accepted. Was it?

3. Bilko rented a fishing boat from a wholesale fish merchant for the purpose of a fishing expedition. He purchased provisions and supplies for the expedition from Wholesale Foods, Inc., and gave as security a bill of sale on all the fish he was to catch on the trip at 8 cents a pound. When the boat docked laden with several tons of fish, the creditors of Bilko attached the fish for the debts owed them by Bilko. Wholesale Foods produced its bill of sale to prove it had title to the fish. Who has superior rights in this case, the creditors or the Wholesale Foods, Inc.?

4. The Blue Goose Cafe served Mrs. Jones a dinner consisting of turkey with dressing. After Mrs. Jones had eaten a part of it, it was discovered that the dressing contained portions of a mouse. Mrs. Jones sued for breach of an implied warranty that in the sale of goods the seller warrants they are fit for human consumption. For this law to be used in this case, serving of food in a restaurant must be a sale. Was this a sale under the Uniform Sales Act?

5. Lasher, the purchasing agent of the Hertz Company, purchased a used bookkeeping machine from the Adams Bookkeeping Service. The selling price of the machine was $3,200. About two weeks later, a representative of the manufacturer of the machine demanded possession of the machine claiming it was only rented to the Adams Bookkeeping Service. He showed Lasher the rental agreement as proof of his statement. What should Lasher have done to avoid this loss?

6. The Fox Fur Shop contracted to sell Adele a fur coat for $4,500. The contract stipulated that the title was to remain with the Fox Fur Shop but that when the contract became a contract of sale, a bill of sale would be issued to Adele. The next day Adele called at the office of Fox Fur Shop to demand a bill of sale. The manager was out, but Mamie, his secretary, attempted to placate Adele. Mamie read the contract and saw that it said, "A bill of sale will be issued as soon as this becomes a contract of sale." Mamie, thinking it was already a contract of sale, issued to Adele a bill of sale. Adele then sold the coat for cash and disappeared. What error did Mamie make?

7. Paul, aged seventeen but married, purchased about $50 worth of groceries from the Burkhart Food Mart on credit. The $50 included $5 for cigarettes. There was a state law making it illegal for a merchant to sell cigarettes to one under 18 years of age. Paul learned of this and refused to pay any part of the $50 since the sales contract is illegal. Was he correct in his contention?

8. Smith entered into a written contract with Denfield to purchase 100 bales of cotton at the market price. Denfield was to pick, bale, and deliver the cotton to Smith's warehouse. Before the cotton was picked, a flood destroyed the entire crop. Who must bear the loss?

9. Before the pecan season opened in Albany, Georgia, Thompson Brothers entered into a contract with Davis, a pecan grower, to purchase all his pecans "at the market price." After Davis had delivered 20,000 pounds of pecans, he asked Thompson Brothers for a settlement. He produced a New York paper showing the market price for pecans in New York to be 19 cents. In Albany they were 17 cents a pound. Could Davis collect 19 cents a pound?

CHAPTER 14

FORMALITIES OF A
SALE

FORM OF CONTRACTS PERTAINING TO SALES

Unless a statute provides otherwise, a sale of property or a contract to sell property may be (1) oral, (2) written, (3) implied from the conduct of the parties, or (4) a combination of two or more of these. Generally the law does not prescribe any particular form for most sales contracts; but many executory contracts of sale and contracts to sell are required by the Statute of Frauds either to be in writing or to meet some other specific requirement. Unless the contracts meet these requirements, the courts will not enforce them.

REQUIREMENTS OF THE STATUTE OF FRAUDS

In addition to the five classes of contracts required by its fourth section to be in writing (page 73), the Statute of Frauds requires, under its seventeenth section, that certain contracts to sell and sales of goods, wares, and merchandise, as well as other forms of personal property, must be in writing.

In the main, the seventeenth section of the Statute of Frauds requires only a few sales contracts to be in writing. The Statute covers only the sale of goods as defined in the preceding chapter. In brief the Statute provides that all sales contracts of goods must be in writing unless the contract comes under one of the following four exceptions:

(1) The amount of the sale is less than the sum fixed by law. The amount varies from state to state as illustrated by the table on page 120. In those states that have adopted the Uniform Commercial Code, the amount is $500.

117

(2) Some of the goods have been accepted and received by the buyer with the intent to retain them; or

(3) Something of value has been given by the buyer to bind the contract or in part payment thereof; or

(4) A note or memorandum of the agreement has been made and signed by the parties to be charged by the contract, or by their authorized agents.

In most of the states, any contract pertaining to the sale of personal property for more than the amount fixed by statute must meet one, but only one, of the four provisions listed above. If it meets either the first or the second provision, the contract, regardless of the amount, may be oral without losing its enforceability. The table on page 120 (which is, of course, subject to statutory change at any session of a state legislature) summarizes the maximum amounts for which sales may be made in the several states, and the District of Columbia, without coming under the Statute of Frauds (that is, the maximum amounts which may be proved orally).

If a contract does not meet the requirements of the Statute of Frauds, it is not void, merely unenforceable. If both parties elect to abide by its terms even though they are not legally bound to do so, neither one can later change his mind.

> ▪ Middlebrooks orally promised to sell the Watkinsville Bank a non-negotiable note he owned as part payment of a loan he owed the bank. He later refused to make the transfer, and the bank sued for breach of contract. Middlebrooks contended this contract was invalid under the Statute of Frauds because it was oral. This was not a sale since the Uniform Sales Act specifically excludes choses in action as goods. Under the Uniform Commercial Code it would not be a sale either.

SALES WITHIN THE STATUTE OF FRAUDS

If a sale is for an amount less than the sum specified in the particular state statute, it is enforceable without reference to the Statute of Frauds. Millions of sales occur daily for amounts less than the statutory sums. If all these had to meet the rigid tests of the Statute of Frauds, the wheels of commerce would be unduly impeded. The purpose of the act is to discourage perjury. The temptation to commit perjury is weak when the amount involved is small. Then, too, one does not engage in litigation simply because he has a right to do so.

If the expense of litigation is greater than the loss sustained, it is cheaper and better to forego enforcing one's rights.

Frequently one makes several purchases the same day from the same seller. The question may then be raised as to whether there is one sale or several sales. In Alabama, for example, all sales of less than $500 may be made by oral contract. If one purchases five items from the same seller in one day, each one having a sale price of less than $500, but in the aggregate they are in excess of $500, must this contract meet the requirement of the Statute of Frauds? If the several items are part of the same sales transaction, it is one sale and must meet the requirement of the Statute. If all purchases are made during the same shopping tour and all are to be delivered at the same time and place, the several items are considered to be part of the same transaction.

ACCEPTANCE AND RECEIPT

An oral contract of sale for any amount is enforceable if there are both an acceptance and a receipt of the goods. If the goods are divisible, acceptance and receipt of any part of them will meet the requirements of the statute. In some sales, such as that of a fur coat, the goods are not subject to division; in other sales, such as of a thousand bushels of wheat, the goods are subject to division.

Acceptance is the assent of the buyer to become the owner of specific goods; *receipt* is taking possession of all or any part of the goods. The receipt may be actual or constructive. If Arnold buys from Taylor a thousand railroad ties stacked along the side of the highway, and Taylor says, "They are yours; haul them away when you are ready," there is a constructive delivery; and the contract does not come under the Statute of Frauds because there was both an acceptance and a receipt.

Sometimes goods are received for the purpose of making an examination. Here the receipt precedes the acceptance. If the goods are afterwards rejected, no contract is consummated. If, however, the buyer asserts ownership by act or word, he indicates an acceptance; and the sale is completed.

PART PAYMENT

A sales contract need not be in writing if a part or all of the purchase price is paid at the time the contract is entered into or at a subsequent date. There need not be a receipt of the goods, only a payment or part payment or something of value to bind the bargain.

Minimum Amounts of Sales to Which the Statute of Frauds Applies

Alabama	$500	Montana	$500
Alaska	500	Nebraska	500
Arizona	500	Nevada [f]	500
Arkansas	500	New Hampshire	500
California	500	New Jersey	500
Colorado [a]	500	New Mexico	500
Connecticut	500	New York	500
Delaware	500	North Carolina [g]	500
District of Columbia	500	North Dakota	500
Florida [b]	500	Ohio	500
Georgia	500	Oklahoma	500
Hawaii [c]	500	Oregon	500
Idaho	500	Pennsylvania	500
Illinois	500	Rhode Island	500
Indiana	500	South Carolina	50
Iowa [d]	500	South Dakota	500
Kansas	500	Tennessee	500
Kentucky	500	Texas [h]	500
Louisiana	No Requirement	Utah	500
Maine	500	Vermont	50
Maryland	500	Virginia [i]	500
Massachusetts	500	Washington [j]	500
Michigan	500	West Virginia	500
Minnesota [e]	500	Wisconsin	500
Mississippi	50	Wyoming	500
Missouri	500		

[a] Effective July 1, 1966; $50 prior to that date.
[b] Effective January 1, 1967; all sales prior to that date.
[c] Effective January 1, 1967; $100 prior to that date.
[d] Effective July 4, 1966; all sales prior to that date.
[e] Prior requirement $50.
[f] Effective March 1, 1967; $200 prior to that date.
[g] Effective July 1, 1967; no prior requirement.
[h] Effective July 1, 1966; no prior requirement.
[i] Effective January 1, 1966; no prior requirement.
[j] Effective June 30, 1967; $50 prior to that date.

The payment need not be in money, but whatever is given must have its value stated in money's worth; otherwise the transaction is a barter, not a sale.

A check, draft, or note is usually not a payment within the meaning of the Statute of Frauds. These are only conditional payments. But if a check is cashed before rescission is attempted, the sale is valid even though it is based on an oral contract. If the seller accepts a check, draft, note, or similar conditional payment as an "absolute" payment, however, the requirement of part payment of the Statute is met. There must be some concrete evidence that the seller is accepting the instrument as an absolute payment. This might be and usually is in the form of an indorsement on a check: "Pay to the order of John Smith without recourse to me if the check is not paid. Adam Stolz." In the absence of proof that the check is being accepted as absolute payment, the courts will interpret the check to be a conditional payment.

A check or a note is a conditional payment in that the seller in substance is saying, "I accept this check as payment only on condition the bank pays it when I present it." A due bill or a nonnegotiable note assigned to the seller may be part payment since there is no warranty that the one primarily liable is solvent and able to pay. The courts, in defining payment, make a distinction between actual payment of the price and a mere promise to pay the price. A promise to pay is not payment.

> ▪ Jones sold Greiner a trailer for $650, and Greiner gave a check
> for $10 as evidence of good faith. One hour later Jones cashed the
> check at the bank on which it was drawn. The next day Greiner in-
> formed Jones that he had changed his mind and would not go through
> with the deal since it was oral. The contract was binding, however,
> because the check had been cashed. Had Greiner notified Jones before
> the check had been cashed, the contract would have been canceled,
> as the check was not a part payment. Had Greiner indorsed a check
> to Jones and he (Jones) had agreed to accept it "good or bad,"
> this check would have been a part payment.

NOTE OR MEMORANDUM

The third factor which may make it unnecessary to have a written contract for the sale of personal property is a written note or memo-randum of the sale. This note is required to be almost as complete as a written contract. It must contain a description of the goods sold, the price, terms, time, and place of delivery, and be signed by the party to be charged, that is, the one to be sued for breach of contract or specific performance. The memorandum need not be formal. Letters, telegrams, invoices, and sales tickets are adequate if they contain the information set out above.

> ▪ Harrison agreed to purchase 10 head of cattle from Roberts,
> Harrison to take possession at Roberts' farm. Before Harrison
> took delivery of the cattle, three of them were killed during an electri-
> cal storm. Roberts wrote Harrison a letter setting forth all the terms of
> the sale and demanded that Harrison carry out his part of the con-
> tract. Harrison replied to this letter and frankly stated that even
> though Robert's letter correctly stated the terms of the sale, he was
> not going to buy the cattle since it was on oral contract. These two
> letters constituted a sufficient memorandum and Harrison was bound.
> The memorandum need not be made at the time of the sale.

The Uniform Commercial Code makes one material alteration in the Statute of Frauds relative to the memorandum. The writing need not be so complete. The specific provision reads, "A writing is not insufficient because it omits or incorrectly states a term agreed upon, but the contract is not enforceable under this paragraph beyond the quantity of goods shown in such writing." In those states that have not adopted the Uniform Commercial Code, such an error in the memorandum would render it ineffective.

CONTRACTS FOR LABOR AND MATERIALS

A contract for labor and materials is not a sale and need not meet the requirements of the seventeenth section of the Statute of Frauds. The courts are in complete accord that service contracts need not be in writing but are divided on the criteria used to distinguish a sale from a contract for labor and materials. There are two rules applied by the various courts in the United States: the Massachusetts rule and the New York rule. Some state courts use one rule, some the other.

(1) **Massachusetts Rule.** Under the Massachusetts rule, when the goods that are made up in accordance with the buyer's order are different from those produced for the general market, the contract is for labor and materials and is not a contract of sale. On the other hand, if the goods are suitable for trade in the ordinary course of business, the agreement is a contract to sell and comes under the Statute of Frauds. This rule, often called the American rule, has been adopted by the Uniform Sales Act and most states follow it.

The Uniform Commercial Code specifically adopts the Massachusetts rule provided the seller has made a substantial beginning of the manufacture of goods or has made commitments for their procurement before he receives any notice of repudiation.

In all cases of contracts for labor and materials there is, of course, a sale of the materials; but labor is a service, and service contracts are not covered by the seventeenth section of the Statute of Frauds. The expression "suitable for the trade" is sometimes difficult to apply. It does not mean that every small change made for a particular buyer converts the contract from a sales contract to one for labor and materials. It must be such a deviation from the standard pattern of the goods that it would be difficult to find another buyer. For example, if a taxi company ordered a fleet of cars but asked the seller to paint them yellow, would this be a sale? No other taxi company might want yellow cabs, but by repainting the cabs would be suitable for sale to other cab companies.

(2) New York Rule. A few states follow the so-called New York rule, which differs from the Massachusetts rule in only one particular. If the goods are not in existence at the time of the contract but are to be manufactured on the order of the buyer, the agreement is a contract for labor and materials regardless of whether or not the goods are suitable for trade in the ordinary course of business.

- Tucker, a cabinet maker, contracted with Hill to make him a black walnut cabinet for $750, Tucker to supply the lumber. The contract was entirely oral. When the cabinet was finished, Hill refused to take it and pay for it. He was bound since this was a contract for labor and materials, not a sale. A contract for labor and materials need not be in writing no matter how much money is involved.

AUCTION SALES

A sale by auction for any amount is valid even though it is from necessity oral. In most states the auctioneer is the special agent for both the owner and the bidder. When he or the clerk of the auction makes a memorandum of the sale and signs it, this binds both parties. The bidder is the one who makes the offer. There is no contract until the auctioneer accepts the offer, which he may do in several ways. The most common way is to cry, "Sold to John Smith." In most auctions, however, the final bid is preceded by several lower bids. If a man makes a bid to start the sale, the auctioneer may refuse to accept this as a starting bid. If he does accept it and then proceeds to ask for a higher bid, he can later refuse to accept this bid as the selling price. The acceptance of a bid is the final fall of the hammer or other usual manner.

The Uniform Commercial Code provides for contingencies lacking in the other laws covering auction sales. If a bid is made "while the hammer is falling" in acceptance of a prior bid, then the auctioneer may at his discretion reopen the bidding or declare the goods sold. His decision is binding.

Goods may be offered for sale "with reserve" or "without reserve." If they are without reserve, then the goods cannot be withdrawn after the bidding starts unless no bid is received within a reasonable time after the auctioneer calls for bids. Goods are presumed to be offered with reserve unless the goods are explicitly put up without reserve.

There are two practices often employed in auction sales that are a species of fraud, and if discovered by either party after the bid is accepted, may vitiate the contract. One is known as "puffing." This is bidding merely to run the price up without any intention of buying. It is done by either the seller or his agent. When the successful bidder learns of this, he may refuse to carry out the terms of the sale. The other fraudulent practice is known as "chilling." This is done by the bidder or his agent to keep the price down. Any artifice or practice that discourages open and free bidding releases the innocent party from the contract.

- Green attended a livestock auction where several registered brood cows were being sold. Green made a deal with two other bidders whereby he would not bid against them if they in turn would not bid on the animals he wanted. This is known as "chilling"; and when the owner learns of it, he may refuse to sell to any of the three bidders.

QUESTIONS

1. Must a contract to sell a chose in action for $50 or more be in writing?
2. Is a check part payment as defined by the Statute of Frauds?
3. If A sells B 1,000 bushels of wheat by oral contract, is a token delivery of one handful sufficient to make the contract valid?
4. What is a constructive delivery of goods?
5. What constitutes part payment?
6. How does a written memorandum differ from a written contract?
7. (a) Can an exchange of letters constitute a memorandum?
   (b) Is a sales ticket that is signed by the buyer a sufficient memorandum?
8. Wherein does a contract for labor and materials differ from a contract of sale?
9. In what particular does the Massachusetts rule differ from the New York rule on contracts for labor and materials?
10. What kind of writing meets the requirements of a note or memorandum for an auction sale?

CASE PROBLEMS

1. Henry and Harriet went shopping at the Shadow Discount House for furniture. They selected a living room suite for $450. After visiting another store, they returned to the Shadow Discount House and selected a dining room suite for $475. The seller was to deliver the furniture the following day at which time payment was to be made. All sales in this state for $500 or more must be in writing to be enforceable. Is this one or two sales?

2. Joel, sales manager for the Dobbs Building Materials Company, sold Wilson $6,000 worth of building materials. Joel wrote down the items on

a purchase order as Wilson listed them. Joel agreed to take in part payment a 60-day draft drawn by Downs Motor Company in favor of Wilson. This draft was assigned in writing to the Dobbs Building Materials Company. Joel interpreted this to meet the requirements of a memo under the Statute of Frauds. Wilson signed nothing else and made no other payment at the time. He later canceled the order and demanded a return of the draft. Was Wilson bound on this contract?

3. Horace purchased a piano from Walden and paid for it by indorsing a check, on which he was the payee, to Walden in payment. On the back of the check, he wrote: "Pay to the order of A. Walden but with no recourse on me if the check is not paid. Signed: John Horace." Walden agreed to accept the check with this indorsement. Does this meet the test of part payment?

4. Duncan made out a purchase order to the Fulton Steel Company for some sheet metal costing $2,700. This order was mailed on July 7. There was no acknowledgment of the order. On August 3 the metal arrived, but in the meantime Duncan had purchased the metal elsewhere. He claims he is not bound on this contract because it is not in writing. Do you agree?

5. The Ferguson Men's Shop sold a suit to Harbottle for $150. Because of Harbottle's odd build, extensive alterations had to be made. In order to keep this sale from coming within the Statute of Frauds, Ferguson quoted the suit as $149.75 and said the alterations would cost 25 cents. Harbottle accepted. Later he refused to take the suit and pay for it, claiming he was not bound because the contract was oral. Do you agree?

6. Carson sold his recorder to Douglas for $350. He gave Douglas the key to the room where the recorder was stored and told Douglas to pick it up when convenient. Before Douglas went for the recorder, the building in which it was stored was destroyed by fire. Douglas now refuses to pay for the set, claiming it is Carson's loss since this was an oral contract. Do you agree?

7. Hammond, manager for a supermarket, ordered by telephone 400 bushels of peaches from Hardigree. He stipulated, "The peaches must be first-grade and free from defects." When the peaches were delivered, Hammond opened one bushel before the truck was unloaded and the peaches seemed to be as ordered. He made no further comment. After the peaches were unloaded and opened, he found they were badly bruised by hail, and every bushel contained some rotten ones. He called Hardigree and asked him to come and get the peaches. Hardigree refused. The peaches remained in the warehouse for ten days while the argument between Hammond and Hardigree as to their rights persisted. During that time the peaches became a total loss. What fundamental error did Hammond make?

8. Mrs. Jane Langley inspected some carpet material on display at the Sinkwich Furniture Mart. The salesman quoted her a definite price per square foot, the carpet material to be cut individually to fit her living room, a wall-to-wall type of carpet. She orally agreed to purchase it. Her living room had a very odd and unusual shape. After the carpet was cut and laid,

Mrs. Langley was keenly disappointed in its appearance. She had faintly remembered from her business law course that an oral sales contract under certain conditions is invalid. She refused to pay for it and demanded that the seller take it up. What were the rights of the parties here?

9. The Glo-Coat Paint Company offered to sell the Lull Paint Store a quantity of paint of various grades and colors. The value of the bulk lot was $5,575. The owner of the Lull Paint Store orally agreed to buy it, but the seller insisted on a written memorandum of the sale to make it comply with the Statute of Frauds. Lull was in a quandary. He really wanted the paint as it was a very good price, but there was a possibility he would sell his paint store in a few days, in which case he would not want it. He drew up a memo as follows: "It is hereby agreed that were I to buy the paint herein described, I will pay cash on the day of delivery, which is to be not later than one week from today." Both parties signed the memo. Lull sold his paint store the next day and notified the Glo-Paint Company that he would not buy the paint. The Glo-Paint Company sued him for breach of contract, alleging that they were inveigled into signing a trick memo. Was the Lull Paint Store liable on this contract?

CHAPTER 15

TRANSFER OF
OWNERSHIP

PASSING OF TITLE

In a sale there is always a specific, definite time when title or owner-ship passes from the seller to the buyer. If the goods are lost, stolen, or damaged, the loss generally falls upon the owner. Also, if there should be a gain or an increase, or a loss or a decrease, the increase or gain inures to the owner, and the decrease or loss is his also. It is important, then, to have definite rules to enable the court to determine when title passes. If the parties expressly state when title is to pass, no dispute need arise. Furthermore, in most cash sales where delivery is made immediately, there is little difficulty in determining when title passes. But if delivery is to be made at a future date, if the goods are not separated from a mass, or if something remains to be done, it frequently is difficult to determine the exact time when title passes.

SELLER'S TITLE

Only the owner of property can pass title to it. If one does not own property, he cannot vest others with good title to it. The seller can pass only such title as he has. A man may steal property and sell it; but no subsequent purchaser can ever acquire title to the property because the real owner has never parted with the title. An innocent purchaser can look only to the seller for damages.

One fundamental exception to this rule is that when one of two innocent persons must suffer loss by reason of the wrongdoing of an-other, the loss should fall on the one whose conduct enabled the wrongdoer to cause the injury. This rule applies in each of the follow-ing four situations.

(1) Transfer of Possession to Agent or Dealer. If the owner of personal property transfers possession to an agent, dealer, commission merchant, or similar person so that he is clothed with the apparent authority to sell, this person has the power to transfer title to an innocent third party. If the courts adhered strictly to the law that only the owner may pass title, many lines of business could not operate. This is especially true of commission merchants, sometimes called *factors,* who take possession of other people's property under a contract to sell it and receive a commission for their services. They can transfer good title to the buyer even though they do not own the property. This same law applies to all firms or persons, whether it is their common business to sell on commission or not, who are entrusted with the possession of personal property in such a way as to indicate that they have the right to sell.

- Williams was a factor merchant dealing mainly in baled cotton. Vinson delivered to him 100 bales of cotton with instructions to hold it until he returned from a trip. One of Williams' salesmen who was unaware of this special arrangement sold the cotton to Dale. Vinson in the meantime had found a buyer for 2 cents a pound higher than Dale paid. In spite of this, Dale got good title to the cotton. Williams, of course, could be sued for damages for breach of contract.

(2) Sale by One Having Only a Conditional Title. In sales on the installment plan whereby the seller retains title until the terms of the sale are complied with, the buyer may sell the goods and under certain conditions pass good title to them. To prevent this loss, the seller must have his conditional sales contract recorded.

- Kaufman purchased an air conditioner for window installation from the Grimes Corporation. It was purchased on the installment sales plan. He later sold the conditioner to Heller for $340 and told him the title was clear. The Grimes Corporation demanded that Heller pay the balance of $300. The sales manager had failed to record the conditional sales agreement in the county clerk's office. Heller, therefore, obtained good title to the conditioner.

(3) Sale by One Who Has Voidable Title. In Chapter 5 it was pointed out that all contracts evidenced by fraud, duress, or undue influence were voidable. If such a voidable contract is a sales contract and if the buyer is the one who committed the wrongdoing, he has only a voidable title. When the seller elects to avoid the sales contract, he has the right to regain both possession and title of the article sold.

If, before he regains title, the buyer resells the article to an innocent purchaser, that purchaser obtains good title even though the seller did not have good title. This would not be true if the first sale was the result of forgery or mistake since then the buyer's title would rest upon a void contract.

- Herblock purchased a piano from Dotson, a minor. Herblock soon thereafter sold the piano to DuBose for $1,400. Dotson then disaffirmed the contract and demanded that DuBose turn the piano over to him. DuBose need not do this since he obtained good title as an innocent purchaser. Dotson's only remedy is to demand the $1,400 from Herblock.

(4) **Negotiable Instruments.** The most important exception pertains to negotiable instruments. This will be discussed fully in Chapters 24 and 25.

TYPES OF GOODS

Under the Uniform Sales Act there are three classes of goods:
1. Ascertained or specific goods
2. Fungible goods
3. Unascertained goods

(1) **Ascertained or Specific Goods.** Goods that are in existence and are specifically selected and set aside by the seller with the assent of the buyer are *ascertained* or *specific goods*. If Smith buys a new car exactly like the demonstrator in color, make, style, and other features with only the motor number differing, this is not specific goods. The exact car to be bought must be ascertained.

(2) **Fungible Goods.** Goods that are in mass, but of the same grade or quality, such as wheat, lumber, and coal, are *fungible goods*. If a man buys 500 bushels of No. 1 wheat out of a bin containing 10,000 bushels of No. 1 wheat, he owns one-twentieth of the mass. This would not be true if the bin contained 10,000 bushels of several grades and the buyer bought only No. 1 wheat. In most states the law considers fungible goods as ascertained goods.

Fungible goods are another form of specific or ascertained goods. The only purpose of listing them as a separate class is to avoid confusing them with unascertained goods, explained in the next paragraph. The law that applies to specific goods applies to fungible goods.

(3) **Unascertained Goods.** If a sales contract involves goods that have not been specifically designated, the contract must from its nature be one to sell, not of sale. This is particularly true of goods that are part of a mass of goods of varying quality and value. Until the goods covered by the contract are separated from the mass, they are *unascertained goods.* They become *specific goods* when they are weighed, counted, or otherwise separated from the mass. Notice the difference in the law relative to ascertained and unascertained goods in rules (1) and (5) in the following section.

INTENTION OF THE PARTIES

It is a well-established rule of law that title to goods passes when the parties intend it to pass. If their intentions are clearly expressed at the time the contract is made, disputes seldom arise. When the parties are silent as to when title is to pass, then the time of passage of title must be inferred from their conduct or the nature of the transaction. Over the years the courts have achieved a high degree of uniformity throughout all the states by adopting seven rules which help in determining the true intention of the parties.

(1) **If Specific Goods Are in a Deliverable State at the Time of the Contract, the Title Passes Immediately.** The average sales contract consists of a brief, definite offer and an equally brief acceptance. The following is a typical illustration taken from an actual case:

- *A* says to *B,* "I will sell you this horse for $50." *B* replies, "I will take him." Neither said anything as to when the $50 was to be paid or when delivery was to be made. Nevertheless, title to the horse passed to *B* as soon as he uttered the words, "I will take him." This is true even though goods are sold on credit or where delivery is expressly stated to be at a future date. The court fixes the time title is to pass if the parties fail to do so.

(2) **If Something Remains to Be Done Before Specific Goods Are Put in a Deliverable State, Title Does Not Pass Until Such Thing Is Done.** It is not unusual for the contract to sell to contain a provision that the selling price is not for the goods in their present state but in a state described in the offer and the acceptance. An example would be an agreement whereby the seller promises to repair and revarnish a sewing machine as a part of the selling price. Title would not pass until the machine is repaired and revarnished.

If the thing that remains to be done is merely weighing, sorting, counting, or measuring to determine the quantity, passing of title in most states does not depend on the performance of this act. If one buys 500 bushels of wheat from a bin of 10,000 bushels of the same grade, for example, the 500 bushels would have to be measured, but title would pass even before this is done unless otherwise agreed upon by the parties to the sale.

- Kirkpatrick sold Himler a color television set for $800. As part of the selling price Kirkpatrick agreed to have it repaired to remove a slight defect in the performance of the set. While the set was at the repair shop, it was stolen. The loss falls on Kirkpatrick since title had not passed.

(3) If Goods Are Delivered to the Buyer on a "Sale or Return" Basis, Title Passes Immediately to the Buyer, but the Buyer May Revest Title in the Seller. The contract may fix the time limit upon the buyer's option to retain or return the goods. If he keeps them beyond this time, such an act constitutes a waiver of his right to return the goods. If no time is fixed by agreement, then a reasonable time will be allowed. What constitutes a reasonable time is a question of fact.

The buyer may expressly waive his right to return the goods before the expiration of either the agreed time or a reasonable time. In that event, the title of the buyer becomes absolute.

- Rochester purchased a second-hand tractor from Fleeman. The agreement stipulated that Rochester was to have the tractor with the right to return it in thirty days if he was not satisfied with it. Ten days after the sale, the creditors of Rochester levied upon the tractor. Since Rochester had not exercised his right to return the tractor before the levy, he could not do so afterwards; the creditors could sell it to satisfy their debts. Had the tractor been stolen or destroyed before Rochester had indicated an intention to return the tractor, the loss would have fallen on him.

(4) If Goods Are Delivered to the Buyer "on Approval," the Title Remains with the Seller until the Buyer Indicates His Approval by Word or Act. In a sale "on approval," the title remains with the seller, and thus the risk of loss must be borne by him. If there is an increase, as is often the case with animals and livestock, the increase belongs to the seller. The title vests in the buyer as soon as he expressly indicates his approval or commits some act which indicates approval.

- Mary Jones purchased an evening gown "on approval" and
  promised to return it in two days if her mother did not like it.
  Mary decided to wear the gown to a formal dance so that she would
  be better able to determine if the gown was becoming to her. The
  next day the gown was stolen through no fault of her own. The loss
  was Mary's because her wearing the gown to a formal dance was an
  act of approval.

When the sales contract provides that the seller may return the
goods but it is not clear whether it is a sale or return or a sale on approval, then the Uniform Commercial Code provides that it shall be
deemed a sale on approval if the goods are bought for use. If they
are bought for resale, then it shall be deemed a sale or return.

(5) **In a Contract to Sell Unascertained or Future Goods by
Description, Title Does Not Pass to the Buyer until the Goods
Have Been Appropriated to the Contract.** If the goods to be delivered have not been ascertained or are not in existence, title cannot,
in most states, pass to the buyer at the time of the sale. They must
first be ascertained or acquired, but this alone does not pass title. They
must be "appropriated to the contract," which means either delivered
to the buyer directly or delivered to a transportation company for
hauling. Title passes as soon as the goods are placed with the transportation company. The parties may, of course, expressly agree otherwise, in which case the goods are appropriated to the contract when
the terms of the contract regarding the passing of title have been
carried out.

- The Grantland Mill Company contracted with Brown to purchase
  several thousand saw logs which Brown had cut. The price was
  to be $37 per thousand board feet, the price to be paid "when the
  logs are placed on the skidway." A fire destroyed many of the logs
  before they were hauled. The loss fell on Brown since the goods had
  not been appropriated to the contract at the time of the loss.

(6) **If the Contract to Sell Specific Goods Requires the Seller
to Deliver the Goods to the Buyer or to a Particular Place, the
Title Does Not Pass until the Goods Reach Their Destination.**
The goods are appropriated to the contract as soon as they are delivered to the buyer or to the place designated in the contract. In
many instances, the goods are shipped C.O.D. The terms C.O.D. have
no effect upon the passing of title. Possession cannot pass to the buyer
until the purchase price is paid, but the passing of title can precede
the transfer of possession.

If the terms are f.o.b. destination, title does not pass until the goods reach the buyer.

- Hinton purchased a house trailer from the Kerr Sales Corporation. The price was $6,500 and the seller agreed for this price to haul it to Hinton's lot and place it on blocks. Hinton paid the purchase price at the time the agreement was made. While the trailer was being hauled to Hinton's lot, a collision caused the trailer to be upset, causing $2,100 damage to the trailer. This loss falls on the seller because title had not passed.

(7) **If the Goods Are to Be Delivered at the Buyer's Expense, as, for Example, When the Terms Are f.o.b. Shipping Point, Title Passes as soon as the Goods Are Delivered to the Transportation Company.** When the terms, however, are f.o.b. shipping point, or in other cases where the goods are to be delivered at the buyer's expense, title passes as soon as the goods have been delivered to the common carrier for transportation unless there is an express agreement to the contrary.

CONDITIONAL SALES

The seller of goods may deliver the possession of the goods to the buyer but retain title to them. Such a sale is known as a *conditional sale*. In a conditional sale the price is usually payable in installments. Common examples of conditional sales are installment sales of automobiles, television sets, refrigerators, and furniture.

The chief purposes of a conditional sale are:

1. To protect the seller against third parties who may purchase the article

2. To obtain a preferred lien against the article for the unpaid purchase price

3. To facilitate a collection if the account is in default

(1) **To Protect the Seller Against Third Parties Who May Purchase the Article.** Possession is presumptive evidence of ownership. If the buyer under a conditional sales contract is inclined to do so, he can sell the article to an innocent third party. If the article was merely sold on credit, but title was permitted to pass, the third party would obtain a title superior to the original seller. Under a conditional sale the seller can assert title to the article even against an innocent third party. Under the common law the seller is not required to record the conditional sales contract in order to protect his interest. A majority

of the states have amended the common law to require the seller to record his conditional sales agreements. This record is constructive notice to everyone that the seller retains title. It is not necessary that the innocent third party actually see the record. Usually there is a conditional sales book in the county or city clerk's office for the recording of conditional sales contracts.

If the article sold on a conditional sales contract is attached to a larger article, complications may arise. As between the seller and the purchaser, the seller may repossess the goods in case of default no matter how much inconvenience or expense it causes the buyer. An example would be a set of truck tires mounted on a truck. The seller may remove the tires if the purchaser defaults in his payments. If the truck also was purchased under a conditional sales contract, the seller of the tires may still repossess them unless the seller of the truck can prove he would sustain a serious injury by the repossession of the tires.

> ▪ Eagen purchased a complete air conditioning unit on the install-
> ment plan and had it installed in his home. Subsequently he
> mortgaged his home for $15,000 to the Prudential Insurance Com-
> pany. When he defaulted in his payments on his air conditioner,
> the seller attempted to repossess it. He was not allowed to do so
> since the mortgage was placed on the home after the air conditioner
> was installed. Had the sale been subsequent to the mortgage, he could
> repossess it provided its repossession did not cause a serious injury
> to the insurance company.

(2) **To Obtain a Preferred Lien Against the Article for the Unpaid Purchase Price.** The creditors of the buyer, after having obtained judgment against the debtor, may proceed to levy on all the assets of the buyer to collect their unpaid claims. In such an event, the seller has a prior lien on the article he sold. The creditors may sell it, but the seller must have his claim paid in full before the other creditors get anything from the proceeds. This is true under the common law, but in those states requiring the agreement to be recorded, no preference exists unless it is recorded or the seller notifies the bidders at the sale of his interest.

(3) **To Facilitate a Collection if the Account Is in Default.** If the seller retains title to personal property under a conditional sales agreement, he has the right in most states to repossess it since it belongs to him. He may use any peaceable means which he deems necessary. If the buyer refuses to return the goods, the seller may resort to court action to compel a return. After the goods are re-

Conditional Sales Agreement, made this __eighth__ day of __March__, 19___, between the

JOHN REGIS CO., Dayton, Ohio, hereinafter called the "Seller," and ____John Burroughs____,

residing at __362 Forest Avenue__, in the city of __Dayton__, State of Ohio. hereinafter

called the "Buyer."

WITNESSETH: That the buyer has this day conditionally purchased from the seller, subject to

the terms and conditions hereof, certain personal property, as listed below:

DESCRIPTION	SERIAL NO.	PURCHASE PRICE
one RCA Television Receiver, Model TC167	A-1575273	$ 412.00
Salesman	Total	$ 412.00

The buyer agrees to pay the seller for said property and the use thereof the sum of __$52.00__

Dollars on the signing of the contract, and __$20.00__ Dollars on the __first__ day of every

__month__ hereafter.

The title in the property above described shall remain in the seller until the terms of this

contract have been fully complied with. In case of any default in the performance of the terms and

condition hereof, or in the event the seller deems itself insecure, the seller shall have the right to

declare the full unpaid amount immediately due and payable and/or retake all the property. Buyer

agrees not to move, sell, mortgage, encumber, pledge, or otherwise dispose of the property until paid

for in full. Upon the performance by the buyer of all the conditions of this contract, title to the prop-

erty is to vest in the buyer. It is mutually agreed that this instrument sets forth the entire contract.

In Witness Whereof, the parties to this instrument have hereunto set their hands and

seals at Dayton, Ohio, on the date hereinabove stated.

READ THIS BEFORE SIGNING.

JOHN REGIS COMPANY

By *Charles H. McConnell*   Signature *John Burroughs*

A Conditional Sales Contract

possessed, some states require the seller to resell the goods and apply
the proceeds on the unpaid purchase price. If the proceeds are less
than the unpaid balance, the seller may sue for the deficit. If there is
an excess, this goes to the buyer after all costs and expenses are paid.
Other states permit a repossession but do not require a resale. The
title revests in the seller, and he is free to do as he chooses.

RISKS

Although title remains with the seller in a conditional sales contract, the risks of ownership fall on the buyer. If the property is destroyed, stolen, lost, or damaged, the buyer still must pay the balance due. This is not true, of course, if the contract provides otherwise.

BULK SALES LAWS

The purpose of state bulk sales laws is to prevent a merchant from defrauding his creditors by purchasing stock on credit and then selling the entire stock to another merchant. The goods can be sold item by item, but not in bulk.

The first requirement under the bulk sales laws is that the seller under oath must deliver to the buyer a written list of all his creditors with their addresses and the amounts owed to each. The second requirement is that the buyer, within a specified time and before taking possession of the goods or paying the purchase price, must notify these creditors of the proposed sale, the price, and conditions. The buyer, having given such notice, has no further liability, and it is the responsibility of the creditors to protect themselves. If they do nothing, the purchaser takes the goods free of the creditors' claims.

The Uniform Commercial Code sets forth specifically how the notice shall be given and the minimum contents of the notice. Any deviation from these minimum requirements is not due notice. The notice must be given personally to each person entitled to it or else mailed to him by registered mail. The Uniform Commercial Code also provides that the transferee (buyer) must give notice to any party who is known to him to have any claim against the transferor (seller) even though this party is not included in the list of creditors supplied by the transferor.

QUESTIONS

1. If John buys a watch for cash and drops it as soon as he starts to put it on his wrist, who must bear the loss if it breaks?
2. Are fungible goods merely another form of unascertained goods?
3. Why is it necessary for the law to fix the time when title passes?
4. What is the purpose of recording a conditional sales contract in the county clerk's office?
5. In a contract to sell specific goods in which the seller must do something to the goods before they are ready to deliver, when does title pass?

6. If a television set is sold on approval, when does title pass?

7. If the Climax Hosiery Mills buys all of John's cotton and John is to pick, bale, and deliver the cotton, when does title pass?

8. (a) If Jones purchases a piano and the seller is to deliver it to 237 Hope Street, when does title pass?

   (b) If the Davis Furniture Exchange buys $10,000 worth of furniture f.o.b. Chicago, when does title pass?

9. In a conditional sales contract, who has the risks of ownership before the conditions are met?

10. What is the purpose of the bulk sales law?

CASE PROBLEMS

1. On December 27 the Hartsfield Lumber Company received a bill of lading and an invoice from the Chicago Aluminum Window Company showing that $5,000 worth of merchandise had been shipped f.o.b. Chicago. The bookkeeper was asked not to record the purchase until the goods arrived, which was January 7, the following fiscal year. The Hartsfield Lumber Company wished to make a loan in January from the bank, and the bank required a balance sheet as of December 31 with an affidavit that it was "true and correct." John, the bookkeeper, made this affidavit and was later indicted for perjury. Was he guilty?

2. Anne and Tom were married. They went to the Lee Furniture Company and selected several items of furniture for their apartment. The total sales price was $2,100. Terms were "cash and carry." They paid for the furniture, and the seller agreed to deliver it for $25. While the truck was on its way to deliver the furniture, it had a collision due to no fault of the driver, and the furniture was almost a total loss. Who must bear this loss, Anne and Tom or the seller?

3. Hunt built his own home without the use of a contractor. He purchased three heating furnaces and an electric hot water heater from the Lee Appliance Company. These items were purchased on the installment plan extending over a period of three years. After the house was completed, Hunt placed a mortgage on it for $14,000. He became ill and could not keep up his payments on the heaters and hot water heater. May the Lee Appliance Company repossess these items?

4. Sooter called by long distance the Sunshine Boat Company to inquire about the price of a particular boat. The price was quoted as follows: "$2,700 at the site of the boat." Sooter did not inquire as to which "site" was meant since he was assured a written offer would be mailed immediately. The written offer contained the words, "at the sight of the boat." Sooter accepted, but the boat was destroyed in transit. The Sunshine Boat Company contended it was Sooter's loss as the secretary merely typed the wrong "sight." Who must bear this loss?

5. Lowe of New York, who owned and operated a supermarket, purchased a carload of lettuce from the Produce Exchange in California. The

seller described the lettuce as "first class." The terms were "f.o.b. Los Angeles." When the lettuce arrived in New York, Lowe examined it and found it to be second class. He refused to pay the freight and accept it. A week went by while Lowe, the railroad, and the Produce Exchange argued as to what disposition should be made of the lettuce. During that week the lettuce deteriorated and became worthless. The purchase price was $3,500; the value of a similar quantity of second-class lettuce was $2,700; and the freight was $400. Discuss the rights of all the parties.

6. Smith sold Ling a radio for $75, cash to be paid within two weeks. Smith agreed to supply two new tubes before delivering the radio to Ling. It was further expressly agreed that the radio should belong to Ling as of the time of the sale even though delivery was not made then. Before delivery was made, the radio was destroyed by fire due to no fault of Smith's. Who had to bear the loss?

7. Mrs. Jones took her three children to the Baxter Tot Shop to purchase each of them a coat preparatory to their starting back to school. She selected a coat for each one, the total purchase price amounting to $110. She paid $50 and agreed to pay the balance when the coats were delivered. The seller was to alter each of the coats to meet each child's measurements. There was no charge for these alterations. He said, "They will be ready on or before Friday." Thursday night the store was burglarized, and the three coats were among those things taken. The coats had been altered, but Mrs. Jones had not been notified. Who must bear this loss?

8. Mary, a widow, took her insurance money which she received upon her late husband's death and purchased The Thrift Dress Shop, hoping thereby to earn a living for her three minor children. The purchase price was $14,500. Soon after she took over the business, she found there were $3,000 in unpaid bills. The seller had assured her all bills were paid. Must Mary pay this $3,000?

9. Coleman was the bookkeeper for the Anawalt Auto Stores. The store sold Brandt four truck tires on a conditional sales agreement. The manager said to Coleman, "After you record the sale, be sure to file the conditional sales contract." He filed it under "Ti" for Tires. They discovered later that the buyer had sold the tires, and the seller planned to take legal action to regain them. In checking at the county clerk's office, it was found that the contract was never filed with the clerk for recording, nor could they find the contract. Could the seller compel the second buyer to pay for them or give up possession?

CHAPTER 16

WARRANTIES OF THE SELLER

NATURE OF WARRANTIES

In making a sale, a seller often "warrants" or "guarantees" that the article will measure up to a certain standard or will operate in a certain manner. The statement of the seller in which he "warrants" or "guarantees" the article is known as an *express warranty*. It is a warranty because it is a representation about the goods; it is express because the seller actually and definitely expresses it. By his warranty the seller agrees in effect to make good any loss or damages that the purchaser may suffer if the goods are not as they are represented.

If a warranty is made at the time of the sale, it is considered to be a part of the contract and is therefore binding. If a warranty is made after a sale has been completed, it must be supported by a separate or additional consideration because it is a promise made by the seller that is not a part of the sales contract.

Certain warranties, such as the seller's right to sell the goods, are imposed on all sellers by law. Since they are not expressed by the seller but are nevertheless an essential part of sales contracts, they are called *implied warranties*.

EXPRESS WARRANTIES

An express warranty need not consist of any particular words to be binding on the seller. The words "warrant" or "guarantee" need not be used. If a statement or a promise is such that a reasonable interpretation of the language leads the buyer to believe there is a warranty, the courts will construe it as such. A seller is bound by the ordinary meaning of his words, not by his intentions.

The seller can use the word "warrant" or "guarantee" and still not be bound by it if an ordinary, prudent man would not interpret it to constitute a warranty. If the seller of a car says, "I'll guarantee that you will not be sorry if you buy the car at this price," no warranty exists as this is mere conjecture, even though the word "guarantee" is used.

REPRESENTATIONS

A *representation* is a statement made prior to the sale for the purpose of inducing the sale. A representation differs from a warranty. To be a warranty there must be two elements in the statement: First, there must be an affirmation about the quality or condition of the article sold; and second, the seller must intend to make this a warranty. Thus every warranty is a representation, but a representation may not be a warranty. For a representation to constitute a breach of contract, it must be both false and material. Furthermore, even if the representation is both untrue and material, it does not constitute a breach of contract unless the buyer relied on the statement.

Most so-called representations are mere "sales talk" or "puffing." The law holds that a seller may praise his wares, even extravagantly, without obligating himself on his statements or representations. If the representations can be classed as "opinions," "sales talk," "puffing," or similar expressions, they do not give cause for legal redress. Some "shady" merchants have made an art of making opinions sound like warranties. A person should not be misled by such borderline expressions as "best on the market for the money," "these goods are worth $10 if they are worth a dime," "experts have estimated that one ought to be able to sell a thousand a month of these," and many others which sound very convincing but which have been held to be mere expressions of opinion.

The second reason why one must distinguish between a representation and a warranty is in the remedy. If there is a breach of warranty, the result is a breach of contract. The innocent party has only one of the remedies described later in this chapter. If it is a false representation, it is a tort or legal wrong and gives the injured party the right to sue for damages over and beyond the contract itself.

If the buyer sues for breach of warranty, the seller is not allowed to prove that he made the statement in good faith. This is irrelevant. If the buyer sues for a tort, alleging a false representation, he must prove the seller made the false statement with a knowledge of its falsity. A tort action for misrepresentation may give the buyer wider legal remedies than a suit for breach of warranty, but it is more difficult to prove.

The rule that a statement of opinion or belief does not constitute a warranty must be qualified. If the seller does not warrant but expresses an opinion that the article is first-class merchandise when he knows that it is not first-class, the statement becomes a warranty. He in substance warrants that his opinion is sincere. Secondly, one who is not an expert may rely on the opinion of one who is an expert. An expert refrigerator mechanic says, "In my opinion this refrigerator will give you good service." The purchaser who knows little or nothing about the mechanics of refrigerators may rely on this expert's opinion.

- Hopkins sold Ringgold an oil heater for his ten-room house. Hopkins tried to explain the meaning of BTU's to Ringgold, but it was not very clear to Ringgold. Ringgold selected a heater, and Hopkins expressed the opinion it would be adequate to heat his house. It proved to be totally inadequate to heat the house. Ringgold had a right to rely on Hopkins' opinion since he seemed to be an expert.

WARRANTIES IN WRITTEN CONTRACTS

In oral contracts it may be difficult to distinguish between a warranty and a representation. They are both made to induce the sale. If the seller, after having made many warranties and many representations, says, "I will sell you this computer for $2,700," and the buyer says, "I accept your offer," this is the sales contract. In reality to make the warranties a part of the oral sales contract, the buyer would have to say, "I accept your offer of $2,700 plus the warranty that it is free of mechanical defects." This is seldom, if ever, done. It must always be done in written contracts, however.

The Uniform Commercial Code modifies the Uniform Sales Act slightly in regard to express warranties and representations. The Code specifically provides that any affirmation of fact or promise made by the seller to the buyer which relates to the goods and becomes part of the basis of the bargain creates an express warranty.

- Abbit, in an attempt to sell Stoval a cotton picking machine, said, "In many experiments this machine has repeatedly picked 18,000 pounds of seed cotton in a 10-hour day. We will guarantee this performance." When the written contract was signed, it did not contain this warranty. The machine would not pick more than 10,000 pounds in a 10-hour day. Stoval could not sue for breach of warranty. He could, however, bring a tort action for false representation.

DEFECTS

Even when the words used constitute an express warranty, no effect will be given to them unless the buyer relied on them or was materially influenced by them in agreeing to the contract. If there are defects that are actually known to the buyer, or defects that are so apparent that no special skill or ability is required to detect them, an express warranty cannot be invoked to cover them. If Ross says, "I guarantee this car to be in first-class condition in every respect," there is no breach of warranty if the car clearly has four bald tires. The courts assume that the clear implication of his words is, "except for the defects which you can clearly see." This would not be true if the seller used any scheme or artifice to conceal the defect. The seller must not do anything that is for the purpose of diverting the attention of the buyer from the defects.

IMPLIED WARRANTIES

An implied warranty differs from an express warranty in that it is created by the operation of law rather than by statements made by the seller. It is implied from the very nature of the transaction and the surrounding facts and circumstances as well as custom and usage. The seller cannot avoid liability by insisting that he made no such warranties unless he expressly stated that he did not warrant it.

The two most common types of implied warranties are:

1. Warranty of title
2. Warranty of quality

(1) **Warranty of Title.** If the seller has goods in his possession at the time of the sale, there is an implied warranty that he either has title to them or has the right to transfer title. In some states the warranty of title applies even though the goods are not in the seller's possession at the immediate time of the sale. If the contract is one to sell, the seller warrants that he will have title to the goods at the time when the title is to pass. Neither of these implications will apply if the buyer personally knows that the seller does not have title or that he is merely selling whatever interest he may have in the goods.

- Webster bought his fiancee an engagement ring from a pawnshop because it was offered at a bargain price. Valerie, his fiancee, was very proud of it and showed it to many people. Ruth recognized it as her engagement ring that had been stolen. She demanded that

Valerie return it to her. Valerie had to part with the ring. Neither the pawnshop nor Webster had good title to it, so Valerie's title was defective.

This rule of implied warranty of title does not hold true when one sells goods in a representative capacity, such as when an executor, a trustee, or a sheriff sells property under an order of the court or in an official capacity. In such a case the buyer assumes the risk that someone having a superior title will claim the article.

If the seller expressly states that he does not warrant the title, the buyer assumes all the risks since the seller did not leave his intentions to be ascertained by implication. Implication is invoked by the courts only when the true intentions of the parties cannot be ascertained.

(2) **Warranty of Quality.** At one time there was no implied warranty of quality. The rule of *caveat emptor,* "Let the buyer beware," was the law of the market place. This is still the primary law that applies to ordinary sales. It applies particularly to what are called "over-the-counter" sales where the buyer can see and inspect the goods. In sales of this kind the law presumes that the buyer can demand an express warranty of quality if he does not trust his own judgment. If he does not avail himself of this bargaining right, he buys without recourse to an implied warranty of quality. There are four exceptions to this rule.

(a) *When Goods Are Bought for a Particular Purpose, There Is an Implied Warranty That They Are Fit for That Purpose.* To avail oneself of this law, the article must be bought for a particular purpose, the purpose must be made known to the seller, and the buyer must rely on the seller's skill and judgment. If these three conditions are met, the merchandise must be fit for the purpose for which it was bought. If any one of these conditions is absent, there is no breach of warranty. This situation frequently arises when one purchases an article by trade name or brand name. If the buyer accepts whatever brand is offered, it must be fit for the purpose for which it was bought. But if the buyer orders by trade name or selects the brand that he thinks most likely will serve his purpose, he does not rely on the seller's skill and judgment.

The Uniform Commercial Code goes one step further and provides for an implied warranty of fitness if the seller has reason to know the purpose for which the article is bought and further knows that the buyer is relying on the skill and judgment of the seller. The buyer need not expressly make this fact known to the seller.

- Westfall, a crippled soldier, ordered an automobile that he could steer while standing, since a spinal injury made it impossible for him to drive while sitting. The car was satisfactory in every particular, but the steering device was so constructed that it was impossible for him to stand while driving. He was not liable for the purchase price because there was an implied warranty that the car was fit for the particular purpose. Westfall had made known to the seller the use to which the article was to be put.

(b) When Goods Are Sold by Sample, There Is an Implied Warranty That the Bulk of the Goods Will Correspond With the Sample in Kind and Quality. When Goods Are Sold by Description, There Is an Implied Warranty That They Will Answer the Description. If the goods fail to conform to the sample or the description, the buyer may reject them.

Just what constitutes a description is often a question of fact to be decided by a jury. Such expressions as "No. 2 wheat," "grade B oak flooring," and "oil base paint" are meaningful descriptions to people in these businesses, and the goods must meet these descriptions. Also when goods are manufactured and sold under trade name, such as Windex, Glo-Coat, and similar trade names, selling goods by these names is by description. If the seller describes goods while the buyer is inspecting them, the sale may or may not be a sale by description depending on the circumstances. If the buyer inspects the goods and a false description is perfectly evident, the law presumes the buyer did not rely on the seller's description. The buyer does not have to inspect the goods to ascertain if the description is true or false. He may, if he chooses, rely on the seller's description. Also if a reasonable inspection would not reveal the false description, there is a breach of warranty even when the buyer inspects the goods.

- Jefferson purchased for his Christmas trade 1,000 sets of visible motors sold by sample under the label Visi-Motors. The sample shown by the salesman was a V-8 auto engine. When the 1,000 sets arrived, they were tractor motors. Jefferson did not have to accept them as they were not like the sample.

The Uniform Commercial Code classifies sales by sample and sales by description as express warranties, not implied warranties. The remedies remain the same, so the Code did not materially alter the law as it is stated in the Uniform Sales Act.

(c) When Goods Are Sold for Human Consumption, There Is an Implied Warranty That They Are Wholesome and Fit for Consumption. It matters not that the buyer inspected the food or failed to indicate that he relied on the seller's skill and judgment.

- Darlene purchased fish from the Bay Shore Fish Market. The fish were highly radioactive and so contaminated that Darlene and her family were made ill. She was entitled to recover damages because of a breach of warranty that the fish were fit for human consumption.

(d) In the Sale of Goods for Resale, There Is an Implied Warranty That the Goods Are of Merchantable Quality Unless the Buyer Assumes This Risk by Inspecting the Goods or Otherwise Showing His Approval. If a dealer orders a carload of lettuce which ordinarily sells for twenty cents a head and he is unable to inspect the lettuce, there is an implied warranty that the lettuce is merchantable at approximately that price. It is not sufficient that the lettuce can be sold at some price.

If the merchant caters to a discerning class of customers, second-grade lettuce might not be marketable at any price to them. In most cases, however, if the goods are salable for an average price, there is no breach of an implied warranty of merchantability. This is true when there is no description, such as first class, or when there is no express warranty.

This warranty does not apply when the sale is an isolated sale by one who is not in the business of manufacturing or growing the particular item.

REMOTE PURCHASER

A suit for breach of warranty is based on a contractual relationship existing between the buyer and the seller. If a manufacturer sells a retailer defective merchandise, and the retailer in turn sells it to the consumer, there is no contractual relationship existing between the manufacturer and the remote purchaser. For this reason, until recently no suit for breach of warranty could be maintained against the manufacturer. The modern trend of court decisions is to give the remote purchaser one of two courses for redress. The first is a suit for damages, not for breach of warranty, but for tort. To do this, the purchaser must prove fraud or negligence on the part of the manufacturer. The other remedy is to treat the retailer as the agent of the manufacturer, thus creating a contractual relationship with the remote purchaser.

These remedies are not yet permitted in all states, but the trend is in this direction.

REMEDIES FOR BREACH OF WARRANTIES

If the seller is guilty of a breach of warranty in the sale of any article, the law allows the buyer to choose one of four remedies. He must weigh all the facts carefully to determine which of these remedies is most advantageous to him. He can have one and only one. These remedies are:

(1) Keep the merchandise and bring suit against the seller for any damages he has sustained. Frequently there has been a breach of warranty, but no damage was sustained. In such case this remedy is of little value.

(2) If the goods were bought on credit, the purchaser may deduct from the purchase price the damages he has sustained. In this event he keeps the goods. If he overestimates the damages, the seller would have to sue the buyer so that the actual damages could be judicially determined.

(3) If title has not passed to the buyer at the time the breach of warranty is discovered, the buyer can refuse to accept the goods and then can sue the seller for any damages he has sustained. He must make sure title has not passed before he attempts to exercise this remedy. Again, if he has not been damaged materially, there is no merit in bringing a suit for damages.

(4) If title has passed to the buyer, he should return the goods or offer to return them, assuming he does not wish to keep them. If the seller refuses to take them back, the buyer should hold them, unless they are perishable, until the respective rights have been judicially determined. While awaiting the outcome, the buyer must not permit the goods to deteriorate. Even if he returns the goods, he may still sue for damages.

QUESTIONS

1. Must a warranty involve a material fact before there can be a breach of warranty?
2. What is the difference between a warranty and a representation?
3. May one make a warranty even though he has no intention of doing so?
4. If an oral warranty is not included when the contract is written up, may the purchaser prove it by oral testimony?

5. Is the statement, "This fish bait is so good you will have to hide behind a tree to put it on a hook," a warranty or sales talk?

6. Is an expression of an opinion ever a warranty?

7. Name the two most common types of implied warranties.

8. What warranty does the seller make when he sells by sample?

9. If the buyer of food for human consumption inspects the food, what liability, if any, does the seller have?

10. What are the remedies for a breach of warranty?

CASE PROBLEMS

1. Mrs. Fuller had a prescription filled at the East End Drug Store. She took the tablets as recommended by the prescription. Because of a poisonous substance in the medicine, she was made seriously ill. She sued both the East End Drug Store and the Fuller Drug Company, the manufacturer, for a breach of warranty. Is either or both liable for damages?

2. Reynolds was the purchasing agent for the Big Apple Supermarket. He visited the Wholesale Produce Exchange and made a memorandum of several items he wished to buy. Because the goods he wished to buy were stored in vast quantities, he was unable to inspect any except the top layers. He walked across the street and telephoned in his order. What was his purpose in placing his order this way?

3. Margaret deposited a dime in a soft drink dispensing machine and purchased a bottled drink. When she had finished drinking about half of it, she discovered a dead insect in the bottle. She sued the local bottling company for damages. Was she entitled to collect?

4. Sullivan was the purchasing agent for the Swanson Clothing Store. While on a New York buying trip, he inspected some suit samples. The seller assured him, "They are the very latest Ivy League style;" "They will sell like hot cakes;" "You will need to reorder before the season is half over." Sullivan purchased 1,000 suits, but the store could sell only 300 suits. The store sued the seller for breach of warranty. Were any or all of these statements warranties?

5. The Elkhorn Motor Sales Corporation sold Kirby a car for $1,200. He was given a written guarantee that the car was in "A-1 condition" and provided that if anything went wrong with the car within 12 months, the Elkhorn Motor Corporation would repair it, charging only the wholesale cost of parts and labor. What is the weakness in this warranty?

6. Branch, a cattleman, purchased from the Hay Seed Company 2,000 pounds of reseeding crimson clover seed. The seller said, "This is the Dixie strain of reseeding clover, and I guarantee you won't have to worry about its reseeding." There are several strains of crimson clover, some reseeding, some not. The Dixie strain is the most reliable. Branch later learned his seed was not the Dixie strain. It did reseed satisfactorily, but Branch could not market his seed as Dixie seed. He sued the Hay Seed Company for breach of warranty. Was he entitled to collect damages?

7. The Virginia Supply Company sold Lewis, a groceryman, 500 bushels of No. 1 Idaho potatoes. The sale was by correspondence. The potatoes were shipped by truck and accepted by Lewis. Four days later, after several customers had complained about the poor quality of the potatoes, Lewis notified the seller that he would not pay for the potatoes and offered to return them, claiming a breach of warranty. Was there a breach of warranty in this case?

8. Young was branch manager for the Free-Fit Shoe stores. He purchased 1,000 pairs of overshoes that were expressly guaranteed to be waterproof and seamless. The shoes delivered had two seams and were not 100 per cent waterproof. The purchase price was $5,000, and Young estimated that the shoes were not worth more than $4,000. The shoes had been purchased on credit. Young kept the shoes and withheld $3,000 from the purchase price as damages. The seller sued for $1,000, admitting the $1,000 damages, and obtained judgment for this amount. What error did Young commit in selecting his remedy?

9. The defendant wrote to the plaintiff for information and prices on a road-finishing machine. In his letter he stated that the machine must be for 16″ x 18″ finishing work on a concrete pavement and "must pass the specifications of the Michigan State Highway Department." The machine that was delivered failed to do the work. The defendant refused to pay the notes that he had given in payment of the purchase price.

(a) Did the purchaser expressly or impliedly make known the purpose for which the machine was to be used?

(b) Did the buyer rely on the seller's skill or judgment?

10. The Heller Typewriter Exchange sold McBroom a secondhand typewriter. McBroom wanted the typewriter just for personal use. He used the "hunt-and-peck" system. The seller assured McBroom that a good typist could attain a speed of 150 words a minute on this machine although he knew it was impossible to make over 80 words a minute. He also guaranteed that it was in perfect condition, that it was "the best buy in town," and that McBroom could no doubt sell it for $15 more than he was paying for it. McBroom later learned that he could buy a similar machine for $5 less and that it was impossible to attain a speed of more than 80 words a minute; otherwise, the machine was just as represented. He offered to return the machine and demanded the return of his money. The seller refused so McBroom brought suit. Who was entitled to win the case?

11. A salesman in an effort to sell a college student an encyclopedia set for $70 showed him proofs of advertisements that were to be run soon fixing the price for the same books at $210. "This is the last chance to buy at this price" was repeated over and over. The salesman also said, "I guarantee that you can pass any business law exam if you learn all the answers in this encyclopedia." The college student bought the books but failed his examination. Also, the price did not go up. The purchaser wished to rescind the contract. Could he do so?

SUMMARY CASES

PART 3

1. John Low and Sons sold to Alfred Low and Company all the halibut that might be caught by the fishing schooner on which they were setting out on a fishing trip. Before the fish were delivered, John Low and Sons went into bankruptcy, and the question arose as to whether or not this sale of the halibut was valid. Was this a valid sale? (Low v. Pew, 108 Mass. 347)

2. The city of Boscobel, Wisconsin, sold two bailers, two engines, two steam pumps, and other equipment to the Muscoda Manufacturing Company. The total selling price was $1,800, $200 in cash and the balance "to be paid before taking out of the plant." This property was located in a frame building. Before the balance of the $1,600 was paid and the property was removed, the building and all its contents were destroyed by fire. The city of Boscobel brought suit to collect the balance due, and the Muscoda Manufacturing Company denied liability on the ground that title to the property had not passed to it at the time of the fire loss. Had title passed? (City of Boscobel v. Muscoda Manufacturing Company, 175 Wis. 62, 183 N. W. 963)

3. The Kramer Brothers offered by wire to sell Hunter Brothers Milling Company, 1,600 sacks of bran at 73 cents a hundred pounds f.o.b. destination. The Hunter Brothers Milling Company accepted by wire, and the bran was shipped by freight in four cars. Only two of the cars arrived, the other two having been destroyed by flood. The buyer sued to recover damages for the failure of the seller to deliver the four carloads as agreed. Is the buyer entitled to damages? (Hunter Brothers Milling Company v. Kramer Bros., 71 Kans. 468, 80 p. 963)

4. Plummer sold a car for $800 cash to Davis. Davis paid for the car by check. Plummer delivered the car to Davis together with a certificate of title but with the understanding that there was to be no sale until the check was cleared through the bank. The check turned out to be a bad check. Davis in the meantime had sold the car to Kingsley who knew nothing about the arrangement between Plummer and Davis. Plummer brought suit against Kingsley to recover the car, claiming that since Davis did not have good title to the car, he could not transfer good title to Kingsley. Did Kingsley obtain good title to the car? (Plummer v. Kingsley, 190 Oregon, 378, 226 P. 2d 297)

5. Saunders purchased a canvas tent from Cowl, paying $250 down. Saunders inspected the tent, but at the time of the inspection it was folded and not easily inspected. Furthermore, the evidence showed that Saunders would not have been able to perceive the defects in the canvas even if he had inspected it thoroughly. The seller stated, "It is to be in good condition when delivered." The tent was so defective that it was in reality worthless. Saunders alleges a breach of warranty and sues to recover his $250. Was there a breach of warranty? (Saunders v. Cowl et al., 201 Minn. 574, 277 N. W. 12)

6. Coburn purchased 25 head of cattle from Regan and paid $1,500 for them by check. Coburn asked Regan to keep the cattle a few days for him as he was not ready to haul them. Regan agreed to do this. Before Coburn came for the cattle, Regan sold them to Drown for $1,550. After Drown had paid for the cattle but before he took possession of them, he was told of the prior deal with Coburn. He hauled the cattle away nevertheless. Coburn then brought suit against Drown to obtain possession of the cattle, claiming that Regan had no authority to sell them as he was neither owner nor the agent of Coburn. Is Coburn entitled to the cattle? (Coburn v. Drown, 114 Vt. 158, 40A 2d 528)

7. Mrs. Hirth, at the request of her mother, Mrs. Burkhart, purchased a can of corned beef from the Great Atlantic and Pacific Tea Company. The beef had been processed by Armour and Company. The can of beef contained imbedded in the meat a piece of tin which Mrs. Burkhart swallowed. She became ill and soon died from the effects of this act. Her next of kin brought suit against both the seller and the processor. The complaint alleged that both were negligent and that both the seller and the processor had committed a breach of warranty. (a) Was either or both guilty of negligence? (b) Was either or both guilty of a breach of warranty? (Burkhart v. Armour & Co., et al., 115 Conn. 249, 161 A. 385)

8. Lentz was a cripple and could walk only with great difficulty. Through an agent he purchased a horse from the Omar Baking Company. The agent made clear to the seller that because of Lentz's physical condition the horse must be gentle. He was assured that the horse was gentle. The first time the horse was hitched to a buggy with Lentz as the driver, it ran away; Lentz received severe injuries that rendered him a helpless invalid. He sued the bakery for doctor bills, pain and suffering, and the loss of earning power, alleging a breach of warranty. Was there a breach of warranty? (Lentz v. Omar Baking Company, 125 Neb. 861, 252 N. W. 410)

9. Braun of Philadelphia contracted to sell and deliver a barge load of coal to McNeal of Burlington, New Jersey. The contract clearly stipulated that the coal was to be delivered by the seller to the buyer at Burlington. The coal was loaded on the barge and shipped. The barge arrived safely and was tied securely to the wharf. Soon thereafter and before McNeal had an opportunity to unload it, the barge sank and the coal was lost. Braun brought suit to compel McNeal to pay for the coal. Who must bear the loss in this case? (McNeal v. Braun, 153 N. J. 617, 23 A. 687)

10. The Standard Stevedoring Company purchased a crane from Jaffe that Jaffe had widely advertised as having a lifting capacity of 15 to 20 tons. There was no evidence that this statement was made orally when an agent of the buyer came to inspect the crane. The seller was aware that the buyer became interested in the crane as a result of the advertising. The purchasing agent of the Standard Stevedoring Company made no attempt to verify the lifting capacity of the crane due to the impracticality of doing so. The purchaser learned after he bought the crane that it would not lift anywhere near 15 to 20 tons and brought suit to rescind the contract. Was there a breach of an express warranty? (Standard Stevedoring Company v. Jaffe, Tenn. App. 302 S. W. 2d 829)

PART 4

BAILMENTS

Preview Cases for Part 4: Bailments

- Branch left his prized piano with his neighbor, Gerdine, while he went on an extensive world tour. Gerdine placed the piano in front of the window in his den because he had no other place for it. The window was left open while Gerdine was away, and a heavy storm poured an enormous amount of water through the open window into the piano, causing much damage to it. Does Gerdine have any liability for the damage to the piano?

- Fleeman borrowed Brown's truck to haul a load of cotton to the cotton gin. After the cotton was ginned, Fleeman drove about ten miles further to another town to get some farm machinery parts. The truck was wrecked on this part of the trip due to no fault on the part of Fleeman. Who must bear the loss for damage to the truck?

- Webster shipped some perishable freight by the Georgia Central Railroad. The freight was intended for Athens, Georgia, but by error in the address it was sent to Athens, Tennessee. Before it could be returned, the freight was a total loss. Who must bear the loss?

- Johnson was traveling by plane to Cedar City. The plane made a brief stop at Cedar City, but Johnson was asleep and did not hear the pilot's announcement. Johnson awoke after the plane had gone 100 miles beyond Cedar City. Is the airline liable to Johnson for the inconvenience he suffered?

- Jason entered the Ridge Manor Motel to register as a guest. He was told there were no vacancies but that he could wait awhile if he wished to see if anyone checked out. This he did. While he was waiting, his baggage was stolen. Is the motel liable for the loss?

These preview cases are designed to serve as a springboard for the study of this part. As you read through each chapter in this part, you will find the actual decisions for all these preview cases. Of course, there are many more such illustrative problems as well as case problems for decision at the end of each chapter. And there are also a number of even more challenging cases for review at the end of the part.

CHAPTER 17

BAILMENTS IN GENERAL

CHARACTERISTICS OF A BAILMENT

A *bailment* is the transfer of possession, but not the title, of personal property (never real property) by one party, usually the owner, to another party on condition that the identical property will be returned to him or his agent at a future date. The one who retains title but gives up possession is called the *bailor*. The one who acquires possession but not the title is called the *bailee*.

Bailments are generally classified as ordinary and extraordinary. *Extraordinary bailments* are those in which the bailee assumes unusual duties and liabilities imposed by law, as in the case of hotelkeepers or common carriers. *Ordinary bailments* include all other bailments.

In a bailment two conditions are always present:

(1) There must be both a delivery and an acceptance of property.

(2) The bailor must expect to get back the same property, though it may be considerably altered in form.

Also, the property may be delivered with the understanding that the bailee is to deliver it to a third party or sell the item for the bailor. In this case the bailee would not expect to get the property back, but would expect it to be disposed of in the way designated. If either one of the preceding conditions is absent, the transfer may be a sale, a barter, or a gift; but it is not a bailment.

Some typical business transactions resulting in a bailment are:

(a) A motorist leaves his car with the garage for repairs.

(b) A family stores its furniture in a warehouse.

(c) A student borrows a dinner jacket to wear to a formal dance.

(d) A hunter leaves his jewelry with a friend for safekeeping while he goes on an extended hunting trip.

THE BAILMENT AGREEMENT

A bailment is based upon an agreement, express or implied, between the bailor and the bailee. If the agreement is the result of written or spoken words, the bailment is express. If the agreement is indicated by the conduct of the parties, the bailment is implied. When a man checks his hat and coat as he enters a restaurant, nothing may be said, but the bailment is implied by the acts of the two parties. When one finds lost property, the bailment is implied by law.

DELIVERY AND ACCEPTANCE

A bailment can be established only if there is delivery accompanied by acceptance of personal property. The delivery and acceptance may be actual or constructive. They are actual when the goods themselves are delivered and accepted. They are constructive when there is no physical delivery of the goods but when control over the goods is delivered and accepted.

There is a constructive delivery when someone finds lost property. The owner does not actually deliver the property to the finder, but the law holds this to be a bailment. A constructive bailment also occurs when property of one person is washed up on the land of another, the latter being constituted the bailee for the goods of the former.

- Dieball had a painting on exhibit at an art show. Hauchin, a furniture merchant, offered to rent it for 60 days to place on display in his store. Dieball wrote out a statement notifying the manager of the art exhibition to deliver his painting to Hauchin. The delivery of this writing to Hauchin constituted constructive delivery.

RETURN OF THE BAILED PROPERTY

In a bailment the bailee must return to the bailor the identical goods bailed. If a farmer delivers wheat to a miller, a bailment is established if he expects to get back flour made from the same wheat. If he expects to get back flour made from any wheat of like grade, there is an exchange of personal property, but not a bailment.

- The Apex Freezer Company delivered 10 home freezers to the Gerhart Appliance Company to be sold on a 20 percent commission. Any freezers unsold were to be returned. This was a bailment even though the contract contemplated that the freezers would never be returned. If they were not sold, they would have to be returned.

CLASSIFICATIONS OF BAILMENTS

For convenience, bailments are usually divided into the following three groups:

1. Bailments for the sole benefit of the bailor
2. Bailments for the sole benefit of the bailee
3. Bailments for the mutual benefit of both parties

(1) **Bailments for the Sole Benefit of the Bailor.** If one is in possession of another's personal property for the sole benefit of the owner, a bailment for the sole benefit of the bailor exists. The bailee receives no benefits in the way of compensation or else it would not be a bailment for the sole benefit of the bailor. Any benefit that the bailee receives must be from the nature of the property and not a part of the contract. For example, a man asks a friend to keep his piano in his home until he, the owner, is able to rent larger quarters. The friend may play the piano and otherwise receive all the benefits of ownership while it is in his possession without this constituting a consideration. If the pleasure which the bailee received from possessing the piano in no way induced him to take care of the piano, there was no benefit, in the eyes of the law, derived from the act. Not all gratuitous services have the possibility of benefit to the bailee. If a farmer agrees, gratuitously, to haul a load of hay to town for a neighbor, this is clearly a bailment for the sole benefit of the bailor.

- Branch left his prized piano with his neighbor, Gerdine, while he went on an extensive world tour. Gerdine placed the piano in front of the window in his den because he had no other room. The window was left open while Gerdine was away and a heavy storm poured an enormous amount of water through the open window into the piano, causing great damage to the piano. This would constitute negligence and subject Gerdine to liability for damages.

Another example of a bailment for the sole benefit of the bailor occurs when one person loses an article and another person finds it. In this case the loser is the bailor, and the finder is the bailee. The finder is under no obligation to take possession of the lost property. During the time that he has possession of the goods as a bailee, even though the bailment is for the sole benefit of the bailor, he nevertheless assumes certain responsibilities. He is liable for lack of reasonable care with respect to the property. After a reasonable time has elapsed and reasonable diligence has been exercised to find the owner, or after statutory requirements have been met, the bailment comes to an end; and the finder becomes the owner of the found property.

(2) **Bailments for the Sole Benefit of the Bailee.** If the bailee has possession and use of another's personal property, and the owner of the property receives no benefit or compensation for its use, a bailment for the sole benefit of the bailee exists. This type of bailment arises as a rule through borrowing someone else's property. The bailee must exercise reasonable care over the property and is liable for negligence if he fails to do so. The bailee is not an insurer of the bailed property since any loss or damage due to no fault whatsoever of the bailee falls upon the owner. If Petras borrows Walker's diamond ring to wear to a dance and is robbed on the way to the dance, the loss falls upon Walker, the owner. Petras was not negligent.

Even though the bailor receives no benefit from a bailment for the sole benefit of the bailee, he must inform the bailee of any known defects. If the bailee is injured by reason of a defect, the bailor is liable for damages, provided he knew of the defect and failed to inform the bailee.

- Davis borrowed his neighbor's bird dog to take on a hunting trip. The dog was very vicious while eating, but the owner did not tell Davis about this characteristic. Davis' five-year old son attempted to play with the dog while it was eating and was bitten severely. The owner was liable for damages even though this was a bailment for the sole benefit of the bailee.

(3) **Bailments for the Mutual Benefit of Both Parties.** The largest volume of bailments are those for the mutual benefit of both the bailor and the bailee. Some common bailments of this type are: machinery left with a mechanic to be repaired, laundry and dry cleaning contracts, the rental of personal property, such as an automobile or a typewriter, and material left with a fabricator to be converted into a finished product for a price. The bailee must take reasonable care of the bailed property.

- Green rented a You-Drive-It automobile from Trestle Motors Company. While driving to Denver, he collided with a car driven by White, and both cars were wrecked. The roads were coated with ice, and at the time of the collision Green was driving down a fairly steep grade at about forty miles an hour. Visibility because of snow was about 200 feet. Green was liable to the Trestle Motors Company for damages to the car. Forty miles an hour, under the conditions described, was faster than an ordinary, prudent man would have driven his own car.

Had the Trestle Motors Company furnished Green with a car which had a defect that caused the accident, not only would Green not have been liable, but the Trestle Motors Company would have been liable to Green for any damages sustained by him. In a mutual-benefit bailment of this type, the bailor must furnish safe property, not just inform the bailee of any known defects.

In most cases of mutual-benefit bailment the bailee makes a charge for services rendered. This is true in all repair jobs, laundry, dry cleaning, shoe mending, and storage bailments. The bailee has a lien, and usually a first lien, against the bailed property for his charges. If these charges are not paid, the bailee is under no obligation to return the bailed goods. After a reasonable time, the bailee may advertise and sell the property for his charges. If any money remains from the proceeds of the sale after expenses and his charges are paid, he must turn it over to the bailor.

If the bailee parts with possession of the property before he has been paid, in most states he loses his lien. If he later regains possession of the same property, his lien is not re-established for the old charges, except in a few states where, by special statute, this right is given to the bailee.

CARE OF BAILED PROPERTY

As a general rule, any loss due to the theft or damage of personal property falls upon the owner. This may not be true in the case of a bailment. Thus it is important to ascertain if there is in fact a bailment. If a bailment exists, the owner may in some instances, in case of loss or damage, shift the burden to the bailee. To do this, he must prove negligence on the part of the bailee.

The degree of negligence required to hold the bailee liable in event of loss or damage according to older decisions varied according to the class of bailment. In a bailment for the sole benefit of the bailee, great care was required, and the bailee was liable in the event he was slightly negligent. In a bailment for the sole benefit of the bailor, the bailee was required to exercise only slight care and was liable only in the event of gross negligence. In a mutual-benefit bailment the bailee was required to exercise ordinary care and was liable in the event he was ordinarily negligent.

But the division of liability according to degrees of care is somewhat misleading in the case of ordinary bailments. The standard is actually the same for all ordinary bailments: *reasonable care under the circumstances*, that is, the degree of care which a reasonable man would exercise in order to protect the property from harm.

The chief factors in determining what is reasonable care in a bailment are (a) time and place of making the bailment, (b) facilities for taking care of the property, (c) nature of the property, (d) bailee's knowledge of its nature, and (e) extent of the bailee's skill and experience in taking care of goods of that kind. The bailee is also liable for the negligence of his employees or servants with respect to the property. Whether or not a bailee is negligent is a question of fact to be decided by a jury.

USE OF THE BAILED GOODS

When a bailment is for the sole benefit of the bailor, the bailee has no right to use the property for his own purpose. This rule may be altered if use of the goods is for their benefit or is necessary to preserve them.

If the bailment is for the sole benefit of the bailee, the use is strictly limited to the use agreed upon by the parties at the time the contract was formed. If the bailee uses the property in any other way, he is liable for any resulting damage regardless of his negligence.

- Fleeman borrowed Brown's truck to haul a load of cotton to the cotton gin. After the cotton was ginned, Fleeman drove about ten miles further to another town to get some farm machinery parts. The truck was wrecked on this part of the trip due to no fault of Fleeman. He must bear the loss, however, since he used the truck for a purpose for which it was not bailed.

If a bailment is for the mutual benefit of both parties, the wrongful use of the property makes the bailee liable for any damages caused by that use.

DUTIES AND OBLIGATIONS OF THE BAILOR

In all types of bailments the bailee has the right to receive bailed property that is safe to keep or use, or to be apprised of the dangerous nature of the article bailed. For example, when *A* borrows or rents *B*'s truck, *B* must inform *A* if the brakes are deficient. If *B* fails to do so and *A* is injured, *B* is liable for damages. When the bailment is for the sole benefit of the bailee, the bailor is liable for any injury due to a failure to inform the bailee of any known defects. The bailor is not liable if the injury is due to an unknown defect. When it is a mutual-benefit bailment, the bailor is liable for any injury caused not only by any known defects if he fails to inform the bailee, but also by any unknown defects. When one rents or leases to another a car, boat, airplane, or other goods, he warrants that the devices are suitable and trustworthy.

BAILEE'S DUTY TO PROTECT PROPERTY

Often bailed property is damaged or destroyed not by any negligence by the bailee in the use of it, but by some act having nothing to do with its use. One of the most common causes of loss is the failure to insure the property. In the absence of a promise supported by a consideration to insure the property, the bailee is under no obligation to insure it. But the bailor may as a part of the contract of bailment obligate the bailee to insure the bailed property. Under such circumstances a failure of the bailee to do so subjects him to full liability for all losses due to a failure to insure.

> ▪ Inglis rented some stage decorations for a play he was staging.
> After the play was over but before the decorations were returned, they were destroyed by fire due to no fault of Inglis. He had no fire insurance on them. In a mutual-benefit bailment the bailee must exercise that degree of care that an ordinary, prudent man would exercise. Since the contract did not require Inglis to insure the property and since Inglis was not negligent, he has no liability to the bailor.

Another cause of loss not due to the use of property is a failure to return it on time or returning it to the wrong party in good faith. In both cases the bailee is liable if the loss is due primarily to this breach of duty to return the property on time to the owner. The bailee is liable for all loss due to the wrongful conversion of the property regardless of negligence.

SALE OF BAILED PROPERTY BY THE BAILEE

Possession of property is not proof of ownership. One who purchases property from a bailee ordinarily does not get good title to it. There are situations, however, where the bailor may not deny that the bailee had the right to sell the property. This is particularly true in goods put out on consignment with a commission merchant or factor. In these cases a mutual-benefit bailment exists even though the bailor does not expect to get the bailed property back. The purpose of the bailment is to have the property sold and the proceeds remitted to the bailor. The bailee has the power to sell all goods under these types of contracts regardless of any restriction upon his right to sell, unless the buyer knows of the restriction.

The bailor may by his act mislead an innocent third person into believing that the bailee owns the property. An instance of this type is shown in the following illustration:

> ▪ Donovan purchased a typewriter from the Dodd Office Equipment Company. He paid for the machine but asked the seller to leave it on display until he was ready to pick it up. Dodd sold it to Dooley. Dooley got good title to it even though the seller was merely the bailee of the typewriter. Donovan's act of making it possible for the Dodd Office Equipment Company to perpetrate a fraud upon an innocent party estops him from denying the company had a right to sell it.

PLEDGE OR PAWN

One type of bailment is the deposit of personal property as security for some debt or obligation. If the security is tangible property, such as livestock, a radio, or an automobile, it is a *pawn*. If the security is intangible property, such as notes, bonds, or stock certificates, it is a *pledge*. In each case the transaction is a mutual-benefit bailment.

QUESTIONS

1. In a contract of bailment, is the owner the bailor or the bailee?
2. (a) If one sends a suit to be cleaned, is this a bailment?
   (b) If one enters a restaurant and hangs his coat on a hook provided for the convenience of the customers, is this a bailment?
3. Give an example of a contract of bailment without an actual delivery of the goods to the bailee.
4. If the owner of a car has it in *B*'s garage and he gives the keys to *C* and instructs him to get the car, is this a bailment?
5. Should a bailee carry fire insurance on the property he has in his possession that belongs to another?
6. What is the extent of liability of a bailor with regard to defects in property loaned for no compensation to the bailee?
7. If Jones loans his car to Smith as a favor and Smith is injured because the car had very defective brakes, what remedy does Smith have against Jones?
8. In a bailment for the sole benefit of the bailor, how may the bailee use the goods?

9. In a bailment for the mutual benefit of both parties, the bailee used the property contrary to the agreement. Is the bailee liable for damages if the property is damaged due to no negligence on the part of the bailee?

10. (a) Define a pawn.
(b) Define a pledge.

CASE PROBLEMS

1. Crutchfield ran the following advertisement in a daily newspaper: "Found one palomino horse. Owner can get it by paying for the cost of this ad and a reasonable price for feed and caring for it." Must the owner pay before obtaining the horse?

2. Ramsey placed an expensive fur with the Snow Fur Storage Company. Ramsey wrote a note to the bailee asking him to deliver the fur to John Harlee. Mrs. Harlee obtained the note, took it to the Snow Fur Storage Company, and asked to receive the fur. Grace, the secretary for the bailee, delivered the fur to Mrs. Harlee. It developed that Mr. and Mrs. Harlee were divorced and neither Mrs. Harlee nor the fur coat could be located. Was the Snow Fur Storage Company liable for this loss?

3. Lucille entered an exclusive coat and dress shop intending to purchase a coat. Preparatory to trying on a coat, she removed the one she was wearing and laid it with her pocketbook on the store counter. The pocketbook, containing $500 in money and a $150 watch, was stolen by an unknown customer. The owner of the dress shop contended he was not liable for the loss because there was no delivery of the articles to him or his agents. Do you agree?

4. The Dupree Garage, over a period of one month, did about $1,500 repairs on several trucks owned by the Brown Trucking Company. The $1,500 repair bill was past due. Two trucks were later brought in for minor repairs. Mr. Dupree refused to let Brown have the trucks until the $1,500 plus the last repair bill was paid. Brown paid the last repair bill and demanded possession of the trucks. Was he within his rights?

5. The Bronson Typewriter Exchange sold an electric typewriter to Holmes, who was to pick up the machine the following day. The next day Holmes telephoned the Bronson Typewriter Exchange and asked that the machine be delivered to 237 Hull Street. Marion, the secretary, attached a memo to the machine showing that it was to be delivered to 237 Hull Street. Because of her poor penmanship, the truck driver read it 237 Hall Street. He delivered it at that address. The machine was stolen before the error was detected. Who must bear the loss, Holmes or the Bronson Typewriter Exchange?

6. The Bailey Transfer and Storage Company received from Hill some household furniture to be stored in their brick warehouse. About one month later the storage company, without Hill's knowledge or consent, moved the furniture to a new location in a less fireproof building. Hill's fire insurance policy showed the location of his furniture as 1416 Main street, the location of the brick warehouse. The policy also contained a clause which limited the company's liability if the property was moved to a new location without the insurance company's consent. The property was destroyed by fire through no negligence on the part of the storage company. The fire insurance company refused to pay. Could Hill collect for the loss from the Bailey Transfer and Storage Company?

7. The Bargain Corner had a stock of merchandise valued at $20,000. Of this amount $15,000 belonged to the proprietor, and $5,000 was stocked on consignment. There was a fire insurance policy of $10,000 on the stock owned by the Bargain Corner proprietor but none on the consigned merchandise. A fire loss results in a damage of $8,000 on the stock, $2,000 of which was on the consigned goods. The proprietor of the Bargain Corner was in no way negligent in causing the loss. Must he use $2,000 of the insurance proceeds to apply on the loss of the consigned goods?

8. Hicks orally sold Smith all his spring lambs and gave Smith one week to take them away. Hicks agreed to care for the lambs without charge until Smith came for them, at which time Smith was to make payment. Two days later the lambs were frozen to death in a blizzard. Hicks made no effort to get them to shelter, and there was some evidence to indicate that he might have saved some of them had he put them in shelter. Smith refused to pay for the lambs. Must he pay for them?

9. Henry asked to borrow his employer's car to drive to Booneville on personal business. There were two roads to Booneville. By the usual route, the distance was ten miles; by the other route, it was twenty miles. Henry went the long way so that he could pick up his girl friend and take her with him. While driving at forty miles an hour around a bad curve, he ran into another car parked on the wrong side of the road. There was conflicting evidence as to whether or not he was driving with both hands. His employer demanded that Henry pay the $575 repair bill. Was he legally bound to pay it?

10. Nixon owned a warehouse used for storing wheat for his customers. Wheat of like grade was deposited in bins, and the owner was given a warehouse receipt showing the number of bushels and grade of wheat left with Nixon. It was the custom to return to the wheat owner the correct number of bushels of wheat of like grade that was left in the warehouse, but no promise was made to return exactly the same wheat. Rice deposited wheat with Nixon, and soon thereafter the warehouse and all the wheat was destroyed. Rice demanded payment from Nixon for the value of the wheat contending there was a sale, not a bailment. Do you agree?

CHAPTER 18

COMMON CARRIERS

DEFINITION

A *carrier* is engaged in the business of transporting either goods or persons, or both. A carrier of goods is a bailee. Since a fee is charged for such service, the bailment is one for the mutual benefit of both parties. The general law of bailments, however, does not apply to all carriers of goods. For this reason it is necessary to classify carriers so that the laws governing each class may be set out.

CLASSIFICATION OF CARRIERS

Carriers are usually classified into two groups:

1. Private carriers
2. Common carriers

(1) **Private Carriers.** A *private carrier* is one who, for a fee, undertakes to transport goods or persons. He does not hold himself out to the public as being able and willing to serve all who apply. He transports only under special instances and special arrangements. Since he conducts his business for profit, he is anxious to serve all as far as it is profitable for him to do so. He is free to refuse service if it is unprofitable, a freedom denied to common carriers. The most usual types of private carriers are taxis, trucks, moving vans, railroads, and ships owned by mining and other companies for transporting their goods only, and private delivery services.

Private carriers' contracts for transporting goods are mutual-benefit bailments, and the general law of bailments as well as of contracts governs them. Under the law of contracts one may limit his liability for his own negligence. In the absence of such a limitation the law of mutual-benefit bailments applies. Any state or city may impose certain limitations upon these private carriers, but such limitations are seldom extensive.

(2) **Common Carriers.** A *common carrier* is one who undertakes to transport goods or persons for all who apply for that service. The nature of the services rendered determines whether or not one is a common carrier. If one's business of transporting goods is extensively affected with a public interest, he will be deemed a common carrier.

A common carrier must serve all who apply without discrimination. If he fails to do so, he is liable for any damages resulting from such a refusal. He may refuse service because it is not one for which he is equipped. For example, an express company does not have to accept lumber for transportation. Also, a common carrier may refuse service if its equipment is inadequate to accommodate additional customers in excess of the normal demands.

Provided he has room, a common carrier of persons must carry without discrimination all fit persons who may apply for passage. He is not, however, required to transport (a) any person who requires unusual attention, unless that person is accompanied by an attendant, (b) any person who intends to cause an injury to the carrier or the passengers, (c) any person who is likely to harm passengers, such as a person with a contagious disease, or (d) any person who is likely to be offensive to passengers, such as an intoxicated person.

The usual types of common carriers of persons are railroads, bus lines, airplanes, ships (both ocean and river), and street railways. Common carriers that are public monopolies are subject to regulations as to prices, services, equipment, and other operational policies. This public regulation is in lieu of competition as a determinant of their prices and services.

One who ships goods by a common carrier is called the *consignor*; the one to whom the goods are shipped is called the *consignee*; and the contract between the parties is called a *bill of lading*.

LIABILITY OF COMMON CARRIER OF GOODS FOR LOSS

With but five exceptions noted below, a common carrier of goods is liable for loss or damage without reference to negligence. He thus approaches the status of an insurer since he assumes the risks inherent in transporting goods.

The common carrier is not liable as an insurer for losses arising from:

1. Acts of God
2. Acts of a public authority
3. Inherent nature of goods
4. Acts of the shipper
5. Acts of public enemy

(1) Acts of God. If the loss to goods being transported is due to floods, snowstorms, tornadoes, lightning, or fire caused by lightning, the carrier is not liable since these are considered acts of God. These acts, however, must be the immediate, not the remote, cause of the damage.

- A flash flood weakened the pillars of a railroad bridge. Soon after the waters began to recede, a freight train started across the bridge, causing it to collapse and plunge into the raging waters. The company did not have the bridge inspected before dispatching the train across. Many carloads of freight were badly damaged by water. The railroad denied liability on the ground this was an act of God. The court ruled that the flood was only the indirect cause of the loss. The direct cause was the failure of the company to inspect the bridge after the flood.

(2) Acts of Public Authority. Any loss to goods being transported due to public authority is borne by the shipper, not the carrier. Illicit goods may be seized by public officials, or health officials may seize goods that are a menace to health. The carrier is not liable for any loss due to these and similar acts.

(3) Inherent Nature of the Goods. Some goods, such as vegetables, are highly perishable. If the carrier uses the most modern methods of refrigeration or other means of minimizing loss, he is not liable for damage due to the inherent nature of the goods. The most common types of loss due to the inherent nature of the goods are: decay of vegetables, fermentation or evaporation of liquids, and the death of livestock as a result of natural causes or the fault of other animals. The loss must have been in no way due to the negligence of the carrier.

(4) Acts of the Shipper. If the loss is due directly to the act of the shipper, the carrier is not liable. The most common cause of this type of loss is improper packing. If the packing is clearly improper, the carrier should refuse to accept the goods. If the improper packing cannot be detected by inspection, and a loss results, the carrier is relieved from liability. Other instances are misdirection of the merchandise and failure to indicate fragile contents.

- Webster shipped some perishable freight by the Georgia Central Railroad. The freight was intended for Athens, Georgia, but by error in the address it was sent to Athens, Tennessee. Before it could be returned, the freight was a total loss. This loss must be borne by the shipper.

(5) **Acts of Public Enemy.** If the loss or damage to goods is the result of organized warfare or border excursions of foreign bandits, the carrier is not liable. This cause of loss has all but vanished in America. Mobs, strikers, and rioters are not listed as public enemies in interpreting this exclusion.

LIABILITY OF CARRIER BEFORE AND AFTER TRANSPORTATION

Frequently, goods are delivered to the carrier before they are ready for transportation. The carrier may be instructed to hold the goods until shipping instructions are received, or the carrier may delay shipment until the freight charges are paid. In either event, the carrier is liable only as a warehouseman, that is, a mutual-benefit bailee. The carrier's role as an insurer does not arise until the goods are ready to be transported.

LIMITATIONS UPON THE CARRIER'S LIABILITY

A carrier may attempt to limit or escape the extraordinary liability imposed upon him by law. This is most often done by a contract between the shipper and the carrier. Since the bill of lading is the written evidence of the contract, the limitations on the carrier's liability are set out in this document. Since the shipper does not have any direct voice in the preparation of the bill of lading, the law requires all carriers to have the printed bill-of-lading form approved before it is adopted. For interstate commerce this approval is given by the Interstate Commerce Commission. The states have similar bodies to regulate purely intrastate commerce. These bodies have approved a few provisions whereby the carriers limit their liability. But in addition to the uniform limitations set out in the printed form of bill of lading, space is left for any additional limitations which the shipper and the carrier may agree upon. All of these acts are governed by the Uniform Bills of Lading Act, adopted in 31 states, and the Federal Bills of Lading Act and the Uniform Commercial Code, adopted by many states, which incorporates the Uniform Bills of Lading Act into the Code. In general the limitations upon the carrier's liability permitted by these acts fall into the following classes:

(1) A carrier is permitted to limit by agreement his loss to a specified sum or to a specified percent of the value of the goods. The freight rates must be uniform for all shippers. Carriers are prohibited from either reducing or raising the rates without prior approval. They may, however, as a consideration for the shipper's agreement to permit the carrier to limit his liability, reduce the rate a reasonable amount. The shipper must be given the right to ship his wares under either rate.

The Uniform Commercial Code provides that the carrier may limit its liability to a value stated in the bill of lading provided the carrier's rates are dependent upon value and the shipper has been given an opportunity to declare a higher value.

(2) Most states permit the carriers to exempt themselves from liability due to certain named hazards. The most common named hazards are: fire, leakage, breakage, spoilage, and losses due to riots, strikes, mobs, and robbers. Some states specifically prohibit an exemption for loss by fire. Before these exemptions are valid, they must be specifically enumerated in the bill of lading or shipper's receipt. In all cases the exemptions are not effective if the loss is due to the negligence of the carrier. No consideration in the form of a reduced rate need be given to justify these limitations.

(3) Livestock shipments create many problems for carriers, and delay in transportation for any cause may result in serious losses or extra expense for feed. Most states allow some form of limitation upon the carrier's liability if the loss is due to a delay over which the carrier has no control.

The Uniform Commercial Code specifically provides that the Code does not change or alter in any way those liabilities imposed upon the carrier for losses not the result of the carrier's negligence. In those cases where the carrier is held liable only for loss due to negligence, the Uniform Commercial Code provides for liability only for ordinary negligence. This does not change the common law, but it does make the rule uniform in those states adopting the Uniform Commercial Code.

DURATION OF CARRIER'S LIABILITY

During most shipments the carrier at one stage of the shipment is an extraordinary bailee and liable as an insurer with the exceptions set out above. At another stage of the shipment, the carrier is an ordinary bailee and thus subject to far less risk. For example, if goods are delivered to a carrier with instructions not to ship until notified to do so, the carrier is an ordinary bailee during this waiting period. If the goods are damaged or destroyed, the carrier is not liable if ordinary care is taken of the goods. This is also true after the goods arrive at their destination if the consignee does not call for them within the time fixed by law. At all other times the carrier is liable for all loss or damage with the exceptions named, regardless of negligence. It is then often of the utmost importance to both the carrier and the shipper or the consignee to know at the time of the loss what class of bailment existed. The problem is to determine the exact moment the carrier's liability as a carrier begins and ends.

(1) **Commencement of the Carrier's Liability.** The carrier often comes into possession of the goods prior to the time they are to be shipped. This is particularly true when the goods are delivered in parts but shipment is not to take place until all goods have been delivered. During this interval, the carrier is an ordinary bailee of those goods in its possession. As soon as everything has been done to make the goods ready for shipment, the carrier becomes liable as an extraordinary bailee.

At other times the goods are delivered, but the shipper asks that shipment be delayed a specified time or until further instructions. During this time the carrier is an ordinary bailee and is liable only for loss due to ordinary negligence.

(2) **Termination of the Carrier's Liability as a Carrier.** When the goods arrive at their destination, the consignee is given a short time to accept delivery of the goods. Express companies must deliver the goods to the consignee's place of business, but railroads need only place the goods in the freight depot, or, in case of car lots, set the car on a siding where the consignee can unload the goods. There are at least three rules that attempt to fix the exact time when the carrier ceases to be an insurer and becomes a mere mutual-benefit bailee:

(a) The Massachusetts rule holds that the carrier becomes a bailee as soon as the goods are placed for delivery. This would be in the freight depot or on a railroad siding. No notice of arrival is necessary.

(b) The New Hampshire rule differs from the Massachusetts rule in only one important respect, namely, that a reasonable time must elapse after the goods have been placed for delivery before the carrier becomes a mere bailee. A reasonable time varies from one to three days, depending on the circumstances. This rule, then, continues the status of the carrier as an insurer during this reasonable time; also under this rule, the consignee is not entitled to any notice of arrival.

(c) The New York rule, and the one most widely followed, goes one step beyond the New Hampshire rule in that it requires the carrier to notify the consignee of the arrival of the goods, and then the carrier remains an insurer for a reasonable time after the notice is given, not just a reasonable time after the goods arrive. Oddly enough most states follow this rule for water carriers even when one of the other rules is used for other types of carriers.

INITIAL AND CONNECTING CARRIERS

Under the federal laws the initial carrier is charged with liability for the loss or damage even though it occurs on a connecting line. The initial carrier may then compel the connecting carrier to reimburse it. Most of the states follow this same rule for intrastate commerce, although in a few states the liability of the initial carrier ends as soon as the goods are delivered to the connecting carrier.

BILL OF LADING

A *bill of lading* is a document of title and is evidence of the contract between the shipper and the carrier. Title to the goods described in the bill of lading may be passed by transferring the bill of lading to the purchaser. Since the bill of lading names the consignee, the carrier should deliver the goods to him only, or to one whom he has designated as the proper person to receive the goods.

The Uniform Commercial Code defines a bill of lading as "a document evidencing the receipt of goods for shipment issued by a person engaged in the business of transporting or forwarding goods, and includes an airbill." It is the contract between the shipper and the transportation company. Title to the goods described in the bill of lading may be passed by transferring the bill of lading to the purchaser. Since it names the consignee, the carrier should deliver the goods to him only, or to one whom he has designated as the proper person to receive the goods.

There are two types of bills of lading:

1. Straight bills of lading
2. Order bills of lading

(1) Straight Bills of Lading. Under this type of bill of lading the consignee alone is designated as the one to whom the goods are to be delivered. The consignee may transfer his rights to another, but as a rule the third party obtains no better title than the shipper or the consignee had. He may under certain circumstances get larger rights than the consignee. If the bill of lading contains a recital as to the contents, quantity, or weight of the goods, the carrier is bound to a bona fide transferee as to the accuracy of these descriptions unless the bill of lading itself indicates that the contents of packages are unknown to the carrier.

As with all assignments, the assignee should notify the carrier of his assignment when the original consignee sells the goods before receipt. The carrier is justified in delivering goods to the consignee if it has received no notice of assignment.

- McDougal shipped by a straight bill of lading 1,000 reams of typing paper to the Yuma Printing Company. The consignee sold this bill of lading to the Guest Printing Company. When the cartons were opened, there were only 800 reams of paper. The railroad must make good the shortage as it should have checked the accuracy of the count.

(2) Order Bills of Lading. Under the common law a bill of lading is not negotiable. Under the Uniform Bills of Lading Act and the Federal Bills of Lading Act, goods may be shipped to a designated consignee or his order, or merely "to the bearer" of the bill of lading. The bill of lading must be presented before the carrier can safely deliver the goods. If the goods are delivered to the named consignee and later a bona fide innocent purchaser of the bill of lading demands the goods, the carrier is liable to the holder of the bill of lading.

The Uniform Commercial Code incorporates the Uniform Bills of Lading Act into the Code so that those states that adopt the Uniform Commercial Code repeal the Uniform Bills of Lading Act. Only minor changes were made in the Code, however. One of these minor changes is that the Code makes a bill of lading negotiable if the goods are consigned to "bearer."

- The Clark Milling Company shipped a carload of flour to Rose and Rogers in South Carolina. The order bill of lading was attached to a draft and sent to a bank at the point of destination. The consignee, without paying the draft or obtaining the bill of lading, was permitted to receive the flour. The carrier was held liable for delivery of the flour without demanding that the consignee present the bill of lading. (N. & W. Ry. Co. v. Aylor, 153 Va. 575)

LIABILITY OF COMMON CARRIER OF PERSONS

The carriers of passengers are not insurers of the passengers' safety, but they are required to exercise the highest degree of care possible, consistent with practical operation. The liability of the carrier begins as soon as the passenger enters the station or waiting platform and does not end until he has left the station at the end of the journey. The degree of care required is only ordinary care while the passenger is in the station. After the passenger boards the bus, train, plane, or other vehicle, the utmost care is required.

RIGHTS OF COMMON CARRIERS OF PERSONS

Common carriers of persons have the right to prescribe the place and time of the payment of fares, usually before boarding the train, bus, or other vehicle. They also have the right to prescribe certain rules of conduct while transporting passengers so long as these are reasonable and for the convenience of the other passengers. They may stop the vehicle and remove any passenger who refuses to pay his fare or whose conduct is offensive to the other passengers. They also have the right to reserve certain coaches or seats for special classes of passengers, usually those who have paid extra for reserved seats.

- Scott boarded a boat for a coastal trip south. When the ship master called for all tickets, Scott could not locate his. Upon his refusal to pay for his passage, he was removed at the first mooring. He sued the ship line owner for damages after he later located his ticket. He did not succeed in his claim for damages since his remedy was to have paid his fare a second time and then apply for a refund.

DUTIES OF COMMON CARRIERS OF PERSONS

A carrier's duty to its passengers consists of two broad groups:

1. Duty to provide reasonable accommodations and services
2. Duty to provide reasonable protection to its passengers

(1) **Duty to Provide Reasonable Accommodations and Services.**
When a traveler purchases a ticket from a common carrier, a contract
is formed between the carrier and the passenger. This contract entitles
the passenger to a seat. If there is no seat available, he may get off
at the next station and demand a refund of his fare. He may also sue
for damages for breach of contract. The carrier must also notify the
passenger of the arrival of the train, bus, or airplane at his destination
and stop long enough to permit the passenger to disembark. A personal
notice is not necessary, only a general announcement. If this is not done
and a passenger is carried beyond his destination, he may sue for any
damages suffered.

(2) **Duty to Provide Reasonable Protection to Its Passengers.**
Common carriers of passengers are not insurers of the absolute safety
of passengers but must exercise extraordinary care to protect them.
Any injury to the passenger by an employee or fellow passengers subjects the carrier to liability for damages, provided the passenger is
without blame. The vehicle must stop at a safe place for alighting,
and passengers must be assisted when necessary for alighting. Transportation may be denied to invalids unless someone accompanies them;
but if accepted, reasonable assistance must be rendered to them.

- Johnson was traveling by plane to Cedar City. The plane made
  a brief stop at Cedar City, but Johnson was asleep and did not
  hear the pilot's announcement. Johnson awoke after the plane had
  gone 100 miles beyond Cedar City. The carrier was not liable for
  Johnson's inconvenience and delay in reaching his destination since
  the pilot announced the arrival at Cedar City.

DEFINITION OF BAGGAGE

Baggage consists of those articles necessary for personal convenience while traveling. Articles carried by travelers on similar missions
and destinations constitute the test rather than what passengers in
general carry. For example, fishing paraphernalia is baggage for a
man on a fishing trip, but not for the ordinary traveler. Also, a lady's
watch is not baggage when carried in a traveling bag by a man. Any
article carried for the accommodation of one who is not a passenger is
not baggage. Samples carried by salesmen are not baggage. The carrier is, of course, liable for the loss of these articles the same as for
baggage, but the passenger is not entitled to have them transported
without extra charge. They are freight, not baggage.

LIABILITY FOR BAGGAGE

The liability of a common carrier for baggage is the same as that of a common carrier of goods. The common carrier is an insurer of the baggage with the five exceptions noted in the section on common carriers of goods. It is necessary to distinguish between baggage retained in the possession of the traveler and that carried in the baggage car or other space. In the first type, the carrier is liable only for lack of reasonable care or for willful misconduct of its agents or employees.

A reasonable amount of baggage may be carried as a part of the cost of the passenger's fare. The carrier may charge extra for an amount in excess of a reasonable value, usually $100.

QUESTIONS

1. What law governs private carriers?
2. Is a common carrier liable for the loss or damage to goods being transported regardless of negligence?
3. Must a common carrier serve all who apply?
4. (a) Name some acts which the law tends to call acts of God.
   (b) Is there a difference between a loss caused by an act of God when the act is the remote rather than the direct cause?
5. What acts of the shipper will relieve a common carrier for liability for loss?
6. When does the common carrier's liability begin?
7. When goods must be transported by two or more carriers before reaching their destination, which carrier is liable?
8. (a) What is a bill of lading?
   (b) What is the difference between a straight bill of lading and an order bill of lading?
9. To what extent are common carriers responsible for the safety of passengers?
10. What is the liability of a common carrier for baggage carried by a passenger?

CASE PROBLEMS

1. The Case Equipment Company purchased 10 tractors from the Case Manufacturing Company. The tractors were shipped by railroad freight with a negotiable bill of lading. The consignee borrowed money on the tractors from Finley Finance Company and indorsed the bill of lading to the lender as security for the loan. When the tractors arrived, they were delivered to the consignee without demanding that he produce the bill of lading. The Finley Finance Company sued the railroad for its loss. Is the railroad liable?

2. Stanley shipped several cartons of books by air freight. In one package was a painting valued at $10,000. The cartons were all marked: "Contents— Books." The carton containing the painting was stolen. Is the carrier liable?

3. The Blue Ridge Airlines had a rule that no dogs were to be taken aboard one of its planes. Miss Wiley persuaded the pilot to make an exception for her tiny Fifi. The little poodle looked so innocent that the pilot permitted Miss Wiley to carry it aboard. It bit a lady passenger severely on the ankle. Did the carrier have to pay damages because of its failure to protect the safety of its passengers?

4. The Devon Seed Company ordered a carload of seed from the Newberry Seed Corporation. When the seed arrived, the car was placed on a siding where the consignee by agreement was to load it onto his truck and at his expense. The car was placed on the siding at 10 a.m., but the Devon Seed Company was not notified that day. During the night a riot occurred, and the seed was thrown out of the car and destroyed by a heavy rain. Loss by riot had not been excluded in the bill of lading. What would be the carrier's liability for this loss under (a) the New Hampshire rule, (b) the Massachusetts rule, (c) the New York rule?

5. The Holland Brothers were large producers of fruits and vegetables. Their farm adjoined the railroad tracks. They built a loading platform beside the tracks and would place their packaged fruit and vegetables on this platform. The railroad had permitted them to do this for several years. The train would stop, and the railroad's employees would load the freight. When the train got into town about twenty miles away, the freight would be weighed and a bill of lading made out. The Holland Brothers loaded the platform with freight and left it for the railroad to pick up. Because of a strike, the train did not run that day, and a hard freeze destroyed all the fruit and vegetables. The railroad refused to compensate the Holland Brothers for the loss, claiming there had been no delivery and receipt of the freight. Was this contention correct?

6. The Baxter Machine Company shipped an expensive machine to the Buford Mining Company in Denver by a straight bill of lading. An agent of the Buford Mining Company called at the office of the Stern Engineering Corporation and offered to sell them the machinery, stating that their plans had been altered and they would have to return it. The Stern Corporation purchased the machinery and received the bill of lading by indorsement. Three days later they inquired of the railroad if the machinery had arrived and were told that it had already been delivered to the consignee, the Buford Mining Company. It developed that this latter company, after it got possession of the machinery, had sold and delivered it to the Rocky Mountain Mining Company. The Stern Engineering Corporation sued the railroad for the value of the machinery, alleging it had delivered the machinery to the wrong party. Was the railroad liable?

7. Hardin delivered 42 bales of cotton to the Georgia Railroad with instructions to hold them until the following day when an additional 58 bales would be delivered, making a total shipment of 100 bales. The 42 bales were stacked on the loading platform. That night a fire destroyed the

42 bales. There was no negligence on the part of the railroad in starting the fire or in preventing its spread. Hardin sued the railroad for the value of the cotton, alleging that it was liable as a common carrier. Was Hardin entitled to collect?

8. Thomas owned a large truck in which he hauled fresh vegetables for a produce exchange from Florida to Atlanta. On the return trip he often carried freight at rates considerably below that charged by the railroad. On one of these return trips, the Glenn Jewelry Company shipped two cases of jewelry valued at $2,500 to its branch store in Orlando. The jewelry was stolen through no fault of Thomas. The Glenn Jewelry Company sued Thomas as a common carrier for the value of the jewelry. Was he liable?

9. A jewelry salesman was traveling on a train to a college town to sell class rings, fraternity and sorority pins, and other types of jewelry to college students. His bag containing $1,000 worth of samples was stolen. The baggage was given to the porter and he stacked it with the baggage belonging to the other passengers. Was the carrier liable for its loss, assuming no extra charge was paid for the baggage?

10. Roberts purchased a ticket for a trip to Denver. He boarded the train and took a seat. When the conductor called for his ticket, he could not locate it. The conductor required him to pay his fare in cash, and Roberts refused. At the next station Roberts was ordered to leave the train, but he refused to do so. The train policeman was called, and Roberts was forceably removed. As a result he was twenty-four hours late in keeping an appointment, resulting in a loss of $20,000. He sued the railroad for the loss plus additional damages for his injured pride in being forceably removed from the train. Was the carrier liable?

11. The Associated Farmers Warehouse Corporation shipped a load of wheat by river boat to St. Louis. The boat struck a tree trunk that had been washed into the river channel by a recent flood. The boat sank, and all the wheat was destroyed. Was the carrier liable for this loss?

12. Mrs. Julia Hasbrouck obtained passage on the New York Central and Hudson Railroad to make a trip to Natick, Massachusetts, to visit her daughter, a college student in that city. In her baggage were four rings valued at about $1,500. Mrs. Hasbrouck was socially prominent and was in the habit of wearing expensive jewelry at all social functions. The baggage was checked with the railroad and the usual excess value was declared and the charges paid. When she arrived at her destination, her baggage was returned to her, but the jewelry was missing. The railroad refused to pay her claim, contending that so much jewelry, four diamond rings, was not properly baggage, and therefore the railroad was not liable for its loss. Was the railroad liable for the loss?

CHAPTER 19

HOTELKEEPERS AS
BAILEES

EXCEPTIONAL BAILMENTS

When a guest registers at a hotel, the hotelkeeper enters into a contract of bailment with him with respect to the guest's luggage and other personal property. From early times, however, the innkeeper has been held to an extraordinary degree of liability for the safety of the personal property of his guest, the traveler, or the transient. Since the hotelkeeper's occupation is that of a public calling, the law exacts from him a higher degree of care than it does from a bailee in an ordinary mutual-benefit bailment. Like those of carriers described in the preceding chapter, the contracts of hotelkeepers are specially designated exceptional bailments. For this reason a hotelkeeper's liability for the safety of a guest's property cannot be determined from the law of bailments in general.

The common law is the basis of most of our laws dealing with hotelkeepers, but as conditions change, the law must change. The traveler today is not at the mercy of the hotelkeeper as was the case prior to our modern system of transportation and communication. Much of the change in the common law has been by statute. Today most states have laws permitting hotelkeepers and motel keepers to limit their liability. These statutes vary so widely that only a few general statements can be made about them. Limitation upon his liability usually is accomplished by some kind of public notice to the guest, usually a notice posted in the guest's room. Some statutes simply declare that the law of mutual-benefit bailments applies. Other statutes require that the hotelkeeper, in order to escape full liability, provide a vault or other safe place of deposit for valuables, such as furs and jewelry. Even with all these statutory modifications of the common law, the hotelkeeper still owes his guest a high degree of care for both his property and his person.

WHO IS A HOTELKEEPER?

Under the old common law an innkeeper was one who provided a traveler with lodging, food, drink, and a stable for the traveler's horses. If any one of these services was not supplied, one was not an innkeeper, and thus not held to strict accountability for the care and safety of the guest. This narrow common law rule has been so modified that today "innkeeper" is synonymous with "hotelkeeper." Today a *hotelkeeper* is one who supplies lodging to transients. He may supply food or entertainment, but providing lodging to the transients is the cardinal test.

THOSE WHO ARE NOT HOTELKEEPERS

Because of the narrow dividing line between a hotelkeeper and one who keeps a boardinghouse, tourist home, or hotel apartment, it is important to know who is not a hotelkeeper. If one provides rooms only or room and board to permanent guests, but does not hold himself out as able and willing to accommodate transients, he is not a hotelkeeper and thus is not held to the strict accountability of the common law. A tourist home is not an inn if the owner does not hold himself out as willing to accommodate all who apply so long as he has room. Some states have held that when a tourist home, by roadside advertising, attempts to attract transients, it is an inn. If the service is provided only seasonally or at infrequent intervals, a tourist home is not an inn. Modern motels, auto courts, and tourist cabin establishments are usually classed as inns. Apartment hotels that cater only to permanent residents are not inns, although a hotel may cater to both permanent guests and transients. In that event, a hotel is an inn.

DUTIES AND LIABILITIES OF A HOTELKEEPER

The duties and liabilities of a hotelkeeper are:

1. Duty to serve all who apply
2. Duty to protect a guest's person
3. Duty to care for the guest's property

(1) **Duty to Serve All Who Apply.** The basic test of a hotel-keeper is that he holds himself out as willing to serve all who apply without discrimination. He is liable for damages to the person rejected. He may turn people away, such as a drunken person who would be highly offensive to his other guests. If his rooms are all filled, he may turn all other applicants away without liability for damages. Today hotels of all classes are so numerous and competition for business is so keen that this duty is seldom breached.

(2) **Duty to Protect a Guest's Person.** A hotelkeeper is not liable as an insurer of a guest's safety. He must use ordinary care for the safety of those who are on his premises as guests, but not for a mere visitor or a patron of the newsstand or lunch room. He must provide fire escapes and also have conspicuous notices indicating the direction of the fire escapes. He is not liable for an injury due to a fire if he was in no way negligent in starting the fire. If he is negligent in preventing the spread of the fire or in directing the guests to fire escapes, he is liable. Fire prevention practices, such as steel doors leading to stair-ways between floors, are required of all hotels. If a fire starts due to no negligence of the hotelkeeper or his employees, he is not liable to the guests for their personal injuries unless they can show that the fire was not contained because of a failure to install the required fire safety features. In one case the court held the hotelkeeper was not liable for the loss of life on the floor where the fire started, but was liable for all personal injuries on the four floors to which the fire spread.

(3) **Duty to Care for the Guest's Property.** The hotelkeeper is an insurer of the guest's property except for losses occurring from:

(a) An act of God
(b) Act of public enemy
(c) Negligence or fault of the guest
(d) The inherent nature of the property itself
(e) Accidental fire, provided neither the hotelkeeper nor his servants are negligent

Under the common law the innkeeper was an insurer of the guest's property unless the loss or damage was due to one of the five acts listed. By statute in every state this liability has been modified to some extent.

The hotelkeeper may provide a safe where a guest may deposit his valuable articles. If the guest fails to do this, the hotelkeeper is released from liability as an insurer. Notice to this effect must be posted either in the room or at the registration desk. Also, most statutes limit a hotel's liability to a designated sum. Other states permit the hotelkeeper to limit his liability by contract with the guest. This is usually done by posting a notice.

WHO ARE GUESTS?

Before a hotelkeeper can be held liable either for injury to the person or for loss of property, the injured party must be a guest. To be a *guest* one must be a transient, not a permanent resident. Also, he must have been received as a guest. If one enters the hotel to attend a ball or other social function or to visit a guest, he himself is not a guest. If one enters a hotel with the intention of becoming a guest, but before registering he changes his mind, he is not a guest. If one enters a hotel with the intention of becoming a guest, but is refused accommodations because of no room, he is a guest and remains one until he leaves the premises.

- Jason entered the Ridge Manor Motel to register as a guest. He was told there were no vacancies but that he could wait awhile if he wished to see if anyone checked out. This he did. While he was waiting, his baggage was stolen. The motel was liable since he entered the premises with the intention of becoming a guest.

LIEN OF THE HOTELKEEPER

A hotelkeeper has a lien on the baggage of his guests for the value of the services rendered. This lien extends also to all wearing apparel not actually being worn, such as an overcoat, a fur coat, or an extra suit. Since the hotelkeeper is an insurer of all goods brought to the hotel by the guest, the lien extends to all these goods even if they do not belong to the guest. The only exception to this rule is that the lien does not attach to the property of another if the proprietor or manager of the hotel knows of the true ownership. Some states have slightly modified by statute these strict common-law rules; but for the most part, they are still in effect.

The lien of the hotelkeeper attaches only to baggage. It does not apply to an automobile, for example. If the hotel provides storage facilities for the guest's car, the car cannot be held if the guest fails to pay his hotel bill. If there is a separate charge for car storage, this charge (but not the room charge) must be paid before the car can be removed.

If the charges are not paid within a reasonable time, the hotel-keeper may sell the baggage or other goods and pay the charges. Any residue must be returned to the guest.

A minor is as fully bound by these laws as an adult. The lien is imposed by law so the minor cannot plead disaffirmance of the contract.

The lien terminates when the property is returned to the guest even though the room charges have not been paid.

- Garson registered at the Ridge Manor Motel in Florida and incurred a hotel bill amounting to $120. He paid the bill by check and departed taking all his baggage and jewelry. The check was returned marked "Insufficient funds." The lien is not re-established by a return of the check.

BOARDINGHOUSE KEEPERS

The laws of a hotelkeeper do not apply to boardinghouse keepers. The boardinghouse keeper has no lien under the common law, but most states have given this right to boardinghouses by statute. The chief difference in the common law relating to a hotelkeeper and a boardinghouse keeper is that the latter need take only ordinary care of the property of the boarder or lodger. He is in no way an insurer. Also, he does not have to accept all who apply. He may choose his clients using whatever test of discrimination he wishes.

At common law the boardinghouse keeper is not given a lien on the goods of a boarder as security for an unpaid account; in some states, however, he is given such a lien by statute. Some of these state laws make it a criminal offense for a boarder owing a board bill to leave his boardinghouse secretly. Under the federal Constitution no one can be imprisoned for a debt. These state laws comply with this constitutional restriction by making the crime consist of "leaving without paying the board bill," not just a failure to pay it.

- Dobson had been a guest at the Georgian Hotel for five days. He secretly left the hotel without paying his bill. The hotel owner had him indicted "for leaving without paying his hotel bill." He was found guilty.

QUESTIONS

1. Is a hotelkeeper a mere mutual-benefit bailee for guests' baggage?
2. Must one actually register at a hotel before he becomes a guest?

3. How may a hotelkeeper avoid liability for the loss of valuables carried by the guest?

4. Who is liable for the injury to a guest by fire if the hotel was in no way negligent?

5. If a guest has $4,000 worth of jewelry and expensive clothes while staying at a hotel and the property is stolen due to no fault of the hotel, who is liable for the loss?

6. If a guest's baggage is held by the hotel as a lien for the payment of the hotel charges, what disposition may be made of the property?

7. What is the chief difference in the law relating to a hotelkeeper and a boardinghouse keeper?

8. (a) Under the common law may a boardinghouse keeper hold a roomer's baggage and clothes for his unpaid room rent?

    (b) May one be imprisoned for leaving without paying his board bill at a boardinghouse?

CASE PROBLEMS

1. Burke registered at the Devon Hotel. He was a minor. He ran up a hotel bill of $75 dollars. The hotel held his baggage and a hi-fi set until the bill was paid. Burke attempted to disaffirm his contract, contending it was not a necessity since he did not have to travel. May he disaffirm?

2. Danner drove up to the King Cotton Motel. An attendant approached and he inquired about a room. He left two traveling bags with the attendant, stating he would return later to register. He changed his mind and returned for his bags. They could not be located. Is the motel liable for this loss?

3. Mr. and Mrs. North took two rooms at a motel fixed for light housekeeping. They were to pay rent by the month and planned to spend the winter in the city. While they were out, a thief entered the room and stole a necklace worth $1,500. They sued the motel owner for the loss. Is he liable?

4. Miss Seagraves, an actress, spent some time at an exclusive hotel in Florida. When she got ready to leave, she had an unpaid hotel bill of several hundred dollars. She was unable to pay the bill, and the hotel notified her that she could not remove her baggage from the room. Although the temperature outside was 96, she put on her expensive mink coat, adorned herself with all her expensive jewelry, and then attempted to leave without her baggage. The hotel contended it was entitled to a lien on her coat and her excess jewelry. Was its contention correct?

5. Martin was a guest in the Savoy Hotel. He deposited his overcoat, baggage, and a few other items with a check girl and received a check stating in bold letters that the hotel would not be liable for any loss of the items checked. The items were delivered by the check girl to the wrong guest, and Martin was never able to locate them. The hotel contended its liability had been limited by contract when the items were checked. Was this contention correct?

6. The Greenway Auto Court had signs along the highway soliciting all travelers to become guests. John L. Hewess, a labor leader, applied for accommodations. Because the owner of the auto court was violently opposed to unions, he refused Hewess accommodations although he had vacant rooms. Hewess sued for damages. Was the Greenway Auto Court liable?

7. The law in Georgia requires all hotels to provide devices to prevent a fire from spreading from one floor to another. A fire of undetermined origin started on the fifth floor of the Fenwick Hotel. Because of open stairways the fire spread quickly to the upper floors, and many guests lost their lives on the fifth, sixth, and seventh floors.

(a) If the hotel was not negligent in starting the fire, was it liable for the loss of life on the fifth floor?

(b) Was it liable for the loss of life on the sixth and the seventh floors?

8. Hawkins registered at a hotel and was assigned a room. During the night the hotel caught fire; neither the hotel nor its employees were negligent. When Hawkins was awakened, he could not leave by the stairway, so he sought the fire escape. Since there were no signs directing him to the fire escape, he could not find it. Seeing no other way out, he jumped from a second-floor window and was injured. All his baggage was destroyed. Hawkins brought suit against the hotel to collect for the value of his baggage and compensation for his injuries. Discuss the rights and obligations of the parties.

9. Rice, a traveling salesman, registered at the Unique Tavern and was assigned a room. Desiring to keep an appointment with a customer before going to his room, Rice had the clerk send his suitcase to his room, where it was stolen through no fault of Rice. What was the liability of the Unique Tavern for the loss of the suitcase?

10. Porter was a guest at the City Hotel. The hotel provided a safe for the deposit of jewels and other valuable articles. Proper notice of this service was posted on the door, according to the provisions of the law. Porter ignored this notice and retained possession of his valuables. They were stolen while he was a guest. He brought a suit for damages.

(a) Was the posting of the notice on the door sufficient, or must the hotel-keeper inform the guests of the protection provided?

(b) In your judgment was the hotelkeeper liable in this case?

11. The Standish Hotel served both transient and permanent roomers. McIntosh rented a room at a fixed rent by the month and occupied the room as a lodger rather than a transient. He was a resident of Portland where the hotel was located. While McIntosh was away for a few days, but still retaining possession of his room, a burglar entered the room and stole clothes and other articles valued in excess of $100. There was no evidence that the hotel was negligent in any way. McIntosh brought suit against the hotel for the value of the stolen property. Was he entitled to recover?

SUMMARY CASES

PART 4

1. Wetmore stored two rugs in the warehouse of B. W. Hooker Co., Inc. There was no charge for this storage as it was done as a favor to Wetmore. Seven years later Wetmore asked for a return of the rugs, but the bailee could not locate one of them. The evidence showed that the Hooker Co. placed the rugs in the same space where it stored its own property. There was no way to account for the disappearance of the rugs. Was the bailee liable for the value of the lost rug? (Wetmore v. B. W. Hooker Co., Inc., 111 Vt. 519, 18 A. 2d 181)

2. Ray F. Veech placed her car in a commercial parking lot owned and run by Drybrough. The car contained a fur coat, but its presence in the car was not called to the attention of the attendant. The charge for parking the car was fifty cents. The coat was stolen, and Veech brought suit against the bailee for the value of the coat. There was no evidence that Drybrough was negligent in handling the car since it was returned safely. (a) Was this a bailment? (b) Was Drybrough liable for the value of the coat? (Drybrough v. Veech, 238 S. W. 2d 996)

3. Tilson was a passenger on interstate railroad to Kansas City from St. Louis. She carried two handbags with her. She gave these handbags to a redcap in the station in St. Louis, and they were stolen. The luggage was later found and delivered to her in Kansas City, but jewelry valued at $2,885 had been taken from the luggage. The carrier operated under a rule approved by the Interstate Commerce Commission whereby a limit of $25 is set for the loss of any one piece of luggage or its contents unless a larger value is declared and an extra charge paid. She sued the carrier for $2,885. Was the carrier liable for the $2,885? (Tilson v. Terminal Railroad Association of St. Louis, 236 S. W. 2d 42)

4. Hamilton shipped two carloads of grapes to Schwalb, the consignee, in New York City. The grapes were packed in boxes so that the contents of the boxes could easily be inspected. A bill of lading was issued on which was this notation: "The property described below, in apparent good order, except as noted (contents of packages unknown)." When the grapes arrived in New York, they were badly damaged and in poor condition. The consignee sued the connecting railroad for the damages. It denied liability on the ground the bill of lading showed the condition of the contents could not be determined at the point of origin. Was the railroad liable? (Schwalb v. Erie Railroad Company, 293 N. Y. S. 842, 161 Misc. 743)

5. Featherstone became a guest at the Pacific Hotel. Some valuables were stolen from his room. The law required all hotelkeepers, if they wished to be relieved from the common-law liability as an insurer of the guest's property, to post three notices in conspicuous places in the hotel. The owners of the Pacific Hotel posted one notice on the wall of the elevator, one on the hotel register, and one in the back of the office where guests had no access. Featherstone brought suit against the owners of the hotel to recover the value of the stolen articles. They denied liability on the ground that they had complied with the statute. Were the owners of the hotel liable? (Featherstone v. Victor and Louise Dessert, 173 Wash. 264, 22 P. 2d 1050)

6. Maher entered the back room at Chapin's Lunch Co. It was crowded, and he had to wait to get a table. The manager told him, "Hang your coat over there, and you will get a seat in a minute." Maher did so. When he finished and went to get his coat, it was gone. On the menu cards were printed statements that the restaurant would not be responsible for coats or other articles lost by its customers. Also, signs were posted to this effect on the wall. Was the restaurant liable? (Maher v. Chapin's Lunch Co., 119 Pa. Super. 213, 180 A. 739)

7. Bohan owned and operated an inn on the Island of Great Tybe. In addition to the inn, he owned and operated a bathhouse on the seashore. His guests and the public in general were encouraged to use this bathhouse. The charge for its use was the same for both the guests of the inn and the public. Mrs. Walpert was a guest at the inn. She became a patron of the bathhouse for a separate fee and while a patron, lost a valuable diamond ring. There was no evidence of negligence on the part of Bohan or his employees. Mrs. Walpert sued Bohan as innkeeper. Was he liable as an innkeeper? (Walpert v. Bohan, 126 Ga. 532, 55 S. E. 181)

8. The Salem Mills Company received a quantity of wheat from Savage. The wheat was stored with the Salem Mills Company's own wheat of the same grade. The contract with Savage provided that if the Company used the wheat for its own purposes, it would either return to Savage an equal quantity of wheat of the same grade and quality or pay for it at the market price. The wheat was destroyed under conditions that might impute negligence to the Salem Mills Company. Savage sued the company, not as a bailee, but as the purchaser of the wheat. Was this a bailment? (Savage v. Salem Mills Co., 48 Ore. 1, 85 P. 69)

9. Healy checked his traveling bag at the checkroom of the defendant railroad's station. On the back of the checking ticket he received was printed in small print the charges for checking and also a clause limiting the railroad's liability to $10 for the loss of any one parcel. This was not called to Healy's attention. Through an error, the baggage was delivered to the wrong person and never was located. Healy brought suit for the full value of the baggage. Was the railroad liable for the full value of the baggage? (Healy v. New York Central and Hudson Railroad, 138 N. Y. S. 287)

10. Gantt was a student at the Aircraft Sales and Service, a privately owned flight school. The school supplied the planes in which students did their flight training. On one flight with Gantt at the controls the plane went out of control and the pilot was unable to bring it under control. It crashed and Gantt was seriously injured. An investigation revealed that a mechanic for the school had left a screw driver in the control mechanism. Gantt sued the school for his personal injuries. Was the bailor liable? (Aircraft Sales and Service v. Gantt, 52 So. 2d 388 Ala. 1951)

PART 5

NEGOTIABLE INSTRUMENTS

Preview Cases for Part 5: Negotiable Instruments

- The Wolfe Trucking Company sold a truck to the Frost Tire Company and received a written nonnegotiable promise to pay the total purchase price of $2,400 in 90 days. The Frost Tire Company sold tires and other products to the Wolfe Trucking Company amounting to $900. Before the 90 days expired, the Wolfe Company sold all its accounts receivable to the Citizens Bank. When the bank demanded payment for the $2,400, the Frost Company attempted to offset its $900 against the $2,400. Should it be allowed to do so?

- O'Kelly forged Cohen's name as drawer to a draft for $3,000 payable to O'Kelly. He presented it to Smith for acceptance. Smith then transferred the draft by indorsement to Berger. Later Smith learned that Cohen's signature was forged and refused to pay the draft when it became due. May he avoid payment?

- Massey made a note payable to Hess or order, and Hess indorsed the note to Frazier. Hess was a minor. When Massey refused to pay the note upon its due date, Frazier brought an action against him. Massey claimed that the minor was not competent to indorse the note and that Frazier could not sue and recover on the note. Should Frazier be allowed to recover?

- Hale drew a check payable to Shane in the amount of $500. Shane cleverly altered the check to $2,500 and negotiated it to McFain, an innocent purchaser who had no knowledge of the alteration. The bank refused to pay the check. From whom may McFain recover?

- Westfall agreed to sign a contract for the purchase of a car from Robinson. Robinson used a trick type of paper which contained the correct terms of the contract to sell. The paper was such that when the true contract was lifted up, it revealed a note for $5,000; and the signature of Westfall was to the note, not the contract to sell. What liability does Westfall have on the note?

These preview cases are designed to serve as a springboard for the study of this part. As you read through each chapter in this part, you will find the actual decisions for all these preview cases. Of course, there are many more such illustrative problems as well as case problems for decision at the end of each chapter. And there are also a number of even more challenging cases for review at the end of the part.

CHAPTER 20

NATURE OF NEGOTIABLE
INSTRUMENTS

DEFINITION OF A NEGOTIABLE INSTRUMENT

A *negotiable instrument* is a written instrument drawn in a special form, which can be transferred from person to person as a substitute for money or as an instrument of credit. Such an instrument must meet certain definite requirements in regard to form and the manner in which it is transferred. Since a negotiable instrument is not money, a person is not required by law to accept one in payment of a debt due him unless he wishes to do so.

HISTORY AND DEVELOPMENT

In the days of sea pirates and land robbers the shipment of money in settlement of debts between traders was a risky business. The need for instruments of credit that would permit the settlement of claims between distant cities without the transfer of money has existed as long as trade has existed.

There were references to bills of exchange or instruments of credit as early as 50 B.C. Their widespread usage, however, began about 1200 A.D. At first these credit instruments were used only in international trade, but they gradually became common in domestic trade.

Prior to about 1400 A.D. all disputes between merchants were settled on the spot by special courts set up by the merchants. The decisions of these courts became known as the *law merchant.* Later the common-law courts of England took over the adjudication of all disputes including those between merchants, but these common-law courts retained most of the customs developed by the merchants and incorporated the law merchant into the common law. Most, but by no means all, of the law merchant dealt with bills of exchange or credit instruments. The colonists brought these laws to America. After the Revolution each state developed the common law dealing with credit instruments in its own way so that by 1890 much confusion existed. In 1895 a commission was appointed by the American Bar Association and the American Bankers Association to draw up a Uniform Negotiable Instruments Law. The commission in 1896 proposed a Uniform Act. This act has since been adopted in all the states but modified and updated for inclusion in the Uniform Commercial Code.

TRANSFER OF NEGOTIABLE INSTRUMENTS

Negotiation is the act of transferring a negotiable instrument, such as a draft, a check, or a promissory note, to another party in such a manner that the instrument is payable to that party. The simplest way for a person who owns a negotiable instrument to negotiate it is to write his name on the back of the instrument and deliver it to the other party. When a person writes his name on the back of a negotiable instrument before delivery, he is said to *indorse* the instrument.

ORDER PAPER AND BEARER PAPER

Negotiable contracts are referred to as paper or commercial paper. How this terminology originated no one knows. All contracts that are negotiable under the Uniform Negotiable Instruments Law are either "order" paper or "bearer" paper. These two classes of paper are fundamentally alike, but there are some basic differences. The person to whom any negotiable contract is made payable is called the *payee*. If a negotiable contract is payable to the "order" of a specific party or business firm, it is called "order" paper. This means the party primarily liable will pay the specific named payee or any other party the original payee may designate, that is, order to be paid. The proof that the one primarily liable has been ordered to pay someone other than the payee is the payee's indorsement on the back of the instrument. If, on the other hand, the instrument reads, "Pay to the order of bearer," this means the one primarily liable may pay anyone who has the instrument in his possession when it falls due. No indorsement is necessary to pass title from one party to another.

When a negotiable instrument is transferred to one or more parties, these parties may acquire rights that are superior to those of the original owner. Parties who acquire rights superior to those of the original owner are known as holders in due course. It is mainly this feature of the transfer of superior rights that gives negotiable contracts a special classification all their own.

The law has clothed negotiable instruments with special advantages as a means to promote and to encourage commerce. How this is done will be more evident as the subject is developed.

CLASSIFICATION OF NEGOTIABLE INSTRUMENTS

The basic negotiable instruments may be classified as follows:

1. Bills of exchange
2. Promissory notes

Inasmuch as these negotiable instruments are discussed in detail in succeeding chapters, a definition of each type will suffice at this time.

(1) **Bills of Exchange.** A *bill of exchange* is "an unconditional order in writing addressed by one person to another, signed by the person giving it, requiring the person to whom it is addressed to pay on demand, or at a fixed or determinable future time, a sum certain in money to order or to bearer." The three main divisions of bills of exchange are drafts, trade acceptances, and checks.

(2) **Promissory Notes.** A *promissory note* is "an unconditional promise in writing made by one person to another, signed by the maker, engaging to pay on demand, or at a fixed or determinable future time, a sum certain in money to order or to bearer."

```
$450.00          Grand Rapids, Mich.____March 20, 19___
Thirty days _____ AFTER DATE___I___ PROMISE TO PAY TO
THE ORDER OF___Johnson Furniture Company___
Four hundred fifty and no/100 _____DOLLARS
PAYABLE AT___Second National Bank___
VALUE RECEIVED WITH INTEREST AT___5 %
No.__85__ DUE April 19, 19.___     Fred H. Hart
```

Promissory Note

There are commercial instruments other than bills of exchange and promissory notes which are usually negotiable. Bonds and certificates of deposit, for example, are negotiable in form under certain circumstances. Whether or not they are negotiable depends upon their wording.

PARTIES TO NEGOTIABLE INSTRUMENTS

Each party to a negotiable instrument is designated by a certain term depending upon the type of instrument. Some of these terms are common to all types of negotiable instruments, while others are restricted to one type only. The same individual may be known by one term at one stage and may be designated by another term at a later stage through which the instrument passes before it is collected. These terms are payee, drawer, drawee, acceptor, maker, bearer, holder, indorser, and indorsee.

Payee. The party to whom any negotiable instrument is made payable is called the *payee.*

Drawer. The person who executes any bill of exchange, such as a draft, a trade acceptance, or a check, is called the *drawer.*

Drawee. The person who is ordered to pay a bill of exchange is called the *drawee.*

Acceptor. When the drawee accepts a bill of exchange, that is, indicates his willingness to assume responsibility for its payment, he is called the *acceptor.* In the case of a sight draft or a check, the drawee indicates his *acceptance* by paying the instrument according to its terms. Time drafts are accepted by writing upon the face of the instrument these or similar words: "Accepted this 10th day of June, 1963. John Daws." This indicates that John Daws is willing to perform the contract according to its terms. This transaction simply means that a creditor has previously extended credit to John Daws and is

Draft

now willing to extend the credit period an additional period of time. The creditor and Daws could have used a promissory note to effect this extension of time. If the original creditor, however, owes some-one himself, he may prefer to extend the time by drawing a time draft on Daws, send it to the party he owes, and let that party present the instrument to Daws for his acceptance. When the draft is accepted by Daws, it has most of the legal aspects of a note. The bookkeeper will record both promissory notes and accepted time drafts as notes receivable.

Maker. The person who executes a promissory note is called the *maker*. He is the one who contracts to pay the amount due on the note. His obligation is similar to that of the acceptor of a time draft.

Bearer. Any negotiable contract may be made payable to "bearer." The payee of such an instrument is the *bearer*. If the payee is "Myself," "Cash," or another similar name, these terms are equivalent to bearer.

Holder. Any person who has possession of a delivered negotiable instrument is called the *holder*. The payee is the original holder.

Indorser. When the payee of a draft, a check, or a note wishes to transfer the instrument to another party, he must indorse it. He is then called the *indorser*.

Indorsee. A person who becomes the holder of a negotiable instrument by indorsement is called the *indorsee*. If he obtains possession of a "bearer" instrument, he is merely another holder unless he required the preceding holder to indorse it. This he can do even though the indorsement is not necessary to transfer title.

NEGOTIATION AND ASSIGNMENT

In some respects negotiation and assignment are the same; in others they are different. In each case there are original parties. In a promissory note, for example, the original parties are the maker (the one who promises to pay) and the payee (the one to whom the money is to be paid). Between the original parties, both a nonnegotiable and a negotiable contract are equally enforceable. Also, the same defenses against fulfilling the terms of the contract may be set up. For example, in either case, if one party to the contract is a minor, he may set up his incapacity to contract as a defense against carrying out the agreement.

Although nonnegotiable and negotiable instruments are alike in the rights given to the original parties, they are different in the rights given to subsequent parties. When a nonnegotiable contract is transferred by assignment, the assignee receives only the rights of the assignor and no more. (See Chapter 10.) If one of the original parties to the contract has a defense that is valid against the assignor, it is also valid against the assignee. When an instrument is transferred by negotiation, however, the party who receives the instrument in good faith and for value will ordinarily have rights that are superior to the rights of the original holder. The nature of these rights and the conditions under which they are received are discussed in later chapters.

> ▪ The Wolfe Trucking Company sold a truck to the Frost Tire Company and received a written nonnegotiable promise to pay the total purchase price of $2,400 in 90 days. The Frost Tire Company sold tires and other products to the Wolfe Trucking Company amounting to $900. Before the 90 days expired, the Wolfe Trucking Company sold all of its accounts receivable to the Citizens Bank. When the bank demanded payment for the $2,400, the Frost Tire Company attempted to offset its $900 against the $2,400. It was allowed to do so, since an assignee takes accounts receivable subject to all defenses the principal had against the assignor.

Under the same facts as stated above, had the Frost Tire Company paid for the truck with a ninety-day negotiable note, then the Wolfe Trucking Company could have negotiated, not assigned, the note to the bank. In that case the bank would have received the note free from any defense of offset. It is this advantage of negotiation over assignment that gives meaning and significance to the law of negotiable instruments.

QUESTIONS

1. Explain the difference between negotiable contracts as instruments of credit and as instruments of collection.
2. What is the one difference in the wording of "bearer" paper and "order" paper?
3. Can a negotiable contract ever be negotiated without an indorsement?
4. How does one indorse a negotiable instrument?
5. Who is the payee of a negotiable instrument?
6. What is the difference between the drawer and the drawee of a bill of exchange?

7. When the drawee accepts the bill of exchange, what is he called?

8. What does the maker of a promissory note contract to do?

9. Who is the indorser of a negotiable instrument? The indorsee?

10. How do assignment and negotiation differ?

CASE PROBLEMS

1. The Adams Company sold Huntley a hi-fi set for $400, and Huntley paid for it by giving a sixty-day nonnegotiable promissory note. Before the note became due, Huntley worked for the Adams Company and earned $350. When the note came due, Adams informed Huntley it had assigned his note to the Comer National Bank, an innocent purchaser, and that he would have to pay the bearer. The Adams Company refused to pay the $350, and Huntley attempted to offset this $350 against the $400 when the bank demanded payment. Can he do so?

Would your answer be different if the note was so worded that it was negotiable in form according to the Uniform Negotiable Instrument Law and the note had been negotiated instead of assigned?

2. Gregory drew a check on the Dayton National Bank for $704.50, payable to "Bearer." Before the check was delivered, it was stolen by Davis and cashed at the bank. Gregory demanded that the bank restore the amount of the check to his checking account. Must the bank do this?

3. (a) Who is the payee in this trade acceptance?

(b) Identify the drawer and the drawee in this instrument.

TRADE ACCEPTANCE

No. 101 .... Peoria, Illinois, March 4, 19....

To Brown Store Company .... Cleveland, Ohio ....

On June 2, 19 ....Pay to the order of.... Ourselves ....
      (DATE OF MATURITY)
Five hundred and no/100 ....Dollars, ($ 500.00 ....)

The obligation of the acceptor hereof arises out of the purchase of goods from the drawer. The drawee may accept this bill payable at any bank, banker or trust company in the United States which he may designate.

Accepted at Cleveland on March 7, 19....

Payable at Pioneer Trust Company Bank By Smith, McCord & Company ....

.... Brown Store Company ....
           (SIGNATURE OF ACCEPTOR)
By D. C. Brown, Pres. .... By A. M. Smith, Treasurer

---

4. Strong of San Diego owed Lawson of Richmond, Virginia, $5,000. Bell of Richmond owed Strong $5,000. Show how by means of a draft, check, or other negotiable instrument Strong could pay Lawson the $5,000 he owes him and collect the $5,000 Bell owes him without sending any money across the country.

5. Smith borrowed $500 from Alexander and agreed to repay it in sixty days with 6 percent interest. When the sixty days were up, Smith tendered Alexander a check for the amount due. The check was payable to Smith and drawn by Lowe.

(a) Was Alexander obligated to accept this check?

(b) If Alexander refused to accept it, would this refusal stop the running of interest?

CHAPTER 21

BILLS OF EXCHANGE

NATURE OF A BILL OF EXCHANGE

A bill of exchange is commonly called a draft. It is drawn or executed by the drawer in favor of the payee, who has the drawer's authority to collect the amount indicated on the instrument. It is addressed to the drawee, who is ordered by the drawer to pay the amount of the instrument when the amount is demanded by the payee or some other party to whom the payee has transferred the instrument by indorsement. The drawee, after he has accepted the instrument, that is, after he has agreed to pay it, becomes the acceptor.

An *inland bill of exchange* is one that shows on its face that it is both drawn and payable in one state. If it cannot be determined on its face either where it is drawn or where it is payable, the holder may treat it as an inland bill of exchange. Inland bills of exchange are frequently referred to as *domestic bills of exchange*. All others are referred to as *foreign bills of exchange*. In Chapter 26 the reason for making the distinction will be set forth fully.

FORMS OF BILLS OF EXCHANGE

There are two principal classes of negotiable instruments—bills of exchange and notes. This chapter deals with bills of exchange. There are several forms of bills of exchange, and employees who handle them must be able to recognize each one. The first step is to learn to recognize each of the three forms of bills of exchange:

1. Drafts
2. Trade acceptances
3. Checks (discussed separately in Chapter 22)

Sight and Time Drafts. Any type of *draft* is a written order drawn and signed by one party (drawer), ordering another party (drawee) to pay either to the payee (who commonly is also the drawer) or to his order a definite sum of money. There are two kinds of drafts to meet the different needs of business:

1. Sight drafts
2. Time drafts

Sight Drafts. A *sight draft* is a draft payable at sight or upon presentation by the payee or holder. It indicates that the amount is either due or past due and that the drawer is demanding payment at once.

| $950.50 | CLEVELAND, OHIO | February 11, | 19 |

At sight-- PAY TO THE

ORDER OF City National Bank, Gary, Indiana

Nine hundred fifty and 50/100--DOLLARS

VALUE RECEIVED AND CHARGE TO ACCOUNT OF

TO L. A. Britton

No 167   Gary, Indiana

GORDON ELECTRIC APPLIANCES

BY B. J. Carter

Sight Draft

Time Drafts. A *time draft* has exactly the same form as a sight draft except that the drawee is ordered to pay the money a certain number of days after date or after sight rather than at sight. In other words, the drawer by drawing a time draft is indicating his willingness to give the drawee an additional credit period.

The payee should present the draft to the drawee for acceptance. Then when the credit period expires, that is, when the draft matures, it must be presented for payment. If the draft reads, "Sixty days after date," it matures or becomes due sixty days after the date of the draft regardless of the date it was accepted.

If the drawee is ordered to pay the draft a specified number of days after sight, it must be presented for acceptance because the due date is calculated from the date of the acceptance, not from the date of the draft. A failure to present such a time draft for acceptance may release the drawer from his liability to the payee. This is the primary reason the two forms must be identified.

USE OF DRAFTS

Negotiable instruments are called instruments of credit and instruments of collection. If *A* sells *B* merchandise on sixty days' credit, the granting of this credit may be handled in one of two ways. First, the amount of the sale may be recorded in the sales journal and the accounts receivable ledger. In this form it is referred to as an open account. Secondly, the buyer may at the time of the sale execute a sixty-day negotiable note in payment of the merchandise. This note then is an instrument of credit. But a time draft may also be used for the same purpose. The term to describe this type of time draft, however, is a *trade acceptance*. The mechanics of drawing up a trade acceptance are quite different from that of a negotiable note. The buyer fills out the note, signs it, and mails it to the seller. The seller fills out the trade acceptance and in most cases mails it to a bank in the buyer's hometown. The bank then presents it to the buyer for acceptance. The bank acts as agent of the seller. When it is accepted, the bank mails it back to the seller and the bookkeeper records it as a notes receivable just as he would do if it were a note. So both are instruments of credit.

A time draft is also an instrument of credit, but the preparation of a time draft may be quite different from that of a note or a trade acceptance. In most cases the payee of a trade acceptance is also the drawer. If a bank is the payee, the bank is merely the agent of the drawer to facilitate collection.

There are always three original but separate parties on the face of a time draft. The reason for this is obvious. As between the drawer of a time draft and the drawee, it is an instrument of credit, that is, the drawer is extending an original credit period. As between the drawer and the payee, the time draft is an instrument of payment because the drawer is paying his debts to the payee by drawing a time draft on one of his customers, the drawee. This is a conditional payment, however, since the drawer, like an indorser on a check, warrants the drawee will pay the draft when it falls due. It is because of this warranty that the payee is willing to take the draft as an instrument of credit. The payee must be very careful not to commit any act that will release the drawer from his warranty.

If the seller in the transaction above is unwilling to extend the original credit at sixty days, he may draw a sight draft on the buyer, who then would be the drawee. The sight draft then is an instrument of collection. In this case, the drawer may make a bank the payee, the bank being a mere agent of the drawer. He may, however, make one of his creditors the payee so that he collects an account receivable and pays an account payable all in one transaction. If the buyer takes the initiative when the account receivable comes due, he will mail to the seller a check, which is a special and different type of sight draft. The negotiable instruments law is very exacting in its demands on the drawing, the presenting, the indorsing, and the honoring of these instruments. Business firms must have an office force that clearly understands these laws to prevent serious losses. Failure to perform any one of the acts in the following paragraphs may cause a financial loss.

PRESENTMENT FOR ACCEPTANCE

All trade acceptances and all time drafts payable so many days after sight must be presented for acceptance by the payee to the drawee. If the presentment for acceptance is improper, the drawer may be released from his warranty that the drawee will pay it. To be a proper acceptance these conditions must be met:

(1) Time. The instrument must be presented for acceptance within a reasonable time. The court decides what is a reasonable time.

(2) Place. The instrument should be presented at the drawee's place of business. If he has no place of business, it may be presented at his home or wherever he may be found.

(3) Hour. It must be presented for acceptance at a reasonable hour on a business day.

(4) Party. It must be presented to the drawee or to someone authorized either by law or by contract to accept for him.

FORM OF ACCEPTANCE

The usual method of accepting a bill of exchange is to write on the face of it these words:

"Accepted July 12, 1963

John Doe."

The drawee may use other words of acceptance, but the words used must indicate an intention to be bound by the terms of the

An Accepted Time Draft

contract. An oral acceptance is not permissible. The written acceptance may be on separate paper, but the payee has a right to treat this as dishonoring the draft if he chooses to do so. A telegram of acceptance has been held to be a valid acceptance if the payee is willing to treat it as accepted.

The word "accepted" and the drawee's name are all that is necessary to constitute a valid acceptance. In one case on record the drawee merely wrote his name across the face. The payee wrote over the drawee's name the word "Accepted." The court held this was a valid acceptance. It is well to remember that the payee is free to return the instrument to the drawer and demand cash if he is not satisfied the acceptance is valid.

The Uniform Commercial Code alters the Uniform Negotiable Instruments Law in one important particular. The Code requires the acceptance to be written on the instrument. Under the Uniform Negotiable Instruments Law, the payee could, if he chose, consider the acceptance proper if it were written in a letter. The Code also provides that the drawee is not considered to have accepted the draft if he destroys it or fails to return it. This is another important deviation from the Uniform Negotiable Instruments Law.

PRESENTMENT FOR PAYMENT

All sight drafts and all accepted time drafts must be presented for payment. The law governing this type of presentment is developed more fully in Chapter 26.

OBLIGATION OF THE ACCEPTOR

When a draft is presented to a drawee for acceptance, he must either accept or return it. If it is not returned within a reasonable time, it is presumed to have been accepted. After the instrument has been accepted, the drawee is unconditionally and absolutely required to pay the amount of the instrument; he is therefore primarily liable for the obligation.

When the drawee accepts a time draft, he makes the following three admissions concerning the drawer:

(1) That the signature of the drawer is genuine

(2) That he owes the drawer the amount shown on the draft

(3) That the drawer has both the capacity and the authority to draw the draft

The drawee, by accepting a draft, also admits the payee's capacity to indorse, but not the genuineness of the payee's indorsement.

Having made these admissions, the acceptor cannot later deny them against a holder in due course.

- O'Kelly forged Cohen's name as drawer to a draft for $3,000 payable to O'Kelly. He presented it to Smith for acceptance. Smith then transferred the draft by indorsement to Berger. Later Smith learned that Cohen's signature was forged and refused to pay the draft when it became due. He could not avoid payment because he admitted the genuineness of Cohen's signature when he accepted the draft. It was then too late to raise the defense of forgery against Berger. He could proceed, of course, against O'Kelly.

TRADE ACCEPTANCE

The *trade acceptance* is a time draft. Its use is confined to the sale of goods. It is a bill of exchange drawn by the seller on the purchaser of goods sold, and accepted by such purchaser. It is drawn at the time the goods are sold. The seller is the drawer, and the purchaser is the drawee. Both the trade acceptance and the time draft in accounting are notes receivable when accepted. The chief difference is that the trade acceptance is always given at the time the goods are sold, and the time draft is usually given at the end of a credit period.

Also, a trade acceptance is never drawn except in a sales transaction; a draft may be used in many types of business transactions. Legally there is no difference between a time draft and a trade acceptance. Also, the bookkeeper treats them both as notes receivable if his firm is the payee and as notes payable if his firm is the drawee. From a bookkeeping standpoint, then, there is no difference between a time draft, a trade acceptance, and a promissory note.

BANKER'S ACCEPTANCE

A trade acceptance is similar to a banker's acceptance. One reason business firms use time drafts and trade acceptances to extend credit to the buyer instead of just "charging" the sale as an accounts receivable is that these negotiable contracts can be discounted at a bank. Discounting simply means the payee sells the contract to a bank for cash. In this way the buyer gets the credit he needs, and the seller gets the cash he needs. An ordinary time draft or trade acceptance is an unsecured loan. If the payee wishes to sell one to the bank, the bank may demand some type of collateral from the payee, the one who usually discounts it. One way to accomplish this is for the buyer, who is the drawee of a trade acceptance, to put up the collateral since he is the one who is asking for credit. He provides whatever security the bank requires; then the bank agrees to accept a draft drawn by the seller. The bank, then, is the drawee, not the buyer. Such a draft is called a *banker's acceptance*. The reason for this arrangement is that the seller, the payee, then can discount the draft for cash much more easily than he could discount one accepted by the buyer.

QUESTIONS

1. What is the difference between a domestic bill of exchange and a foreign bill of exchange?
2. Name three forms of bills of exchange.
3. Name two types of drafts and indicate characteristics of each.
4. Why is a bank usually made the payee of a sight draft?
5. If an instrument is properly presented for acceptance, what conditions must be met?
6. When the drawee accepts a time draft, what admissions does he make concerning the drawer?
7. What is a trade acceptance?
8. Must a time draft payable thirty days after sight be presented for acceptance?
9. Where should a time draft be presented for acceptance?

CASE PROBLEMS

1. Scott wished to purchase $10,000 worth of merchandise from Dover on six months' credit. Dover needed the cash but did not wish to take a trade acceptance since he could not discount it at the bank without collateral, and he had no acceptable collateral. Explain in detail how Scott and Dover might complete this transaction satisfactorily.

2. White received in the mail a sixty-day time draft drawn by Jardine, one of White's customers, ordering London to pay White $5,000. White sent his secretary, Jeanne, to London's office to get it accepted. London was out when Jeanne arrived, and no one knew what to do about it. Finally, John, the bookkeeper, agreed to accept since his accounts payable ledger showed London owed White the $5,000. When the draft came due, London refused to pay it, claiming the bookkeeper had no authority to accept the draft for him. Jardine refused to pay White, claiming he was released because he had never been notified that the draft had been dishonored. What errors were made in this transaction?

3. Harold owed Jenkins $2,700. To pay it he drew a sixty-day time-sight (60 days after sight) draft on Henderson, one of his customers. When Jenkins received the draft, dated April 2, he filed it. On June 1, he presented the draft to Henderson for payment. Henderson refused to pay it, claiming he should merely accept it since it had never been presented for acceptance. Jenkins refused to let him accept it, and notified Harold the draft had been dishonored for nonpayment. Must Harold pay Jenkins?

4. Benson Brothers had an order from Holman of Cincinnati for $2,500. He wanted to purchase merchandise on sixty days' credit. Holman's credit was good, but he had the reputation of always denying that he received all the merchandise or claiming an error of some kind. Benson Brothers were willing to sell him the merchandise on credit but wanted to forestall any contention about the amount owed. Explain how they might accomplish this.

5. Dalton owed Harper and Son $3,200. When the account came due, he was unable to pay it. He drew a time draft on Turner for $3,200 and sent it to Harper and Son. Hand, the bookkeeper for Harper and Son, presented the draft to Turner for acceptance, and Turner wrote this on the draft: "The face of this draft is the correct amount I owe Harper and Son. A. Turner." Was this a proper acceptance?

6. Thomas J. Granger executed the following instrument:

Chicago, Ill., April 10, 19—

At sixty days' sight pay to the order of Charles Hudson five hundred dollars ($500) and charge the same to the account of

To Albert W. Morris
   St. Louis, Mo.   Thomas J. Granger

(a) Must this draft be presented for acceptance?
(b) To whom should it be presented?
(c) When should it be presented?
(d) If the drawee was out when it was presented and his secretary accepted it, would this be a proper acceptance?
(e) If the draft was presented on Sunday at the drawee's home, would this be a proper presentment?

(f) The drawee took the draft, and the next day returned it by mail with this memo attached: "I will pay this draft when it comes due. A. W. Morris." Was this a valid acceptance?

(g) If Hudson was not satisfied unless Morris wrote an acceptance on the face of the draft, what should he do?

(h) When Hudson received the draft with the acceptance written on a separate paper, he notified Granger that this was unsatisfactory and demanded that Granger pay him. Granger did this. Two months later Morris paid Hudson and Hudson accepted the money but never remitted it to Granger. Must Morris pay Granger?

7. The following draft was sent to Milton V. Gray:

Denver, Colo., June 20, 19—

At sight pay to the order of Rocky Mountain National Bank for collection one thousand dollars ($1,000), and charge to the account of

To Milton V. Gray
Billings, Mont. R. W. Tate & Co.

(a) Who is the drawer of this draft?

(b) Who is to pay the draft?

(c) Must this draft be presented for acceptance?

8. (a) If the draft in the foregoing case read "At ten days' sight," would it require presentment for acceptance? If it were accepted on June 25, when would it be due?

(b) If this draft read "Ten days after date pay . . . ," would an acceptance be necessary? If it were accepted on June 25, when would it be due?

CHAPTER 22

CHECKS

CHECKS

A *check* is a bill of exchange drawn on a bank and payable on demand. In many ways a check is similar to a sight draft, the drawee being a bank instead of an individual or a business firm as is the case with a sight draft. There are, however, several differences between a check and a sight draft.

(1) The death of the drawer of a check automatically revokes the authority of the bank, the drawee, to pay it. This is not true of a sight draft. If the drawee of a sight draft dies, the administrator of his estate must pay it to the payee.

(2) The drawer who draws a sight draft on a drawee with whom he has no funds commits no crime. It is a fraud, and in most states a crime also, to draw a check on a bank in which the drawer has no funds.

(3) If the holder of a check delays presentment for payment beyond a reasonable time, the drawer is released, provided he can prove an injury due to the delay. If the delay causes no injury, he remains liable until the Statute of Limitations has run on the check. Hence, he must keep funds in the bank for an indefinite period of time. Delay in presenting a sight draft can discharge the drawer regardless of injury.

(4) Presentment by the holder of a check for certification, that is, acceptance, discharges the drawer and all indorsers. This is not true of other bills of exchange.

(5) Acceptance (certification) of a check by the bank constitutes a warranty that the drawer has sufficient funds to pay it and that these funds are being earmarked for payment. No such warranty is given by the acceptor of a draft.

(6) A sight draft is an assignment, that is a sale, to the payee of a debt owed to the drawer by the drawee. When the drawer once assigns this debt to the payee, he cannot stop payment on it. The drawer can stop payment on a check any time prior to its payment by the bank.

CARLSON ADVERTISING, INC.
1112 Brookhaven Drive

No. *78*   64-22 / 610

Atlanta, Georgia _*July 22*_ 19 *63*

PAY TO THE ORDER OF _*The Daily Mirror*_ $ *110.53*

One hundred ten and 53/100 ———————————————— DOLLARS

Merchants Bank
ATLANTA 3, GEORGIA

J. L. Harvey
Treasurer, CARLSON ADVERTISING, INC.

⑆0610⑈0022⑆ 8140⑈662⑈

Check

SPECIAL KINDS OF CHECKS

There are four special types of checks, each one having a distinguishing characteristic:

1. Certified checks
2. Cashier's checks
3. Bank drafts
4. Voucher checks

(1) **Certified Checks.** A *certified check* is an ordinary check which an official of the bank, the drawee, has accepted by writing across the face of the check the word "certified," or some similar word, and signed. Either the drawer or the holder may have a check certified. The effect of having it certified is to establish a primary liability on the part of the bank. The bank not only thereby guarantees the genuineness of the drawer's signature but warrants that the drawer has sufficient funds to cover the check and that these funds have been earmarked in an amount equal to the check.

If the drawer has the check certified before delivering the check to the payee or holder, he merely adds, but does not substitute, the bank as a copromisor of payment. The drawer remains fully liable if the bank refuses or is unable to pay it. If the holder, however, has it certified, he substitutes the bank for the drawer as the one liable for its payment. The drawer is released from liability.

■ Sherman Matney gave Garner a $10,000 check on a Grundy bank.

Garner, not wishing to cash the check and carry the cash while traveling, had it certified. Before Garner arrived at his destination, the bank failed and its assets were insufficient to pay all its depositors. Garner was the loser since he could have received the cash at the time he had the check certified.

Had Matney been the one who had the check certified and mailed it to Garner, the drawer, Matney, would have remained liable, provided Garner was diligent in presenting it for payment.

(2) Cashier's Checks. A check that a bank draws on its own funds and that is signed by the cashier or some other responsible official of the bank is called a *cashier's check*. Such a check may be used by a bank in paying its own obligations, or it may be used by anyone else who wishes to remit in some form other than his own check.

(3) Bank Drafts. A *bank draft* is a check drawn by one bank on another bank. It is customary for banks to keep a portion of their funds on deposit with other banks. A bank, then, may draw a check on these funds as freely as any corporation may draw checks.

(4) Voucher Checks. A *voucher check* is one with a voucher attached. The voucher lists the items of an invoice for which the check is means of payment. It is customary, in business at least, for the drawer of the check to write on it such words as "In full of account," "For invoice No. 1622," or similar notations. These notations make the checks excellent receipts when they are returned to the drawer. The voucher check is a device to extend the space on which to make a notation for which the check is issued. In most cases the voucher part of the check is made in duplicate. The payee detaches his copy of the voucher before depositing the check. The drawer files his copy so that both parties have identical records relative to the purpose for which the check was drawn.

POSTDATED CHECKS

A check dated July 1, but drawn on June 21, is a *postdated check*. It is in effect a ten-day sight draft when so drawn. If the payee is willing to accept such a check, and funds are in the bank on July 1 to cover it, the transaction is a legitimate one. If a check is postdated for the purpose of defrauding someone, the drawer is guilty under the bad check laws.

BAD CHECKS

A check drawn on a bank in which the drawer has no funds is a *bad check*. Such act is a crime under the bad check laws in all states. If one gives a bad check in payment of an existing debt, as a rule no serious harm has been done. The debt merely remains unpaid just as if no check had been given. Some states do not make this a crime. If one induces another to part with money or other property, however, the drawer commits a fraud. Some states make the act equivalent to larceny. If the drawer can prove that there was no intent to defraud, no crime has been committed. The burden of proving this is on the drawer.

PRESENTMENT OF A CHECK FOR PAYMENT

Checks, unlike other bills of exchange, are given as immediate payment of accounts, not as an instrument of credit. For this reason, they should be presented for payment within a reasonable time after receipt. As a rule a "reasonable time" is interpreted to mean during banking hours of the next business day after it is drawn. If the payee and the bank are in different towns, then the payee should forward it for presentment not later than the next business day after it is drawn. In rural communities these times may be somewhat longer.

When the drawer gives a check, he should have funds in the bank to cover it. As far as the drawer is concerned, the payee could hold the check for months and still present it for payment. If the delay has not injured the drawer in any way, he cannot complain. If the bank should become insolvent, however, the payee's recovery would be limited to the drawer's pro rata share in the assets of the insolvent bank. This might mean that the payee could recover nothing on the check. The effect of delay is quite different with indorsers. If the holder through indorsement waits an unreasonable length of time to present the check for payment, all indorsers are discharged whether they have suffered a loss or not.

LIABILITY OF THE BANK

When money is deposited in a bank, a debtor-creditor relationship is created. The bank agrees to return the loan to the depositor on demand. The bank further agrees to pay any part of the loan to any party to whom the depositor orders it to pay. If the depositor draws a check payable to a specific payee and the bank refuses to pay the check, the bank breaks its contract with the drawer, but the payee cannot sue the bank since a check is not an assignment of the debt. The payee's only remedy is to return to the drawee and demand payment of the debt by another medium. The drawer may sue the bank for breach of contract if he has been damaged in any way.

STOPPING PAYMENT ON A CHECK

The drawer of a check may stop payment on a check anytime before it is paid. Either by law or by contract with the bank the drawer must give notice in writing to stop payment. The bank usually waives this requirement if an oral notice is followed up immediately by a written notice. If the payee indorses the check to an innocent purchaser, the drawer may still stop payment on it. The innocent holder, however, may sue to recover the amount of the check either from the payee-indorser or from the drawer. He cannot sue the bank.

If a bank pays a check after it has been properly notified not to pay it, the drawer may sue for recovery of the face of the check. As a general rule, the stop-payment notice is effective for only six months, unless renewed. If the bank pays it after this period, assuming the notice has not been renewed, it is not liable to the drawer.

BANK'S LIABILITY TO DEPOSITOR

When one deposits money in a bank, he is merely loaning money to the bank with the understanding that the money will be returned on demand to the party or parties the depositor orders the bank to pay. If the bank pays out any of this money contrary to the order of the depositor or without his order, the bank can be held liable for the loss. The most common causes for wrongful payment are:

(1) The depositor's signature is forged on a check. It is the bank's responsibility to recognize the drawer's signature. The bank, of course, carries full insurance to protect it against these losses.

(2) Alteration of the check by raising the amount. The bank is liable for the amount by which the check was raised over that written by the drawer. The drawer must not be negligent in writing the check so that the alteration can be made without detection. The drawer should be careful to mark out all unused blank spaces.

(3) The Uniform Commercial Code provides that a bank may at its option pay a check presented for payment more than six months after date.

The bank must act in good faith. If it refuses to pay the check, the bank incurs no liability to the depositor.

(4) The Uniform Commercial Code provides that a bank is not liable if it pays a check after the drawer's death if the bank had no knowledge of his death. After the bank has knowledge of the drawer's death, it may continue to pay and certify his checks for ten days unless notified by a qualified party not to do so.

QUESTIONS

1. Does the death of the drawer of a check revoke the bank's authority to pay it?
2. Is a check an assignment of the funds of the drawer to the drawee?
3. May a bank refuse to honor a check when presented for payment without giving any reason for its refusal?
4. What is a voucher check?
5. If a check is drawn for $10 and the drawee raises it to $100 and the bank carelessly fails to detect the alterations, must the drawer suffer the loss?
6. If the drawer's signature is forged to a check and the check is cashed, must the bank reimburse the depositor?
7. What is the difference between a check and a sight draft?
8. If the holder of a check has it certified, who is liable?
9. If one bank has some of its funds deposited in another bank and draws a check on these funds, what is this type of check called?
10. What may be the effect of a delay in presentment for payment of a check?

CASE PROBLEMS

1. Roger and Molly had a joint bank account. Molly wrote a check on the account in payment of a fur coat. Roger learned of the purchase before the check was deposited. Since he disapproved of the purchase, he notified the bank to stop payment on the check. The bank refused to do so unless Molly joined in giving notice. Was the bank within its rights?

2. Halleman drew a check on the Crawford National Bank for $500. By careless writing he left spaces so that it was easy to add a two before the $500 to make it $2,500, and the word "twenty" before "five hundred." The bank paid the altered check for $2,500, and Halleman sued the bank for the $2,000 loss. Must the bank make good this loss?

3. Benton drew a check for $400 in favor of Aiken. The check was held by Aiken for one month before he presented it to the bank for payment. During the latter part of this month, the bank failed. The bank was not

insured by the Federal Deposit Insurance Corporation, and Aiken was able to collect only $100 on the check. May he look to Benton for the other $300?

4. Hartsfield owed Huff and Company $1,900. He wrote on a post card these words:

The First National Bank
   Pay to the order of Huff and Company $1,900
                                    Cordially yours,
                                      A. W. Hartsfield.

He put a stamp on this post card and mailed it to Huff and Company. Since the owner of this company was on vacation, the bookkeeper held the post card until his employer returned about two weeks later. In the meantime The First National Bank went into receivership, and the assets of the bank were sufficient to pay only $900 on the post card. Who must bear the $1,000 loss, Hartsfield or Huff and Company?

5. Davison drew a check on June 7 payable to Lester Hardware Company. He dated the check June 12 and asked the Lester Hardware Company to hold the check until June 12 before cashing it, stating he would have the money to pay it in the bank at that time. The Lester Hardware Company deposited the check on June 8, and it was returned marked "Insufficient Funds." Davison was indicted for giving a bad check. Was he guilty?

6. Holston Tobacco Company received a check by indorsement from Davis, a customer. The check was misplaced by the auditor, and it was two weeks before it was located. The check was immediately deposited but was returned because the drawer had no money in the bank. Must Davis make this check good?

7. Donaldson had a check for $800 drawn by Harvey on the Acton Bank. Since Donaldson was leaving on an extended trip and did not care to carry $800 in cash with him, he had the check certified. The bookkeeper at the bank by error showed that Harvey's balance was $875, when in reality it was $185. Before the check was cashed, the bank auditor discovered the error and the bank refused to pay the check. Must the bank pay the full $800?

8. Dotson drew a check on the First National Bank for $375, payable to Adkins. At the time the check was drawn, Dotson had sufficient funds in the bank to cover the check.

(a) If Adkins held the check without presenting it for payment, would this delay justify Dotson's drawing the money out of the bank at the end of four months?

(b) If during the four months the bank became insolvent and a receiver was appointed, was Dotson released from liability?

CHAPTER 23

PROMISSORY NOTES

NATURE OF A PROMISSORY NOTE

Any written promise to pay money is a promissory note, but it may not be a negotiable instrument. To be negotiable, a note must contain the essential elements discussed in Chapter 24.

It is not necessary to use the word "promise" in a note, but the substitute word or words must literally mean "promise." Such expressions as "I will pay" and "I guarantee to pay" have been held to constitute a "promise to pay."

The two original parties to a promissory note are the maker, the one who signs the note and promises to pay, and the payee, the one to whom the promise is made. If the payee transfers the note, he becomes an indorser; the new holder becomes the indorsee.

LIABILITY OF THE MAKER

The maker of a promissory note (1) expressly agrees that he will pay the note when it is due, (2) admits the existence of the payee, and (3) warrants that the payee is competent to transfer the instrument by indorsement.

■ Massey made a note payable to Hess or order, and Hess indorsed the instrument to Frazier. Hess was a minor. When Massey refused to pay the note upon its due date, Frazier brought an action against him. Massey set up the defense that the minor was not competent to indorse the note to Frazier and therefore Frazier could not sue and recover on the note. The court held that Frazier could recover. Massey, by making the note payable to Hess, a minor, warranted the competency of Hess to negotiate the paper.

TYPES OF NEGOTIABLE NOTES

Any contract the wording of which corresponds to the definition of a note set out in the early part of this chapter is a negotiable note. Many types of notes are known by special names; thus one who deals with them must know what they are and what their special characteristics are. These classes are:

1. Bonds
2. Interest coupons
3. Chattel mortgage notes
4. Collateral notes
5. Real estate mortgage notes
6. Judgment notes
7. Debentures

(1) **Bonds.** A *bond* is a written contract obligation, generally issued by a corporation, a municipality, or a government, which contains a promise to pay a sum certain in money at a fixed or determinable future time to order or to bearer. It may contain, in addition to the promise to pay, certain other conditions and stipulations. If it is issued by a corporation, it is generally secured by a deed of trust on the property of the corporation.

Bonds, which are more formal than ordinary promissory notes, may be classified as (a) registered bonds, and (b) coupon bonds.

A *registered bond* is recorded under the name of the purchaser by the organization issuing it to guard against its loss or destruction. When a registered bond is sold, a record of the transfer to the new bondholder must be made under the name of the new holder of the bond.

A *coupon bond* is so called because the interest payments are made by means of small notes or coupons attached to the bond itself. Coupon bonds are usually payable to the bearer; as a result, they can be negotiated by delivery.

(2) **Interest Coupons.** A ten-year coupon bond with interest payable semiannually has twenty interest coupons attached. At the end of each six months, the holder detaches one interest coupon. This coupon may be negotiated like a check or a negotiable promissory note. The coupon contains a promise to pay to the bearer a definite sum of money on demand and thus may be classed as a special type of promissory note.

(3) **Chattel Mortgage Notes.** A *chattel* is personal property, as distinguished from real estate. A *chattel mortgage note* is a promissory note secured by a chattel mortgage on personal property, usually tangible personal property. The debtor keeps possession of the property. In some states he also retains title to the property; in others he keeps possession but gives title to the creditor, that is, the payee of the note. The mortgage provides that in the event the note is paid, title to the chattel reverts to the debtor. In those states where title never rests in the creditor, in the event of default in the payment of the note, the creditor must sell the chattels and apply the proceeds to the note. If there is any residue, it goes to the debtor. If the mortgagee transfers title to the chattels to the creditor, in the event of default, he may sue to get possession of the chattels. In most states chattel mortgage notes are fully negotiable.

In some states, however, Illinois for example, the courts hold that chattel mortgage notes are not negotiable on the theory they are to be paid from a specific fund. This is especially true where the note itself states that the note is secured by personal property described in the note. If the chattel mortgage is a legal document entirely separate from the note and this document is recorded in the county clerk's office, then there is no need for the note to make reference to this chattel mortgage. The negotiability of the note would in no way be affected by the chattel mortgage contract.

(4) **Collateral Notes.** A *collateral note* is a note secured by personal property; but unlike a chattel mortgage note, the debtor must deposit with the creditor the personal property, that is, the collateral. The collateral usually consists of stocks, bonds, or other written evidences of debt, but it may be any type of personal property. In the event of default, the creditor must comply strictly with the state law relative to selling the collateral. Any surplus remaining after all costs and the note are paid is payable to the debtor, that is, the maker of the note.

(5) **Real Estate Mortgage Notes.** A *real estate mortgage note* is in all respects the same as a chattel mortgage note except that the property given to secure the note is specific real estate rather than personal property. The owner of the real estate retains possession of it; but in the event of default by the mortgagor the holder of the note may sell the real estate. This subject is treated more fully in Chapter 45.

(6) Judgment Notes. In several states the law permits the use of *judgment notes,* which include a confession of judgment clause. This clause empowers the holder of the note to go into court and obtain judgment in the event the note is in default. The maker need not be summoned into court nor receive any notice. Except for this confession of judgment clause, these notes are ordinary promissory notes.

(7) Debentures. An unsecured bond or note issued by a business firm is called a *debenture.* A debenture, like any other bond or note, is nothing more nor less than a promissory note. It may be embellished with gold-colored edges, but this adds not a penny to its value. A debenture is usually negotiable in form, but like any other note, it is the wording on the bond that determines whether or not it is negotiable, not its name.

CERTIFICATES OF DEPOSIT

The Uniform Commercial Code does not classify a certificate of deposit as a note. The Code defines a *certificate of deposit* as "an acknowledgment by a bank of a receipt of money with an engagement to repay it." A certificate has all the elements of a note except it does not contain the word "promise." A certificate of deposit cannot be considered a bill of exchange since it does not contain an order to pay. The Uniform Commercial Code changes the terminology slightly but not the law.

QUESTIONS

1. Must a promissory note contain the word "promise" to be enforceable?
2. Who is the payee of a note?
3. What are the obligations of the maker of a promissory note?
4. What is a bond and by whom are bonds usually issued?
5. What is the difference between a registered bond and a coupon bond?
6. How many coupons are there on a fifteen-year coupon bond if the interest is payable quarterly?
7. (a) Define a chattel.
   (b) What is a chattel mortgage note?
8. (a) What is a collateral note?
   (b) Of what does the collateral usually consist?
9. How does a real estate mortgage differ from a chattel mortgage note?
10. What is a judgment note?

CASE PROBLEMS

1. Dwight loaned Burns $2,000. Burns executed a promissory note payable six months from date. To secure the note Burns signed a chattel mortgage on his office equipment. Dwight filed this chattel mortgage and note in his office safe but did not record the chattel mortgage in the county clerk's office. The note did not recite the fact that it was secured by a chattel mortgage. Burns sold his business to Duncan, but Duncan did not assume Burns' debts. Later Dwight attempted to sell the office equipment to satisfy the note. Does he have the right to do this?

2. Dover borrowed $10,000 from Carlton and signed a collateral promissory note for the loan. The collateral consisted of "Bearer Coupon Bonds." Carlton's secretary filed the bonds and the note in a folder in the regular file cabinet instead of placing them in the safe. The bonds were stolen and cashed. Dover refuses to pay the note unless Carlton returns the bonds. Is he within his rights?

3. Darlington purchased some office machines from the Tifton Corporation with a written warranty that the equipment would be kept repaired without cost for 12 months. The machines were of poor quality and required frequent extensive repairs. The seller refused to make these repairs in compliance with its warranty. At the time of the purchase Darlington executed a judgment note for $5,700. He wished to offset these repairs against the note when the time came to pay it. Show how the Tifton Corporation can prevent his doing this.

4. A bond salesman called on Mrs. Dale in an effort to sell her some 8 percent debenture bonds. The bonds were impressive looking with gold-colored edges and signed with an impressive seal of the issuing corporation. Mr. and Mrs. Dale had $4,000 worth of government E bonds which paid only 3¾ per cent. Mrs. Dale cashed them and bought the debenture bonds. Point out some factors that may make this a very unwise move.

5. Hart purchased $20,000 worth of registered bonds from Wirth. He put them in his safe deposit box and paid no more attention to them. After two years he became concerned because he had received no interest checks. Why had he not received interest checks?

6. Henderson borrowed $6,000 from Byrd. He deposited with Byrd six $1,000 coupon bonds as collateral for this loan. Before the loan was repaid, the semiannual coupons became due. Byrd detached them and deposited them in his personal bank account. When Henderson started to pay Byrd the $6,000 note, he demanded that he receive credit for the $150 in coupons. Byrd claims the coupons belonged to him. Who is correct?

7. Darter owned fifty $1,000 coupon bonds, the interest payable semiannually. On one of the due dates of the interest coupons, Darter detached them, intending to cash them at the bank. Before he did so, they were stolen, and the thief cashed them at the Bank of Fargo. Darter sued the bank for reimbursement, claiming it should not have paid the coupons to the thief. Was Darter correct in his contention?

CHAPTER 24

ESSENTIALS OF

NEGOTIABILITY

REQUIREMENTS

The Uniform Negotiable Instruments Law sets forth seven definite requirements as to form with which an instrument must comply in order to be negotiable. If any one of these requirements is lacking, the contract is not negotiable even though it may be valid and enforceable as between the original parties to the instrument. These seven requirements are:

1. The instrument must be in writing and signed by the party executing it.

2. The instrument must contain either an order to pay or a promise to pay.

3. The order or the promise must be unconditional.

4. The instrument must provide for the payment of a sum certain in money.

5. The instrument must be payable either on demand or at a fixed or determinable future time.

6. The instrument must be payable to the order of a payee or to the bearer of the instrument.

7. The payee (unless the instrument is payable to bearer) and the drawee must be designated with reasonable certainty.

(1) **A Signed Writing.** A negotiable instrument must be written. The law does not, however, require that the writing be in any particular form. The instrument may be written with pen and ink or with pencil; it may be typed or printed; or it may be partly printed and partly typed. If an instrument is executed with a lead pencil, it

meets the legal requirements of negotiability; but a person might hesitate to accept it because of the ease with which it could be altered without detection.

There is little value to an unsigned form of any kind. On a negotiable instrument, as on other forms, a signature must be placed in order to show the intent of the promisor to be bound. The natural place for a signature is in the lower right-hand corner, but the location of the signature and its form are wholly immaterial if it is clear that a signature was intended. The signature may be written, typed, printed, or stamped. It may be a name, a symbol, a mark, or a trade name. The signature, however, must be on the instrument. It cannot be on a separate paper which is attached to the instrument.

From a legal standpoint, an odd or fictitious signature will bind the maker of a negotiable note as effectively as his real name. Here again, however, the question may later be raised as to whether or not the instrument is "complete and regular on its face" if the signature is of an odd nature. If any feature of the instrument is out of the ordinary, its legal negotiability may be nullified by prudent business customs.

The signature may be signed by another person who has been given authority to perform this act. When an agent signs for his principal or when an officer signs for his corporation, care must be taken not to make himself wholly liable or jointly liable with his principal or corporation. The two signatures below are the correct ones to use.

(a) The Acme Corporation   (b) *A. B. Jones*
By *A. B. Jones*   for The Acme
                                                    Corporation

Below are some odd or irregular but valid signatures:

His
(a) Richard ✕ Cooper
Mark

(b) "I, Thomas Morley," written by Morley in the body of the note but signed on the typewriter in the usual place for the signature.

(c) "Snowwhite Cleaner," the trade name under which Glendon Sutton operates his business.

The drawer of a bill of exchange, the drawee of a draft, the maker of a note, and all indorsers may sign these instruments in person or by an agent. When an agent signs the name of the principal to one of these instruments, he should make certain that he follows the safe manner of signing as an agent. The one sure, safe method is as follows:

Harold DeWitt

By Claude Firestone

The Uniform Commercial Code adds a section not found in the Uniform Negotiable Instruments Law. It reads as follows: "Except as otherwise established, the name of an organization preceded or followed by the name and office of an authorized individual is a signature made in a representative capacity." This reduces the possibility that an agent may be held liable as a joint maker of a note if he fails to sign the note exactly as illustrated above.

(2) An Order or a Promise to Pay. A bill of exchange, such as a draft, a trade acceptance, or a check, must contain an order to pay. A polite request or a suggestion to another to pay does not constitute an order. If the request is imperative and unequivocal, it is an order even though the word "order" is not used.

A promissory note must contain a promise to pay. The word "promise" need not be used—any equivalent words will answer the purpose—but the language used must show that a promise is intended. Thus the words "This is to certify that we are bound to pay" were held to be sufficient to constitute a promise.

(3) Unconditional. The order or the promise must be absolute and unconditional. Neither must be contingent upon any other act or event. If Baron promises to pay Noffke $500 "in sixty days, or sooner if I sell my farm," the contract is negotiable because the promise itself is unconditional. In any event he promises to pay the $500 in sixty days. The contingency pertains only to the time of payment, and that time cannot exceed sixty days. If the words "or sooner" were omitted, the promise would be conditional, and the note would be nonnegotiable. It is well to emphasize here again, however, that a contract may be valid even though nonnegotiable.

If the order to pay is out of a particular fund or account, the instrument is nonnegotiable. For example, "Pay to the order of Leonard Cohen $5,000 out of my share of my father's estate" would be a conditional order to pay. The order or the promise must commit the entire credit of the one primarily liable for the payment of the instrument.

(4) A Sum Certain in Money. The instrument must call for the payment of money and money alone. It need not be American money, but it must be some national medium of exchange. It cannot be in scrip, gold bullion, bonds, or similar assets. Frequently, the instrument provides for the payment of either money or goods. If the choice lies with the holder, such a provision does not destroy its negotiability. If the option to pay in goods lies with the drawer or the maker, the contract is not negotiable, but it may be enforced unless there is some valid defense to it.

- Sixty days after date I promise to pay to the order of Ira Rasmussen $500 or 250 bushels of wheat at his option.

  Signed—*Frank Birchmore*

  This note is negotiable because it is at the option of the payee, Rasmussen. If the words "his option" were changed to read, "my option," the note would not be negotiable.

The sum payable must be a certain amount that is not dependent upon other funds or upon future profits.

- In consideration for recommending Varney for a certain job, Fulton received the following instrument: ". . . we hereby agree to pay you the sum of $1,059 ninety days from date; the amount to be paid out of our profits on the 3 East 40th Street job." The court held that the statement on the note that the money was to be paid out of a particular fund destroyed its negotiability.

Not only must the contract be payable in money to be negotiable, but the amount must be certain from the wording of the instrument itself. A note for $5,000 provides that all taxes which may be levied upon a certain piece of real estate will be paid. This destroys its negotiability. The amount to be paid cannot be determined from the note itself. A provision providing for the payment of interest or exchange charges, however, does not destroy negotiability. Other terms which have been held not to destroy negotiability are provisions for cost of collection, a 10 percent attorney's fee if placed in the hands of an attorney for collection, and installment payments.

Frequently, through error, a negotiable instrument calls for the payment of one sum in figures and a different amount in words. The amount expressed in words prevails because one is less likely to err in writing this amount. Also, if anyone should attempt to raise the amount, it would be much simpler to alter the figures than it would be the words.

(5) **Payable on Demand or at a Fixed or Determinable Future Time.** An instrument meets the test of negotiability as to time if it is payable on demand—as in a demand note, or at sight—as in a sight draft, or when no time is specified—as in a check.

If the instrument provides for payment at some future time, the due date must either be fixed or so definitely stated that the due date can be determined. The date must be sure to arrive.

- Vaughn gave Marx an instrument containing the following provision: "I promise to pay Marx the sum of $450 when my son reaches the age of twenty-one." Such a condition rendered the instrument nonnegotiable because the time of payment was dependent upon a condition that might not happen. In other words, Vaughn's son might never reach the age of twenty-one.

- If Riggs promises to pay Burton $500 "sixty days after my marriage," the instrument is not payable at a determinable future time because the event is not certain to occur. If the words "after my death" were used instead of "after my marriage," the time would be determinable because the event is bound to occur.

The Uniform Commercial Code has made one important change in the law. If an instrument is payable "30 days after my death," it is not negotiable even though the date is certain to arrive. Under the Uniform Negotiable Instruments Law, such a wording would not have destroyed the instrument's negotiability.

In promissory notes there is often included either an acceleration clause or a prepayment clause. An acceleration clause is for the protection of the payee, and the prepayment clause is for the benefit of the maker or drawee. A note or a draft is usually not a gift though we often incorrectly speak of "giving" a person a note. The instrument is usually executed and delivered in settlement of some contract that has just been consummated, such as an installment sale. A typical accelerating clause provides that in the event one installment is in default, the whole note shall become due and payable at once. This does not destroy its negotiability.

Another accelerating clause stipulates that if the maker or the drawer defaults in carrying out the terms of a collateral contract, the instrument shall become due at once. Courts are divided on this clause, but the majority hold that this destroys its negotiability since the note calls for some act other than the payment of money.

Most prepayment clauses give the maker or the drawee the right to prepay the instrument in order to save interest. This does not affect the negotiability of the instrument.

(6) Payable to Order or Bearer. The two most common words of negotiability are "order" and "bearer." The instrument is *payable to order* when some person is made the payee and the maker or drawer wishes to indicate that the instrument will be paid to the person designated or to anyone else to whom he may transfer the instrument by indorsement.

It is not necessary to use the word "order," but it is strongly recommended. A note payable to "Smith and assigns" was held to be nonnegotiable. If it had been payable to "Smith or assigns," it would have been negotiable. Also "Pay to the order of the holder" would be negotiable, but some people might hesitate to accept a check or other bill of exchange containing such wording. The law looks to the intention of the maker or the acceptor. If the words used clearly show an intention to pay either the named payee or anyone else whom he designates, the contract is negotiable.

The other words of negotiability, *payable to bearer,* indicate that the maker or the acceptor of a bill of exchange is willing to pay the person who has possession of the instrument at maturity. The usual form in which these words appear is thus: "Pay to bearer" or "Pay to Lydia Lester or bearer." There are other types of wording that render a contract a bearer instrument. For example, if the payee is a fictitious person, it is a bearer instrument even though it contains the word "order." For example, "Pay to the order of Payroll" is a bearer instrument. The same is true if it is payable to "Cash," "Holder," or a name that is clearly fictitious and that fact is known to the drawer.

The reason a clear distinction must be made between "order" negotiable contracts and "bearer" contracts is that title to the latter may be obtained by delivery only, while title to "order" instruments can be obtained only by indorsement and delivery.

(7) Payee and Drawee Designated with Reasonable Certainty. When a negotiable instrument is payable "to order," the payee must be so named that the specific party can be identified with reasonable certainty. For example, a check which reads, "Pay to the order of the Treasurer of the Virginia Education Association" is not payable to a specific party, but that party can be ascertained with reasonable certainty; and the check is negotiable. If, on the other hand, the check is payable "to the order of the Treasurer of the Y.M.C.A." and there are three such organizations in the city, it would not be possible to ascertain with reasonable certainty who the payee is; and the check would not be negotiable.

If a check dated September 23 is made payable to Pete Dickens and Dickens dies on September 22, the check is void. A negotiable contract cannot be made payable to a dead person. If a check is made payable "to the administrator of Clark's estate," the payee is designated with reasonable certainty.

The drawee of a bill of exchange must likewise be named or described with reasonable certainty so that the holder will know to whom he must go for an acceptance or payment.

EXECUTION AND DELIVERY

The Uniform Negotiable Instruments Law states: "Every contract on a negotiable instrument is incomplete and revocable until delivery of the instrument for the purpose of giving effect thereto." Without this delivery there can be no force or effect to the contract. To constitute delivery the maker or drawer must give over control of the instrument to the holder for the sole purpose of giving effect to it, that is, making a binding obligation according to its terms. There can be a delivery without its being absolute, that is, without the delivery giving effect to the contract. If the delivery is made with the understanding, oral or written, that the instrument is not to become effective until some condition is met, this condition must be met before any liability arises under the contract. This is true only between the primary parties. If a negotiable instrument is completely filled out and possession of it is obtained illegally, there is no contract between the primary parties, but a remote purchaser, that is, an indorsee who has no knowledge of the nondelivery, can collect from the one primarily liable. This would also be true for a conditional delivery.

DELIVERY OF AN INCOMPLETE INSTRUMENT

If a negotiable instrument is only partially filled out and signed before delivery, the maker or drawer is liable if the blanks are filled in according to instructions. If the holder fills in the blanks contrary to the authority given him, the maker or drawer is liable to the original payee only for the amount authorized.

CONSIDERATION

Negotiable instruments, like other contracts, must be supported by a valid consideration. In the hands of an innocent purchaser, consideration is conclusively presumed. It is not necessary to recite in the contract that there is a consideration to support it. Frequently, such a recital is made, and this may destroy negotiability.

A reference to the consideration in a note that does not condition the promise does not destroy negotiability. The clause "This note is given in consideration of a typewriter purchased today" does not condition the maker's promise to pay. If the clause read, "This note is given in consideration for a typewriter guaranteed for ninety days, breach of warranty to constitute cancellation of the note," the instrument would not be negotiable. This promise to pay is not absolute, but conditional. Also, if the recital of the consideration is in such form as to make the instrument a part of another contract, the negotiability of the contract is destroyed.

- Mott inserted this statement in a note: "This note is a part of an agreement dated January 19, 1921." The court held that tying up the contract, which constituted the consideration for the note, with the note so that it all constituted one contract destroyed the negotiability of the note.

NONESSENTIALS OF NEGOTIABILITY

Since the purpose of the Uniform Negotiable Instruments Law is to encourage the transfer of negotiable instruments freely from hand to hand, no minor detail is permitted to destroy an instrument's negotiability. Some details held to be nonessential are:

The instrument need not be dated. The omission of a date may cause considerable inconvenience, but the date is not essential. The holder may fill in the correct date if the space for the date is left blank. If an instrument is due thirty days after date, and the date is omitted, the instrument is payable thirty days after it was issued or delivered. In case of dispute the date of issue may be proved.

The Uniform Commercial Code changes the wording of the law as set out in the Uniform Negotiable Instruments Law by stating that the negotiability of the instrument is not affected "by the fact it is undated, antedated, or postdated."

The name of the place where the instrument was drawn or where it is payable is not specified. For contracts in general, one's rights are governed by the law where the contract is made or where it is to be performed. This rule makes it advisable for a negotiable instrument to stipulate the place where it is drawn and where it is payable, but neither is essential for its negotiability.

QUESTIONS

1. If a negotiable contract is signed in pencil, is it negotiable?
2. Must the signature of the maker on a negotiable contract be in the lower right-hand corner?
3. Does an acceleration clause in a note destroy its negotiability?
4. If a check is stolen after it is partially filled out and is completed by the thief, is the drawer liable on it?
5. Must a check be dated in order to be negotiable?
6. When must a negotiable instrument be payable?
7. Explain the difference between "payable to order" and "payable to bearer."
8. Why is it important to designate the payee and drawee with reasonable certainty?
9. If an instrument is not supported by consideration, is it negotiable or nonnegotiable?
10. Is negotiability of an instrument affected if the name of the place where the instrument was drawn is not specified?

CASE PROBLEMS

1. Claude Holmes signed a note that contained this clause: "This note is to be paid from the proceeds of the sale of my home." At the time the note was signed, Holmes had a contract to sell his home. Madison, the payee of the note, negotiated it for value before it was due to the Garret Auto Mart in payment of a car. Holmes never paid the note; the Garret Auto Mart sued Madison, the indorser. Is he liable?

2. An accepted time draft read as follows: "Sixty days after the presidential election, pay Adam Horton $2,700." This draft was negotiated soon after its acceptance to the Cates Land Company as a partial payment for some timber land. When the draft came due, the drawee was bankrupt, and the Cates Land Company sought to make the drawer reimburse it for the $2,700. Can it do so?

3. The sales manager of the Snead Motors, Inc., sold Henry Amos a new car for $2,800. Amos tendered in payment a check on which he was the payee. The check was not dated. The sales manager interpreted this to mean it was nonnegotiable. Amos contended it was negotiable. As a result Amos became angry and refused to buy the car. Who was right?

4. The Harbin Hosiery Mills, Inc., was a family-owned corporation. The president, James Harbin, borrowed $50,000 from the bank on a six-months note. He signed the note:

James Harbin, Owner
Harbin Hosiery Mills, Inc.

His intention was to commit the credit of the corporation for the loan, but not his personal estate. The corporation went into bankruptcy, and the note was unpaid. The bank sued, contending that James Harbin was personally liable on this note. Is he personally liable?

5. Is the following note negotiable?

Sixty days after Easter I obligate myself to pay Globe, Inc., or bearer, the sum of $5,000 out of the proceeds of the sale of my GMC stock.

Glen Tinsdale

---

6. (a) Is the following draft negotiable?

To Lennox, Inc.

At sixty days' sight pay upon demand to John Ray $1,000 in gold bullion.

Henry Adams

(b) John Ray took this draft in payment of an account owed to him by Henry Adams. Lennox, Inc., accepted the draft on November 20, but he never paid it. Ray now wishes to hold Adams liable. Can he do so?

7. Is the following instrument negotiable?

Sixty days after my death I bind my heirs to pay to the Treasurer of the Y.M.C.A., or to anyone else whom he may designate, the sum of $5,000 with interest from the date of my death.

Signed: Albert Sloan

---

8. Stanley was manager for the Anawalt Furniture Company. A customer selected furniture amounting to $700 and tendered in payment a check payable to the customer and drawn by A. W. Green. The check was for $750 in figures, but in words it stated: "Seven Hundred and No/100 dollars." The customer offered to indorse it and accept $700 as the correct figure. Stanley interpreted this discrepancy to mean the instrument was not complete and regular on its face and therefore it was not negotiable. He refused to accept it and lost the sale. Was Stanley correct in his interpretation?

9. Lamb executed a note for $7,000 payable to Sam Storey. The note was regular in every way except that it contained this clause; "payable within two years from date with 6% interest, but if paid within one year, no interest is to be charged." Storey sold the note before maturity to Hanson. Before Hanson could collect this note from Lamb, he had to prove it was negotiable. Was it negotiable?

CHAPTER 25

NEGOTIATION AND
DISCHARGE

NEGOTIATION DEFINED

Negotiation is the transferring of a negotiable instrument in such a way as to constitute the transferee the holder of the instrument. The negotiation is usually, but not always, for the purpose of transferring title to the holder. Bearer instruments may be negotiated by delivery without any indorsement. This effectively invests ownership in the holder. In practice an indorsement is usually required even for bearer paper, although this adds nothing to the legality of the negotiation. It merely preserves a written chronological record of all negotiations. If the instrument is payable to "order," there can be a negotiation only by indorsement and delivery. The indorsement is the contract between the indorser and the indorsee or holder. The nature of the contract is fixed by the type of the indorsement.

PLACE OF INDORSEMENT

The usual place to indorse a negotiable instrument is on the back of the form. If the indorser's signature appears elsewhere and it cannot be determined in what capacity he signed, he will be considered an indorser. In any event, the indorsement must be physically attached to the contract. One may not wish to assume the liabilities of an indorser even though the instrument is negotiable. In that event he can assign it by writing out the assignment on a separate piece of paper.

If the maker or drawer misspells the name of the payee, the payee should first indorse exactly as the name appears on the instrument, and immediately following this, he should write his name correctly.

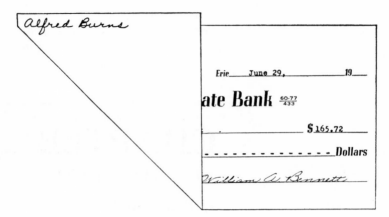

An Indorsed Check Folded to Show the Position of the Indorsement

KINDS OF INDORSEMENTS

The Uniform Negotiable Instruments Law lists five types of indorsements:

1. Blank indorsement
2. Special indorsement
3. Qualified indorsement
4. Restrictive indorsement
5. Conditional indorsement

(1) Blank Indorsement. As the name indicates, a *blank indorsement* is one having no words other than the name of the indorser. If the instrument is bearer paper, this type of indorsement preserves this status so that the new holder legally may pass good title to another holder without indorsing it. The one primarily liable on the instrument is bound to pay the person who presents it to him for payment on the date due. This may be a thief or other unauthorized party, provided he does not know the bearer is a thief or the finder of a lost instrument.

If the instrument is order paper, then a blank indorsement creates the same risks to the indorsee that the holder of bearer paper runs. One who steals or finds order paper cannot pass title to it without forging the payee's name. But if the order instrument is indorsed in blank before it is stolen or lost, the thief or the finder can pass good title without indorsing it. The risks involved in handling an instrument indorsed in blank can be minimized as shown in the following paragraph and in the section on special indorsements.

Indorsement in Blank

If the office force of a business firm is aware of these risks relative to bearer paper and paper indorsed in blank, the firm may be spared these risks in the following ways: (1) The drawer, if it is convenient, can be requested to make the instrument order paper from its inception; (2) If the firm becomes the indorsee by a blank indorsement, this indorsement may be converted to a special indorsement by writing over the indorser's signature these words: "Pay to the order of Mays, Inc." This in no way alters the contract between the indorser and the indorsee. The instrument cannot now be negotiated except by indorsement and delivery.

(2) Special Indorsement. A *special indorsement* designates the particular person to whom payment is to be made. The holder must indorse it before he can further negotiate it. He may, of course, indorse

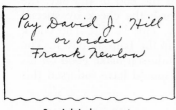

Special Indorsement

the instrument in blank, which makes it bearer paper. Each holder has the power to elect either a blank or a special indorsement. If the paper is bearer paper at the time of issuance either because it is stated to be payable to "bearer" or because the payee is fictitious, it stays bearer paper and can never be converted into an order instrument by means of a special indorsement.

If bearer paper is indorsed specially, it may nevertheless be further negotiated by delivery alone. The contract of the special indorser does not inure to the benefit of any indorser except to the one to whom he indorsed it. This is not true of an indorsement of order paper. The holder of order paper may sue all indorsers jointly, or he may sue any of them separately. If the last indorser is held liable to the holder, he in turn may seek reimbursement from any or all prior indorsers.

(3) Qualified Indorsement. A *qualified indorsement* has the effect of qualifying, that is, limiting the liability of the indorser. For example, if an agent receives checks in payment of his principal's claims which are made payable to the agent personally, the agent should and can

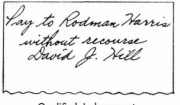

Qualified Indorsement

elect to use a qualified indorsement. This is done merely by adding to either a blank or special type of indorsement the words "without recourse" immediately before the signature. This releases the indorser from liability for payment if the instrument is not paid because of insolvency or mere refusal to pay. The indorser still warrants that the instrument is genuine, that he has good title to it, that all prior parties had capacity to contract, and that the instrument to his knowledge is valid. If the agent wishes to avoid these liabilities, his recourse is to return the check to the drawer and at the same time request that a new one be made out to the principal.

- Henderson was a special agent for the Cates Realty Company. One of his duties was to collect the rent from the occupants of rental properties handled by the Cates Realty Company. One of these tenants made a check for the rent payable to "John Henderson." When Henderson turned in his receipts at the end of the day, the accounting department asked him to indorse the check by special indorsement to the Cates Realty Company. This he did. The check was returned as the drawer had no funds in the bank to pay it. The Cates Realty Company demanded that Henderson make good on his special indorsement. This he must do. He should have indorsed this by a qualified indorsement.

(4) **Restrictive Indorsement.** A restrictive indorsement is just what the name implies. It places some restrictions upon the indorsee.

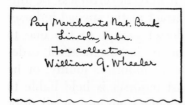

Restrictive Indorsement

It passes title to him but prohibits further negotiation of the instrument. The indorsement would then read: "Pay to Henry Felt only." This gives Felt title to the instrument, so he may assign it to someone else, but he cannot negotiate it.

The second type of restriction is far more common and quite different in effect. This type of indorsement transfers possession but not title to the instrument. It makes the indorsee merely the agent of the indorser. In this case the indorsement reads: "Pay to the Cairo National Bank for collection." This indorsement transfers possession, but not title, to the indorsee. The Cairo

National Bank is merely the agent of the indorser. When it collects the money, it holds the proceeds in trust for the indorser. If the Cairo bank finds it necessary to transfer the instrument to another bank for collection, it may do so; but the second bank is merely the sub-agent of the indorser. It, too, must hold the money in trust for the indorser. This point becomes extremely important when the collecting bank goes into receivership before the proceeds are remitted to the indorser. In that event the receiver must pay the entire proceeds to the indorser. He does not collect his pro rata share of the net assets as do the other creditors of the insolvent bank.

The Uniform Commercial Code modifies this law by specifically providing that a restrictive indorsement does not prohibit the further negotiation of the instrument.

(5) **Conditional Indorsement.** The indorser by *special indorsement* may wish to impose a condition precedent to the payment. In this event the indorsee may not receive full payment until the condition is met. The condition, of course, is binding only between the indorser and subsequent purchasers. The maker of a note or the acceptor of a draft may disregard the condition and pay the holder. Should the instrument be dishonored by nonpayment, the holder must look to the indorsers. In this event, the condition must be met before collection from the indorsers is possible. If the party primarily liable does pay the holder before the condition is met, the holder must hold the money in trust for the indorser who imposed the condition until the condition is met. The maker or the acceptor cannot be sued for wrongful payment since the indorser cannot impose an additional obligation upon the one primarily liable.

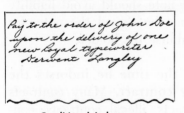

Conditional Indorsement

CONTRACT OF AN INDORSER

Although each type of indorsement is a slightly different contract, all of these contracts have many provisions in common. The Uniform Negotiable Instrument Law writes out the terms of these contracts. An indorser, merely by signing his name, indicates his intention to be bound by the terms of the contract. These terms for all indorsers are as follows:

(1) The indorser warrants that the instrument, whether a check, note, or draft, is genuine and in all respects what it purports to be. If it purports to be a check for $500 drawn by Smith on the Bonner State Bank and payable to Danner, the indorser warrants that there has been no forgery, alteration, or other irregularity in the check. He warrants that it is exactly what it appears to be. If it is not as it is warranted to be, he can be sued by the holder for breach of warranty.

(2) The indorser warrants that he has good title to the instrument. This warranty is to provide the new holder with assurance that the person indorsing it to him did not steal the instrument, or find it, or come into possession of it in any unlawful manner.

(3) The indorser warrants that all prior parties had capacity to contract. If a minor, an insane person, or other incompetent person draws a check, executes a note, or indorses any negotiable contract, he is no more liable for his act than he is on any other type of contract. He may plead his incapacity to contract as an absolute defense to his contract. The indorser by this warranty assures the holder that all parties whose names appear on the instrument were competent to contract. If the maker of a note should avoid liability on the ground of drunkenness at the time he signed the note, for example, the indorser would have to reimburse the holder.

(4) The indorser warrants that at the time he indorses the instrument, it is a valid and binding contract. Many contracts prove defective and void. Sunday contracts, illegal contracts, contracts entered into by a mistake as to the existence of the subject matter of the contract, and many others are void. A negotiable instrument given in payment of a gambling debt is no more binding on the primary party than any other type of contract for a similar payment. Also, a negotiable instrument might be valid at the time it is accepted but subsequently becomes invalid. This warranty protects the holder against any of these infirmities in the contract.

(5) The indorser warrants that the instrument will be paid upon proper presentment at the proper time and place. This is the key warranty. Without it few people would be willing to accept negotiable contracts by indorsement because they would not be much better off than an assignee.

Two of the five types of indorsements set out above do not unqualifiedly and unconditionally make warranty number five. A qualified indorser warrants that he will make good on the instrument if it is not paid by the one primarily liable for any one of the first four warranties. If it is dishonored for nonpayment merely because the one primarily liable cannot pay even though he owes it, then the qualified indorser does not warrant he will pay it. If the failure to pay is due to any one of the conditions set out in the first four warranties, then the qualified indorser does bind himself to make good on his indorsement.

Also, one who makes a conditional indorsement does not make warranty number five without reservation. The indorsee in a conditional indorsement must meet the conditions set out before he can look to the indorser for reimbursement.

OBLIGATION OF NEGOTIATOR OF BEARER PAPER

Bearer paper need not be indorsed when negotiated. Mere delivery passes title. One who negotiates a bearer instrument by delivery alone does not guarantee payment, but he is liable to his immediate purchaser only as a warrantor of the genuineness of the instrument, of his title to it, of the capacity of prior parties, and of its validity so far as he knows. These warranties are the same as those made by a qualified indorser, except that the warranties of the qualified indorser extend to all subsequent holders, not just to the immediate purchaser. But since negotiable instruments are not legal tender, no one is under any obligation to accept bearer paper without an indorsement. By requiring an indorsement even though not necessary to pass title, the holder protects himself by requiring the one who wishes to negotiate it to assume all the obligations of an indorser by indorsement.

- Sands was the maker of a bearer negotiable note which he delivered to Holt. Subsequently, Burks became the holder with the note showing these indorsements:

  Dorsey Harber
  Wayne Finley

Holt had passed title to the note by mere delivery to Weston Dupree, and Dupree had delivered to Harber without indorsement. The maker was insolvent and unable to pay the note when it fell due. Burks can look only to Finley for reimbursement, and Finley can look to Harber. Harber, on the other hand, had received it from Dupree without indorsement, so he can look only to the maker.

The Uniform Commercial Code introduces one entirely new provision relative to indorsements. If the indorser adds to his indorsement the words "payment guaranteed," then any holder upon default by the one primarily liable may proceed against the indorser without resort to any other party. If the indorser adds the words "collection guaranteed" to his indorsement, then the holder cannot proceed against the indorser until he has brought suit against the one primarily liable and has been unable to collect on the judgment.

DISCHARGE OF THE OBLIGATION

Negotiable instruments may be discharged by payment, by cancellation, or by alteration. Payment at or after the date of the maturity of the instrument by the party who is primarily liable constitutes proper payment. Cancellation consists of any act that indicates the intention to cancel the instrument. A cancellation is not effective, however, when it is made unintentionally or by mistake. A party to a negotiable instrument is discharged from liability if the instrument is materially altered without his consent. If such an instrument gets into the hands of a holder in due course, however, the holder in due course may collect according to the original terms of the instrument, and not according to its altered terms.

- Hale drew a check payable to Shane in the amount of $500. Shane cleverly altered the check to $2,500 and negotiated it to McFain, an innocent purchaser who had no knowledge of the alteration. The bank refused to pay the check. McFain can recover $500 from Hale since this was the original amount of the check. He could then sue Shane for the $2,000.

The obligations of the parties may be discharged in other ways, just as in the case of a simple contract. For example, the parties will be discharged from liability if they have been judicially declared bankrupt or if there has been the necessary lapse of time provided by a statute of limitations.

Frequently a negotiable instrument is lost or accidentally destroyed. This does not discharge the obligation. The party obligated to pay it has a right to demand the instrument's return if this is possible. If this cannot be done, then he has a right to demand security from the holder adequate to protect the payer from having to pay the instrument a second time. The security usually takes the form of an indemnity bond.

QUESTIONS

1. What is negotiation?
2. How may bearer instruments be negotiated?
3. Where should one indorse a negotiable instrument?
4. Name five kinds of indorsements and give an example of the proper use of each one.
5. Why is it usually undesirable to indorse a check in blank?
6. If an instrument that is payable to "bearer" is indorsed by special indorsement, what must the second holder do in order to pass title to it?
7. If a check is made payable to John Atkins, agent for the Branch Insurance Agency, when it should have been made payable to the agency, how should John indorse it when he delivers it to the agency? Why?
8. How may one indorse a check so that the indorsee cannot negotiate it?
9. Give an illustration of the proper use of a qualified indorsement.
10. If one indorses a check by a conditional indorsement and the bank pays it without requiring the indorsee to meet the conditions, is the bank liable to the indorser?
11. If one loses a negotiable instrument, is there any way he can collect it?
12. If bearer paper is indorsed by special indorsement, may the indorsee pass good title to it by delivery alone?

CASE PROBLEMS

1. Darrow was a collector for the Beusse Loan and Investment Company. One borrower paid his note of $502.84 by check made payable to Darrow. At the end of the day Darrow turned in his collections, and the bookkeeper discovered the check had been erroneously made payable to Darrow. He suggested that Darrow indorse it by special indorsement, and this Darrow did. The check proved to be a bad check, and Darrow was required to make the check good. What knowledge of law set out in this chapter would have helped Darrow avoid this loss?

2. Wood was the payee of a time draft for $3,200. He mailed the draft to James Hill for collection. Wood indorsed the draft as follows: "Pay to the order of James Hill only." Hill collected the draft and placed the $3,200 in his personal checking account and mailed his personal check to Wood. Hill owed the bank a note for $5,000 that was past due. It refused to honor any more checks on Hill's account and applied his balance to the note. Indicate specifically what errors Wood committed.

3. Richards owed Griffith $4,000. He executed a negotiable note as follows: "Ninety days after date I promise to pay to Bearer $4,000 with 6% interest from date.

Signed: E. J. Richards

This note was lost by Griffith. The finder transferred it by delivery alone to Hopkins. Griffith ordered Richards not to pay the note to Hopkins, but

Richards ignored this order and paid it anyway. May Griffith compel Richards to pay him? What could Griffith have done to avoid this loss?

4. Fortson was the payee of a check for $802.63. He transferred it to Samuel for value and indorsed it as follows: "Pay to the order of A. Samuel without recourse."

Signed: Ben Fortson

The drawer of the check stopped payment on the check because he was a minor and wished to disaffirm his contract. Samuel demanded that Fortson reimburse him for the check. Must he do so?

5. Marsh purchased a hi-fi set from Comer and paid for it by giving Comer a ninety-day note for $400. When the note came due and Marsh wished to pay, Comer claimed he had accidentally burned it up but offered to give Marsh a written receipt certifying it had been paid in full. Marsh agreed to accept this receipt. The next day Stacy presented the note to Marsh and demanded payment. Marsh produced his receipt, but Stacy contended this receipt did not affect his right to collect. Was Stacey right in his contention?

6. Paul Chapman, as the administrator of his uncle's estate, was required to collect all debts due the estate. One of the estate's debtors paid his debt of $1,100 by check made payable to Paul Chapman. Chapman indorsed this check as follows: "Pay to the order of Paul Chapman, Administrator of John Chapman's Estate. Paul Chapman." This check was never paid because the drawer had insufficient funds in the bank. Later demand was made on Paul Chapman that he pay this $1,100 out of his personal funds because of his special indorsement. Was he personally liable for it?

7. McDonald was the payee of a note for $3,500, signed by Garrard. He entered into a contract with Bell which provided that Bell was to accept the note by assignment so that McDonald would not be liable as an indorser. This was agreeable to Bell, but they were uncertain how to make the assignment. They decided to write on the note these words: "I hereby assign all my rights and interest in this note to John Bell. (Signed) Alex Mc-Donald." Later Bell transferred the note by blank indorsement to Saye. The note was not paid by Garrard, and Saye sued McDonald as an indorser. He claimed he was only an assignor and therefore not liable under the warranties of an indorser. Was this contention correct?

8. Inez Katz owned and operated the Thrift Dress Shop, an exclusive dress shop. She sold an expensive gown to Mrs. Gene Shopen who paid for it by drawing a sight draft on Josiah Shopen for $1,100. Miss Katz sent this sight draft to Herman Shobelt, an attorney, for presentment for collection. She indorsed it as follows: "Pay to the order of Herman Shobelt. (Signed) Inez Katz." Shobelt collected the draft, but before he remitted the proceeds to Miss Katz, he was declared bankrupt. He had deposited the money in a special account, intending to remit by check from this special account. The question arose as to whether or not this $1,100 was a part of Shobelt's estate to be taken over by the receiver in bankruptcy. What do you think?

CHAPTER 26

HOLDERS IN DUE COURSE

HOLDERS IN DUE COURSE

Negotiable instruments would have no advantage over ordinary contracts if the remote parties could not be given immunity against many of the defenses which might be made against simple contracts. To enjoy this immunity, the holder of a negotiable instrument must be a *holder in due course*. The term "innocent purchaser" is also used to describe a person who is a holder in due course. Neither term can be used to describe any one but the holder of a negotiable instrument who has obtained it under these conditions:

1. The instrument must be complete and regular on its face.
2. It must not be past due at the time of the negotiation.
3. The holder must take the instrument in good faith and for value.
4. At the time the instrument is negotiated, the holder must have no notice of any infirmity in the instrument or any defect in the title of the person who negotiated it.

(1) **Instrument Regular on Its Face.** Checks, notes, and drafts, the most common types of negotiable paper, are usually printed with blank spaces that are to be filled in by the person executing them. The instruments are regular when these spaces have been filled in properly and the instrument is signed. Any material deviation from this regular practice makes the instrument irregular, and the holder takes it subject to all the defenses which the maker or acceptor can make against the original holder. If he has no defenses, the irregularity does not necessarily render the contract unenforceable.

Blank notes generally have a space for the rate of interest. If a note is noninterest bearing, this space could be crossed out with x's. If this is done, and then "8%" is later written over the "x's," the note is not regular, and the holder cannot be considered innocent. He is charged with notice that this may have been done subsequent to the delivery. If it later develops that the maker wrote the "8%" before delivering it, the contract is enforceable if there are no other defenses. The holder, however, cannot enjoy the privileges of an innocent purchaser. The irregularity is a warning signal to a prospective purchaser. It he does not heed it, he cannot claim immunity to any defenses.

- Magee was the payee of a time draft payable 60 days after date and accepted by Homer. Magee indorsed this draft before it was due for value to Lester. The time was written: $\frac{"90}{60}$ days after $\frac{\text{sight."}}{\text{date}}$
  The drawee refused to pay the draft when it came due, claiming he had already paid it to Magee. If Lester is an innocent purchaser, then Homer cannot raise the defense of payment against him. If he is not an innocent purchaser, the defense of payment is just as good against Lester as it is against Magee. Lester's status hinges on whether or not this draft is "complete and regular on its face." It is complete, but it is not regular. Lester is not an innocent purchaser.

(2) Instrument Not Past Due. One who takes an instrument that is past due cannot be an innocent purchaser. If it is due and unpaid, there must be a reason. It is the duty of the prospective purchaser to ascertain that reason. If he fails or neglects to do so, he forfeits the privileges of a holder in due course. If the note is dated and payable in a fixed number of days or months, the instrument itself indicates whether or not it is past due.

If the instrument is transferred on the date of maturity, it is not past due but would be overdue on the day following the due date. If it is payable on demand, it is due within a reasonable time after it is issued. What is a reasonable time "depends upon the nature of the instrument, the usage of trade or business with respect to such instruments, and the facts of the particular case." For example, if a demand note is given in temporary settlement for merchandise purchased for which the usual terms are 2/10, n/60, a reasonable time would be approximately sixty days.

(3) For Value. This requirement does not mean that one must pay full value for a negotiable instrument in order to be a holder in due course. As a matter of fact, one who purchases a negotiable contract at a discount can qualify as a holder in due course. The law states that he must take it "for value and in good faith." If the instrument is offered at an exorbitant discount, that fact may be evidence that the purchaser did not buy it in good faith. It is the lack of good faith that destroys one's status as a holder in due course, not the amount of the discount.

If the payee of a negotiable instrument for $3,000 offered to transfer it for a consideration of $2,700, and the purchaser had no other reason to suspect any infirmity in the instrument, he can qualify as a holder in due course. He took the instrument in good faith. If, on the other hand, the holder had offered to discount the note $1,000, the purchaser could not take it in good faith because he should suspect that there is some fatal infirmity in the contract because of the large discount.

As so often occurs, the purchaser pays for the instrument in cash and other property. The discount is concealed in the inflated value placed on the property taken in payment. The test always is: Were there any circumstances that should have warned a prudent man that the instrument was not genuine and in all respects what it purported to be? If there were, the purchaser did not take it in good faith.

The Uniform Commercial Code rewords these rules slightly, but the legal effect remains the same. The Code eliminates the concept of consideration in defining value. One who takes a negotiable instrument as a gift cannot qualify as an innocent purchaser.

- Smallwood executed a ninety-day note for $5,000 in favor of Greene. The note was in payment of a bookkeeping machine which Greene had guaranteed would save the services of one bookkeeper. This guarantee was absolutely false. Greene, knowing he could not collect because of this breach of warranty, sold the note before maturity to Hargrove for $3,000 cash and $2,000 worth of stock, par value, in a Canadian uranium mine. The stock at the time had no known market value and later proved to be absolutely worthless. When Hargrove demanded payment on the note, Smallwood refused to pay because of the breach of warranty. The sole question is whether or not Hargrove is an innocent purchaser, that is, did he take it for value and in good faith?

(4) No Knowledge of any Infirmity in the Instrument. When one takes a negotiable instrument by negotiation, to obtain the rights of an innocent purchaser he must have no knowledge of any infirmity in the instrument. As between the primary parties on a negotiable instrument, any act, such as fraud, duress, mistake, illegality, which would make any other type of contract either void or voidable will have the same effect on a negotiable instrument. Many of these defects, as will be seen in the next chapter, are eliminated as defenses if the instrument is negotiated to an innocent purchaser. To qualify as an innocent purchaser one must have no knowledge either directly or indirectly that any of these defects in the contract exist. The following case illustrates this point:

> ▪ Sellers and Bell were engineers for an oil prospecting company. Their occupation was well known by Harley. Sellers told Harley they had discovered unmistakable signs of oil on a tract of land Sellers owned. He offered the land to Harley for $20,000. If there was no oil on it, its true value was $1,000. Bell knew Sellers was misrepresenting the facts to Harley although he took no part in the deal. Harley bought the land, giving Sellers $5,000 in cash and a 12-month negotiable note for $15,000. Sellers immediately sold the note to Bell for $14,000. The question is whether or not Bell can qualify as an innocent purchaser. He cannot because he knew at the time the note was negotiated to him that Harley, the maker, would very likely plead fraud as a defense to the note.

The first holder in due course brings into operation for the first time all the protections which the law has placed around negotiable instruments. When these protections once accrue, they are not easily lost. Consequently, a subsequent holder may avail himself of them even though he himself is not a holder in due course. For example, Adams, without consideration, gives Bryce a negotiable note due in sixty days. Before maturity Bryce indorses it to Cordell under conditions which make Cordell a holder in due course. Ten days after maturity Cordell sells the note to Gray, but Gray is not a holder in due course since he did not obtain the note before maturity. If Gray is not a party to any wrongdoing or illegality affecting this instrument, he acquires all the rights of a holder in due course. This is true because Cordell had these rights, and when Cordell sold the note to Gray, he sold all of his rights, which include the right to collect the amount due and the right to be free from the defense of no consideration.

DUTIES OF THE HOLDER

As has been pointed out before, the prime significance of the Uniform Negotiable Instruments Law is that the purchaser of a negotiable instrument may obtain rights greater than the payee had. Even if he gets no greater rights, he may, and in most cases does, obtain greater advantages.

Stevens purchases an automobile from Griffin for $900 and gives in payment this note: "Sixty days after date I promise to pay Archibald Griffin or order $900. Harold Stevens." What are Griffin's rights? If there was no fraud in the transaction or other infirmity in the contract, Griffin's simple right is to collect $900 on the due date of the note. Like all property rights this one may be sold. If Griffin, the payee, sells his rights to Comer, a holder in due course, does Comer obtain rights superior to Griffin? If Griffin's rights were perfect, Comer could obtain no greater rights. If Griffin, in order to sell the car, had made fraudulent representations about it, his right to collect $900 is reduced by the amount of damages which Stevens sustained. In this case Comer does get greater rights than Griffin had.

Under all circumstances Comer would obtain greater advantages than Griffin had. In order to collect the $900, Griffin could look only to Stevens. If Stevens is insolvent and unable to pay, Griffin's rights may prove to be worthless. Comer, however, has the right to look to both Stevens and Griffin for payment. His chances of collecting are twice as great as Griffin's, but through ignorance or lack of diligence, Comer may lose a substantial part of these rights.

The holder of a negotiable instrument has duties to perform in order to preserve his rights as an innocent purchaser:

(1) He must present a bill of exchange for acceptance when its form requires an acceptance.

(2) He must present an accepted bill of exchange, a bill of exchange that need not be accepted, such as a sight draft or check, and a note for payment

(3) If any of these contracts are dishonored either by nonacceptance or nonpayment, the holder must notify all indorsers and the drawer of bills of exchange of that dishonor.

The presentment of the instrument and the notice of dishonor must both be done at the proper time, at the proper place, and in the proper manner.

PROPER PRESENTMENT FOR ACCEPTANCE

Not all drafts must be presented for acceptance, but all of them, except sight drafts, should be presented for acceptance. Presentment for acceptance must be made:

(1) When the draft is made payable a certain number of days after sight

(2) When the draft is made payable at some place other than the drawee's place of business or residence

(3) When the draft expressly stipulates that it must be presented for acceptance

The presentment for acceptance in these cases must be made at the proper time, which is a reasonable time after the bill is drawn. The courts interpret what constitutes a reasonable time depending on the circumstances in each particular case. Prudence, not the law, requires that the presentment be made at the next business day after the bill is received by the payee.

The presentment for acceptance must be made at the proper place, which is the drawee's place of business or his residence. If he cannot be found there, it may be presented anywhere he can be found. If he cannot be located with reasonable diligence, the failure to present it does not release the drawer and the indorsers, if any.

The bill must be presented by the payee or his agent to the drawee, his agent, or anyone else having the power to accept. If the drawee, for example, is dead, the administrator of his estate has the power to accept the bill.

The holder has the responsibility of determining whether or not the one who accepts as the agent of the drawee has the authority to accept. If there is any doubt about his authority and this doubt cannot be resolved, the only safe course is to notify the drawer that the draft has been dishonored.

PROPER PRESENTMENT FOR PAYMENT

All bills of exchange and all notes must be presented for payment. The law is even more exacting in this type of presentment than in the presentment for acceptance. This presentment must be made at the proper time, at the proper place, and in the proper manner.

The presentment for acceptance must be made within a reasonable time, but the presentment for payment must be made on the due date. It must not be done one day early nor one day late. If the due date falls on Sunday or a holiday, the presentment for payment must be made the following day. It not only must be made on that day, but it must be made during reasonable hours of that day. If the payer is a business firm, this will be during business hours.

Naturally sight drafts, checks, and demand notes do not have a due date. For demand notes the due date is a reasonable time after the date of issue. For all other instruments the presentment for payment must be made within a reasonable time after the last negotiation.

The presentment for payment must be made at the proper place. If a place of payment is stated in the instrument, presentment must be made at that place. If no place of payment is stipulated in the instrument, it must be presented at the payer's place of business if he has one. If he has no place of business, it may be presented anywhere he can be found.

The presentment for payment must be made in the proper manner. This means that the holder or his agent must present the instrument in person to the proper party. The holder must have the instrument in his possession and be able and willing to cancel it and to return it when payment is received.

WHEN PRESENTMENT FOR ACCEPTANCE OR PAYMENT IS EXCUSED

Sometimes the presentment for acceptance may be either delayed or excused. If the payee of a time draft, for example, learns before presentment that the drawee will not accept the draft, he may treat this knowledge as a dishonor and notify the drawer accordingly. The presentment for payment may be waived. This is usually done by inserting a provision in the instrument itself to this effect. If the drawee of a draft or the maker of a note cannot be located with reasonable diligence, either presentment for acceptance or presentment for payment may be excused or delayed. Mere inconvenience will not excuse a holder from presenting a negotiable instrument for payment at the proper time. Failure must be due to conditions beyond the holder's control.

EFFECTS OF A FAILURE TO PRESENT FOR ACCEPTANCE OR PAYMENT

The drawer of a draft is by his act assigning an amount of money due him to a payee in payment of a debt due the payee, unless the drawer and the payee is the same person, or the payee is the agent of the drawer. In these latter two instances the draft is a collection technique. When the draft is in payment of a debt, the presentment for acceptance is to notify the drawee that an assignment of the funds due the drawer has been made. Thereafter the drawee cannot safely pay the drawer. The drawer, however, remains fully liable to the payee until the draft is paid by the drawee if the payee properly presents the draft for acceptance and gives proper notice of dishonor if it is not accepted. The effect of a failure to present a draft for acceptance is to release the drawer from all liability to the payee or holder. If the instrument is a check, a failure to present it properly by the holder releases all indorsers absolutely, and it releases the drawer to the extent of his loss by reason of the improper presentment for payment.

The party primarily liable on a draft is the drawee and on a note, the maker. A failure to present a negotiable instrument for payment to the party primarily liable has no effect on his liability. The only exception to this rule is that when a draft or note is made payable at a particular place, a failure to present it properly at this place releases the party primarily liable from any payment of interest after the due date, provided he was able and willing to make payment on that date.

NOTICE OF DISHONOR

If a negotiable instrument has been dishonored by nonacceptance or nonpayment, *notice of* this *dishonor* must be given to the drawer and to each indorser. The drawer or any indorser who has not been given notice will be discharged from liability. Notice is not required if the instrument is nonnegotiable.

The notice of dishonor for domestic instruments is not required to be in any special form; it may be in writing or it may be oral. The only requirement is that the notice must identify the instrument sufficiently and must indicate that it has been dishonored.

The notice of dishonor must be given within a reasonable time. It may be given personally or by mail. If the parties live in the same place, notice of dishonor must be given before the end of the day after the day of dishonor. When the parties live in different places, notice by mail must ordinarily be posted not later than the day after the day of dishonor. Proper mailing of the notice constitutes due notice, even if the notice is lost in the mail.

> ■ Dodd was the holder of a draft drawn by Duncan and payable to Dennis. Dennis has indorsed the draft to Dodd by a special indorsement. The draft was properly presented for payment on the due date, and it was dishonored. The draft was a domestic bill. On the following day Dodd called Duncan by long-distance telephone,

identified the draft, and informed him that it had been dishonored. Two days later he wired Dennis and notified him of the dishonor. Both tried to avoid liability on the grounds of improper notice of dishonor. Dennis is correct in his contention, but Duncan is not. The forms of the notices are correct since this is a domestic bill of exchange, but Dodd waited too long to notify Dennis and thus released him from all liability on his indorsement.

PROTEST

Notice of dishonor must sometimes be in the form of a protest. A *protest* is a formal declaration made in writing by a notary public in behalf of the holder of a negotiable instrument, attesting that it has been presented for acceptance or payment and that acceptance or payment was refused. The certificate of protest, signed and sealed by the notary, is accepted as evidence of the facts of presentment, demand, nonacceptance or nonpayment, and notice of dishonor. A protest must ordinarily be made on the day and at the place of dishonor.

Any negotiable instrument may be protested at the election of the holder. Although it is not necessary to protest inland or domestic bills of exchange, such bills may be protested. Foreign bills of exchange (including checks), however, must be protested for nonacceptance or nonpayment. If a foreign bill is not protested, the drawer and the indorsers will be discharged from liability for payment.

The certificate of protest must be attached to the protested instrument or must contain a copy of the instrument. It must specify:

(1) The time and the place of presentment

(2) The fact that presentment was made and the manner in which it was made

(3) The demand made and the answer given, or the fact that the maker or the acceptor could not be found

(4) The cause of or the reason for the protest

NOTICE OF PROTEST

Notice of the protest must be given to the parties not later than the day following the protest. No special form of notice is necessary. Any notice that informs the parties of the demand and the nonacceptance or the nonpayment is sufficient. The drawer or the indorser to whom notice of the protest is not given is ordinarily discharged from liability unless he has waived notice of protest.

The State of SOUTH CAROLINA RICHLAND **County, ss.**

Columbia, June 1, 19

Take Notice, *that a* check *for* $ 25.88

dated May 28, 19

drawn by M. R. French

in favor of L. C. Baldwin

on the South Carolina National Bank

~~*accepted by*~~

indorsed by L. C. Baldwin and the Peoples First National Bank

was this day presented for payment *which was refused, and therefore was this*

day Protested, by the undersigned Notary Public, for non payment

The holder therefore looks to you for payment thereof, together with interest, damages,

costs, etc., you being payee *thereof.*

H. J. Stevenson

To L. C. Baldwin, Charleston, S. Car. *Notary Public*

Certificate of Protest

It should be remembered, however, that the instrument may contain a clause in which the drawer and the indorsers waive presentment, notice of dishonor, protest, and notice of protest.

The Uniform Commercial Code changes the Uniform Negotiable Instruments Law slightly with reference to the time of the notice. The Code provides that the notice of dishonor must be given not later than midnight of the third business day after dishonor or receipt of notice of dishonor. The Code eliminates the term "reasonable time" which courts tended to interpret to be the next business day after dishonor or notice of dishonor.

QUESTIONS

1. Who is a holder in due course?
2. On a draft the term "60 days" is marked out and over it is written, "90 days." Can one become a holder in due course of this draft? Why?
3. When is a "demand note" past due?
4. What are the duties of a holder of a negotiable instrument?
5. When should a draft be presented for acceptance?
6. How long after a negotiable instrument has been dishonored either by nonacceptance or nonpayment does the holder have to notify the indorsers of the dishonor?
7. In what manner must the notice of dishonor be given?
8. What is the effect of a failure of an indorser to receive notice of dishonor?

9. What must a certificate of protest specify?
10. What procedure should be followed by the holder after a certificate of protest has been completed?

CASE PROBLEMS

1. Lowe, manager for the Harper Building Supplies Corporation, received the following draft from Agnew, a customer, in payment of an account.

July 27, 19—

Two months after date pay to the order of J. W. Agnew $2,104.52 and charge to the account of

Robert E. Finch

To: H. V. Kincaid
Memphis, Tenn.

This draft had been duly presented to Kincaid and accepted by him. It was indorsed by Agnew on September 26. Lowe presented this draft for payment the next day, and payment was refused. Lowe immediately notified Agnew and Finch of the dishonor. Both Agnew and Finch denied any liability on the instrument, pleading improper presentment for payment. Was their defense valid?

2. Miss Holmes, secretary to the president of Heintz, Inc., was sent to the office of the Pablo Ranch to present a draft drawn by the Dayton Boat Company for acceptance. When she arrived, the owner was not in the office. His secretary agreed to accept the draft since the accounts payable ledger indicated the amount was owed. When the draft came due, the owner of the Pablo Ranch refused to pay it, claiming his secretary had no right to accept it. Heintz, Inc., then sued the Dayton Boat Company who denied liability because it had not been properly notified of the dishonor. Is this contention correct?

3. The Daytona Yacht Club was the indorsee of a negotiable note for $5,000 signed by Clarke as maker and indorsed by Courts. The note had this clause in it: "Payable at the Second National Bank of Daytona." On the due date, the holder presented the note for payment at the office of Clarke. He refused to pay, claiming he was defrauded by the payee. The Daytona Yacht Club notified Courts immediately of dishonor. Both Clarke and Courts now refuse to pay, claiming improper presentment for payment. Is either or both right in this contention?

4. Range was the indorsee on a check drawn by A. Dince of Atlanta, Georgia, on a Dallas, Texas, bank, and payable to Carson of Houston. The check was dishonored on Monday, July 3. On July 5 Range sent Carson a registered letter notifying him of the dishonor. Carson now denies liability on his indorsement, claiming he was not notified at the proper time and in the proper manner. Was he?

5. Leeburn obtained title to a note by indorsement from Terry. The time of the note had been clearly changed from 120 days to 60 days. Jones, the

maker, had really made this change before he signed the note, but Leeburn did not know this at the time. The maker refused to pay the note on the due date because he had returned the merchandise for which the note had been given in payment. If Leeburn is an innocent purchaser, the maker could not deny liability to Leeburn for this reason. Was Leeburn an innocent purchaser?

6. Tillman was the indorsee of a draft for $3,264.80 drawn by Stafford and payable to Kent. Tillman purchased the draft from Kent ten days before it was due for $2,800. Kent claimed he was desperate for cash and for that reason was offering Tillman a bargain. The drawee had paid the draft in advance, and Kent had promised to mail it to him. He refused to pay Tillman. For Tillman to be able to collect this draft from the drawee, he must qualify as an innocent purchaser. Can he?

7. Miss Drew, secretary to the Barber Equipment Company, was sent to the office of the Bates Construction Company to collect a draft for $7,500, due that day. When she arrived at the office, she was told that Mr. Barber, the only man in the firm who had the authority to pay it, was out of town. The draft had these words on it, "Payable at the First National Bank of Dublin." Ten days later Miss Drew returned to the office and presented the draft to Mr. Barber for payment. He failed to pay it because of financial embarrassment. Six months later, when he was sued on the draft, he denied liability for both principal and interest, claiming the draft was not properly presented for payment. Was he liable for both the principal and the interest from the due date of the draft?

8. The Sparks Cordage Company sold merchandise to Sanderson amounting to $475. The terms called for a 60-day trade acceptance with bill of lading attached. After the merchandise was shipped, a 60-day trade acceptance was drawn, the bill of lading was attached, and the two sent to the Tri-State Bank with instructions to deliver the bill of lading to Sanderson upon his acceptance of the trade acceptance. When the bank presented the trade acceptance, Sanderson claimed the amount should have been only $425 and wanted to qualify his acceptance so as to obligate himself only for this amount. The bank claimed such a qualified acceptance was in reality a dishonor of the bill and refused to deliver to him the bill of lading. Was the bank correct in its action?

CHAPTER 27

DEFENSES

WHO MAY MAKE A DEFENSE?

There are both immediate and remote parties to negotiable instruments. The immediate parties to a note are the maker and the payee, and the remote parties are the indorsers. All the indorsers are liable on the note, and all of them may make a defense against paying it. In the case of a draft, the drawer, the payee, and the drawee, who later becomes the acceptor if it is a time draft, are the immediate parties. When the draft is accepted, the drawer assumes the legal status of an indorser if the draft is payable to a third party. The maker of a note or the drawee or acceptor of a draft is the one from whom the holder will first demand payment. If he refuses, the holder demands payment from one of the indorsers. We will discuss first the defenses which the maker or the acceptor may make against the holder.

PERSONAL DEFENSES AND REAL DEFENSES

The defenses which the maker or the acceptor may make against the holder are classed as personal and real. If the holder is not an innocent purchaser or a holder in due course, either a real or a personal defense will bar recovery. He has no more privileges or immunities than the original payee. If he is a holder in due course or if he derives his title through a holder in due course, however, personal defenses are of no avail against him. He takes the instrument free from all personal defenses. The real defenses, however, are good against the whole world. If established, they are a complete bar to recovery regardless of one's status as a holder in due course.

The Uniform Commercial Code eliminates the terms "personal" and "real" defenses but does not change the law in any way relative to these defenses.

PERSONAL DEFENSES

Personal defenses are good against all holders except holders in due course. The one thing which makes this group of defenses peculiar to negotiable instruments is that they will not suffice to bar recovery even if true when made against an innocent purchaser. We have already discussed most of them in preceding chapters and found that any one of them renders a contract other than a negotiable instrument either void or voidable. It is this feature which gives negotiable instruments their privileged status among all other contracts. There are three links in the chain: the instrument must be negotiable; the holder must be an innocent purchaser; the defense must be personal. The common personal defenses are:

1. Duress
2. Undue influence
3. Misrepresentation
4. Nondelivery of a completed instrument
5. Fraud
6. Lack of consideration
7. Payment or part payment
8. Setoff and counterclaim

(1) **Duress.** Duress, as explained in Chapter 5, is the act of obtaining one's consent to a contract by force or by the threat of force.

(2) **Undue Influence.** Undue influence, as explained in Chapter 5, is a form of mental coercion or pressure brought to bear through the close personal relationship existing between the contracting parties.

(3) **Misrepresentation.** *Misrepresentation* is an innocent misstatement or concealment of a material fact.

(4) **Nondelivery of a Completed Instrument.** If an instrument is stolen, lost, or otherwise wrongfully taken after it is completely filled out but before it is delivered by the maker or the drawer, delivery is not considered to have been made. Nondelivery is a personal

defense, and the instrument is therefore collectible in the hands of a holder in due course but not in the hands of others.

(5) Fraud. Fraud relating to the formation of a negotiable instrument is a personal defense not good against a holder in due course.

- Crane offered to sell Yardley his car for $500 and stated that the car just recently had a complete overhauling of the engine and transmission. Yardley, relying upon this false statement, accepted the offer to his detriment. Crane suggested that Yardley sign a memorandum of the agreement pending final consummation of the sale. Crane, by trickery, substituted a negotiable note for $1,000 which Yardley signs.

  There was fraud in the sale which preceded the signing of the instrument. This type of fraud is a personal defense and is of no avail against a holder in due course.

We shall observe later that fraud which results in a mistake as to the nature of the agreement signed renders the agreement void and that such a defense is therefore valid against all holders. This type of fraud is covered under (4) of Real Defenses, page 251.

(6) Lack of Consideration. Negotiable instruments, like all other contracts, must be supported by a consideration. In the hands of a holder in due course, consideration is presumptive. A note made as a gift cannot be collected by court action by the original holder, but a holder in due course can collect it.

(7) Payment or Part Payment. If the maker of a note or the drawee of a draft pays the full amount of the instrument, or any part of it, before maturity and, because of carelessness or neglect, fails to see that the proper notation is made on the instrument, he may be compelled to pay the instrument a second time. If the instrument is acquired by a holder in due course after such a payment without the proper notation having been made, the defense of payment will not be good against that holder. A receipt for the payment will not be sufficient.

- Mitchell was the drawee of a ninety-day draft for $2,000, payable to Aldredge. Mitchell sold Aldredge a trailer truck for $7,200, but allowed him credit for the $2,000 even though the draft was not yet due for thirty days. Aldredge said, "I'll mail the draft to you in a day or two." Aldredge had actually negotiated the draft to Brown, an innocent purchaser. When Brown presented it for payment on the due date, Mitchell denied liability because he had already paid it through a credit allowance. The court ruled he had to pay Brown and then seek reimbursement from Aldredge. Payment is a personal defense and cannot be used against an innocent purchaser.

(8) Setoff and Counterclaim. If the maker of a note or the acceptor of a draft given for the purchase of merchandise later returns a part of the merchandise, he has a right of setoff against the seller. The right is lost, however, if the seller transfers the instrument to a holder in due course.

- Tonne buys merchandise from Larson valued at $500 and later sells Larson merchandise valued at $100. He has a counterclaim against Larson for $100. If Tonne gave Larson a negotiable note for $500 and Larson transferred it to a holder in due course, Tonne could not make his counterclaim against the holder in due course.

REAL DEFENSES

Real defenses are defenses of a somewhat unusual character that concern not the merits of the transaction, but rather the nature of the instrument itself. They are sometimes called absolute defenses because they are good against even a holder in due course. They are:

1. Personal incapacity to make an enforceable contract
2. Illegality
3. Forgery and alteration
4. Fraud in the inception
5. Lapse of time under a statute of limitations
6. Nondelivery of an incompleted instrument
7. Usury
8. Mistakes which render a contract void

(1) Personal Incapacity to Make an Enforceable Contract. This defense relates to minors, insane persons, and all other persons legally incompetent to contract.

(2) Illegality. If statutes have declared certain instruments void, no enforceable rights under them can be acquired against the maker, drawer, or acceptor. This rule applies especially when statutes have declared void negotiable instruments given in payment of gambling transactions. General indorsers of such instruments must pay damages for breach of the warranty of validity.

(3) Forgery and Alteration. A forgery is an absolute defense. It is quite evident that a person cannot be compelled to pay a negotiable instrument that he did not sign. If a material alteration has been made in a negotiable instrument, the party who made the alteration will not be permitted to recover. A holder in due course who received the instrument after it was altered may recover the amount due on the original instrument. A material alteration is one that affects:

(a) The sum payable, either principal or interest
(b) The time, the place, or the date of payment
(c) The number or the relationship of the parties

In the case of both forgery and alteration, the bank is liable to the drawer of checks if through the bank's negligence the forgery or alteration is not detected. In the absence of negligence, the depositor sustains the loss. Even when the bank is negligent, the depositor must notify the bank within a reasonable time after the forgery or alteration is discovered. What is a reasonable time is fixed by statute in many states and by court decisions in others. The time varies from two months to one year.

(4) Fraud in the Inception. Fraud in the inception, which is one of the mistakes that render an agreement void, is a real defense. It exists when a person is induced by fraud, without negligence on his part, to sign a negotiable instrument that he believes is an instrument of some other character. Since the party primarily liable has no intention of creating a negotiable instrument, none is created.

- Westfall agreed to sign a contract for the purchase of a car from Robinson. Robinson used a trick type of paper which contained the correct terms of the contract to sell. The paper was such that when the true contract was lifted up, it revealed a note for $5,000 and the signature of Westfall was to the note, not the contract to sell. This was fraud in the inception or execution and constituted a real defense, good against the whole world, provided the maker was not negligent. When a trick or device such as this is used, there is no negligence if an ordinary person could not detect the trick.

(5) Lapse of Time under a Statute of Limitations. This defense relates to instruments that have been outlawed by the expiration of a statutory period.

(6) Nondelivery of an Incompleted Instrument. If the negotiable instrument is incomplete and is not delivered, no contract is ever formed; and even a holder in due course cannot collect. To be a real defense, the instrument must be both incomplete and nondelivered. If it is incomplete but is delivered, the defense is personal.

If the maker or the drawer of a negotiable instrument that is incomplete—that is, one on which blanks have been left—delivers it to another, he gives the holder implied authority to fill in the blanks and to complete the instrument in accordance with his directions. The signer is bound on the instrument if the blanks are filled in in accordance with the authority given. The signer is liable even though the instrument was completed in a manner contrary to his directions, however, if the instrument is negotiated to a holder in due course.

(7) Usury. *Usury* is charging an interest rate in excess of the maximum rate fixed by law. The law on this point is not uniform, but in most states usury at the inception of the note is a real defense.

(8) Mistakes Which Render a Contract Void. In Chapter 5 we discussed the mistakes that render a contract void. These mistakes made in the execution of a negotiable instrument constitute a good defense against even a holder in due course.

DEFENSES OF THE INDORSERS

The preceding discussion of defenses relates to the defenses which only the maker of a note or the acceptor of a draft may make against a holder in due course. When the holder presents a negotiable instrument for payment and is refused, his next step is to demand payment from the indorsers. He can demand payment from them, either individually or jointly, regardless of the reason which the maker or the acceptor may give for not paying it. One or more of the indorsers, however, may have a tenable defense to make.

On June 26, 19—, I promise to pay to John Doe or order $500.

Richard Roe

This note was indorsed as follows:

> *Pay to the order of Adam Smith*
> *John Doe*
> *Pay to the order of Henry Ratcliffe*
> *Adam Smith*
> *Pay to the order of Bernard Beck*
> *Henry Ratcliffe*

I IS THE INSTRUMENT NEGOTIABLE?	II IS THE PARTY A HOLDER IN DUE COURSE?	III WHAT IS THE NATURE OF THE DEFENSE?
The instrument must: 1. Be in writing and signed by the party executing it. 2. Contain either an order or a promise to pay. 3. Make the order or the promise unconditional. 4. Provide for the payment of a sum certain in money. 5. Be payable on demand or at a fixed or determinable future time.* 6. Be payable to the order of a payee or to the bearer of the instrument. 7. Designate the payee and the drawee with reasonable certainty. * On demand or at a fixed future time according to U. C. C.	1. The instrument must be complete and regular on its face. 2. It must not be past due at the time of the negotiation. 3. The holder must take the instrument in good faith and for value. 4. The holder must have no notice of any infirmity in the instrument or any defect in the title of the person who negotiated it.	PERSONAL DEFENSES: 1. Duress. 2. Undue influence. 3. Misrepresentation. 4. Nondelivery of a completed instrument. 5. Fraud. 6. Lack of consideration. 7. Payment or part payment. 8. Setoff and counterclaim. REAL DEFENSES: 1. Personal incapacity to contract. 2. Illegality. 3. Forgery and alteration. 4. Fraud in the inception. 5. Lapse of time under a statute of limitations. 6. Nondelivery of an incompleted instrument. 7. Usury. 8. Mistakes which render a contract void.

Important Features of the Law of Negotiable Instruments

On June 26, Bernard Beck presents the note to Richard Roe for payment, and payment is refused. Beck can now look to any one or all of the indorsers for payment. To do this, however, he has the note duly protested, and notice of dishonor and protest is given to each of the indorsers. Let us assume that Ratcliffe reimburses Beck. Ratcliffe then demands and receives payment from Smith; and Smith in turn goes back to Doe for reimbursement.

If Beck serves notice of dishonor, or notice of protest on Ratcliffe only, then Ratcliffe, in order to preserve his right to proceed against Smith and Doe, should give notice to them. If Beck gives the notice to Smith and Doe, Ratcliffe need not do so.

If we assume the same facts except that Beck gave Doe and Smith notice of dishonor and protest but not Ratcliffe, then Ratcliffe would be the one to plead no notice as a defense. This would be a good defense for him, but it would not release Smith and Doe from liability since their rights were in no way jeopardized by Beck's failure to give notice to Ratcliffe.

The note may provide for a waiver of presentment for payment, as well as protest and notice of dishonor and protest, by the maker and all indorsers. In such event, the law as described above would not apply.

If notice of dishonor and protest is impossible, and the holder exercises all due diligence in an effort to give notice, then a failure to receive the notice is not a good defense. The last indorser is known to the holder, but his address may be unknown. The holder may not know any of the other indorsers or their addresses. In this event he is required only to use due diligence in trying to notify them.

QUESTIONS

1. Name the primary parties in (a) a note, (b) a time draft, (c) a check.
2. State in one sentence the chief privilege of a holder in due course of a negotiable contract.
3. Is it any advantage to be the holder of a negotiable instrument even though one is not a holder in due course?
4. What is the difference between a real defense and a personal defense?
5. Name and explain three personal defenses.
6. Who may collect a completed instrument that has been lost or stolen before it is delivered?
7. Name and explain three real defenses.
8. When does fraud in the inception exist?

9. What is the effect upon a holder in due course if the instrument is incomplete and is not delivered?

10. When the holder presents a negotiable instrument for payment and it is refused, what is his next step?

CASE PROBLEMS

1. Caroline Debbs was a private secretary to General Neal W. Butter. One of her duties was to reconcile his personal bank account each month. One month three checks had been clearly altered, but she delayed reconciling his statement. She was not exactly sure how to make a reconciliation and had not been able to make one for the two preceding months. The law in her state provided that all forgeries and alterations must be reported to the bank in 60 days. She did not report them for 95 days and would not have discovered them then had it not been for the fact that General Butter gave a check in payment of his country club dues that was returned as a bad check. This mortified General Butter, and he threatened to sue the bank. Must the bank or General Butter bear this loss?

2. Stanton purchased a color television set and gave in payment a $512.60 ninety-day negotiable note. Johnson, the payee, indorsed the note by a qualified indorsement before maturity to Butler Brothers in part payment of a piano. The salesman for Butler Brothers knew Stanton well and was aware he was only eighteen years old. When the note came due, it was properly presented to Stanton for payment, and he refused on the grounds he was a minor. Johnson claims he is not liable because of his qualified indorsement. Is either Stanton or Johnson bound to pay Butler Brothers?

3. Dobbs gave his favorite daughter, Peggy, a note for $10,000, due and payable on April 1, 1950, her 21st birthday. Peggy was only sixteen at the time. She immediately negotiated the note in full payment of a sports car. When the note came due, her father refused to pay it, claiming lack of consideration. The cost of the car was $6,500. May Dobbs set up the defense of lack of consideration against the holder?

4. Landry accepted a ninety-day time draft payable to Case and drawn by Holt. Landry accepted the draft as part payment for the purchase of the D & E Cafeteria. Holt, when he sold the cafeteria to Landry, showed him his receipts averaging $30,000 a month. These records had been padded so that they materially overstated the profit prospects from the operation of the cafeteria. Case sold the draft to Bagget, an innocent purchaser. Landry refused to pay the draft, pleading fraud. Is this defense good?

5. Dewey of Salem, Oregon, purchased a boat from Morse. At the time the contract was made the boat was supposedly in a boathouse on a lake in Idaho. Dewey gave a check for $3,500 in payment of the boat. Morse indorsed the check immediately to Wayne. A few hours after the sale, Morse received a wire informing him that the boathouse and the boat were destroyed in a fire the day before the sale. When he learned of this, Dewey stopped payment on the check. Wayne sued both Morse as indorser and Dewey as the drawer. Is either or both liable?

6. Garrett gave Brooks the following note:

Date _____

Six months after date I promise to pay E. Brooks or order, $1,572.84 with ____% interest from date in payment of one lot purchased by deed of even date and his promises to clear the lot of debris.

A. Garrett

Brooks induced Garrett to give him this note through fraud. He sold the note to Smith, an innocent purchaser. Smith, in turn, sold it to Jones who knew of the fraudulent nature of the transaction, but was not himself a party to it. Jones sued Garrett for the note, and Garrett attempted to plead fraud as a defense. Would the court permit him to offer this defense?

7. Davis filled out a note payable to Mullins. It was complete in every respect except that the amount was omitted, pending a determination of the exact amount. Mullins stole the note, filled in the amount spaces for $1,000, and then sold it to Fortune, an innocent purchaser. Could Fortune collect the note from Davis?

What would your answer be if it had been completed before Mullins obtained possession of it?

8. Allen signed a note on June 1 payable on demand for $100 at 10 percent interest. The maximum rate of interest in that state is 6 percent, and the penalty for usury is rendering the whole contract null and void. On December 1, Dodge, the payee, sold the note to Ford for value. Allen refused to pay the note on demand. Ford waited one month and then notified Dodge that the note had been dishonored. He later sued both Allen and Dodge for the value of the note. What defense, if any, could either defendant offer?

SUMMARY CASES

PART 5

1. The following instrument was signed by Bushred Buek:

"For value received I promise to pay John Peron, or bearer, five hundred seventy-five dollars and fifty cents, it being for property I purchased of him in value at this date, as being payable as soon as can be realized of the above amount for the said property I have this date purchased of said Peron, which is to be paid in the course of the season now coming." The sole question to be determined was: Is this instrument negotiable in form? If you were asked to accept this instrument by indorsement in payment of merchandise, would you accept it if you knew the indorser's credit was good? (Cota v. Buek, 7 Metc. [Mass.] 588)

2. The following note was on a printed form but with the parts under-scored being in the handwriting of Cecelia W. Donohoe:

"I, Cecelia W. Donohoe, after date, August 30th, promise to pay to the order of Richard Donohoe, Thirteen Thousand and Seventy Dollars and 86/100 Dollars without defalcation, value received, with interest at 6%. Witness my hand and seal."

Hester Johnson,
Notary Public

There was no signature in the space normally reserved for the signature of the maker. The sole question to be decided here is: Was this instrument signed as required by the Uniform Negotiable Instruments Law? (Donohoe's Estate, 271, Pa. 554)

3. Haskin drew a check payable to himself and then indorsed it as follows: "Pay to the order of Mrs. Mary Hook for the benefit of her son." The drawer died, and the executor of his estate refused to honor the check, claiming that there was no consideration to induce the indorsement. The sole question to be decided was whether or not this indorsement must be supported by a consideration. (Hook v. Pratt, 78 N. Y. Court of Appeals 498)

4. A check was drawn by the Havana Canning Company for $125, payable to George Wells. The check was regular in every detail except that in the lower left-hand corner were these words: "For berries to be delivered to us June 8th." This check was indorsed by George Wells to an innocent purchaser. The drawer wished to raise a defense to the payment of it a breach of warranty, a personal defense. Before he could raise this defense, he had to establish the fact that this check was nonnegotiable because of this notation. Did this notation constitute a conditional order to pay? (First National Bank of Marianna v. Havana Canning Company, 195 So. 118, 142 Fla. 554)

5. Berry executed a promissory note payable to William C. Stepp. The note was in perfect order. Stepp indorsed the note before maturity as follows: "I hereby transfer my right to this note over to W. E. McCullough.

(signed) William C. Stepp." The maker failed to pay the note, and Mc-Cullough brought suit against Stepp the indorser. His defense was that the indorsement was a qualified indorsement and, therefore, he was not liable since the maker's only reason for not paying was insolvency. Was this a qualified indorsement? (McCullough v. Stepp, 91 Ga. App. 103, 85 S. E. 2d 159)

6. Producers Consolidated Oil drew the following bill of exchange:

$260.06   Mexico, Mo.
                    April 1, 1921

One Hundred and eighty days from date hereof, pay to the order of the Producers Consolidated Oil Company, $250 at office of Savings Bank of Mexico, Mo., for petroleum products sold to drawee. With interest hereon at the rate of 8 percent from date.

            The Producers Consolidated Oil Company

On April 1 this instrument was duly and properly accepted by Ralph Dobyns and A. L. Hendrix as joint acceptors. The payee negotiated the instrument to Clay and Funkhouser Banking Company for value and before maturity. There were two questions to be decided in this case: (1) Was the instrument negotiable in form? (2) Was the Clay and Funkhouser Banking Company a holder in due course? (Clay and Funkhouser Banking Company v. Dobyns, 255 S. W. 946)

7. A check was drawn by Fellsway Motors, Inc., on October 25, made payable to Therrien. Therrien then drew a line through the "5" in "25" to make it look like Oct. 28. The line was in a different color of ink from the rest of the check, and the change in the number was perfectly evident. On October 29 Therrien indorsed the check to Manuel Medeiros for value and in good faith. Before the check was paid, payment was stopped by the drawer. The key question to be decided in the case was whether or not Medeiros was a holder in due course. (Medeiros v. Fellsway Motors, Inc., 96 N. E. 2d 170)

8. Stevens was the maker of several notes in favor of Snow. Snow indorsed them by blank indorsement and placed them in his desk, intending to send them for collection. Stevens stole them from the desk and sold them, that is, discounted them at the Massachusetts National Bank. The question raised in this case was whether or not the bank could obtain good title to the notes from a thief. What was the chief error in this case? (Massachusetts National Bank v. Snow, 187 Mass. 159, 72 N. E. 959)

9. In August, 1949, Hier executed a negotiable note for $1,075, payable to the Washington Fixtures and Equipment Company. The note was to be paid in installments, the first installment to be due December 1, 1949, with a provision that if any installment was not paid on time, the entire balance should become due and payable at once. The first installment was not paid. On December 23, the payee indorsed the note to the Federal Glass Company, Inc. for value. When Hier was sued by the holder, he wished to plead fraud and a breach of warranty. The holder claimed he was not required to defend himself against such a defense. What fundamental error did some employee for the Federal Glass Company commit in this case? (Hier v. Federal Glass Co., Inc., Mun. Ct. App. D. C. 102, A. 2d 840)

10. The Washington Motor Company, a corporation, executed a note in favor of W. A. Sinkey. The note before delivery was indorsed in blank by Herman Steffens and some other directors of the corporation. Some time after the note became due, Steffens died. Up to the time of Steffens' death, Sinkey had made no presentment of the note for payment to the Washington Motor Company nor had any notice of dishonor ever been given to him prior to Steffens' death. Sinkey brought suit against Dorthea Steffens, the executrix of Herman Steffens' estate, and the other indorsers. Judgment for whom? (Steffens v. Sinkey, 43 Ohio App. 355, 183 N. E. 288)

11. J. M. Carver executed a negotiable note in favor of J. W. Crafton. The note was in payment of a gambling debt. Crafton indorsed the note by blank indorsement to the Wachovia Bank and Trust Company. Carver denied liability on the note when it came due because it was for a gambling debt. The holder immediately made demand upon Crafton for payment under his indorsement. Was either Carver or Crafton liable to the holder for this note? (Wachovia Bank and Trust Company v. Crafton, 181 N. C. 404, 107 S. E. 316)

12. The Jonesboro Rice Milling Company drew a draft on McGill Brothers Rice Mill Co. The draft was duly accepted by the drawee. The draft was then discounted by indorsement by the Jonesboro Milling Company, the payee. The indorsement of the payee was made by Franklin W. Cohen and Harry E. Bovay, the owners. The draft was properly presented on the due date and was dishonored, but no notice of dishonor was ever received by Bovay. The notice of dishonor was addressed to: "Jonesboro Rice Mill Co., Jonesboro, Ark., Attention Mr. Bovay." Mr. Bovay claims he never received the notice. Was the notice of dishonor properly addressed to Bovay? (Harry E. Bovay v. Fuller, Circuit Court of Appeals, Eighth Circuit 63 F. 2d 280)

13. Brewer made a note payable to the Murphy Motor Company. There was a provision in the note that it was payable at the Planters' Bank of Clarksdale. The note was negotiable in form. Cutrer indorsed this note as an accommodation to Brewer. The Murphy Motor Company negotiated the note before maturity to the Automobile Sales Company. When the note came due, the holder took it to Brewer's office and presented it for payment, and payment was refused. This was on the due date. The next day the holder notified each indorser that the note had been presented at Brewer's office and payment was refused. The holder then sued the indorsers for payment. (a) Was there a proper presentment for payment? (b) Was there a proper notice of dishonor? (c) Had you been the employee of the Automobile Sales Company whose job it was to handle this transaction, what specific law or laws would you need to know in order to perform your duty satisfactorily? (Brewer et al. v. Automobile Sales Company, 147 Miss. 603)

14. Yates and Gray were makers of a negotiable note which was negotiated several times before maturity. The first indorsement was by Horton. Linn, the last holder, presented the note for payment to Yates and Gray, and payment was refused. Linn, the holder, immediately notified the last indorser of the dishonor. In the notice of dishonor to the last indorser were included notices of dishonor for all the other indorsers, including Horton, the first one. As he received the notices of dishonor each indorser mailed them to the next preceding indorser. For some reason Horton never received his notice. He denied liability on two grounds: First, he never received his notice; second, the notice that was alleged to have been mailed to him was not sent the next business day after dishonor as required by law. When there are several indorsers, must each one receive notice of dishonor not later than the next business day after the dishonor? (Linn v. Horton, 17 Wis. 157)

PART 6

AGENCY AND EMPLOYMENT

Preview Cases for Part 6: Agency and Employment

- Slaughter had a checking account with the Citizens Bank. The Bank was not authorized to honor any checks except those with Slaughter's signature. Over a period of six months Mrs. Slaughter signed her husband's name on dozens of checks and signed them: "by Mrs. Slaughter." Mr. Slaughter notified the bank to stop honoring his wife's checks and demanded that the bank restore to his account all checks drawn by her. Should the bank be required to do so by the court?

- Hawkins was the manager of the Three Bar Ranch. The owner went on a world tour and left Hawkins in complete charge. Hawkins used the proceeds from the sale of cattle to buy and sell cattle at the public sales barns. His gross profits from these speculations amounted to $3,800 and his losses to $1,400, leaving a net profit of $2,400. When the owner returned and learned of these speculations, he demanded the $3,800 in profits. Is he entitled to recover?

- Kent, a construction manager of Master Builders, Inc., was told to build a filling station on a particular lot. He was to bear all costs himself and be reimbursed plus 10 percent of the cost upon completion. When the job was half finished, the city stopped him since a zoning ordinance prohibited all business property on this particular lot. Was Kent entitled to be reimbursed by Master Builders, Inc?

- The Cheyney Hardware Company owed Hanson $4,200. Hanson was appointed the agent for the Cheyney Company to collect certain accounts receivable with instructions to keep the first $4,200 and remit the balance to Cheyney. After Hanson had collected $1,000, Cheyney attempted to discharge him. Did the Cheyney Company have the right to do so?

- Dexter was employed as a welder in the Safe Machine Shop. Space was inadequate, making it necessary to pile sheet steel and I-Beams on the floor. Dexter tripped over some of this material, and the flame from the welding machine touched his face, causing him to lose sight in one eye. Is the employer liable for Dexter's injury?

These preview cases are designed to serve as a springboard for the study of this part. As you read through each chapter in this part, you will find the actual decisions for all these preview cases. Of course, there are many more such illustrative problems as well as case problems for decision at the end of each chapter. And there are also a number of even more challenging cases for review at the end of the part.

CHAPTER 28

CREATION OF AN
AGENCY

NATURE OF AGENCY

When one party, known as a *principal*, appoints another party, known as an *agent*, to enter into contracts with third parties in the name of the principal, a contract of *agency* is formed. By this definition at least three parties are involved in every contract which an agent negotiates, the principal, the agent, and the third party. This feature of agency distinguishes it from all other types of employment relationships. The principal, the agent, or the third party may be a person, a partnership, or a corporation.

IMPORTANCE OF AGENCY

Because of the magnitude and the complexity of our modern industry, many of the important details pertaining to business transactions must be delegated by the owners of businesses to agents for performance. The relation creating this delegation of powers is governed by the general principles of law pertaining to contracts.

The underlying principles of partnerships and joint-stock companies are dependent upon an application of the law of agency, and the business of a corporation can be carried on only through agents. Much of the business of banks, manufacturing enterprises, and similar businesses is carried out by agents.

Even in the performance of ordinary routine matters by individuals, agents are necessary in order to bring one person into a business contractual relationship with other persons. Thus a farmer who sends an employee to town to have a piece of machinery repaired gives the latter the authority to enter into a contract that binds the farmer to the agreement. This case is an application of the maxim that "whatever a person does through another, he does himself."

WHAT POWERS MAY BE DELEGATED TO AN AGENT?

As a general rule, all those things that one has the right to do personally he may do through an agent. There are, however, certain acts which are of such a personal nature that the courts will not permit them to be delegated to others. The law insists that if these acts are performed at all, they must be performed by the one who, because of the personal nature of such acts, should do them. Some of the acts that are considered personal and that may not be performed by an agent are voting in a public election, executing a will, making an affidavit, painting a portrait, and representing a client in a lawsuit.

What one may not lawfully do himself may not be done through another. Thus no person can authorize an agent to commit a crime, to publish a libelous statement, to perpetrate a fraud, or to do any other act that is illegal, immoral, or opposed to the welfare of society. For example, an agreement to act as an agent to help another to secure a public office through improper means or to defraud the public cannot be enforced.

OTHER TYPES OF EMPLOYMENT RELATIONSHIPS

There are two other types of employment relationships:

1. Independent contractor
2. Employer and employee, originally referred to in law as master and servant

(1) **Independent Contractor.** An *independent contractor* is one hired to perform some tasks for a fixed fee but is independent of the control of the employer as to the means by which he performs the contract. He is merely held responsible for the proper performance of the contract. The contract does not create either a principal-agent relationship or an employer-employee relationship, yet is easily confused with either of these relationships. The most usual type of independent contractor relationship is in the building trades.

- Pope entered into a contract with Bruce to build a house for Bruce for $20,000, the house to conform to prescribed blueprints and to be completed within three months from date. Bruce has no control over Pope during the construction. His only rights are to insist it conform to the blueprints and be finished within three months. This is a typical independent contractor relationship.

There are many reasons why one must not confuse a contract of employment with a contract of independent contractor. In the first place, an employer may be held liable for any injuries his employees negligently cause to third parties. This is not true of independent contractors. In the second place, there are several laws an employer must comply with relative to his employees. He must withhold social security taxes on their wages, pay a payroll tax for unemployment compensation, withhold federal income taxes, bargain with his employees collectively when properly demanded, and many others. None of these laws apply when one contracts with an independent contractor. He is the employer of those employed by him to perform the contract.

(2) **Employer and Employee.** The main difference between an employee and an agent is that an employee does not have the power to bind his employer on a contract while an agent does have that power. Furthermore, an employee does not owe his employer the same degree of loyalty and good faith required of an agent. For this reason an agent may be sued by his employer, the principal, for all damages due to a lack of good faith, while under identical circumstances, a mere employee would not be liable.

- Vaughn employed Pearson to fix his automobile. While Pearson was working on it, a prospective purchaser, thinking Pearson was the owner, offered him $2,000 for the car. Pearson bought the car from Vaughn for $1,800 and then sold it immediately to the interested party. As an employee, Pearson would not have to account to his employer for this profit. Such an act, however, would be a breach of good faith on the part of an agent.

CLASSIFICATION OF AGENTS

Agents may be classified as follows:

1. General agents
2. Special agents

(1) **General Agents.** A *general agent* is one who is authorized to carry out all of his principal's business of a particular kind, or all of his principal's business at a particular place even though it is not

all of one kind. A purchasing agent and a bank cashier are examples of general agents who perform all of the principal's business of a particular kind. A manager who is in full charge of one branch of a chain of shoe stores is a general agent who transacts all of his principal's business at a particular place. In this capacity he buys and sells merchandise, employs help, pays bills, collects accounts, and performs all other duties. He has a wide scope of authority and the power to act on his own initiative.

A general agent has considerable authority beyond his contract of employment. He has in addition to his contractual authority that authority which one in his position customarily has. This is sometimes called *customary authority*. One who knows the extent of an agent's contractual authority cannot rely upon customary authority.

(2) **Special Agents.** A *special agent* is one who is authorized by his principal to transact some specific act or acts. He is invested with only limited powers which he may use only for a specific purpose. The authorization may cover just one act, such as buying a house; or it may cover a series of acts which are mere repetitions, such as selling admission tickets to a movie. A special agent has little or no customary authority. If a special agent exceeds his contractual authority, the principal is usually not bound.

SPECIAL TYPES OF AGENTS

There are several special types of agents. In general these are special agents, but because of the nature of their duties, their powers may exceed those of the ordinary special agent:

1. Factors
2. Factors del credere
3. Brokers
4. Attorneys in fact

(1) **Factors.** A *factor* is one who receives possession of another's property for sale on commission. The commission merchant is the largest class of factors. He may sell in the name of his principal, but the usual practice is for him to sell in his own name. When he collects, he deducts his commission or factorage and remits the balance to the principal. The third party as a rule is aware that he is dealing with an agent by the nature of the business or by the name of the business.

The words "Commission Merchant" usually appear on all stationery. He has the power to bind the principal for the customary terms of sale for the type of business he is doing. In this regard his powers are slightly greater than those of the ordinary special agent.

(2) Factors Del Credere. A *factor del credere* is a commission merchant who sells on credit and guarantees to the principal that these accounts are good. This is a form of contract of guaranty, but the courts have ruled that the contract need not be in writing as required by the Statute of Frauds since the agreement is a primary obligation of the factor.

(3) Brokers. A *broker* is a special agent whose task is to bring the two contracting parties together. Unlike the factor, he does not have possession of the merchandise. In real estate and insurance he generally is the agent of the buyer rather than the seller. If his duty is merely to find a buyer, or sometimes a seller, he has no authority to bind the principal on any contract.

(4) Attorneys in Fact. An *attorney in fact* is a general agent who has been appointed by a formal contract. Of all types of agents, he has the greatest authority. Although a real estate agent can enter into a contract of sale that binds his principal, he does not have the power to execute the deed and sell the land; but an attorney in fact may be empowered to execute the deed as well. Some types of business, such as American Lloyds Insurance companies, can act only through attorneys in fact. Their powers are coextensive with the principal's. The appointment of an attorney in fact must be by formal contract.

EXTENT OF AUTHORITY

An agent's authority is from its very nature somewhat indefinite. There are many borderline acts which are difficult to determine as to whether or not they come within an agent's authority. These acts are a frequent source of litigation.

As a general rule, a general agent has authority to transact two classes of acts: those clearly within the scope of his actual or contractual authority, and those outside of this scope which appear to third parties to be apparently within the scope of the agent's actual authority.

As to innocent third parties, the powers of a general agent may be far more extensive than those granted to him by his principal. Secret limitations upon a general agent's authority are not necessarily binding upon a third party who has no knowledge of them; but if the third party knows of them, he is bound by them.

> - The owner of a radio shop employed a general agent to sell radios and instructed him to sell for cash only. If the agent disregarded this instruction and sold a radio on credit at reasonable terms of payment, the contract would have been binding upon the principal. Since it is the custom of radio shops in general to sell on credit, the purchaser had a right to presume that this agent had authority to sell on credit. This is frequently called *customary authority.*
>
> If the salesman had taken a car in payment of the radio and had agreed to pay the purchaser $150 for the difference in value, the principal would not have been bound. This would clearly have been beyond even the apparent scope of the agent's authority, and the purchaser would have had no right to assume that the agent had such authority.

The foregoing rules apply only to general agents. Almost the opposite is true of special agents. The third party is required (1) to ascertain if the party is in fact a special agent and (2) to determine the powers of the agent. If a man represents himself to be the agent of another for the purpose of selling the car of that other person, the very nature of the transaction indicates that he is at most a special agent. The prospective purchaser must seek assurance from the principal as to the agent's authority.

Furthermore, where it is admitted that the agent has such authority and that the prospective customer is aware of it, the agent has no apparent authority to sell any other property of his principal. The very nature of the transaction notifies the customer that the agent is empowered to sell only the car. This leads to the conclusion that a special agent can bind his principal only when he has been expressly empowered to do so, unless the principal is present and by his silence implies additional authority.

WHO MAY APPOINT AN AGENT?

Every person who is legally competent to act for himself may act through an agent. This rule is based upon the principle that whatever a person may do for himself, he may do through another. Hence corporations, partnerships, unincorporated clubs and societies, as well as individuals, may appoint agents.

In general the appointment of an agent by a minor is considered void; some states, however, have broken away from this strict rule and hold that the appointment of an agent by a minor is merely voidable, as in the case of the minor's ordinary contracts.

WHO MAY ACT AS AN AGENT?

Ordinarily any person may be appointed to act as an agent, provided he has sufficient intelligence to carry out his principal's orders. Corporations, partnerships, and joint stock companies may act as agents also.

There are some types of transactions which cannot be performed by an agent unless he meets certain requirements. For example, in many states a realtor must possess certain definite qualifications and must, in addition, secure a license to act in this capacity. Unless he does this, he is disqualified to act as an agent in performing the duties of a realtor. Nor can anyone act as an agent if he also has an interest in the subject matter which is adverse to that of his principal, unless, of course, the principal is aware of the agent's interest.

CREATION OF AN AGENCY

There are several ways in which the relationship of agency may be created. They are usually created by:

1. Appointment
2. Ratification
3. Estoppel
4. Necessity

(1) **Appointment.** The usual way of creating an agency is by appointment. The contract may be oral or written, formal or informal. There are some instances, however, where the appointment must be made in a particular form. The contract appointing an agent must be in writing if the agency is created to transfer title to real estate. Also, if an agent's authority is to extend beyond one year from the date of the contract, the contract is required by the Statute of Frauds to be in writing. If an agent is appointed to execute a formal contract, such as a mortgage, the contract of appointment must be formal.

A written instrument indicating the appointment of an agent is known as a *power of attorney*. If a power of attorney is to be recorded,

Power of Attorney

Know All Men By These Presents: *that* I, Gene Dorsey of Boise, Idaho

have made, constituted and appointed and by these presents do *make, constitute and appoint*

James Turner

      my   *true and lawful attorney for*   me   and in   my   *name, place and stead to*

represent me in the operation of my lumber mill in the State of Idaho

Hereby giving and granting unto   my   said attorney   *full and whole power and authority in and*

about the premises; and generally to do all and every act and acts, thing and things, device and devices, in the law what-

soever needful and necessary to be done in and about the premises, for   me   *and in*   my   *name to do, execute*

and perform as large and amply, to all intents and purposes, as   I   *might or could do, if personally present;*

and an attorney or attorneys under   him   *for the purpose aforesaid, to make and substitute, and the same to*

remove and revoke at   his   *pleasure, hereby ratifying and confirming as good and effectual, in law and in equity,*

all that.   my   *said attorney or*   his   *substitute   shall lawfully and legally do by virtue hereof.*

In Witness Whereof, I   *have hereunto set*   my   *hand   and seal   the* tenth

day of March   *in the year of our Lord one thousand nine hundred and*

Sealed and Delivered in Presence of

Glenn Gordon

Travis Taylor

Gene Dorsey   (SEAL)

  (SEAL)

A Power of Attorney

it must also be acknowledged before a notary public or other officer authorized to take acknowledgments. An ordinary form of power of attorney is shown above.

(2) **Ratification.** The approval by one person of an act previously done by another in the former's name without authority is known as *ratification*. The unauthorized act may have been done by an assumed agent who purported to act as an agent without real or apparent authority, or it may have been done by a real agent who exceeded his apparent authority. The supposed principal in such a case is not bound by the act unless and until he ratifies it. The effect of the ratification is that the ratification relates back to the date of the act done by the assumed agent; hence the assumed agent is put in the same position as if he had had authority to do the act at the time the act was done by him.

The essential elements of a valid ratification are:

(a) The one who assumed the authority of an agent must have acted for the party who attempts to ratify the act.

(b) The unauthorized act must have been committed in the name of the alleged principal.

(c) The one attempting to ratify must have been capable of authorizing the act at the time the act was done. Thus an act of a promoter cannot be ratified by a corporation that is formed subsequently. Since the effect of the ratification is that the ratification is thrown back to the day the act was done, the corporation cannot ratify the act of the promoter because it was not in existence at the time of the act.

(d) The one attempting to ratify must be capable of authorizing the act at the time he gives his approval of the act.

(e) The one attempting to ratify must have knowledge of all material facts.

(f) The one attempting to ratify must approve the entire act.

(g) A valid ratification once made cannot later be withdrawn.

(h) The act that is ratified must be legal.

(3) Estoppel. Agency by ratification and agency by estoppel are often confused. In agency by ratification the principal is bound because he intended to be bound; otherwise he would have refused to ratify the act of the person who assumed to act as his agent. In *agency by estoppel* the principal is bound regardless of the fact that there was no intention to be bound. This liability arises when a person by words or conduct leads another person to believe that a third party is his agent. The principal is held liable for the purpose of preventing an injustice to parties who have been misled by the acts or the conduct of the principal.

> ▪ Slaughter had a checking account with the Citizen's Bank. The bank was not authorized to honor any checks except those with Slaughter's signature. Over a period of six months Mrs. Slaughter signed her husband's name on dozens of checks and signed them: "by Mrs. Slaughter." Mr. Slaughter notified the bank to stop honoring his wife's checks and demanded that the bank restore to his account all checks drawn by her. The court held that because he allowed six months to pass without protesting, he was estopped to deny she had the authority to sign his name to checks. Had he protested as soon as he learned of the act, the bank would have had to make good the checks so drawn.

(4) Necessity. The relationship of agency may be created by necessity. A husband is bound to support his wife and minor children. If he fails to provide them with necessaries, the wife may pledge the husband's credit, even against his will. Agency by necessity may also arise from some unforeseen emergency. Thus the driver of a bus operating between distant cities may pledge the owner's credit in order to have needed repairs made and may have the cost charged to the owner.

QUESTIONS

1. What is an agency?
2. Name the parties who are involved in a contract which an agent negotiates.
3. Why are most business transactions carried on by agents?
4. What acts can never be delegated to an agent?
5. How does an independent contractor differ from an agent?
6. What is the difference between an employee and an agent?
7. What is a general agent?
8. What is customary authority?
9. Name two reasons why it is most important to distinguish between an agent and a broker.
10. May corporations act as agents?
11. Is a wife always the agent of her husband?
12. In order for a principal to ratify an unauthorized contract of an agent, must the agent have pretended to act for the principal?

CASE PROBLEMS

1. McDowell was business manager for the WTUW radio station. Philips, representing himself as the agent of the Hartsfield Oil Company, presented to McDowell an advertising program to run for two weeks over the station. The charge agreed upon was $800. After the program was completed, McDowell sent a bill to the Hartsfield Oil Company. The company denied liability on the ground that Philips did not have the authority to place advertising contracts with the station. The facts showed that Philips' actual authority was to call on stations selling the Hartsfield products, to recruit new agents for the company, and to build goodwill for the oil company whenever possible. Was this authority broad enough to empower him to contract for advertising campaigns?

2. The Kinsey Machine Tool Company shipped by its own truck a truck load of machine tools from its plant in New Jersey to Jacksonville, Florida. On the way the truck driver had several flat tires, and one tire blew out because the truck was overloaded. He stopped in Richmond and purchased twelve new heavy duty tires and tubes, a complete set for the truck, and had the tire company install them. He charged the tires to the Kinsey

Machine Company. When the bill was received, the company refused to pay it, claiming the truck driver was only an employee, not an agent. Was the purchaser liable for the tires?

3. Hinton entered into a contract with Barnett whereby Barnett was to paint a building Hinton owned for $1,100, Barnett to furnish all materials and to pay for all labor. The work was to be completed within 30 days; otherwise, Barnett was free to work as he pleased. Barnett hired Dinkler to assist with the painting. A ladder on which Dinkler was standing broke; he fell to the sidewalk and was seriously injured. The ladder was clearly not safe to use. Is Hinton liable to Dinkler for damages?

4. Denny was employed by a mimeograph manufacturing company to sell new mimeograph machines. The company's usual selling terms provided for trading in old mimeograph machines. Denny sold the Comet Letter Service two new machines and agreed to take six secondhand typewriters as a part of the purchase price. The company refused to abide by the contract. Must it do so?

5. Paulson employed Darwin as a special agent to sell an automobile repair shop and filling station he owned. Darwin was specifically instructed to sell for cash only with possession to be given to the buyer within sixty days. Darwin entered into a contract with Laster to buy the business for one-third cash and the balance to be paid in three equal installments with possession to be given in ten days. Paulson refused to sell on these terms. Is he bound on the contract the agent made for him?

6. Courts was a stock salesman for a proposed new corporation. Courts sold Carlton 1,000 shares of stock for $50,000 and agreed to take in payment Carlton's small firm in bulk and make Carlton a director in the new corporation. After the corporation was formed, Carlton refused to go through with the transaction, claiming Courts had no authority to make such a contract. Through its board of directors the corporation ratified Court's action. Does this ratification make the contract valid?

7. Gutherie was the manager of a drugstore owned by Mrs. Fowler. Gutherie entered into a contract with Comstock to sell the drugstore in bulk for $18,000, claiming he was the owner. After the contract was written and signed, Comstock learned that Mrs. Fowler was the owner. She had not authorized Gutherie to make the contract, but she ratified the agreement. Is Comstock bound on the contract after it is ratified?

8. Knowles delivered two valuable antiques to Harbin, a licensed factor for antiques. Harbin sold the two items to Mrs. Fort for $1,400. Knowles was dissatisfied with the price received and attempted to recover the items from Mrs. Fort, claiming Knowles could not transfer title to them since he was clearly not the owner. Is this contention sound?

9. Mary had an invitation to attend the Magnolia Ball, the leading social event on the college campus. She purchased a gown for the occasion from a department store for $510 and charged it to her father. Her father refused to pay for it on the basis that his daughter had no right to make the contract in his name. The department store contended Mary was her father's agent by necessity. Was she?

CHAPTER 29
OPERATION AND
TERMINATION OF
AN AGENCY

OPERATION OF AGENCY

Every contract creates rights, duties, and obligations on the part of all the contracting parties. These rights, duties, and obligations are set out in the contract. In a contract of agency, the law imposes upon the agent certain duties even though they are not set out in the contract. Likewise, the relationship of agency creates specific duties and obligations which the principal owes to his agent even though these are not specifically enumerated in the contract. In turn, the same relationship imposes upon both principal and agent certain duties and obligations to third parties. An examination of these duties and obligations will reveal the importance of the relationship of agent and principal as well as the necessity for each party in the relationship to be fully cognizant of both his rights and his duties.

AGENT'S DUTIES TO HIS PRINCIPAL

An agent owes the following important duties to his principal:

1. Loyalty and good faith
2. Obedience
3. Skill and diligence
4. Accounting

(1) **Loyalty and Good Faith.** The relationship of principal and agent is fiduciary in nature; that is, the principal must trust the agent

to perform his duties according to contract. The relationship of agent and principal calls for a higher degree of faith and trust than do most contractual relationships. For this reason the law imposes upon the agent the duty of loyalty and good faith, and deprives him of his right to compensation, reimbursement, and indemnification when he proves disloyal to his principal or acts in bad faith. The interests of the principal must be promoted by the agent to the utmost of his ability.

Loyalty and good faith are abstract terms that give the courts wide latitude in interpreting what acts constitute bad faith or a breach of loyalty. Such acts as secretly owning an interest in a firm that competes with the principal, disclosing confidential information, selling to or buying from himself without the knowledge of the principal, and acting simultaneously as the agent of a competitor are acts which the courts have held to be a breach of good faith. If the agent acts in bad faith, not only may he be discharged, but the principal may recover any damages which he has sustained. Also, the principal may recover any profits the agent has made while acting in bad faith even though the principal was not damaged by the act.

> ▪ Hawkins was the manager of the Three Bar Ranch. The owner went on a world tour and left Hawkins in complete charge. Hawkins used the proceeds from the sale of cattle to buy and sell cattle at the public sales barns. His gross profits from these speculations amounted to $3,800 and his losses to $1,400, leaving a net profit of $2,400. When the principal returned and learned of these speculations, he demanded the $3,800 in profits. Hawkins was required to turn over $3,800 to the principal. He could not offset his losses against the profits. This is the penalty for a breach of good faith.

(2) **Obedience.** An agent may have two types of instructions from his principal: one is routine and the other is discretionary. In all routine instructions the agent must carry them out to the letter. An illustration is an instruction not to accept any payments made by check. The agent is liable for any losses incurred by reason of disobeying instructions. He is not justified in disobeying such instructions under any conditions.

If the instruction is a discretionary one, the agent must use the best judgment of which he is capable. For example, if the agent is instructed to accept checks, he is not liable for a bad check when in his judgment the drawer of the check was solvent and reliable. If he accepts a check, however, which he has reason to believe is bad, he will be liable for any loss which the principal sustains by reason of this act.

(3) **Skill and Diligence.** One who acts as an agent must possess the skill required to perform his duties and must be diligent in performing the skill. There is an implied warranty that the agent has such skill and will exercise such diligence in the contract of agency. Any breach of this warranty subjects the agent to a liability for damages for the loss by reason of the breach.

As a general rule, an agent may not delegate any of his authority or appoint subagents unless the acts delegated are necessary to perform his duties as an agent. As a rule, an agent is appointed because of his own peculiar skill to perform the duties of an agent. If he delegates any of these duties or appoints subagents, the principal may be forced to accept the services of unskilled people. In addition to making contracts for his principal, an agent may have certain clerical duties to perform, such as recordkeeping. These duties can be delegated. In many types of businesses, such as real estate and insurance, it is customary for agents to employ subagents. It is assumed the principal condones this practice when it is customary. Also, the contract may specifically provide for subagents. In this case, the agent must use skill and diligence in appointing competent subagents and remains liable to the principal for their breach of good faith or lack of skill.

- Dover was an agent for the Gaines Tractor and Equipment Company. He sold a tractor for $2,417.84 to White. White was the payee of a sight draft for $2,500 on which the words "or order" were clearly marked out. White indorsed this sight draft in full payment of the tractor and was given the difference in change. The drawee was bankrupt and unable to pay the draft when presented for payment. Since the draft was nonnegotiable in form, the negotiation in substance was an assignment in which there is no warranty of payment because of insolvency. When Dover accepted this position, knowing he would have to deal with negotiable instruments, he warranted he had the skill to handle them competently. He was liable to his principal for this loss.

(4) **Accounting.** The duties of an agent include the keeping of a record of all money transactions pertaining to the agency. He must account to the principal for any money and property of the latter that may come into his possession. Money should be deposited in a bank in the name of the principal, preferably in a bank other than that in which the agent keeps his own personal funds. If the deposit is made in the name of the agent, any loss that may be caused by the failure of the bank will fall on the agent. The agent must keep per-

sonal property belonging to the principal separate from his own. If the agent commingles the property of both of them in such a manner that it cannot be separated, the principal will have the right to the entire mass.

- Wright, as collecting agent for the Home Loan Company, collected $2,784.65. He deposited the money in his personal account in a local bank. Wright was behind over $3,000 in alimony payments to his ex-wife. She levied on this bank balance before it was remitted to the principal. She was within her rights since this bank balance in the name of the agent is the property of the agent and can be levied on for his debts. He still owes the principal for his collections since he has never accounted to the principal for the $2,784.65.

PRINCIPAL'S DUTIES TO HIS AGENT

The principal has four important duties in respect to his agent:

1. Compensation
2. Reimbursement
3. Indemnification
4. Abide by the terms of the contract

(1) **Compensation.** The compensation due the agent is determined by the contract of employment. As in most other contracts, this provision may be either express or implied. If the amount is clearly and expressly stated, disputes seldom arise. If one is asked to serve as an agent but no amount of compensation is stated, the customary rules apply. This is especially true when one acts as an attorney or an accountant. If there are no customary rules, a reasonable rate will be fixed by the court according to the character of the services rendered. Frequently, the compensation is on a contingent basis, such as a percentage of the selling price, provided a sale is made. In such a case, no matter how much time is expended by the agent, he cannot collect compensation from his principal unless a sale is made.

- The Devon Motor Company promised Fletcher a reasonable commission on all sales of cars which Fletcher might make. Fletcher sold one for $2,400 and then demanded a 33⅓ percent commission. So long as this agreement remained executory, it was void because the offer was not specific enough to accept. After a car was sold, however, the Devon Motor Company had to pay a customary commission for the sale. If the commission in that locality was 20 percent, then Fletcher could collect this amount but no more.

(2) **Reimbursement.** Any expenses incurred or disbursements made by the agent from his personal funds as a necessary part of the agency is the liability of the principal. The agent is entitled to reimbursement. If, for example, the agent had to pay from his personal funds a $100 truck repair bill before he could continue his mission, he would be entitled to reimbursement. If, on the other hand, he had to pay a $50 fine for speeding, the principal would not be required to reimburse him. Any expense incurred as a result of an unlawful act must be borne by the agent.

(3) **Indemnification.** A contractual payment made by the agent for the principal is an expense of the principal. If the payment is made by the agent, not by reason of a contract but as a result of a loss or damage due to an accident, the principal must indemnify the agent. He reimburses him for expenses and indemnifies him for losses and damages. If an agent is fined for an act done at the request of the principal and the agent is ignorant of the illegal nature of the act, then the principal must indemnify the agent. Under the old maxim "Ignorance of the law is no excuse," seldom can an agent plead ignorance of the law successfully.

- Kent, a construction manager of Master Builders, Inc., was told to build a filling station on a particular lot. He was to bear all costs himself and be reimbursed plus 10 percent of the cost upon completion. When the job was half finished, the city stopped him since a zoning ordinance prohibited all business property on this particular lot. Kent was entitled to reimbursement in this case since he had a right to assume the principal had checked the zoning laws.

(4) **Abide by the Terms of the Contract.** Many an agent's compensation is on a contingent basis, that is, the agent is to be paid only on condition that he carries out the terms of the agency. This is often impossible unless the principal conforms to the contract. For example, if the agent is to sell by sample and be paid a commission on all sales, he must be furnished samples. He must be given the opportunity to earn his contingent fee or commission. In real estate agencies this creates peculiar problems. If the owner of land merely lists his land with the agent, either the owner or any other real estate agent may sell the property. In this case the first agent has no complaint. If the owner makes the first agent his exclusive agent for selling the land, the owner cannot list the property with another agent, for that would deprive the exclusive agent of his contractual opportunity

to earn his commission. The owner, however, may sell the land himself. A third variant of this type of agency is the "exclusive sale" agency. In this case neither another agent nor the owner can sell the property while the agency remains in effect.

AGENT'S LIABILITIES TO THIRD PARTIES

Ordinarily, whenever an agent performs his duties, he thereby binds the principal but not himself. In his relations with third parties, however, an agent may make himself personally liable on contracts and for wrongs in several ways:

(1) If an agent contracts in his own name and does not disclose the name of the principal, he becomes liable to the same extent as though he were the principal.

(2) An agent may make himself personally liable to the third party by an express agreement to be responsible.

(3) If a person assumes to act for another without authority, or if one exceeds or materially departs from the authority that he was given, he is personally liable to those with whom he does business. The latter situation may arise when an agent is overzealous in effecting what he may think is a desirable contract.

(4) If an agent signs a contract in his own name, he will be held liable. He will not escape this liability by writing the word "Agent" after his name or by signing his name and then indicating that he is the agent for a certain person. Such words merely describe the agent.

(5) An agent is personally liable for fraud or any other wrongdoing, whether it was caused by disobedience, carelessness, or malice, or whether it was committed on the order of the principal.

PRINCIPAL'S DUTIES AND LIABILITIES TO THIRD PARTIES

The principal is ordinarily liable to third parties for contracts made within the apparent scope of a general agent's authority and within the actual scope of a special agent's authority. When the agent enters into an unauthorized contract that is not within the apparent scope of his authority, the principal is not bound unless he subsequently ratifies the contract.

The enforceability of any contract may be denied, not because the agent did not have the authority to make the contract, but on the ground that he exceeded his authority or violated his instructions. In such a case the test is: Did a reasonably prudent man have a right to believe the agent had the authority to make a contract with these provisions? If the answer is in the affirmative, the principal is bound by the contract. For example, if the manager of a furniture store sells a suite of furniture on credit contrary to the authority granted to him, the principal is bound to fulfill the contract with the third party, provided the latter did not know of the limitation upon the agent's authority. The agent is then liable to the principal for any loss sustained.

The principal, as well as the agent, is liable for an injury to the person or the property of a third party that was caused by the negligence or the wrongful act of the agent in the course of his employment. When the agent steps aside from the business of his principal and commits a wrong or injury of his own to another, the principal is not liable unless he ratifies the act.

TERMINATION BY ACTS OF THE PARTIES

Agencies may be terminated by acts of the parties or by operation of law.

The chief ways by which an agency may be terminated by acts of the parties are by:

1. Original agreement
2. Subsequent agreement
3. Revocation
4. Renunciation by the agent

(1) **Original Agreement.** The contract creating the agency may specify a date for the termination of the agency. In that event, the agency is automatically terminated on that date. Most special agencies, such as a special agency to sell an automobile, are terminated because their purpose has been accomplished.

(2) **Subsequent Agreement.** An agency may be terminated at any time by a mutual agreement between the principal and the agent.

(3) **Revocation.** The principal may revoke the agent's authority at any time, thereby terminating the agency. One must distinguish between the right to terminate the agency and the power to do so. The principal has the right to terminate the agency any time the agent breaches any material part of the contract of employment. If the agent,

for example, fails to account for all money collected for the principal, the agent may be discharged; and the principal incurs no liability for breach of contract. The principal, on the other hand, has the power, with one exception, to revoke the agent's authority even though the agent has complied fully with his part of the contract. Under these circumstances, however, the principal becomes liable to the agent for all damages which he sustains by reason of the unjustifiable discharge. This is the agent's sole remedy because he cannot insist upon the right to continue to act as an agent even though he has done nothing to justify a termination before the end of the contract period. The only exception to this rule is an agency coupled with an interest.

Interest may take one of two forms: (1) interest in the authority, and (2) interest in the subject matter. An agent has interest in the authority when he is authorized to act as an agent in collecting funds for the principal with an agreement that the agent is not to remit the collections to the principal but to apply them on the debt owed to the agent by the principal. In the second case, the agent has a lien on the property of the principal as security for a debt and is appointed as agent to sell the property and apply the proceeds on the debt.

- ▪ The Cheyney Hardware Company owed Hanson $4,200. Hanson was appointed the agent for the Cheyney Hardware Company to collect certain accounts receivable for the principal with instructions to keep the first $4,200 and remit the balance to the principal. After Hanson had collected $1,000, the principal attempted to discharge him. The principal cannot terminate this agency until Hanson has collected at least $4,200.

(4) **Renunciation.** Like the principal, the agent has the power to renounce the agency at any time. If the agent abandons the agency without cause before the contract is fulfilled, he is liable to the principal for all losses due to the unjustified abandonment.

TERMINATION BY OPERATION OF LAW

An agency may be terminated by operation of law. The chief ways in which this may occur are:

1. Subsequent illegality
2. Death or incapacity
3. Destruction
4. Bankruptcy
5. Dissolution
6. War

(1) **Subsequent Illegality.** Subsequent illegality of the subject matter of the agency terminates the agency.

(2) **Death or Incapacity.** Death or incapacity of either the principal or agent terminates the agency. For example, if the agent loses his power of speech so that he cannot perform his principal's business, the agency is automatically terminated.

(3) **Destruction.** Destruction of the subject matter, such as the destruction of a house by fire that was to be sold by the agent, terminates the agency.

(4) **Bankruptcy.** Bankruptcy of the principal terminates the agency. In most cases bankruptcy of the agent does not terminate the agency.

(5) **Dissolution.** Dissolution of a corporation terminates an agency. This is equivalent to death since a dissolution of a corporation is a legal death.

(6) **War.** When the country of the principal and that of the agent are at war, the agent's authority is usually terminated or at least suspended until peace is restored. When war makes performance impossible, the agency is terminated.

NOTICE OF TERMINATION

When an agency is terminated by an act of one party, the principal must give notice to third parties with whom the agent has previously transacted business and who would be likely to deal with him as an agent. This does not mean that the notice should always be given. If the nature of the agency is such that the agent could not injure the principal's business, notice of termination may safely be omitted. For example, if the agent's duty is to sell cars, he cannot sell any cars if he has no access to them after the agency is terminated. If, on the other hand, the agent's duties are to collect accounts, he may continue to collect even after he is discharged. To prevent this, notice should be given.

When an agency is terminated by the operation of law, notice need not be given either to the agent or to third parties. Since the law has put a stop to the agency, it also relieves the parties from the necessity of giving notice.

QUESTIONS

1. What duties does an agent owe his principal?

2. What two types of instructions may a principal give his agent?

3. What does an agent warrant when he accepts his job?

4. How should an agent deposit his principal's money in a bank?

5. If the agent and the principal do not set the amount of the agent's compensation at the time the contract is performed, how is the amount determined if the agent and the principal cannot agree?

6. If an agent must pay agency expenses out of his personal funds in order to complete his mission, what is the liability of the principal?

7. If an agent grossly exceeds his authority when contracting with a third party, who is held liable on the contract?

8. If an agent commits a fraudulent act on the instructions of the principal, who is liable to the third party for damages?

9. What is the principal's liability in regard to third parties for injuries caused by the negligent acts of his agents?

10. How may an agency be terminated?

CASE PROBLEMS

1. Heckman was an agent to sell Porter's country manor for $60,000. Johnson contacted Heckman and asked him to find him a property of certain descriptions and agreed to pay him 5 percent of the purchase price if he found a desirable place. Without disclosing to Johnson that he also was the agent to sell Porter's property, Heckman persuaded Johnson to buy the Porter mansion. After the sale was consummated, Johnson learned of Heckman's status as an agent for both parties and refused to pay Heckman his 5 percent commission. Must he pay?

2. Gordon's, Inc. was a national organization with a large field force of salesmen supervised by district sales superintendents. The head office prepared a Salesman's Manual, a copy of which was given to each salesman when he was employed. He was told to obey all instructions in the manual. One of these instructions read as follows: "Each day the salesman must deposit all collections before closing hours of the bank, make out a duplicate deposit slip, and mail one of these to the Main Office." One week one of the district sales superintendents met one of his salesmen each day about noon, had lunch with him, and inquired as to how much money the salesman had collected that day. Then he said, "I am returning to the head office as soon as we finish lunch. You let me have the money, and I'll take it in with me." Five of the salesmen did this, and the sales superintendent never returned to his office. The salesmen were sued by Gordon's and the bonding company for the amount of money embezzled by the supervisor. Must each salesman make good the loss to the extent of his collections?

3. The Scott Investment Company owned a housing project consisting of about 200 private dwellings. Langdon was the manager for this project. One of his duties was to keep each property properly insured. He was a secret partner in an insurance agency with his mother-in-law. He placed all insurance with this agency. There was no evidence that he purchased any more insurance than was necessary nor was there any excessive charge of any kind. When the principal learned of Langdon's ownership of the agency, it demanded his share of the profits on all policies placed on the 200 dwellings. Was the Scott Investment Company entitled to these profits?

4. Bursham was a sales agent and representative for a jewelry manufacturer. In calling on retailers he carried several thousand dollars' worth of samples at all times. He was dismissed but refused to return the samples. He sold them for $1,000 above the manufacturer's selling price and kept all the money. (a) Must he remit to the principal any or all of the proceeds? (b) Does the $1,000 profit belong to the principal or to the agent?

5. Tolbert was a sales agent for a vacuum cleaner distributor. Among other instructions he was told not to accept checks in payment of a machine "unless in your opinion the check is good." Tolbert sold one machine for $85 and was paid by check. The check was dishonored and the principal demanded that Tolbert make good the loss. Tolbert contended that since the man "looked honest," he was justified in thinking the check was good. Did Tolbert obey instructions?

6. Watson was employed by Whitworth as his agent at a salary of $12,000 a year plus expenses while traveling. Watson worked the first month and during that time he filed an expense account of $75 for each day he worked, although some days he did not leave town. Whitworth discharged him and refused to pay him any salary or reimburse him for expenses. Watson sued for one year's salary plus one month's traveling expense. Discuss their rights.

7. Wright was employed by Tucker as his agent. One of his duties was to present drafts for acceptance and payment. One draft for $1,284.72 was "payable at the Cross Keys National Bank." The draft was accepted on June 7 and payable ninety days after that date. On September 6, Wright went to the office of the drawee and presented it for payment. Payment was refused and three days later Wright notified the drawer of the dishonor. Did Wright have the skill necessary to perform correctly the duties for which he was employed?

8. Drake acted in the capacity of a general agent for the D & E Grocery Company. One of Drake's duties was to collect each week from the company's charge customers. Drake was discharged. Without the knowledge of the company, he made several collections after his discharge and failed to account for the money. The D & E Grocery Company demanded that its customers pay a second time. Must they pay again if they had already paid Drake?

CHAPTER 30

EMPLOYER AND
EMPLOYEE

NATURE OF THE EMPLOYMENT CONTRACT

Over a period of many decades the common law developed many rules governing the relationship between an employer and his employee, frequently called the master and servant relationship. Not only have the terms "master" and "servant" been largely abandoned, but the laws governing their relationship have also been greatly modified. In every state there remain remnants of the common law which still apply to the employer-employee relationship. Even the modern legislation modifying this relationship did not revolutionize the common law. Many of its features dealing with safe working conditions and other aspects of the employment contract have been retained in modern labor legislation. These new laws do not cover all employees. In every state there is a small core of employees who still have their rights and duties determined largely by the common law master-servant concept. The common law was slanted heavily in favor of the employer, but it did not leave the employee helpless. Many of the well-established principles of the common law are still in force. This chapter will deal primarily with the common law as it relates to employers and employees.

CREATION OF EMPLOYER AND EMPLOYEE RELATIONSHIP

The relationship of employer and employee arises from the contract of employment, either express or implied. As a rule, the relationship arises only from an express contract. The common law was jealous of the right of the employer to hire whom he pleased and of the right of the employee to choose freely his employer. The relationship of employer and employee could not be imposed upon anyone without this assent. Thus, if one voluntarily performs the duties of a servant, he cannot by that act subject the employer or householder to assume the liability of a master. But if a man accepts the proffered services of another in such a way as to imply a willingness to hire him, he will be bound as an employer even though the contract is implied.

In the event an employee is discharged without cause, the employer must pay him up to the end of the contract period. Seldom is the length of the contract period mentioned when the employer-employee relationship is created. It is usually implied by the terms of compensation. If the employee is paid by the hour, he may be discharged without liability at the end of any hour. If he is paid by the week or by the month, as is usually the case with secretaries, stenographers, and many other office employees, the term of employment is one week or one month as the case may be. With the monthly paid employees, the term of employment may depend on the way the compensation is quoted. If the quoted salary is $3,600 a year, the term of employment is one year even though the employee is paid once a month.

The terms of the employer-employee contract, other than the compensation, are seldom stated. They are determined by law.

UNION CONTRACTS

As indicated previously, the employer-employee relationship can come into existence only as the result of a contract, express or implied. Formerly the employer contracted individually with each employee. Under this condition two employees doing the same kind of work might receive radically different rates of pay. The contract of employment came into existence by an offer and an acceptance. Theoretically it was a personal matter with each employee whether he was willing to work for less money than a fellow employee doing the same work. Men with large families and great responsibilities tended to be meek in direct ratio to their responsibilities. This tended to hold wages in general down. Out of this and other economic factors grew the union movement and collective bargaining or contracting in many industries. An agent of the employees speaks and contracts for all the employees collectively. As a general rule, a contract is still made individually with each employee, but the union contract binds the employer to pay certain wages and work each employee only a certain number of hours.

DUTIES AND LIABILITIES OF THE EMPLOYER

The employer under the common law had five well-defined duties:

1. Duty to exercise care
2. Duty to provide a reasonably safe place to work
3. Duty to provide safe tools and appliances
4. Duty to provide competent and sufficient employees for the task
5. Duty to instruct employees with reference to the dangerous nature of employment

(1) **Duty to Exercise Care.** The employer under the common law is not an insurer of the employee's safety. He is liable for negligence in the care of his employees. He must exercise that degree of care which the nature of the business demands. He is not liable, however, for injuries resulting from the hazardous nature of the business itself. The courts generally use two tests to determine if the employer has used the degree of care required. First, did he use that degree of care which an ordinary, prudent man under similar circumstances would use? Second, did he act under the particular circumstances as an ordinary, prudent man? If the answer is "yes" in both instances, then the employer is not liable for the resulting injuries to the employees. If the nature of the business is highly hazardous, then the employer must exercise a high degree of diligence to prevent accidents to his employees.

(2) **Duty to Provide a Reasonably Safe Place to Work.** The employer is required to furnish every employee with a reasonably safe place to work. What is a safe place depends upon the nature of the work. A coal mine is a dangerous place; but if it is made as safe as the nature of coal mining permits, the employer is not liable for accidents under the common law. Most states have statutory laws supplementing and modifying the common law for hazardous industries. When one of these statutory laws and the common law conflict, the statutory law prevails.

- ▪ Dexter was employed as a welder in the Safe Machine Shop. Space was inadequate, making it necessary to pile sheet steel and I-beams on the floor. Dexter tripped over some of this material, and the flame from the welding machine touched his face, causing him to lose sight in one eye. The court held the employer liable in this case since the accident was directly caused by the failure of the employer to provide safe working conditions.

The safe place to work includes not only the particular spot where the worker performs his duties but the whole premises which the employee may use in the course of his employment.

(3) Duty to Provide Safe Tools and Appliances. The tools furnished the employees by the employer must be reasonably safe. This rule applies also to the machinery and appliances. Safe does not mean, of course, free from all danger. Some types of machinery and appliances are dangerous even under the best working conditions possible. The employer is required to use only ordinary care, relative to the nature of the work, in providing safe tools and machinery. He is not bound to discard old tools in order to install the latest and safest devices. If experience has shown that certain appliances or devices are dangerous and that newer devices have eliminated or greatly minimized the hazardous nature of the tool or device, then an employer must provide the safer method.

(4) Duty to Provide Competent and Sufficient Employees for the Task. Both the number of employees and their skill and experience affect the hazardous nature of many jobs. A task which is safe when performed by four men may be highly hazardous when only three men attempt it. Furthermore, the task may be safely performed by three men who are competent, but the same task may be very hazardous when one of the men is inexperienced. The employer is liable for all injuries to employees when the direct cause is due either to an insufficient number of workers or to the lack of skill of some of the workers. The employer is required to know the safe number of men required for each task. He also must have knowledge of the skill required to perform the task in a safe manner and make sure that each employee actually possesses that skill.

■ The Baxter Lumber Company was engaged in buying saw logs and cutting them into lumber. To get to the saw, the logs had to be stacked on a machine and then rolled onto the saw carriage for cutting. Baxter hired Burton to roll the logs onto the carriage. The job was exceptionally hazardous unless performed by an experienced man. Burton was totally inexperienced in this work. As a direct result of his inexperience, a pile of logs was loosened and rolled violently against the saw carriage, knocking the saw operator against the moving saw. He lost both legs. The Baxter Lumber Company was held liable for his injury since the cause of it was traced directly to the inexperience of Burton.

(5) Duty to Instruct New Employees. In all positions where machinery, chemicals, electric appliances, and other modern production instruments are used, there are many hazards of various degrees. The dangerous nature of these instruments may be perfectly evident to an experienced worker but not to an inexperienced worker. A machine that is perfectly safe to operate when the operator is skilled may be very hazardous when operated by one who is new at the job. One need not be told that a buzzing saw is dangerous if touched. How much instruction, then, if any, must be given to a new employee depends upon his experience, the nature of the machinery or chemical, and the degree to which the danger is self-evident to even an inexperienced employee. The law requires the employer to give that degree of instruction which each particular case requires. If a worker is injured while on the job, the cause of the injury must be traced directly to the failure on the part of the employer to give adequate instruction.

LIABILITIES OF THE EMPLOYER TO THIRD PARTIES

The employer is liable under certain circumstances for injuries to third parties which are caused by his employees. To be liable, the employee must have committed the injury in the course of his employment. If the employee, on his own initiative, injures a third party, and the injury was not a result of his work on his job, then the employee is personally liable, but the employer is not. The employer will be liable, however, if he ordered the act which caused the injury, or if he had knowledge of the act and assented to it. Finally, the employer is liable for the torts of his employees when these torts are due to his own negligence in not enforcing safe working procedures or in not employing competent employees.

- The Benten Wrecking Company instructed its employees not to throw timbers from the roof of the building it was wrecking unless one employee was on the ground to see that no one was in danger. The employees ignored this instruction and threw a large timber from the roof, injuring a man walking along beside the building. The company was liable for this injury even though the employees ignored their instructions.

EMPLOYEE'S DUTY TO HIS EMPLOYER

The employee owes certain duties to his employer. He must perform his duties faithfully and honestly. In skilled positions the worker must perform the task with ordinary skill. He must not reveal trade secrets or confidential information. In the event an employee breaches any of these duties, the employer's only remedy is to discharge the employee. He cannot, as in the case of agency, sue the employee for damages.

Many troublesome cases arise when an employee invents a new device during working hours with the use of company facilities. If the discovery or the invention is merely incidental to the employee's duties, then the invention belongs to him; but the employer may use it without the payment of royalties. The employer cannot sell the invention or exercise any right in it except to use it in his own plant.

If the employee's job is to use the employer's facilities to invent new devices or discover new chemical properties, then the invention or discovery belongs exclusively to the employer and may be patented only in his name.

Finally, an employee may by express contract waive his right to any invention made in the course of his employment. This contract is enforceable.

COMMON-LAW DEFENSES OF THE EMPLOYER

Although the common law imposed many duties upon the employer to protect the worker on the job, it allowed several defenses that were sufficient to defeat practically all claims for compensation for injuries sustained on the job. The four most common ones were:

1. Contributory negligence rule
2. The fellow-servant rule
3. The assumption-of-the-risk rule
4. The nonsurvivorship rule

(1) **Contributory Negligence Rule.** Under the common law if a worker sustains an injury on the job, he can sue his employer for damages. To establish liability, he must prove breach of duty on the part of the employer, namely that he failed to provide safe working conditions, or one of the other duties set out on page 287. The employer can escape liability for this breach of duty if he can establish the fact that the employee's own negligence contributed to the accident. If the employee could have avoided the injury by the exercise of due diligence, he is not entitled to collect damages from the employer.

(2) **The Fellow-Servant Rule.** If an employee is injured on the job and he himself was in no way negligent, the employer may still avoid being held liable by proving that the injury was caused by a fellow servant. A *fellow servant* is an employee who has the same status as the injured worker and is working with him. A foreman is not a fellow servant, nor is an employee in a different department even though he has the same status as the injured worker. The justification of this rule is that the employees assume this risk when they accept employment.

(3) **Assumption-of-the-Risk Rule.** Every type of employment in industry has some normal risks. Employees assume these normal risks by voluntarily accepting employment. This does not excuse the employer from the duty of providing safe working conditions; but even after this is done, many types of jobs, such as coal mining, are hazardous. If the injury is due to the hazardous nature of the job, the employer cannot be held liable. Even when the employer fails to provide the safe tools or safe conditions of employment, the employer is not liable if the employee could easily see the hazardous condition and did not protest. He is assumed to have waived his right to demand safe working conditions.

(4) **The Nonsurvivorship Rule.** The three preceding rules apply when the worker receives a nonfatal injury. If the injury is fatal, suit cannot be maintained by a surviving heir or spouse. This rule simply states that the right to damages, after all, is the loss of future wages. If a worker sustains a nonfatal injury that incapacitates him for six months, his damages are six months' wages. The nonsurvivorship rule is based on the theory that if a worker is fatally injured, he has not lost any future wages.

The nonsurvivorship rule has been repealed outright by all states and the other three rules have been modified in some degree by most of the states. Only a few generalizations can be made about the modifications. All states now have passed workmen's compensation laws as described in the following paragraphs. These laws almost without exception repeal the common-law defenses for all workers covered by workmen's compensation laws. In no state are all employees covered by workmen's compensation laws. For the uncovered employees the defenses have not been repealed but modified slightly to favor the employee. For example, many state laws now provide that contributory negligence is no longer an employer defense if the job is hazardous. Employees working for common carriers in interstate commerce are covered by federal laws. These common-law defenses have not been repealed by the federal workmen's compensation laws as has been the case with the state workmen's compensation laws. They have been modified, however, as will be seen in the section that follows.

MODERN LAWS DEALING WITH INDUSTRIAL ACCIDENTS

The federal government and all the states have passed laws repealing or modifying materially the common law relative to industrial accidents. The chief laws of this class are:

1. Federal Employers' Liability Act
2. State Workmen's Compensation Laws

(1) Federal Employers' Liability Act. Advances in technology brought about by the Industrial Revolution made it necessary for society to modify the common law to eliminate much injustice and hardship. One of the earliest acts along this line was the Federal Employers' Liability Act to govern the liability of common carriers engaged in interstate commerce. This act has been amended several times, the provisions of the present act being:

(a) An employee of a common carrier may collect damages caused by the negligence of a fellow employee or from any defect in the equipment that is due to the negligence of the carrier. This greatly modified the common-law fellow-servant rule.

(b) The contributory negligence of the injured worker does not bar recovery as under the common law, although such negligence may diminish the amount of damages.

(c) If an employee is fatally injured, the right to sue for damages survives to the next of kin. Under the common law the right to sue lapsed with the death of the worker.

(d) Contracts by the employer to limit or circumscribe the carrier's liability under the Act are void.

In addition to this act a few other federal laws deal with safety regulations and compensation for injuries. The most important of these are the Federal Coal Mine Safety Act, the Federal Safety Appliance Act, and the Longshoremen's and Harbor Workers' Act, a workmen's compensation law to cover maritime workers who are not covered by a state workmen's compensation law.

(2) **State Workmen's Compensation Laws.** The state workmen's compensation laws deny the employer the three common-law defenses of contributory negligence, fellow-servant rule, and assumption of the risks of the industry rule. The theory back of them is that the cost of an injury to a worker should be borne by society in general, regardless of the cause, provided the injury arises in the course of his employment. In a few states willful negligence and intoxication bar recovery if these acts are the direct cause of the injury.

The general nature of the workmen's compensation laws is to fix a sum to compensate for every type of injury, such as the loss of an eye, a limb, or a life. The worker, or his next of kin in case of death, need only prove that a particular injury was received in the course of employment. The law, itself, fixes the amount due. No formal trial is necessary, only an informal hearing before an examiner. In most cases, it is not necessary to employ counsel. Even though the amount allowed for the injury is often very small, yet the net amount received by the worker is considerably higher than under the old law where court costs and attorneys' fees consumed a large share of all awards.

Some states make the laws apply only to hazardous jobs; others make them cover all employees except domestic servants, farm help, government workers, and casual workers. The common-law rules apply to all workers in the state except those specifically covered by these laws.

QUESTIONS

1. In what important respect are employees distinguished from agents?
2. Are contracts of employment ever required to be in writing? If so, when?
3. How has collective bargaining affected the employer-employee relationship?
4. If a mine owner fails to brace the slate roof of the mine properly and, as a direct result of this failure, a miner is injured, who is liable for the injury?
5. What is the duty in regard to the safety of the tools the employer furnishes?
6. What is the employer's liability concerning the number of competent employees he must provide for each task?
7. May an employee ever bind his employer on a contract?
8. Must an employer provide all the very latest safety devices?
9. May an employer sue an employee for lack of loyalty and good faith?
10. If an employee invents some device on the employer's time, does he have exclusive right to it?

11. Have the state workmen's compensation laws repealed the common law of employer liability for injuries for all workers?

12. Under the Federal Employers' Liability Act, does contributory negligence on the injured employee's part bar recovery?

CASE PROBLEMS

1. Hawthorne was employed by Combs to help float a raft of saw logs down the Levisa river to its confluence with the Ohio river. The river was in flood stage and contained several dangerous rapids. Hawthorne was aware of these conditions, as he had rafted logs on the river before. The raft was broken apart on one rapid and Hawthorne was seriously injured. There was evidence that the raft was not secured by the best methods of constructing rafts. Was Combs liable to Hawthorne for damages?

2. Cheney was a chauffeur for Carter. While taking Carter to the airport to catch a plane, Cheney had a collision with a truck and was seriously injured. Carter was late and kept urging Cheney to drive faster. The collision was caused by a combination of too much speed, faulty brakes which Cheney was supposed to keep in good order, and Cheney's attempt to pass a car without adequate view of oncoming traffic. Is Carter liable to Cheney for damages?

3. Keller was color blind. He was employed by Koner to operate a crane. The foreman had a red light signal to notify the crane operator when to stop and a green light to tell him to proceed with the operation. While the red light was flashing, Keller continued to operate the crane and as a direct result of this, House was injured. Is Koner liable for this injury?

4. Lawson was injured by the moving parts of a piece of machinery. The injury could not have happened had a guard been placed over the moving part. It developed that a guard had been provided but that it had been removed by the previous operator of the machine. Lawson was not aware a guard had ever been on the machine. The employer knew when he assigned Lawson to the machinery that the guard was off. Is Lawson entitled to damages under the common law?

5. Kline was employed by the Keller Machine Shop. As a direct result of his particular job, he invented a machine that was a vast improvement over the one he was using. He worked on his new machine occasionally on company time and with company materials although his job was to operate the machine, not invent a new one. Kline patented his machine and then attempted to prevent the Keller Machine Shop from using it unless he was paid a royalty on the machine. (a) Must the Keller Machine Shop pay Kline to use one of the new machines? (b) Can the Keller Machine Shop manufacture the new machine and license other shops to use it? (c) Can Kline be prevented from patenting the new machine and marketing it in any way he sees fit?

CHAPTER 31
LABOR LEGISLATION

INTRODUCTION

Since 1930 more laws dealing with industrial relations have been passed by the federal government than had been passed during the entire history of the Republic. Although these laws together with the court interpretations of them are for the most part beyond the scope of a course in business law, some basic knowledge of them is valuable.

THE FAIR LABOR STANDARDS ACT

The Fair Labor Standards Act had two major objectives. The first objective was to place a floor under wages so that all employees engaged in interstate commerce would be paid a minimum wage regardless of economic conditions. The second objective was to discourage a long work week and thus spread employment. The first objective was accomplished directly by setting a minimum wage of 25 cents an hour. This minimum wage has been raised by stages through amendments to the act. The second objective was achieved not by fixing the maximum number of hours to be worked each week but by requiring the employers to pay time and a half for all hours over 40 hours. An employer may work his employees, other than women and children, any number of hours a week if he is willing to pay the overtime wage.

EXCLUSIONS FROM THE ACT

Not all workers are covered by the provisions of the Fair Labor Standards Act. There are three classes of exclusions:

1. Employees working for firms engaged in intrastate commerce are not covered by the act. This is not a specific exclusion in the act but is the result of the constitutional provision giving Congress power to regulate interstate commerce, not intrastate commerce.

2. A large number of employees who are engaged in interstate commerce are not covered by the act since certain businesses are specifically excluded. These exclusions are rather numerous. Other exclusions apply to the type of position rather than the nature of the industry. An example of the first type of exclusion is agricultural processing, such as canning, processing, or ginning. Examples of the second type of exclusion are executives, administrators, and outside salesmen.

3. The maximum hours provisions only do not apply to employees in that part of the transportation industry over which the Interstate Commerce Commission has control, to any employee engaged in the canning of fish, and to individuals employed as outside buyers of poultry, eggs, cream, or milk in their natural state.

These types of exclusions are given merely to indicate the complexity of the Act and the nature of the problems faced by business firms that must comply with its provisions.

CHILD LABOR PROVISIONS OF THE FAIR LABOR STANDARDS ACT

The Act forbids "oppressive child labor." The employment of children under 16 years of age is for the most part prohibited. This rule does not apply to parents or guardians, to newspaper delivery boys, or to certain types of employment specified by the Secretary of Labor as not being oppressive child labor. Those between the ages of 16 and 18 are not permitted to work in industries declared by the Secretary of Labor to be particularly hazardous to health.

CONTINGENT WAGES

Many types of employment call for the payment of wages on a commission basis or on a piece-rate basis. Many sales people receive a commission on sales made rather than a salary. If the commissions earned in any one week are less than the minimum wages for the hours worked, then the employer must add to the commission enough to bring the total earnings to the minimum wage. The same is true for those on a piece-rate basis. These types of incentive wages are not prohibited, but they cannot be used to evade the minimum wage provisions of the Act.

THE LABOR MANAGEMENT RELATIONS ACT

The Fair Labor Standards Act was designed primarily to do for the unorganized segment of labor what the organized segment of labor achieved through collective bargaining. The collective bargaining process is often a violent process. It may include strikes, picketing, boycotts, lockouts, sabotage, plant removals, and many other practices that disturb the free flow of commerce. The Labor Management Relations Act was not designed to eliminate any of these acts, but to bring them under the control of a federal agency and the courts to prevent abuses.

The Act applies to all employers engaged in business affecting commerce between and among the states with the following specific exceptions:

1. The railroad industry, which is under the Railway Labor Act of 1947
2. Agricultural laborers
3. Domestic servants
4. Supervisory employees who are considered a part of management
5. Government employees

MAJOR PROVISIONS OF THE ACT

There are five major provisions of the Labor Management Relations Act. These five provisions are:

1. The National Labor Relations Board
2. A declaration as to the rights of employees
3. A declaration as to the rights of employers
4. A prohibition of employers' unfair labor practices
5. A prohibition of certain unfair union practices

(1) The National Labor Relations Board. The Labor Management Relations Act provides for a National Labor Relations Board of five members appointed by the President. This board hears complaints of unfair labor practices of employers and also complaints made by both employers and employees of unfair union practices. If the board finds that an unfair practice exists, it has the power to seek an injunction to enjoin the practice. In strikes affecting the national welfare, the board is empowered to seek an injunction postponing the strike for eighty days. The board conducts investigations, supervises elections among employees for union recognition and for the union shop, and receives union financial reports. In addition to the board's function, a general counsel is appointed by the President. This general counsel is entirely independent of the board in prosecuting complaint cases, but in most other matters he acts as the chief legal advisor to the board.

(2) A Declaration as to the Rights of Employees. The Labor Management Relations Act, like the National Labor Relations Act, sets forth the following list of rights which the employees have:

(a) To organize

(b) To bargain collectively through their own chosen agents

(c) To engage in concerted action; that is, strike, for their mutual aid and protection

(d) Of an individual employee to join or not to join a union as he wishes unless a majority of all workers vote for a union shop

(3) A Declaration as to the Rights of Employers. The Labor Management Relations Act gives the employer many important rights which he did not have under the National Labor Relations Act. The most important of these rights are:

(a) To petition for an investigation when he questions the union's rights to speak for the employees

(b) To refuse to bargain collectively with foremen and other supervisory employees

(c) To institute charges before the board of unfair labor practices by the unions

(d) To sue unions for breaches of the union contract whether the breach is done in the name of the union or as an individual union member

(e) To plead with his workers to refrain from joining the union provided no threats are used. These provisions were included to "equalize" the rights of the employer and the employee on the assumption that the National Labor Relations Act gave the workers an undue advantage

(4) A Prohibition of Unfair Labor Practices by Employers.
The chief acts which are declared to be unfair practices by employers are:

(a) Interfering in the exercise of the rights granted employees

(b) Refusing to bargain collectively with employees when they have legally selected a representative

(c) Dominating any labor organization or contributing financial support to it

(d) Discriminating against or favoring an employee in any way because of his membership or lack of membership in the union

(e) Discriminating against an employee because he has filed a complaint against his employer

All of these unfair practices were also prohibited under the National Labor Relations Act. The board, when it finds the employer guilty of any of these acts, usually issues a "cease and desist order." If the cease and desist order is not effective, an injunction may be obtained.

(5) A Prohibition of Unfair Union Practices. The National Labor Relations Act did not list any unfair union practices. The new act listed seven specific acts which unions and their leaders may not engage in:

(a) Any coercion or restraint of workers in the exercise of their legally expressed rights

(b) Interference with the employer in his selection of a bargaining agent

(c) Refusal to bargain collectively with the employer

(d) Charging excessive initiation fees and discriminatory dues and fees of any kind

(e) Barring a worker from the union for any reason except the nonpayment of dues

(f) Secondary boycotts or strikes in violation of law or the contract

(g) Attempts to exact payment for services not rendered

These are the abuses which the advocates of a new labor law to replace the National Labor Relations Act claimed were widespread. The board, as well as the general counsel, was empowered to investigate all charges that any of these abuses existed and to take the necessary legal action to abate them. The most effective method of dealing with them is an injunction.

FEDERAL SOCIAL SECURITY ACT

The Federal Social Security Act has four major provisions:

1. Old Age and Survivors Insurance
2. Old Age Assistance
3. Unemployment Compensation
4. Taxation to finance the act

(1) **Old Age and Survivors Insurance.** In Chapter 39 on life insurance, both life insurance and annuity insurance are defined and illustrated. The first provision of the Social Security Act provides for the payment by the Social Security Board of decreasing term life insurance to the dependents of a covered worker who dies before the age of retirement. This is called Survivors Benefits. If the worker lives to the age of 65 and retires, then he and his wife draw a retirement annuity known as a Joint and Last Survivor Annuity as described in Chapter 39. This is the old age part of the provision. Both parts of the first provision are properly called insurance because they shift risks that life insurance companies will assume for a fee. The survivors insurance covers the risk of the breadwinner's dying prematurely, leaving those who depend on him without a source of income. The old age benefits cover the risk of outliving one's savings after retirement. These are exactly the same risks assumed by life insurance and annuity insurance contracts.

Who Is Covered? The Social Security Act was passed in 1935 and has been amended at almost every session of Congress since then. Today practically everyone is covered by the life and annuity insurance provisions of the act. Doctors by their own request are for the most part excluded. Employees in state and local governments, including public school teachers, may be brought under the coverage of the Act by means of agreements between the state and the federal government. Before these workers can be covered by this agreement, a majority of the eligible employees must vote in favor of the coverage.

Farmers, professional people, such as lawyers, and self-employed business people are for the most part covered by this provision of the Act. Self-employed people who net less than $400 a year are excluded. Also specifically excluded are certain types of work of close relatives, such as a parent for a child, work by a child under 21 for his parents, employment of a wife by her husband, but the Act covers self employment by a wife.

Eligibility for Retirement Benefits. To be eligible for retirement benefits, one must meet these requirements:

(a) Be fully insured at the time of retirement
(b) Be 62 years of age or older
(c) After reaching the age of retirement have applied for retirement benefits. If one elects to start drawing benefits at age 62, there is a penalty in the form of a reduction in benefits depending on how many months one is short of age 65. To be entitled to the maximum retirement benefits, one must wait until age 65 to apply for the benefits.

Eligibility for Survivors Benefits. To be eligible for retirement benefits one must be fully insured at the time he retires. He is fully insured if, when he reaches retirement age, he has one quarter of coverage (earned any time after 1936) for each two full calendar quarters after 1950. At least 6 quarters of coverage are necessary in every case. When he has earned 40 quarters of coverage, he is fully insured for life. In this case it is not necessary that he be working at the time he applies for retirement benefits. If he is not fully insured at retirement age, he may continue to work until he has enough quarters to be fully insured.

When a worker dies before he achieves a fully insured status, his family is entitled to survivors benefits if he was currently insured at the time of his death. One is currently insured if at the time of his death he has at least 6 quarters of coverage during the 13-quarter period ending with the quarter in which he dies or the quarter in which he becomes entitled to old-age insurance benefits.

Calculating Retirement Benefits. As the first step in calculating one's retirement benefits, his average monthly income from the time he was first covered by social security to the time of retirement must be calculated. Before this is done, there are two adjustments that may need to be made. First, the insured may request that five years of his employment be excluded in calculating his average monthly wage. The higher this wage, the higher the retirement income. If one as a college student earned $80 a month while in college but earned $350 a month or more after that, he can have this $80 a month excluded and the months during which he earned it also excluded. This will give him a higher average monthly income and consequently a higher retirement income than he would have without the exclusion.

Second, the law allows a worker what is called a "disability freeze." If at any time during one's working career he is disabled and unable to earn any income for a considerable period, his average monthly income would be reduced. This is true because his earnings would be listed as zero for the months of disability, but the months would not be excluded in calculating the total number of months covered. If a worker is totally disabled for six months or more, he may ask that this entire period of disability be ignored in calculating his average monthly income.

Also one may exclude from his work coverage the five consecutive years of coverage in which he had the lowest income or no income at all in a covered industry. This exclusion helps to keep one's average monthly income high, thus enabling one to receive a larger annuity than he would otherwise receive.

Survivors Benefits. If the insured dies before reaching 65, his widow, dependent children, and dependent parents may be eligible for survivors benefits. The insured's primary benefit is calculated as though he had retired. Then the widow draws three fourths of the husband's benefit if she has a child under 18 years of age.

If the deceased's widow has only one child under 18, the child draws three fourths of the father's primary benefit. If there is more than one child under 18, each child draws one half of the father's primary benefit plus an equal share in an additional one fourth, with the provision that the benefits for the family do not exceed $254 a month or 80 percent of the father's average monthly income, whichever is less.

The parents of the deceased may draw three fourths of his primary benefit. For the parents to draw these benefits, however, the son must have been fully insured when he died and the parents must have been dependent on the deceased son's income.

In addition, a lump sum payment of $255 or three times the deceased's primary benefit, whichever is less, is paid to the widow or widower.

The 1956 amendment to the Social Security Act provides for disability payments under certain conditions. When one becomes so severely disabled that he is unable to continue working, he can qualify for disability payments if (a) he is both fully and currently insured at the time of disability, and (b) he has 20 quarters of coverage in the 40 calendar quarters before the beginning date of his disability. The disability benefits are calculated exactly as though the disabled worker had reached 65 and retired. The disability must be so severe that it prevents any substantial gainful employment, must have continued for 6 months, and must be expected to continue indefinitely.

(2) Old-Age Assistance. Since many people for various reasons are not covered by the insurance feature of the Social Security Act, other means of assistance are provided for people over 65. Each state was left to adopt its own pension system, and the federal government agreed to match any state pension up to 75 percent of the first $20 and 50 percent of the remainder. This is a noncontributory system. Need is the only test, whereas with old-age insurance feature need is not considered.

(3) Unemployment Compensation. In handling unemployment compensation, the federal government cooperates with the states, which set up their own rules for the payment of unemployment benefits. Payments of unemployment compensation are made by the states and not by the federal government.

Federal Law. Every employer of four or more persons (except employers of the exempted classes) must pay a federal tax on his payrolls. No tax is levied on the employee.

Under the provisions of the federal act, no payment of benefits can be made to any individual with regard to unemployment that occurs within two years after the beginning of the time when contributions were required by the state in which he lived. Twenty-two states began the payment of unemployment compensation benefits in January, 1938; most of the other states began the payment of these benefits by January, 1939.

State Laws. Naturally the unemployment compensation laws of the various states differ in many respects. They are alike, however, in providing for raising funds by levies upon employers.

The state unemployment compensation laws apply in general to workers in commerce and industry. Agricultural workers, domestic servants, governmental employees, and the employees of nonprofit organizations formed and operated exclusively for religious, charitable, literary, educational, scientific, or humane purposes are not included under the laws.

Prior to World War II the maximum benefit under the act was $15 a week and the maximum number of weeks for which unemployment would be paid was twenty-six weeks. Since the War most states have liberalized both these provisions.

In order to be eligible for benefits, a worker must meet the following requirements:

(a) He must be available for work and registered at an unemployment office

(b) He must have been employed for a certain length of time within a specified period in an employment covered by the state law

(c) He must be capable of working

(d) He must not have refused employment for which he is reasonably fitted

(e) He must not be self-employed

(f) He must not be out of work because of a strike or a lockout still in progress

(g) He must have served the required waiting period

(4) Taxation to Finance the Plan. To pay the life insurance and the annuity insurance benefits of the Social Security Act, both the employer and the employee are taxed an equal percentage of all income earned in any one year up to a maximum of $4,800. The current rate of the tax is 3⅜ percent. Both the maximum income and the rate may be changed at any session of Congress. The unemployment compensation part of the act is financed by a payroll tax of a maximum of 3 percent. In most states this tax is borne entirely by the employer. The Old Age Assistance part of the act is paid for by general taxation. No specific tax is levied to meet these payments.

QUESTIONS

1. What was the chief purpose of the Labor Management Relations Act?

2. What act prohibited "oppressive child labor"?

3. Are all workers covered by the Fair Labor Standards Act?

4. Under the National Labor Management Relations Act of 1947, what power does the board have in a strike affecting the national welfare?

5. (a) If an employer refuses to bargain collectively with his employees, is this an unfair labor practice?
   (b) Name some unfair labor practices by employers.

6. What are the unions' rights in regard to initiation fees and dues?

7. What workers or income recipients in America are not covered under the old-age retirement part of the Social Security Act?

8. Who may benefit if the insured dies before reaching 65?

9. What is the "disability freeze" in the Social Security Law?

10. What is the purpose of allowing a worker to eliminate from his social security coverage the five consecutive years of lowest income?

11. Does the Social Security Law cover loss of income due to disability?

CASE PROBLEMS

1. John was employed by the Ritz Hotel for $20 a week plus his tips. Tips amounted on the average to $40 a week. After John had worked six months, he demanded that the hotel pay him the minimum wage, exclusive of tips, for the six months he had been working. Must the hotel pay?

2. Mary was a secretary in a large business establishment. Due to a severe reduction in business, she was laid off. She registered with the public employment office and applied for unemployment compensation. Before her payments began, the employment office found her another position equally as good as her former position except that she would have to work two Sundays per month. She refused to accept the job because of the Sunday work. The employment office ruled she was ineligible for unemployment compensation because of this refusal. Was she?

3. The Fenton Model Airplane Company made kits for model airplanes, boats, and cars. It sold some finished products. To make the finished products ready for sale, it contracted with high school and business college boys to make the kits into finished products. Each boy would take a given number of kits home, and when he returned them all finished, he was paid a fixed sum for each item. After several months John became dissatisfied with the amount he was earning and demanded that he be paid the minimum wage for the number of hours he worked on the models. The company insisted he was an independent contractor and, therefore, not entitled to minimum wages. Is the company's contention correct?

4. The Independent Carpenters Union was a local union made up of all the employees of the Grace Sheet Metal Company who worked in any way with wood. The president of the company contributed $500 a month to the union so it would not have to charge its members dues. Some of the members who wanted to be represented by the National Carpenters' Union, a dues-paying union, filed a complaint with the National Labor Relations Board charging the company with an unfair labor practice. Is this an unfair labor practice?

5. Abbot had three children, aged one year, three years, and four years. His wife was 29. Abbot died at age 30. During his entire working career, he had earned $4,800 a year or more except for two years in which he was totally unemployed due to a serious illness. How much will Mrs. Abbot collect in survivors insurance benefits by the time the youngest child becomes 18?

6. The teachers of Clarke County wish to be covered by Social Security. The County School Board refuses to consider placing them under Social Security. What act, if any, can the teachers take to obtain coverage?

7. The Walton Wax Company employed about 400 workers at the peak of its business load. When business became slack, instead of shutting down, it went on a two-day week for everyone. The workers insisted that the company shut down completely until business picked up so that the workers would be eligible for unemployment compensation. May they compel the company to do this?

8. Crawford owned a cotton gin and cotton storage company. At the peak of the cotton picking season he employed twenty or more workers, but only four employees had full-time work. Often when there was a long line of trucks waiting to have the cotton ginned, he would keep running until midnight. Some of the workers would work fourteen hours a day. They brought suit to compel Crawford to pay them minimum wages and time and a half for overtime. Are they entitled to this relief?

SUMMARY CASES

PART 6

1. J. F. Powell was an agent for the Continental Oil Company. The job was to call on local dealers to explain the company's advertising program, to call on them to get new business, and to increase the old business. His territory covered about 12 counties. He placed an advertising program with C. C. Baxter, owner of radio station KFPL. This program consisted of 26 electrical transcriptions called the "Conoco Listeners' Hour." The company refused to pay for the advertising and Baxter sued. Was the company bound on this contract? (Continental Oil Company v. Baxter, 59 S. W. 2d 463)

2. Samuel Leviten, a commission merchant in New York City engaged the brokerage firm of Bickley, Mandeville and Wimple, Inc. of Chicago to make short sales for him on the Chicago Merchants' Exchange. These brokers at one time covered some short sales by making purchases for Leviten without his knowledge or consent. Leviten was later notified of their act but made no protest for several days. He later brought suit for damages against the brokers alleging that they violated their contract with him. Did Leviten's silence constitute a ratification? (Leviten v. Bickley, Mandeville and Wimple, Inc., 35 F. 2d 825)

3. Alfred S. Dale was the owner of an apartment building in Bismarck. He ordered some beds from Sears, Roebuck and Company. When the beds arrived, he contracted with Nelson to install one of them in one of the apartments. Claude Newman rented the apartment. The bed collapsed and Newman was seriously injured. Nelson did not follow instructions in installing the bed. He used wood screws instead of the lag screws which the seller had recommended for the installation. This was the direct cause of the collapse. Was Nelson an employee or independent contractor? (Newman v. Sears Roebuck Co. and Dale, 43 N. W. 2d 411)

4. Raymond was the agent of Davies in the management and operation of Davies' farm. He brought suit to collect for his unpaid salary of $2,187.35 and $439.99 for money he advanced from his personal funds. Davies denied all the liability on the grounds of breach of good faith. Raymond was secretly a stockholder in Farmers' Cooperative Exchange. He purchased many farm supplies from this corporation for the principal and at one time received a bonus for these purchases in the form of 7 shares of stock. He did not reveal this fact to Davies. Was this act a breach of good faith? (Raymond v. Davies, 293 Mass. 117, 199 N. E. 321)

5. Moore was a real estate broker in Fargo. He approached Olsen, owner of some real estate, relative to selling the real estate. Olsen agreed to pay him 5 percent commission if he would sell it. Moore introduced one Flatt as a prospective purchaser who wished to use the property as a summer resort. The sale was finally consummated to Flatt for $15,000. Olsen then learned that the true purchaser was Pettibone who also owned and operated a summer resort on the same lake where the Olsen property was located. Moore was secretly Pettibone's agent. Upon learning these facts, Olsen brought suit to rescind the contract. May Olsen rescind this contract? (Olsen v. Pettibone, 168 Minn. 414, 210 N. W. 149)

6. McDonnell was the general agent of the Seaboard Air Line Railway at Savannah, Georgia. Among his other duties McDonnell was to issue bills of lading and to notify consignees when freight has arrived. McDonnell fraudulently forged several bills of lading purporting to have originated in Charleston, S. C. He notified Gleason, a cotton factor in Savannah, that cotton consigned to him had arrived. He then induced Gleason to pay him a large sum of money for this non-existing cotton. Gleason, upon learning of the forged documents, brought suit against the principal to recoup his loss. Was the principal liable for the fraudulent act of its agent? (Gleason v. Seaboard Air Line Railway, 278 U. S. 349, 49 S. Ct. 161)

7. The International Seaman's Union had a contract with the Peninsular and Occidental Steamship Company. At the time this contract was signed, there was no other union claiming to represent the seamen. Later the National Maritime Union began organizing the crew and obtained a majority of the crew as members. A strike resulted over the issue as to which union should represent the crew. About 150 members of the crew who engaged in sitdown strikes and threatened to sabotage the ship were dismissed. The dismissed members of the crew filed a complaint with the National Labor Relations Board, alleging the ship owners had engaged in an unfair labor practice by dismissing them for union activity. The board found the steamship company guilty and ordered the dismissed crew members restored to their jobs with back pay. The ship owners alleged that the crew members were dismissed for their mutiny and threatened sabotage, not for their union activity. Did the steamship company commit an unfair labor practice? (The Peninsular and Occidental Steamship Co. v. National Labor Relations Board, C. C. A. 5, 98 F. 2d 411)

8. Curtis applied to the Phelps Dodge Corporation for employment. His application was turned down because he was a member of a labor union. After vainly seeking work for some time, he brought an action before the National Labor Relations Board, alleging an unfair labor practice. The Board found the company guilty and ordered the company to employ Curtis and pay him for the wages he would have earned had he been employed. The company appealed this ruling in the U. S. Circuit Court. The question to be answered in this case is: If "firing" a man for union activity is an unfair labor practice, should refusing to hire a man for the same activity be an unfair labor practice? (Phelps Dodge Corp. v. National Labor Relations Board, 313 U. S. 177)

9. Eleanor Beard conducted a business whereby she supplied materials to women from which they made comforters and quilts. Before delivery the material was stamped with special designs. The women were to take the material home and do the work at their leisure. When the quilts were completed, they were returned, and payment was made according to the contract price. The Collector of Internal Revenue classified these workers as employees and compelled Beard to pay social security taxes on their earnings. Beard appealed to the Federal Court to recover these taxes on the ground these parties were independent contractors, not employees. Were they employees? (Glenn, Collector of Internal Revenue v. Beard, 141 F. 2d 376)

10. John P. Finnegan was the driver of a truck for the New York Tribune, Inc. On his way to deliver a truckload of paper, he collided with a bus driven by Sauter. When Sauter got out of the bus, an argument ensued between Sauter and Finnegan. Finnegan became very angry and kicked Sauter in the face, causing a very painful injury. Sauter then sued the employer of Finnegan, the New York Tribune, Inc., for damages for this unprovoked assault. Was the employer liable for this act of its employee? (Sauter v. New York Tribune, Inc. et al., 305 N. Y. 442, 113 N. E. 2d 790)

11. A telegraph operator in a railway station was asleep when a freight train passed by his station. Because of this, the operator did not hear the train. Later he was called by another operator to inquire if the freight train had passed his station and he assured the operator that it had not. On the basis of this assurance, a train was dispatched over a single track line, heading toward the station the train had passed. The two trains later had a head-on collision causing the death of Dixon, the fireman. Dixon's estate sued the railroad for damages because of Dixon's death. Was the railroad company liable? (Northern Pacific Railroad Company vs. Dixon, 194 U. S. 338)

PART 7

PARTNERSHIPS

Preview Cases for Part 7: Partnerships

- Roger and Dwight purchased 150 acres of pulpwood. They
  agreed to cut it and sell it, and, after paying all costs and expenses, to divide the remaining receipts "fifty-fifty." While hauling
  the pulpwood to the loading yard, Dwight negligently injured
  Carlton. Carlton sued both Roger and Dwight as partners. Should
  both Roger and Dwight be held liable?

- Reed was a partner in the engineering firm of Reed and Dudley.
  Because of carelessness, as well as incompetency, Reed miscalculated the dimensions of steel piers for a bridge. As a result of
  this lack of care and skill, the firm was held liable for a $30,000
  loss. May the firm hold Reed liable?

- The net profits after paying partners' salaries of the partnership
  of Carlton, Gutherie, and Knowles was $40,000. Knowles and
  Gutherie insist that the $40,000 be retained in the business for ex-
  pansion to meet competition. Gutherie insists upon withdrawing his
  share. Does he have the right to do so?

- The widow Jones left some bearer bonds and other valuables
  with the partnership firm of Flannagan and Boyd for safekeeping.
  Boyd cashed some of the bonds and used the money for his personal benefit. Is the firm liable to Mrs. Jones? Is Boyd liable to the
  firm?

- O'Day and Ferber own a patent on a new piece of farm machinery. They form a partnership to continue for five years to
  manufacture and market the machinery. After two years they sold
  only ten pieces of machinery, and the purchasers of these were
  highly dissatisfied. O'Day wished to liquidate and call an end to the
  undertaking while they could still avoid bankduptcy, but Ferber
  insisted on continued operation until the end of the partnership
  agreement. What legal steps may Day take to end the partnership?

*These preview cases are designed to serve as a springboard for the study
of this part. As you read through each chapter in this part, you will find the
actual decisions for all these preview cases. Of course, there are many more
such illustrative problems as well as case problems for decision at the end of
each chapter. And there are also a number of even more challenging cases for
review at the end of the part.*

CHAPTER 32

FORMATION OF A
PARTNERSHIP

WHAT IS A PARTNERSHIP?

A *partnership* is an association of two or more competent persons who have combined their money, property, or labor and skill, or some or all of them, for the purpose of carrying on some lawful business for their joint profit.

The partnership must be formed for the purpose of operating a lawful business. If the business is unlawful, the attempt to form a partnership to operate such a business is void. Furthermore, a partnership may not be formed for the purpose of conducting a lawful business in an illegal manner.

Since the purpose of a partnership must be to conduct a trade, business, or profession for profit, a hunting club, a sewing circle, a trade union, a chamber of commerce, or other nonprofit association cannot be treated as a partnership.

ADVANTAGES OF THE PARTNERSHIP

By the operation of a partnership, capital and skill may be increased, competition may be lessened, labor may be made more efficient, the ratio of expenses per dollar of business may be reduced, and management may be improved. It is not certain that all these advantages will accrue to every partnership, but the prospect of greater profits by reason of them is the incentive which leads to the formation of a partnership.

DISADVANTAGES OF THE PARTNERSHIP

The most important disadvantages are:

(1) The unlimited liability of each partner for the debts of the partnership

(2) The relative instability of the business because of the danger of dissolution by reason of the death or withdrawal of one of the partners

(3) The divided authority among the partners, which may lead to disharmony

CLASSIFICATION OF PARTNERSHIPS

Partnerships may be classified as follows:

1. Ordinary partnerships
2. Limited partnerships
3. Trading and nontrading partnerships

(1) Ordinary Partnerships. When two or more persons voluntarily contract to pool their capital and skill to conduct some business undertaking for profit, with no limitations upon their rights and duties, an *ordinary partnership* is created. This is the oldest type of business combination and is still widely used today. This type of business organization is governed by the common law except in those states which have adopted the Uniform Partnership Act.* The purpose of this act is to bring about uniformity in the partnership laws of the states.

(2) Limited Partnerships. A *limited partnership* is one in which one or more partners have their liability for the firm's debts limited to the amount of their investment. This type of partnership cannot operate either under the common law or the Uniform Partnership Act. Such a partnership cannot be formed without a specific state statute prescribing the conditions under which it can operate. If the limited partnership does not comply strictly with the enabling statute, the courts hold it to be an ordinary partnership.

---

* The Uniform Partnership Act has been adopted in Alaska, Arizona, Arkansas, California, Colorado, Delaware, Guam, Idaho, Illinois, Indiana, Kentucky, Maryland, Massachusetts, Michigan, Minnesota, Missouri, Montana, Nebraska, Nevada, New Jersey, New Mexico, New York, North Carolina, North Dakota, Ohio, Oklahoma, Oregon, Pennsylvania, Rhode Island, South Carolina, South Dakota, Tennessee, Utah, Vermont, Virginia, Washington, West Virginia, Wisconsin, and Wyoming.

(3) **Trading and Nontrading Partnerships.** A *trading partnership* is one engaged in buying and selling merchandise. A *nontrading partnership* is one devoted to services, such as accounting, medicine, dentistry, law, and similar professional services. The chief reason for making the distinction is that the members in a nontrading partnership usually have considerably less apparent authority than the partners in a trading partnership. For example, one partner in a nontrading partnership cannot borrow money in the name of the firm and bind the firm. One dealing with a nontrading partnership is charged with considerably more responsibility in ascertaining the actual authority of the partners to bind the firm than is a person dealing with a trading partnership.

WHO MAY BE PARTNERS?

Since a partnership is based upon a contract, any person who is competent to make a contract is competent to be a partner. A minor may become a partner to the same extent to which he may contract about any other matter. His contracts are voidable by him; but since he is the agent of the other partner or partners, he can bind the partnership on contracts within the scope of the partnership business. On the other hand, the adult partners cannot as a rule bind the minor if he wishes to avoid personal liability. If the partnership has incurred debts, all the assets of the partners, including those of the minor, are subject to application on these debts. This is an exception to the minor's right to disaffirm his contracts.

KINDS OF PARTNERS

The members of a partnership may be classified as follows:

1. General partner
2. Silent partner
3. Secret partner
4. Dormant partner

(1) **General Partner.** A *general partner* is one who is actively and openly engaged in the business and is held out to everyone as a partner. He has unlimited liability in respect to the partnership debts. He holds himself out to the public as a full-fledged partner, assumes all the risks of the partnership, limits none of his rights, and assumes all the duties of an owner. This is the usual type of partner.

(2) Silent Partner. A *silent partner* is one who takes no active part in the management of the business. He limits his rights as a partner to the sharing of the profits in the ratio agreed upon. As a general rule, the other partners offer him two inducements to invest his money but to take no active part in the management. The inducements are limited liability and no share of the losses. To have his liability limited, he must make known to all creditors the extent of his limitations, and the creditors must contract with the firm with notice of such limitations. He performs more the function of an investor than that of an entrepreneur.

(3) Secret Partner. A *secret partner* is an active partner who attempts to keep his status as a partner concealed from the public. His motives are to escape the unlimited liability of a general partner and at the same time to take an active part in the management of the business. Should his relationship to the firm become known to the public, however, he would not escape unlimited liability. He differs from the silent partner in two respects: (1) he is unknown to the public; and (2) he takes an active part in the management of the business. He may feign the status of an employee or he may work elsewhere; but he meets frequently with the other partners to discuss management problems.

(4) Dormant Partner. A *dormant partner* (sometimes referred to as a *sleeping partner*) usually combines the characteristics of both the secret and the silent partner. He is usually unknown to the public as a partner, and he takes no part in the management of the business of the firm. When he becomes known to the public as a partner, he is liable for the debts of the firm to the same extent as a general partner. He foregoes his right to participate in the management of the firm. In return he receives a limitation on his liability so far as the other partners are able to effect it. He may, in addition, agree to limit his income to a reasonable return on his investment, since he contributes no services.

CREATION OF A PARTNERSHIP

A partnership is the result of a contract, express or implied, just as all other business commitments result from a contract. The partnership contract must meet the five tests of a valid contract as set out in Chapter 3. A partnership may also be created by law when two or more parties act in such a way as to lead third parties to believe that a partnership exists. This manner of formation is treated more fully under "Implied Partnership Agreements" and "Partnerships by Estoppel" later in this chapter.

ARTICLES OF COPARTNERSHIP

In the absence of a statute to the contrary, a written contract providing for the formation of a partnership need not be in a particular form. The written agreement is commonly known as *articles of copartnership*. Partnership articles may vary according to the needs of a particular situation, but ordinarily they should contain the following:

(1) The date
(2) The names of the partners
(3) The nature and the duration of the business
(4) The name and the location of the business
(5) The individual contributions of the partners
(6) The sharing of profits, losses, and responsibilities
(7) Keeping of accounts
(8) The duties of the partners
(9) The amounts of withdrawals of money
(10) Unusual restraints upon the partners
(11) Provisions for dissolution and division of assets
(12) Signatures of partners

IMPLIED PARTNERSHIP AGREEMENTS

Under certain circumstances a partnership may be implied by the acts of the individuals. The parties may not intend to form a contract of partnership, but the court may infer such an intention under certain circumstances. Almost without exception an implied partnership arises only as it relates to third parties. Seldom have the courts held that there is a partnership between A and B because B implied by his acts that he was accepting A's offer to form a partnership. Third parties may very well be misled, however, by B's actions into thinking that there is a partnership relation existing between A and B. Such an implied partnership exists, however, only as it relates to third parties who were misled by A's and B's acts. Some acts which may under certain circumstances imply a partnership are:

(a) An agreement to share net profits and net losses

(b) A loan with an understanding that the creditor will accept a percentage of the net profits until the interest and principal are paid

(c) An agreement between the owners of community property to share gross returns

All of these acts create what is sometimes called *prima facie* evidence of a partnership. This simply means that standing alone any of these agreements may constitute a partnership. This presumption of a partnership may be overcome by the introduction of evidence proving no partnership was intended.

PARTNERSHIP BY ESTOPPEL

Closely related to implied partnerships are partnerships by estoppel. An implied partnership is based on some agreement between two or more parties which agreement is closely akin to the articles of copartnership. As a rule, a partnership by estoppel is not based on contract, but on words or acts that mislead innocent third parties into thinking a partnership exists. The parties have no intention of forming a partnership, but their words or acts are such that the courts interpose themselves between the innocent third parties and the partners so that they are "stopped" from denying that a partnership exists.

> ▪ Brinkley was a retired merchant. While he was in business, he had bought vast quantities of merchandise from a particular wholesaler. His credit with the wholesaler was excellent. Hartman, in the presence of the credit manager of the wholesale firm, said, "Mr. Brinkley and I have formed a partnership and will be ordering some merchandise from your firm soon." Brinkley did not deny this statement. Soon thereafter Hartman sent in an order amounting to more than $5,000 on 90 days' credit. The account was never paid and the wholesaler sued Brinkley. He is liable since his silence estops him from denying that a partnership exists.

PARTNERSHIP FIRM NAME

A firm name is not a legal necessity or requirement for a partnership, but it is useful as a matter of convenience and for the purpose of identification. Any name that does not violate the rights of others or that is not contrary to law may be adopted by the firm and may be changed at will by agreement. In some states it is not permissible to use the name of a person who is not a member of the firm, or to use the words "and Company" unless the term represents a partner. Many of the states permit the use of fictitious or trade names. Some states permit use of a fictitious name but require the firm to register its name, address, purpose, and the names and addresses of the partners.

At common law a partnership cannot bring a suit at law or be sued in the name of the firm, but by statute or court rule a partnership may sue or be sued either in the firm name or in the names of the partners. Under the common law real property may be held in the names of the partners, but under the Uniform Partnership Act it may be held and conveyed in the name of the firm.

PARTNER'S INTEREST IN PARTNERSHIP PROPERTY

There are three classes of joint ownership of property. *Joint ownership* exists when the survivor of one of two joint owners gets full title to all the property upon the death of one. In *common ownership* each owner can sell his share without the consent of the other owner, and upon the death of one party, the surviving co-owner does not get title to the deceased owner's part as in joint ownership. His share goes to his heirs. A partner is a *tenant* or *owner in partnership*. This type of ownership differs fundamentally from the other two types. A surviving partner does not get full ownership upon the death of the other partner as is the case in joint ownership. One partner is not as free to sell his interest in partnership property as is the case with common ownership. The personal creditors of one partner in most states cannot sell specific pieces of property of the partnership to satisfy personal debts, nor can they sell a fractional part of specific assets as would be possible under common ownership. The personal creditors of one partner can sell only his pro rata share of the partnership, not specific assets. Each partner owns, and can sell, only a pro rata part of the partnership as an entity. The purchaser of one partner's share cannot demand that the other partners accept him as a partner.

JOINT-STOCK COMPANIES

A *joint-stock company* is in some respects similar to a partnership, but the ownership is indicated by shares of stock, as in a corporation. The ownership of these shares may be transferred without dissolving the association, thus overcoming one of the chief disadvantages of the general partnership. The joint stockholders are still liable, jointly and severally, for the debts of the firm while they are members, and for this reason, joint-stock companies do not offer the safeguards of a corporation. These joint-stock companies are permitted to operate in some states by special statutes authorizing them, or in some states, without statute, as a common-law association.

JOINT VENTURES

These are joint undertakings for profit between two or more parties that have most of the features of a partnership but are not so classified. A sharecropping agreement, or a farm lease "on the halves" are examples of joint ventures. The farm owner puts up the land, the tenant puts up the equipment, and the two share both expenses and receipts. This is not a partnership, however.

> ■ Roger and Dwight purchased 150 acres of pulpwood. They agreed to cut it and sell it, and, after paying all costs and expenses, to divide the remaining receipts "fifty-fifty." While hauling the pulpwood to the loading yard, Dwight negligently injured Carlton. Carlton sued both Roger and Dwight as partners. Roger was not liable since this was a joint venture, not a partnership.

QUESTIONS

1. For what purpose may a partnership be formed?
2. (a) What are the advantages of a partnership?
   (b) What are the disadvantages of a partnership?
3. What are the different classes of partnerships?
4. Are partnerships in your state governed by the common law or by the Uniform Partnership Act?
5. (a) Who may be a partner?
   (b) May a minor be held to his contract creating a partnership?
6. (a) What are the classifications of partners?
   (b) How is a partnership formed?
7. How might two or more parties be held to have formed a partnership when they had no intention to form one?
8. Are partners liable for the negligent acts of the other partners committed in the course of their employment?
9. If there are three members of a partnership, may two of them "fire" the third one and still keep his investment in the firm?
10. Does every partner have an equal right to work for the firm?

CASE PROBLEMS

1. Goldberg in applying for credit states that he is a partner in the firm of Goldberg and Rowan. Credit was extended to him on the basis of this assertion. It developed that two months prior to this transaction, Goldberg had sold his interest in the firm to Rowan, but Rowan had retained Goldberg's name in the firm. Is Rowan liable on this debt after Goldberg defaults ` because of insolvency?

2. Mathis and Lyons were employed by the Twin Bar Ranch to manage the ranch for the owner and to receive as compensation two thirds of the net profits plus living quarters. The Dale Feed Company knew of their receipt of a share of the profits and sold feed to the Ranch on the assumption that Mathis and Lyons were partners. Were they?

3. Grider and Greene were partners in a CPA firm. One of their largest clients was in a tight financial situation. Grider offered to buy some stock the client owned by paying him one third cash and giving him a twelve-month note for the balance. The note was signed:

Grider & Greene
By Grider

The stock became worthless, and Greene refused to pay any part of the note. Grider claims it is a partnership debt since he made the deal to build goodwill for the firm. Must Greene pay his share of the note?

4. Gordon was urged by McLain and Meyer to form a partnership. Gordon was profitably employed and did not wish to undertake a new enterprise. McLain and Myers proposed that if he would invest $15,000 in the firm, they would make him a full-fledged member, guarantee him 2 percent on his investment before they received any profits, and would not reveal to the public that he was a member of the firm. McLain and Meyer were to manage the business. The partnership was organized along the lines mentioned. The firm went bankrupt. A creditor learned of Gordon's relationship with McLain and Meyer and sued him as a partner. Is he liable?

5. Moody, Meek, and Mack were desirous of jointly entering into a business enterprise of marketing home appliances. They knew of the unlimited liability rule of partnerships and wished to avoid this risk. They formed a joint-stock company as a common-law association, and each one took shares of stock equal to his investment. The firm became insolvent, and Moody and Meek were personally insolvent. The creditors of the joint-stock company attempted to hold Mack personally liable for the firm's debts. Can they do so?

6. Dennison and Morse were partners operating a road construction business. They owned several expensive road scrapers, dirt movers, and other machinery incident to road construction. When Dennison became personally insolvent, his personal creditors attempted to sell some specific pieces of machinery belonging to the partnership to satisfy Dennison's personal debts. May they do so?

7. Perry, store manager for one of a chain of supermarkets, secretly entered into a partnership with Allen to operate an independent supermarket. He invested half the capital but took no part in the management of the firm. He was to receive 8 percent on his investment guaranteed, and one fourth of any additional profits. The firm became insolvent, and the creditors learned of Perry's status. Perry claimed he was a limited partner, while the creditors contended he was a dormant partner. What was the significance of making this distinction?

8. Dince, Strahorn, and Gilbert operated an ordinary partnership. Gilbert died leaving a wife but no children. The two surviving partners agreed to employ Mrs. Gilbert at $200 a month and to give her the share of profits which Mr. Gilbert would have received had he lived. At the end of five years, the firm was to belong solely to Dince and Strahorn. During this five years, Mrs. Gilbert was to have all the powers of a partner, and the name Dince, Strahorn, and Gilbert Clothiers was to remain unchanged. At the end of two years, the firm was insolvent. The creditors sued Mrs. Gilbert personally for the debts of the firm. Was she liable?

9. Taffell and Taylor jointly own a building that rents for $800 a month. They pay all expenses and divide the balance evenly. Taylor has an automobile wreck in which two people are killed. Suit is brought against him and Taffell for $100,000, alleging that a partnership existed. Was this a partnership?

10. Watford owned, as a sole proprietor, a hardware store. He had three sons who had helped him in the business when they were not in school. After they finished school, they devoted full time to the business. No salaries were ever paid, but each one was permitted to withdraw a stipulated amount each week. This arrangement continued for five years, and then the sons sued in a court of equity for an accounting and a dissolution of the partnership. Other than the use of the three sons as helpers, no change in the operation or management of the business was ever made. Was this a partnership?

11. Rich operated the Home Radio Shop and employed Smith as a clerk. A salesman for the Plymouth Radio Manufacturers took the shop's order for $1,500 worth of radios. Rich, in an effort to boost his credit standing, introduced Smith as his partner in the business. The seller had previously sold goods to Smith and knew his credit was good. Smith did not deny the statement of Rich that they were partners. The Home Radio Shop became bankrupt, and the seller sued Smith for the $1,500. Were Rich and Smith partners?

CHAPTER 33

OPERATION OF A PARTNERSHIP

DUTIES OF PARTNERS

Someone has said that our partnership laws reflect everything noble in our society. The truth of this statement is evident when one lists the duties which the law says each partner owes to his co-partners. These duties leave no room for sharp practices in the partners' dealings with each other. The law imposes upon each partner the utmost fidelity in all his relationships with his fellow partners. If any partner is remiss in his duty, the other partners have ample legal recourse to redress the wrong.

The four most common duties which the partner owes to the others are:

1. Duty to exercise good faith
2. Duty to use care and skill
3. Duty to conform to the partnership contract
4. Duty to keep records

(1) **Duty to Exercise Good Faith.** Partners owe each other and the firm the utmost good faith. Since each partner is the agent of the firm, the relationship of principal and agent prevails. This relationship is a fiduciary one, so that strict fidelity to the interests of the firm must be observed at all times. No partner may take unfair advantage of his copartners. Any personal profits earned directly as a result of one's connection with the partnership must be considered profits of the firm. If the personal interest or advantage of the partner conflicts with the advantage of the partnership, it is the duty of the partner to put the firm's interest above his personal advantage.

- Rucker owned a bakery. He formed a partnership with Dillon to open a cafeteria, Dillon to be a secret partner. Rucker purchased from his own bakery all the pastries used in the cafeteria and charged the regular prices. Dillon did not know of Rucker's ownership of the bakery. Rucker had to account to the partnership for all profits he made on the sale of pastries to the cafeteria. Keeping his ownership of the bakery secret was not an act of good faith.

(2) **Duty to Use Care and Skill.** Each partner must use reasonable care and skill in conducting the firm's business. Any loss resulting to the firm because of a partner's failure to use adequate care and skill in transacting business must be borne by that partner. If the partnership supplies expert services, such as accounting services or engineering services, then each partner must perform these services in a manner that will free the firm from liability for damages for improper services. However, honest mistakes and errors of judgment do not render a partner liable individually nor the partnership liable collectively.

- Reed was a partner in the engineering firm of Reed and Dudley. Because of carelessness, as well as incompetency, Reed miscalculated the dimensions of steel piers for a bridge. As a result of this lack of care and skill, the firm was held liable for a $30,000 loss. Reed in turn was personally liable to the firm for the loss.

(3) **Duty to Conform to the Partnership Contract.** Anyone who enters into a contractual relationship with another has a duty to abide by the terms of the contract. The partnership contract must be observed scrupulously because of the fiduciary status of the partnership type of business organization. Each partner has the power to do irreparable damage to his copartners should he choose to betray their trust in him. For this reason, the law holds each partner to the utmost fidelity to the partnership agreement. Any violation of this agreement gives the other partners at least two rights: First, they can sue the offending partner for any loss resulting from his failure to abide by the partnership agreement; second, they may elect also to ask the court to decree a dissolution of the partnership. A trivial breach of the partnership agreement will not justify a dissolution, however.

- Hanks, Haley, and Friddle formed a partnership to conduct a jewelry store. The articles of copartnership stipulated that Hanks was to have the exclusive right to do all the buying for the firm. Contrary to this agreement, Haley purchased $20,000 worth of jewelry for the firm. Hanks had previously bought an adequate stock of merchandise. Because of a rapid drop in prices, the firm lost $5,000 on the merchandise that Haley purchased. Haley was liable to his partners for this loss.

(4) Duty to Keep Records. Each partner must keep such records of partnership transactions as are required for an adequate accounting. If the articles of copartnership provide for the type of records to be kept, a partner's duty is fulfilled when he keeps such records, even though they may not be fully adequate. Since each partner must account to the partnership for all his transactions for purchases, sales, commission payments, receipts, and all other business transactions, this accounting should be based upon written records.

RIGHTS OF PARTNERS

Every partner, in the absence of an agreement to the contrary, has five well-defined rights:

1. The right to participate in management
2. The right to inspect the books at all times
3. The right of contribution
4. The right to withdraw advances
5. The right to withdraw profits

(1) Right to Participate in Management. In the absence of a contract limiting his rights, each partner has the right by law to participate equally with the others in the management of the partnership business. Because the exercise of this right often leads to disharmony, it is considered one of the basic disadvantages of the partnership type of business organization; but it deserves to stand as a prime advantage because the investor maintains control over his investment, even though his control may often be exercised in a foolish manner. The right of each partner to a voice in management does not mean a dominant voice. In all routine day-to-day managerial decisions, the views of the majority are decisive. The major decisions, however, must be by unanimous consent.

- Meeks, Harold, and West pooled their money and formed a heating and air conditioning business. Meeks was an advertising expert but knew nothing about air conditioning. Harold was an automobile salesman, and West had years of experience in the heating and air conditioning business. The articles of copartnership did not state how the work was to be shared. Meeks and Harold wanted to buy a building, but West insisted on renting. Meeks and Harold claimed that since they constituted a majority voice, West's ideas could be ignored. This contention was unsound. All major decisions must be by unanimous decision. Buying property in which to operate the business might endanger the financial position of the firm. West has a veto over this act.

(2) **Right to Inspect the Books.** Each partner must keep a clear record of all transactions he performs for the firm, the firm's books must be available to all partners, and each partner must explain on request the significance of any record he makes that is not clear. All checks written must show the purpose for which they are written. There must be no business secrets among the partners.

(3) **Right of Contribution.** If one partner pays a firm debt from his personal funds, he has the right to demand a pro rata contribution from each of the other partners. Such payments made by one partner must be for the ordinary and proper conduct of the business.

(4) **Right to Withdraw Advances.** No partner is entitled to withdraw any part of his original investment without the consent of the other partners. If one partner, however, makes additional advances in the form of a loan, he has a right to withdraw this loan at any time after the due date. Also, he is entitled to interest on this loan unless there is an agreement to the contrary. A partner is not entitled to interest on his capital account. It is, therefore, desirable to keep each partner's capital account separate from his loan account.

(5) **Right to Withdraw Profits.** Each partner has the right to withdraw his share of the net profits at the end of the year. If any part of a partner's share of the profit is not withdrawn, it may be transferred to his capital account. This is a form of advance, however, and may be withdrawn the following year without the consent of the other partners.

- The net profits after partners' salaries of the partnership of Carlton, Gutherie, and Knowles was $40,000. Knowles and Gutherie insist that the $40,000 be retained in the business for expansion to meet competition. Gutherie insists upon withdrawing his share. He is within his rights. Each partner is the sole judge as to what disposition is to be made of his share of profits.

LIABILITIES OF PARTNERS

A partner's liabilities are of two kinds:

1. Contractual liabilities
2. Liability for torts

(1) Contractual Liabilities. Every member of a general partnership is liable individually for the debts of the firm. If one partner incurs a liability in the name of the firm that is beyond both his actual and implied authority, however, he is personally liable, but the firm is not. The firm also is not liable for illegal contracts made by any member of the firm since everyone is charged with knowledge of what is illegal. Thus, if a partner in a wholesale liquor firm contracted to sell an individual a case of whiskey, the contract would not be binding on the firm in a state where individual sales are illegal for wholesalers.

(2) Liability for Torts. The partnership is liable for all torts committed by each partner if the tort is committed in the course of his services to the partnership. If the tort is due to the gross negligence of the partner, he may be required to indemnify the other partners, but this does not bar the injured party from suing the partnership.

- The widow Jones left some bearer bonds and other valuables with the partnership firm of Flannagan and Boyd for safekeeping. Boyd cashed some of the bonds and used the money for his personal benefit. The partnership was liable to Jones for the injury even though Boyd in turn would be liable to reimburse Flannagan for any loss which he sustained.

NATURE OF PARTNERSHIP LIABILITIES

The partners are jointly liable on all partnership contractual liabilities unless the contract stipulates otherwise. They are jointly and severally liable on all tort liabilities. For joint liabilities the partners must be sued jointly. If the firm's assets are inadequate to pay the debts, the partners are, of course, liable individually for the full amount. If all the partners but one are insolvent, the remaining solvent partner must pay all the debts even though the judgment is against all of them. The partner who pays the debt has a right of contribution from the other partners, but he may lack the power to collect it because of their insolvency.

Withdrawing partners are liable for all partnership debts incurred up to the time they withdraw unless these partners are expressly released from liability by the creditors. New partners admitted to the firm under the common law are liable only for the debts incurred after admission unless they agreed otherwise. Under the Uniform Partnership Act and the Bulk Sales Laws, each incoming partner is liable for all debts as fully as if he had been a partner when the debt was incurred, except that this liability for old debts is limited to his investment in the partnership. Withdrawing partners may contract with incoming partners to pay all old debts, but this is not binding on creditors.

IMPLIED POWERS OF A PARTNER

In the absence of an agreement providing otherwise, each partner has the implied authority to bind the firm, and with it the individual members and the property of the firm, by any act committed within the scope of the partnership business in a transaction with a third party. If the authority of the partners is restricted by an agreement, notice of the restriction must be given to third parties to be effective. If that is not done, a third party may hold the partners liable on a contract made with one of them. Among the implied powers of a partner are the following:

(1) To compromise and release a claim against a third party

(2) To receive payments and to give receipts in the name of the firm

(3) To employ agents and employees whose services are needed in the transaction of the partnership business, or to discharge them

(4) To draw and indorse checks, to make notes, and to accept drafts

(5) To insure the property of the partnership, to cancel insurance policies, or to give proof of loss and to collect the proceeds

(6) To buy goods on credit or to sell part or all of the stock of the partnership, provided this is done in the regular course of business

POWERS NOT IMPLIED

Among the acts that a partner does not have the implied power to do and for which he must obtain the unanimous consent of all the partners in order to bind the firm are the following:

(1) To assign the assets of the firm for the benefit of creditors

(2) To indorse a negotiable instrument as an accommodation

(3) To submit a partnership controversy for arbitration

(4) To discharge a personal debt by agreeing that it will be set off against one due the firm

(5) To dispose of the goodwill of the business, or to do any other act that would make impossible the continuance of the business

This restriction covers such items as the admission of a new partner, the addition of a new line of business, the dropping of an old line, changing the locations of the business, or any other act that might result in an adverse effect that would make the continuance of the business impossible. Any partner can block any of these major changes.

SHARING OF PROFITS AND LOSSES

The articles of copartnership usually specify the basis upon which the profits and the losses are to be shared. This proportion cannot be changed by a majority of the members of the firm. If the partnership agreement does not fix the ratio of sharing the profits and the losses, they will be shared equally and not in proportion to the contribution to the capital. In the absence of an agreement to the contrary, the majority of the partners may order a division of the profits at any time.

QUESTIONS

1. What duties does each partner owe his copartner?

2. If one partner, as a result of his membership in the firm, is able to make a personal profit, must he share this profit with the other partners?

3. If A and B form a partnership for the purpose of operating a public accounting office, who is personally liable if A, through his ignorance of accounting principles, loses $1,000 of the firm's money?

4. What records must a partner keep of the transactions he performs for the partnership?

5. Is the right of each partner to participate in management equally with the other partners an advantage or disadvantage of the partnership type of business?

6. Does a partner have the right to inspect firm records at all times?

7. If one partner makes a loan to the firm, when may he withdraw this money without the consent of the other partners?

8. What are a partner's liabilities?

9. What are the implied powers of a partner?

10. If the partnership contract does not set out the method of dividing profits and sharing losses, how are these distributed?

CASE PROBLEMS

1. Hacket, Hammond, and Harper each invested $15,000 in an insurance agency. Each one was to handle a specified function of the business. Salaries of $500 each were to be drawn at the end of each month. After the partnership had operated for two years, during which time the net profits after salaries were $15,000, Hacket and Hammond wanted to retain all profits in the business and add a real estate agency. They would then enter into an ambitious suburban real estate development program. Hacket and Hammond were to handle these added duties and receive an additional $500 a month salary. Harper was to receive no increase. Harper refused to agree to these proposals. Hacket and Hammond insisted that the majority should rule and attempted to ignore Harper's objections. Could these changes be undertaken without Harper's consent?

2. Day, Dolwin, and Farmer operate a partnership engaged in the laundry and dry cleaning business. Each one has $40,000 invested in the business. In addition Day has loaned the business $10,000. At the end of the year the net profits are $25,000. Day and Farmer want to use the profits to install new machinery although the machinery they now have is good. The new machinery has a few modern gadgets which they think will tend to improve their profits. Cash equal to their reserve for depreciation account has been invested in common stock of various corporations. Dolwin insists this stock should be sold and used to purchase new machinery when necessary. He claims he needs his share of the profits to send his four sons to school and insists upon withdrawing his profits. Does he have the right to do so?

3. Albright was a dormant partner in the firm of Town Talk Cleaners. The other two partners managed the firm and kept all records. Albright wanted to inspect the books because he suspected that the other partners were defrauding him. They refused to permit Albright to inspect the books since he had only suspicion, not proof, that something was wrong. Was this a justification for refusing to permit a dormant partner to inspect the books?

4. Anthony and Bill were partners in a tax consultant enterprise. Anthony had a few clients whom he served on Saturdays and at night. The fees they paid him were not turned over to the partnership bookkeeper. Anthony contended that any income he had for services performed on his own time after working hours was his personal income. Was this contention sound?

5. Langford and Palmer were partners in a neon sign installation service. One of their best customers, the Sunset Drive-In Theater, needed credit to build a new drive-in theater in an adjoining town. Langford without Palmer's

knowledge or consent indorsed in the name of the partnership as an accommodation indorser a note to the Citizens Bank for $15,000 with the owner of the Sunset Drive-In Theater as the maker. The note was never paid; the bank sued the partnership on the indorsement. Is the partnership liable?

6. Pressman and Jordan own and operate an insurance agency as a general partnership. Neal, an experienced underwriter for a large insurance company, is approached by Pressman to purchase the agency since Jordan is sick and unable to work. Pressman without Jordan's knowledge or consent enters into a contract with Neal to sell the agency in bulk for $40,000. Neal paid one half down and agreed to pay the balance by turning over to Pressman and Jordan 10 per cent of the commissions earned until the balance was paid. Neal resigns his position and operates the agency one month before Jordan, due to his illness, learns of the sale. He repudiates the contract and demands that Neal restore control and management to the partnership. Discuss the rights of the parties.

7. Fargo, Denton, and Howell were the three owners of a partnership selling and servicing boats. Over a period of two years there were many bitter disputes over management policies. Usually Fargo was a minority of one against Denton and Howell. Howell read in a law book that one of the disadvantages of a partnership was disharmony among the partners due to the rule of unanimity. Howell and Denton propose that the partnership incorporate. Fargo asks your advice. What would you tell him?

8. Pringle and Whyte were partners in a drug business. The articles of copartnership provided that each partner might draw $50 each week as his share of the profits of the business. Pringle became seriously ill, and as a result Whyte was compelled to work overtime to take care of the business. Because of the extra work he performed, Whyte drew a larger amount of money each week.

(a) Did Whyte have the right to draw a larger sum?

(b) If Whyte found it necessary to employ another person, would the wages of this person be considered an expense of the firm or would they be deducted from the amount Pringle drew?

(c) While Pringle was ill, was he entitled to as much of the profits as though he had worked all the time?

9. Gotesky and Grant were partners in a public accounting firm. Gotesky audited a firm's books in such a careless and negligent manner that the firm lost $4,000 by relying on the inaccurate audit. The partnership was required to pay damages of $4,000. Was Gotesky required to reimburse Grant?

10. Collins and Conwell were partners in a men's clothing store. Each invested $12,000. At the end of the first year the profits were $10,000 and each partner drew out $3,600. The balance of the profits were distributed equally to their capital accounts. The following year Collins wished to draw out the remaining $1,400 of his profits plus $1,100 of his original investment. Was he able to do this without Conwell's consent?

CHAPTER 34

DISSOLUTION OF A
PARTNERSHIP

DISSOLUTION AND TERMINATION OF A PARTNERSHIP

If one member of a going partnership withdraws for any reason, the partnership relation is dissolved, but the business may continue to operate. This change is called a dissolution. If, because of the dissolution, the partners wind up their affairs and cease all operations, the partnership is terminated. All business transactions except liquidation then cease, and the partners abandon their rights and duties under the articles of copartnership.

DISSOLUTION BY ACTS OF THE PARTIES

A partnership is dissolved by act of the partners in the following ways:

1. Agreement
2. Withdrawal or alienation
3. Expulsion

(1) **Agreement.** At the time the partnership agreement is formed, the partners may fix the time when the partnership relation will cease. Unless the agreement is renewed or amended, the partnership is dissolved on the agreed date. If no date for the dissolution is fixed at the time the partnership is formed, the partners may by mutual agreement dissolve the partnership at any time. Even when a definite date is fixed in the original agreement, the partners may dissolve the partnership prior to that time. The agreement to dissolve under this condition must be by unanimous consent.

Sometimes no date is fixed for terminating the partnership, but the agreement sets forth the purpose of the partnership, such as the construction of a building. In this event the partnership is terminated as soon as the purpose has been achieved.

(2) Withdrawal or Alienation. The withdrawal of one partner at any time and for any reason dissolves the partnership. In a partnership for a definite term, any partner has the power to withdraw at any time, but he does not have the right to withdraw. He is liable for any loss sustained by the other partners because of his withdrawal. If no termination date is fixed in the articles of copartnership, a partner may withdraw at will without liability unless a sudden withdrawal would result in an irreparable damage to the firm. The withdrawing partner is entitled to receive his capital, undistributed profits, and any loan upon his withdrawal.

If a termination date is fixed in the articles of copartnership or by subsequent agreement, the withdrawing partner breaches his contract by withdrawing prior to the agreed date. He is then not entitled to demand immediate reimbursement for his capital investment. The remaining partners may offset any damages sustained as a result of the withdrawal against the withdrawing partner's capital.

Closely related to the withdrawal of a partner is the alienation of his interest either by a voluntary sale or an involuntary sale to satisfy personal creditors. If the sale is voluntary, it does not of itself dissolve the partnership. The purchaser does not become a partner by purchase since the remaining partners cannot be compelled to accept as a partner anyone who might be "persona non grata" to them. The buying partner has a right to the capital and profits of the withdrawing partner, but he does not have the right to participate in the management.

If the sale of one partner is involuntary and is made to satisfy creditors, the sale dissolves the partnership.

(3) Expulsion. The articles of copartnership may and should contain a clause providing for the expulsion of a member, especially if there are more than two members. This clause should spell out clearly the acts for which a member may be expelled and the method of settlement for his interest. In the absence of a proviso to this effect in the original agreement, no member of a partnership may be expelled for any reason. The expulsion of a member dissolves the partnership but does not terminate the business since the remaining members can continue operation under a new name. This is very desirable for firms enjoying good profits.

DISSOLUTION BY COURT DECREE

Under certain circumstances the court may issue a decree dissolving a partnership. The chief reasons justifying such a decree are:

1. Insanity
2. Incapacity
3. Misconduct
4. Futility

(1) **Insanity of a Partner.** If a partnership is formed for a specified period of time and one member becomes insane before the termination of that time, the other members of the partnership may petition a court of equity to dissolve the partnership. It cannot be dissolved by agreement since this agreement must be by unanimous consent, and the insane member is incompetent to enter into a binding contract of dissolution.

If the other members dissolve the partnership without the insane member's consent, he can sue them for breach of contract upon regaining his sanity. The sane members may avoid liability by obtaining a court decree dissolving the partnership because of the insanity of one member. The dissolution is made under the supervision of the court so as to protect the insane member's rights. Such a dissolution may or may not result in a termination of the business also. If the sane members of the firm desire to continue the business of the firm under a new name, and the interest of the insane member is not jeopardized thereby, the court may order a dissolution but not a termination.

(2) **Incapacity of a Partner.** Insanity, as described in the preceding section, is one type of incapacity which always justifies a dissolution of a partnership by decree of the court. There are other types and degrees of incapacity. Each incapacity must be considered upon its merits as to whether or not it justifies a dissolution. The test is whether or not the incapacity makes it impossible for the partner to perform the services to the partnership which the original partnership agreement contemplated. A member of an accounting firm who loses his eyesight would probably be incapacitated for his work to the

extent of justifying a dissolution. The court, not the partners, must be the judge in each case as to whether or not the partnership should be dissolved.

The incapacity as a rule must be permanent, not temporary. A temporary inability of one partner to perform his duties is one of the risks which the other partners assumed when they formed the partnership and does not justify a court decree in dissolving the partnership.

(3) Misconduct. If one member of a partnership is guilty of misconduct that is prejudicial to the successful continuance of the business, the court may, upon proper application, decree a dissolution of the partnership. Typical illustrations of such misconduct are habitual drunkenness, dishonesty, persistent violation of the partnership agreement, irreconcilable discord among the partners, and abandonment of the business by a partner.

- Gann and Saye were partners in a dry cleaning business. The partnership had three more years to run as provided by the articles of copartnership. Every weekend Saye would become intoxicated but was always sober by Monday morning. There was no evidence that his addiction to drink had any adverse effect on the business. Gann was a teetotaler and wanted to dissolve the partnership. Saye would not agree to a voluntary dissolution, and Gann petitioned the court to decree a dissolution. The court refused, since Saye's drinking was always on his own time and did not harm the business.

(4) Futility. All business partnerships are conducted for the purpose of making a profit. When it is clear that this objective cannot be achieved, the court may decree a dissolution. One partner cannot compel the other members to assume continued losses after the success of the business becomes highly improbable and further operation appears futile. A temporarily unprofitable operation does not justify a dissolution. It is only when the objective reasonably appears impossible to attain that the court will issue a decree of dissolution.

- O'Day and Ferber own a patent on a new piece of farm machinery. They form a partnership to continue for five years to manufacture and market the machinery. After two years they sold only ten pieces of machinery, and the purchasers of these were highly dissatisfied. O'Day wished to liquidate and call an end to the undertaking while they could still avoid bankruptcy, but Ferber insisted on continued operation until the end of the partnership agreement. O'Day petitioned the court to decree an immediate dissolution. This the court did on the ground the patented article had no market and the undertaking was probably futile.

DISSOLUTION BY OPERATION OF LAW

Under certain well-defined circumstances, a partnership will be dissolved by operation of law. No decree of the court is necessary to dissolve the partnership. The law itself achieves this purpose. The most common examples are:

1. Death of a partner
2. Bankruptcy
3. Illegality

(1) **Death of a Partner.** The death of one member of a partnership automatically dissolves the partnership. A representative of the deceased may act to protect the interest of the heirs, but he cannot act as a partner. This is true even when the articles of copartnership provide that the partnership is not to be dissolved by the death of a member. A dead man cannot be a partner, nor can he appoint an agent to act for him because death also terminates the relationship of principal and agent.

The articles of copartnership can provide for an orderly process of dissolution upon the death of a member. Thus, a provision that the surviving partners shall have twelve months in which to liquidate the firm and pay over the deceased partner's share to the heirs is binding. This is not, however, a continuation of the partnership.

(2) **Bankruptcy.** When an individual is declared a bankrupt, he is discharged from most of his debts, including those connected with the partnership. Thus, bankruptcy dissolves the partnership. The rule in equity could not be otherwise. If a partner could be adjudicated a bankrupt for his personal estate and remain solvent in his partnership estate, his creditors could be defrauded. The trustee in bankruptcy has the right to assume control of the bankrupt partner's share of the partnership business, but the trustee is not a partner. The trustee merely stands in the place of the partner to see that the creditors' interests are protected.

(3) **Illegality.** Many types of business are legal when undertaken, but because of a change in the law, they may later become illegal. This is particularly true in the alcoholic beverage field. If a partnership is formed to conduct a lawful business and later this type of business is declared illegal, then the partnership is automatically dissolved. If a partnership is formed for the purpose of operating an

insurance underwriting business, the partnership is dissolved by a law restricting this type of business to corporations.

- Smith and Combs formed a partnership to operate a tavern. Subsequent to the formation of the partnership, the county in which it was located voted in a local option election to prohibit the sale of alcoholic beverages within the county where the partnership business was located. Since the business is now illegal, the partnership was dissolved by operation of law.

EFFECTS OF DISSOLUTION OF A PARTNERSHIP

Dissolution of a partnership does not necessarily mean the liquidation of the business. The firm may continue to operate as a new partnership, as a sole proprietorship, or as a corporation. Until the new business is formed, a partnership that has been dissolved for any reason cannot engage in any new business unless that is necessary to liquidate the firm. If a part of the assets of the firm are goods in process and additional raw materials must be purchased before the goods in process can be converted into finished goods, these raw materials may be purchased.

Anyone who extends credit to the partnership after he has received notice of the dissolution cannot look to partnership assets for collection. The liquidating partner becomes personally liable for these debts. The liquidating partner or partners are trustees of the firm's assets and must account for all funds in existence at the time of liquidation. As a general rule, the partner in charge of liquidation is entitled to reasonable compensation for his services in connection with the liquidation of the firm.

NOTICE OF DISSOLUTION

When a partnership is dissolved, a new firm is frequently established. Such a change may not become known to creditors and other third parties who have done business with the old firm. For the protection of these third parties, the law requires that in certain cases they must be given actual notice of the dissolution. If notice is not given, every member of the old firm may be held liable for the acts of the former partners that are committed within the scope of the new business.

Notice is usually given to former creditors by mail. The withdrawing partner or partners must be prepared to prove that this notice

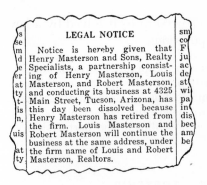

LEGAL NOTICE

Notice is hereby given that Henry Masterson and Sons, Realty Specialists, a partnership consisting of Henry Masterson, Louis Masterson, and Robert Masterson, and conducting its business at 4325 Main Street, Tucson, Arizona, has this day been dissolved because Henry Masterson has retired from the firm. Louis Masterson and Robert Masterson will continue the business at the same address, under the firm name of Louis and Robert Masterson, Realtors.

A Newspaper Notice of the Dissolution of a Partnership

was actually received by the creditors. As a means of proof, a registered letter with a return receipt attached is the safest form of notice. It is sufficient to give the general public notice by publication. This would be adequate also for former creditors if it could be established that they read the publication. If the name of the firm included the name of the withdrawing partner, he should, of course, have his name removed from the firm name from all stationery so that he may avoid further liability with regard to the business.

In the following instances notice is usually not deemed necessary:

(1) To those who were partners
(2) When the partnership was dissolved by the operation of law
(3) When the partnership was dissolved by a judicial decree
(4) When a dormant or a secret partner retired

In those states that have adopted the Uniform Partnership Act, notice is required in some cases even when the dissolution is by operation of law or by decree of court unless the dissolution is due to bankruptcy or illegality. This is particularly important when the partnership is terminated by the death of a partner. His executor or administrator must give the notice to prior creditors and the general public if the business is to be continued under a new partnership agreement. If he does not give this notice, the administrator may be held personally liable for the loss to the heirs.

DISTRIBUTION OF ASSETS

After the termination of a solvent partnership, the partners are entitled to participate in the assets remaining after the debts are paid to creditors. The distribution of the remaining assets among the partners is usually as follows:

(1) Partners who have advanced money to the firm or have incurred liabilities in its behalf are entitled to reimbursement.
(2) Each partner is next entitled to the return of the capital that he contributed to the partnership.

(3) Any assets remaining are distributed equally, unless there is an agreement in the partnership contract that provides for an unequal distribution.

When a firm sustains a loss, the loss will be shared equally by the partners, unless there is an agreement to the contrary.

QUESTIONS

1. Must a partnership business dissolve every time there is a change in ownership?
2. If a partnership is to run five years, may one partner withdraw at the end of two years without incurring any liability to the other partners?
3. If the administrator of a deceased partner's estate does not give notice to prior creditors of the termination of the partnership, may he be held personally liable for losses due to this failure to give notice?
4. What are the rights of a person who buys a partner's interest in the firm?
5. In the absence of a specific provision in the partnership contract, may one partner be expelled by the other members?
6. If one member of a firm becomes ill and cannot perform his share of the work, what recourse do the other partners have?
7. What is the remedy for the innocent partners if one of their members conducts himself in such a way that the good name of the business is seriously damaged?
8. When one member of a partnership dies, what effect does this have on the partnership?
9. If a partner is declared personally bankrupt, what effect has this upon the partnership?
10. After the termination of a solvent partnership, how are the assets divided?

CASE PROBLEMS

1. Randolph and Holcomb formed a partnership to operate a private school for girls. The Tug River Wholesale Grocery Company extended credit to the firm over a period of two years. The partnership was subsequently incorporated, but no notice of this fact was ever given to the creditors except on the letterhead of the school's purchase orders and other papers. The school became insolvent, owing the Tug River Wholesale Company $26,000. The company sued Randolph and Holcomb personally on the debt. The bookkeeper admitted he knew the school had incorporated, but the evidence showed that the owner of the wholesale firm did not. Are Randolph and Holcomb personally liable for this debt?

2. Mize and Duvall formed a partnership to prospect for uranium. The partnership was dissolved at the end of one year by agreement, and due

notice was given of the dissolution. Mize borrowed $2,000 from Lawson and executed the firm's note for this loan since the money was to be used to facilitate the liquidation of the partnership. May Duvall deny all liability on the note?

3. Dotson and Horne were partners. They admitted Henderson to the firm upon the payment of $15,000. For this payment he received a one-third interest. At the time Henderson was admitted, the old partnership owed $20,000. One of these creditors was Paulson; the debt of $1,200 owed by the old firm was dated June 5. On July 7, after Henderson was admitted to the firm, the new firm incurred a debt to Paulson of $1,500. On August 1, the bookkeeper sent a check to Paulson for the $1,800 "on account." The bookkeeper applied it on the $1,500. The new firm became insolvent, and Henderson claims he is not liable for any part of the $1,200 since the bookkeeper should have paid it instead of the new debt. Must Henderson pay the remaining $900 out of his personal estate, assuming this is the only remaining source open to Paulson?

4. Burson and Barber form a partnership to run for 10 years. There is a provision in the articles of copartnership stating that in the event one partner dies, the surviving partner shall continue operation of the partnership for one year. Barber died and Burson, pursuant to this provision, operated the firm for one year during which time the firm lost $30,000. Must Barber's heirs bear one half of this loss?

5. Smith, Combs, and Dennis were partners in a law firm. Smith was appointed judge of the Superior Court. There was a state law stating that it is illegal for an attorney who is also a judge to be a member of a law firm. The Stacy Furniture Company sold some office furniture and office equipment in the sum of $1,584.75 to the firm of "Smith, Combs, and Dennis," upon Combs' order. The debt was never paid, and the Stacy Furniture Company attempted to hold the partners personally liable, alleging no notice of termination was ever received. Are Smith and Dennis, either or both, personally liable for this account?

6. Andrews and Averitt operated a shoe store as a partnership. Andrews became seriously ill, and the court decreed a dissolution and a liquidation. The Snow Shoe Company sold $3,000 worth of shoes to the firm upon Averitt's order even though its manager, Henry Griffith, had notice of the dissolution. The account was never paid, and the Snow Shoe Company insisted upon the right of sharing in the firm assets along with other partnership creditors. Was it entitled to do so?

7. Kelley, Love, and Marler form a partnership to operate a men's clothing store. The firm operates several years and is very profitable. Marler becomes insane and appears to be beyond hope of recovery. Mrs. Marler enters into a contract with Kelley and Love to dissolve the partnership. Kelley and Love pay her Marler's share of the partnership assets. Kelley and Love operate the new partnership for three years during which time their net profits are $36,000. Marler, having regained his sanity, now demands one third of these profits. Is he entitled to them?

8. Adams and Diehl conducted a printing establishment as a partnership under the name of The Economy Print Shop. Diehl withdrew, and Miss Haley, the secretary-bookkeeper, was instructed to send notices of dissolution to all creditors. She did so but overlooked one paper company from which the partnership had in the past bought a considerable quantity of paper on credit. About two weeks after the dissolution, Adams ordered $1,000 worth of paper from the paper mill that had not received notice of dissolution. The order was made on a new type of order blank from which Diehl's name had been removed. Other than this, there was nothing to indicate any change in the business. The account was never paid; the paper mill sued Diehl personally. Was Diehl liable?

SUMMARY CASES

PART 7

1. J. Morris conducted a business under the name of J. Morris and Co. After his death, his two sons, Irving Morris and Jacob Morris continued the business under the same name and at the same place. Jacob Morris signed all checks, and Irving Morris did the selling. Both at various times purchased merchandise on credit from the Sunset Broom and Brush Co. This latter company assigned its accounts receivable to Bedell. J. Morris & Co. failed to pay its account and Bedell sued Irving Morris and Jacob Morris as partners. Jacob Morris denied liability on the ground that he was never a partner. There was little or no evidence that he ever expressly agreed to become a partner. Was Jacob Morris a partner by estoppel? (Bedell v. Morris, 63 Calif. A. 453, 218 P. 769)

2. Cornell and Sagouspe were partners in a ranch and livestock enterprise. The partnership agreement stipulated that each partner was to withdraw profits from time to time but that the withdrawals were to be equal. No mention was made of salaries. Cornell brought suit to have the partnership dissolved and to have an accounting. Sagouspe claimed accrued salary over a nine-year period of $16,475 for himself and $8,237.50 for his wife. Cornell and his wife were to be allowed only $3,522.50 for the two of them. This disparity of salaries was due to the fact that Sagouspe lived at the ranch and devoted much more time to it than did Cornell and his wife. Was Sagouspe entitled to a larger share of the profits than Cornell? (Cornell v. Sagouspe, 53 Nev. 145, 295 P. 443)

3. Beals sold a large tract of timber to Bennett on the following terms: $4 per thousand board feet plus 1/3 of the sales receipts over $21 per thousand. This 1/3 was referred to as 1/3 of the profits, but the profits were arbitrarily fixed at the excess of sales over $21 per thousand board feet. The Worden Company extended considerable credit to Bennett during the logging operations. These debts were never paid. The Worden Company sued Beals as a partner. Did this agreement constitute Beals a partner? (Worden Co. v. Beals, et al., 120 Ore. 66, 250 P. 375)

4. Askew was a partner in the Austin Company. Mrs. Silman was a customer of the Austin Company during the time Askew was a partner but was never a creditor. Askew withdrew from the partnership and gave notice to the public of this withdrawal by a newspaper advertisement. Mrs. Silman never saw the advertisement. Over two years after Askew's withdrawal, Mrs. Silman extended credit to the partnership, thinking Askew was still a partner. She brought suit against Askew since the debt was never paid. Is Askew liable to Silman for this debt? (Askew v. Silman, 95 Ga. 678, 22 S. E. 573)

5. The L. Katz and Company was a partnership consisting of Katz and Brewington. Katz kept control of the books and refused to allow Brewington to inspect them. He also insisted upon managing the business, and refused to permit Brewington to have access to the business or have a voice in its management. Katz did this because he supplied all the capital, even though profits were to be divided equally. Brewington brought an action to compel Katz to give him access to the books. Was Brewington entitled to have access to the books? (Katz v. Brewington, 71 Md. 70)

6. Yost, Campbell, and Sewell formed a partnership operating under the name of the Independent Lumber Company. Freeman purchased Campbell's interest in the firm. At the time of the purchase there were many debts outstanding. Freeman knew of these debts but did not agree to become liable for them. New debts were incurred after the date of purchase. Freeman denied liability for both the old debts and the new debts on the ground that he never intended to become a partner, but intended to form a corporation with Yost and Sewell. Was Freeman liable for both the old and the new debts? (Freeman v. Hutting Sash & Door Company, 105 Texas 560)

7. Green, Casey, and James were partners. Casey died. His personal estate was insolvent at the time of his death. Emanuel, a partnership creditor, brought an action against Casey's estate to collect the partnership debt. Casey's individual creditors claimed they had priority over Emanuel. Prior to Emanuel's action the partnership became insolvent, and the remaining partners were also personally insolvent. Was Emanuel entitled to share in the personal estate of Casey? (Emanuel v. Bird, 19 Ala. 596)

PART 8

CORPORATIONS

Preview Cases for Part 8: Corporations

- DeFoe purchased the Mitchell Shoe Store from John Mitchell. As a part of the contract, Mitchell agreed not to enter the retail shoe business in that town for two years. One month after the sale, Mitchell formed a corporation, in which he was the principal stockholder, to enter the retail shoe business in the same town. Would the court issue an injunction against the corporation to prevent it from doing business?

- The charter of the Well Pump and Supply Company set forth that the corporation was "to engage in the boring of wells, installing pumps, selling pumps and supplies, and the servicing of these pumps." The board of directors entered into a contract with the Board of Supervisors of Buchanan County to hard surface three miles of county roads. May a stockholder apply to the court for an injunction to prohibit the corporation from fulfilling the contract?

- The following paragraph appeared in the prospectus of the Bankers Securities Corporation, a new company being organized in Georgia: "The Board of Directors has agreed to pay Ray Smythe one share of B voting stock for each share of A nonvoting stock sold, but not to exceed 20 percent of the authorized issue." What is the meaning and significance of this paragraph?

- Gable was a director in the LeVisa State Bank. For five years he never attended a directors' meeting, and he never examined the company's books or records. The president and the cashier of the bank managed it in a careless and negligent manner, causing the bank to go into receivership. Does Gable have any personal liability for the losses suffered by stockholders?

These preview cases are designed to serve as a springboard for the study of this part. As you read through each chapter in this part, you will find the actual decisions for all these preview cases. Of course, there are many more such illustrative problems as well as case problems for decision at the end of each chapter. And there are also a number of even more challenging cases for review at the end of the part.

CHAPTER 35

NATURE OF A
CORPORATION

WHAT IS A CORPORATION?

A *corporation* is "an association of individuals united for some common purpose, and permitted by law to use a common name and to change its members without dissolution of the association." This definition was given in an early decision by the Supreme Court of the United States and is still considered a satisfactory definition of the term "corporation." Unlike a partnership, a corporation need not be organized for the purpose of making and sharing profits. It may be organized for any lawful purpose, whether that purpose is for pleasure or profit.

A corporation is known in law as an "entity," that is, something that has a distinct existence separate and apart from the existence of its individual members. Chief Justice Marshall defined a corporation as "an artificial being, invisible, intangible, and existing only in contemplation of law." Under certain circumstances, the courts may disregard the entity concept of the corporation. If the corporation is used as a device to enable a person to do what he cannot do in person, the entity will be ignored.

- DeFoe purchased the Mitchell Shoe Store from John Mitchell. As a part of the contract, Mitchell agreed not to enter the retail shoe business in that town for two years. One month after the sale, Mitchell formed a corporation, in which he was the principal stockholder, to enter the retail shoe business in the same town. The court enjoined the corporation from entering the business on the ground Mitchell was using this device to evade his contract.

A corporation is considered an artificial person that has been substituted for the natural persons who are responsible for its formation and who manage and control its affairs. Hence, when a corporation makes a contract, the contract is made by and in the name of this legal entity, the corporation, and not by and in the name of the individual members. It has all the rights and powers of an individual. It can sue and be sued, it can be fined for violating the law, it has recourse to the constitution to protect its liberties, and in most other respects it enjoys the same prerogatives as an individual.

IMPORTANCE OF CORPORATIONS

Corporations have been in existence for a long time, but essentially they are the product of the last century. The rapid expansion of industry from small shops to giant enterprises required large amounts of capital. Few men had enough money of their own to build a railroad or a great steel mill, and men hesitated to form partnerships with any but trusted acquaintances. In addition, even though four or five men did form a partnership, insufficient capital was still a major problem. The need was for hundreds or even thousands of men, each with a few hundred or a few thousand dollars, to pool their capital for concerted undertakings. The corporate form of business was well adapted to meet this need. It not only provided the necessary capital but also freed the investors from the risks and restraints of partnerships by specifically limiting each investor's liability to his original investment.

It is evident that our mass-production enterprises could not have expanded to their present size except through corporate financing. Small enterprises still offer opportunities; but experience has demonstrated that certain businesses that require much capital, such as a steel mill, an automobile manufacturer, or a railroad, can best be operated by a corporation.

DIFFERENCES BETWEEN PARTNERSHIPS AND CORPORATIONS

There are many differences between the law governing partnerships and that governing corporations. For the investor particularly, these differences are extremely important. For example, three men with $20,000 each can form a partnership with a capital of $60,000. We saw, however, in the chapters on partnership, how each partner risks losing not only this $20,000 but also everything else he may own since he is personally liable for all partnership debts. If a corporation is formed and each investor contributes $20,000, this amount is the maximum he can lose since he is not liable for the corporate debts beyond his investment.

This advantage of the corporation over the partnership is offset by at least one important disadvantage. In a partnership each partner has an equal voice in the management of the business. Furthermore, he is the sole judge as to whether or not his share of the profits should be withdrawn or left in the business. In a corporation the men who own or control a majority of the common stock have not merely a dominant voice in management but the sole voice. If there are fifteen stockholders but one owns 51 percent of the common stock, he is free to run the corporation as he sees fit. He alone decides whether or not profits are to be paid out as dividends or retained in the business. He must not act in an arbitrary and capricious manner, but otherwise there are but few restraints on him. The owners of the minority stock have no right to employment in the business; in fact they may even be prosecuted for trespassing if they enter upon the corporate property. The person who invests his savings in a business in the hope of becoming "his own boss" may not find the corporate type of business organization the most desirable unless he can be sure of controlling a majority of the voting stock.

PUBLIC CORPORATIONS

Corporations may be classified as public and private. A *public corporation* is one formed to carry out some governmental function, such as a city, a state university, or a public hospital. The powers and functions of public corporations are not comparable with private corporations conducted for profit. Public corporations are created by the state primarily for the purpose of facilitating the administration of governmental functions. They are an excellent device for fixing the limit of any public administrator's authority.

Some public bodies, such as school boards, board of county commissioners, and similar bodies are not true public corporations but have many similar powers, such as the right to sue and be sued, own, buy, and sell property, and to sign other contracts as an entity. They are called *quasi corporations,* quasi having the meaning "as if" or "in the nature of."

PRIVATE CORPORATIONS

Private corporations are those formed by private individuals to perform some nongovernmental function. They in turn are classified as:

1. Nonstock corporations
2. Stock corporations

(1) **Nonstock Corporations.** A *nonstock corporation* is one formed by private individuals for the purpose of conducting some charitable, educational, religious, social, or fraternal service. These corporations are not organized for profit, nor is membership in them evidenced by stock ownership. There is no stock issued. The corporation, however, is a legal entity like any other corporation, and can sue and be sued as a corporation, can buy and sell property, and otherwise operate as any other corporation. Membership in these corporations is acquired by agreement between the charter members in the beginning and between the present members and new members thereafter.

A nonstock private corporation that has for its sole purpose some charitable undertaking may be called an *eleemosynary corporation.*

(2) **Stock Corporations.** In terms of number and importance, stock corporations organized for profit constitute the chief type discussed in this text. Membership in a *stock corporation* is represented by shares of stock. The extent of one's rights and liabilities is determined by the number of shares of stock owned and by the charter and the bylaws of the corporation.

OTHER CLASSES OF CORPORATIONS

Corporations may be classified in other ways depending on the purpose of the classification. Thus we may need to classify them as domestic or foreign corporations. A corporation is a *domestic corporation* in the state where it received its initial charter; it is a *foreign corporation* in all other states. If it is incorporated in another country, it may be referred to as an *alien corporation.*

Corporations may also be classified as de jure and de facto. A *de jure corporation* is one that has fulfilled every requirement of the state corporation laws where it received its charter. It is a corporation in both fact and law. A *de facto corporation* is one in fact but not in law. It has failed to comply with some minor requirement of the law governing the formation of corporations, but otherwise acts as a corporation. Only the state can question the status of a de facto corporation. Its contract with the state is not complete, and the state may bring an action to cancel its charter.

FORMATION OF A CORPORATION

The initial stage of forming a corporation is usually taken by one who acts as the promoter. A lot of preliminary work must be done before the corporation comes into existence. The incorporation papers must be prepared, a prospectus drawn up and approved by the Securities and Exchange Commission and by the appropriate state officials, the stock must be sold, and many contracts entered into for the benefit of the proposed corporation. It is always contemplated that the corporation will take over these contracts of the promoter, but the promoter may be personally liable on these contracts pending the formation of the corporation.

CORPORATE LIABILITY ON PROMOTER'S CONTRACTS

Ratification is a term well defined in the law of principal and agent. Some courts have tried to apply this law to the contracts of the promoter and the corporation. One well-defined principle of ratification is that at the time of the contract there must be a principal capable of ratifying the contract. This condition does not exist with the promoter's contracts since there is at that time no corporation. The courts now almost without exception follow the principle of adoption rather than ratification. After the stock is sold, the stock subscribers are called into a stockholders' meeting, the charter is adopted, and a board of directors is elected. The corporation is now a legal entity. Through its board of directors it can adopt the contracts made by the promoter for the benefit of the corporation. Adoption by the corporation of the promoter's contracts is in reality novation. In all cases of novation, an original party to a contract is not released until the other party consents. This remains true of the adopted contracts.

The promoter may avoid personal liability on many contracts made for the benefit of the corporation by including a provision in the contract that he is not to be held personally liable after the corporation adopts the contract.

ADOPTION OF EXPENSES

Along with the adoption of the promoter's contracts, the corporation may or may not adopt the expenses of the promoter in organization of the corporation. It is customary for the corporation after it comes into existence to reimburse the promoter for all necessary expenses in forming the corporation. This may be done by a resolution passed by the board of directors. If the corporation does not expressly agree to pay these expenses, it may be held to have done so by implication by accepting the benefit.

A SIMPLIFIED PROCEDURE

To avoid many difficulties in adopting a promoter's contracts, reimbursing for expenses, and compensating him for his services, the corporation may be formed by a small group who will act as a board of directors. Before any major contracts are made, such as rental agreements, or any except a few nominal expenses have been incurred, the corporation becomes a legal entity. All contracts can be made in its name. This is particularly important in the sale of stocks. If the stock salesmen sell stock in a proposed corporation, the subscription is merely an offer to buy. This offer may be revoked anytime prior to acceptance in most jurisdictions. The corporation is the offeree, and it cannot accept until the stock is sold and the charter accepted. If the stock is sold in a corporation already in existence, it can accept all subscriptions immediately and make them binding contracts. If the promoter is to receive a stock option for his services, the corporation can make such a contract with him before the services are performed. Usually, though not necessarily, the promoter expects to become president of the new corporation. This method assures him of the presidency before all the stock is sold. Most state laws provide a minimum amount of stock must be sold and paid for before the corporation can begin operations. In Georgia this minimum amount is $2,000 and this can be paid for with a promissory note. So these laws seldom provide any roadblock to this procedure. If they do, the corporation can be organized in any state the promoter chooses, and then operate in any other state it chooses as a foreign corporation.

THE CHARTER

The *charter* is a written document setting forth the facts prescribed by law for the issuance of a charter and asserting that the corporation has complied with these legal requirements. This charter is the base on which rests all the authority of the corporation. It is a contract between the corporation and the state. So long as the corporation complies with the terms of the contract, the state cannot alter the charter in any material way without obtaining the consent of the stockholders.

Some courts have further held that a charter is a contract between the corporation and the stockholders, as well as between the stockholders and the state. This makes the charter a three-way contract. When the incorporators meet, elect a board of directors, and begin business, acceptance of the charter is presumed, and all parties are bound by it.

POWERS OF A CORPORATION

A corporation has three classes of powers:

(1) Charter powers
(2) Incidental powers
(3) Implied powers

Charter Powers. The express powers of a corporation are found in its charter. The charter is a contract between the corporation and the state. So long as the corporation complies with the charter the state cannot without cause cancel it or alter it without the consent of the corporation.

The charter is also a contract between the corporation and the stockholders. When the charter is accepted by the stockholders, all parties are bound by it. It prescribes the nature of the corporation, the classes of stock, and the preferences among different classes of stock, if any.

Incidental Powers. Certain powers that are always incidental to a corporate existence are:

1. To have a corporate name
2. To have a continuous existence
3. To buy, sell, and hold property
4. To make bylaws and regulations
5. To sue and be sued in the corporate name
6. To have and use a corporate seal

(1) Corporate Name. A corporation must have a corporate name. The members may select any name they wish, provided it is not contrary to the statutes or is not already used by another firm or corporation within the state. Many of the states have statutes regulating corporate names, for example, by requiring the name to begin with "The" and to end with "Company," or to be followed by the word "Incorporated" or an abbreviation thereof.

(2) Continuous Existence. During the period for which the charter was granted, the existence of the corporation is continuous. This is one of the features of a corporation that makes this form of organization valuable. The death of a member does not dissolve the organization. Sometimes this characteristic is referred to as perpetual or continuous succession.

(3) Property Rights. A corporation has the right to buy, sell, and hold property that is necessary in its functioning as a corporation and that is not foreign to the purpose for which it was created. Such power is usually given by statute or by the charter.

(4) Bylaws and Regulations. Rules and regulations are necessary to govern and to determine the future conduct of the organization. They must conform to the statutes and must not be contrary to public policy.

(5) Legal Actions. Another power that has long been considered incidental to corporate existence is the power to sue in the corporate name. Since a corporation may be composed of hundreds or thousands of stockholders, it would be a very cumbersome task, if not an impossible one, to secure the consent of all the stockholders each time a suit was to be brought by a corporation. A corporation may likewise be sued in the corporate name.

(6) Corporate Seal. A corporation has the incidental power to have and to own a seal. Under the common law the corporation was required to use its seal in most of its transactions. The rule now is that a corporation need not use its seal except (a) in executing deeds and other written instruments that require the use of a seal when executed by natural individuals, or (b) in carrying out transactions where the use of the seal is required by special statutory requirements.

Implied Powers in General. In addition to the powers that are incidental to or expressly conferred upon all corporations, a corporation has also the implied power to do all acts that are reasonably necessary for carrying out the purpose for which the corporation was formed. A corporation may borrow money and contract debts if such acts are necessary for the transaction of the corporate business. It may make, indorse, and accept negotiable instruments. It has the power to acquire and convey property, and to mortgage or lease its property in case such transactions are necessary for carrying on its business.

As a general rule, a corporation does not have implied power to enter into a contract of partnership; nor does it have the power to enter into a contract of guaranty.

ULTRA VIRES CONTRACTS

Any contract entered into by a corporation that is not authorized by any of its three classes of powers (charter powers, incidental powers, and implied powers) is an *ultra vires contract.* These contracts are called ultra vires because they go beyond the powers of a corporation. If the contract is wholly executory or wholly executed, most courts do not disturb them. They will not enforce a wholly executory ultra vires contract for either party, nor permit a rescission by either party if the contract is wholly executed. If the contract is executed by one party but executory to the other party, most courts permit the performing party to recover a reasonable amount for his performance.

A stockholder may obtain a court order, an injunction, to bar a corporation from undertaking a contemplated ultra vires act. The stockholders cannot intervene, however, if the act has already been executed. The state may revoke the charter of a corporation for an ultra vires act, but this is merely a penalty and in no way affects the rights of the parties to the ultra vires contract.

- The charter of the Well Pump and Supply Company set forth that the corporation was "to engage in the boring of wells, installing pumps, selling pumps and supplies, and the servicing of these pumps." The board of directors entered into a contract with the Board of Supervisors of Buchanan County to hard surface three miles of county roads. The court upon application by a stockholder issued an injunction prohibiting the board from fulfilling this contract as it was an executory ultra vires contract.

QUESTIONS

1. What is the main difference between a corporation and a partnership?
2. Is the entity concept of a corporation ever ignored by the court?
3. If one wishes to go into business for himself so he can "be his own boss," is he more likely to achieve his objective as a partner or as a stockholder in a corporation? Explain.
4. What is meant by adoption of a promoter's contracts?
5. What are the rights of the stockholders who control a majority of the common stock in a corporation?
6. If one person owns 49 per cent of the stock in a corporation, does this fact automatically give him a right to work for the corporation?
7. When may the state alter the charter of a corporation?
8. What information is usually included in the articles of incorporation?
9. What powers does a corporation have other than those expressly set out in its charter?
10. What action may the state take if a corporation engages in an ultra vires act?

CASE PROBLEMS

1. Perdue was the promoter for the formation of an auto finance corporation. The plan of incorporation called for the sale of $1,000,000 worth of common stock. Perdue leased for five years a building to be used for the company's main place of business. The lease was in the name of Perdue, but the lessor understood the purpose of the lease since he had subscribed for 100 shares of stock. The rent amounted to $900 a month. After the corporation was formed, the board of directors refused to abide by the lease and leased instead another building. (a) Is the corporation bound on the lease made by the promoter? (b) Is the promoter personally bound on this lease?

2. Mr. and Mrs. Land and their son John proceed to organize a family corporation to be known as The Right Way Laundry. The business began operating with all three parties actively engaged in carrying on the business while the incorporation papers were being drawn up. Neither the charter nor the certificate of incorporation was ever issued by the state, and no stockholders' meeting was ever held. Mr. Land borrowed $10,000 from the bank and signed the note:

> Right Way Laundry
> By Henry Land, President

The note was never paid, and the bank sued Mrs. Land as a partner. Was this a partnership?

3. The Hudson Truck Lines, a corporation, leased ten trailer trucks instead of buying trucks. The corporate charter provided that the scope of the

corporation's business was to own and operate an interstate truck freight business. A stockholder brought a suit to prohibit the corporation from leasing the trucks, claiming the contract was an ultra vires act. Do you agree?

4. Bisher and Furman formed a corporation to manufacture and market athletic equipment. They employed a stockbroker to obtain subscriptions to the $100,000 authorized capital stock. After all the stock had been fully subscribed, Bisher as copromoter, made contracts in the name of the corporation amounting to $11,000. Over half of the subscribers canceled their subscriptions. Since additional subscribers could not be found, the enterprise fell through. What serious blunder did Bisher and Furman commit in this undertaking?

5. Ten stockholders owned all of the stock in the Frost Tire Company, a company specializing in recapping tires. The company was only modestly successful. At a special stockbrokers' meeting, nine of the stockholders vote to sell all the assets of the tire recapping business and use the proceeds to start manufacturing "camel backs," the strip of rubber used to recap tires. The tenth stockholder brought suit to enjoin the corporation from engaging in this new enterprise. Was this the proper action?

6. Donaldson, who owned two large farms devoted to the production of livestock, had two sons, John and Henry. He wanted to take them into business with him in such a way that he would keep one of the farms exclusively for himself and operate the other one as a partnership or corporation. He was told that under a partnership arrangement both farms could still be subjected to liability for the debts of the partnership. To avoid this, the three of them drew up a corporation type of contract, providing for shares of stock, a board of directors, and all the other requirements of a corporation. They did not obtain a charter, however, nor did they attempt to comply with the state corporation laws. They did file a federal and state corporation income tax return each year. The firm, due to the bad management of the two sons, became heavily indebted, and the creditors brought suit to collect. The firm's assets were wholly inadequate to pay the firm's debts. The creditors then sought to hold the father personally liable for these debts. Was he liable?

7. A group of fifty dairy farmers formed a corporation for the purpose of marketing milk and other dairy products. The charter stipulated that it was authorized to bottle and market whole milk in the city of Auburn. Soon the question arose as to whether or not the corporation could do any of these acts: (a) buy milk from farmers other than the fifty members; (b) make and sell ice cream; (c) make and sell butter and cheese; (d) buy and operate a freezer locker plant in conjunction with its milk plant; (e) buy a dairy farm in the name of the corporation to produce milk for sale by the corporation; (f) to operate a feed store for the convenience of the stockholders in purchasing dairy feed; (g) to own and operate the Dairy Queen, a restaurant, selling only dairy products, such as ice cream, milk shakes, and other dishes consisting mainly of milk or milk products. Which of these acts were permissible under the charter, the incidental, or the implied powers of the corporation?

8. The Blue Stone Coal Company, a corporation, voted through its board of directors to use its surplus to construct a hotel to be operated for a profit. After the hotel was completed and in operation, a stockholder brought an action to compel the board of directors to sell the hotel. Was this the proper action?

9. The Big Ben Railroad, a corporation, signed a contract with the Hodgsen Fertilizer Corporation to run an experimental farm to test the various types of fertilizer manufactured by Hodgsen. The Hodgsen Corporation sued the railroad for $10,000, the amount owed for fertilizer bought for the experiments. The railroad claims it is not liable because the contract was an ultra vires act. Was this defense valid?

10. A corporation organized in New Jersey was issued a charter authorizing it to engage in highway construction. Soon after the corporation's organization, it was lowest bidder on a state road construction job and the contract was duly let to the corporation. Later the state attempted arbitrarily to avoid the contract, claiming a corporation was not entitled to the protection of the Federal Constitution protecting individual citizens against the abridgement of their contractual rights. Do corporations enjoy the same constitutional protections as individual citizens?

11. Childs, Clyatt, and Collins formed a partnership dealing in antiques. Each invested $20,000 in the business. It was a very profitable enterprise but was endangered by the constant bickering among the three partners. As a solution to their problem, they incorporated, each taking $20,000 worth of stock in the corporation. In addition, the corporation was authorized to sell an additional $21,000 worth of stock, $7,000 worth for each stockholder. When Clyatt and Collins refused to buy any more stock, Child's mother-in-law bought the other shares. In electing a board of directors each of the original stockholders put up a separate slate. Child's slate won all places. The board of directors discharged Clyatt and Collins from their jobs and denied them all access to the business. From Clyatt's and Collins' point of view, did the corporate type of business organization overcome the so-called weaknesses of the partnership type?

12. A corporation was formed for the purpose of manufacturing and selling jewelry. It owned its own building. The directors found that they had more space than was needed for their business, and they decided to rent one of the floors for office purposes. One of the stockholders opposed the idea, contending that such an act would be ultra vires. Was the stockholder right in his contention in this case? Why?

13. Dempsey, Carpenter, and Rhinehart owned all the stock in the Mathis Lumber Company. They voted unanimously to authorize the board of directors to guarantee the faithful fulfillment of a construction contract by the Dade Construction Company. Did the corporation have the power to do this?

CHAPTER 36

MEMBERSHIP IN A
CORPORATION

CAPITAL STOCK

The *capital stock* of the corporation is the amount authorized by the charter and the articles of incorporation. This stock is subscribed and paid for by the members. It generally is not necessary that all the capital stock of a corporation be subscribed and paid for before the corporation begins operation. The amount of capital stock authorized in the charter cannot be altered without the consent of the state and the stockholders.

The capital stock is divided into units called *shares*. These shares may have a set value of one dollar, ten dollars, one hundred dollars, or any other amount not prohibited by law.

MEMBERSHIP

Membership in a corporation is acquired by the ownership of one or more shares of stock. The members are known as *stockholders*. The shares of stock may be obtained by subscription either before or after the corporation is organized, or they may be obtained by gift or purchase from another stockholder. The amount of ownership, that is, the number of shares owned, is evidenced by a stock certificate.

STOCK CERTIFICATE

A *certificate of stock* is the owner's receipt for the money he has invested in the corporation. It is not considered as property in itself, but only as evidence of the owner's rights in the corporation. It shows on its face the number of shares represented, the par value of each share if there is a par value, and the signatures of the officers.

KINDS OF STOCK

Stock is divided into many classes. The classes are determined by the laws under which the corporation is organized. The two principal classes of stock are:

1. Common stock
2. Preferred stock

(1) **Common Stock.** *Common stock* is the simplest form of stock issued. The owners of common stock are entitled to a pro rata share of the profits after prior claims have been satisfied. If a corporation has issued 5,000 shares of common stock, the owner of 100 shares is entitled to 1/50 of the profits that are made available to the common stockholders. Unlike the partners in a partnership, the owners cannot receive the profits until they have been made available in the form of a dividend declared by the board of directors.

The common stockholders generally have full right to manage and operate the corporation, but they cannot perform this function as individual stockholders or as a group. They must elect agents or directors, who in turn appoint the managers, usually though not necessarily from the stockholders. The stockholders who are not employed by these managers to work for the corporation have no more rights in determining the operating policies than has an outsider.

(2) **Preferred Stock.** *Preferred stock* differs from common stock in that some sort of preference is granted to the holder of this stock. The preference may pertain to voting, to the division of profits, to the division of assets upon dissolution, or to any two or more of these preferences in combination. The most valuable preference is the preference as to profits.

The fact that particular stock is called preferred stock does not tell much about what preference the holder really has. It may be preferred as to assets only, which gives the holder no advantage except in the event of liquidation. It may be preferred as to dividends only, but not as to assets in the event of liquidation. The most common type is that which gives preference both as to dividends and assets; but even here the stock may be either first preferred, second preferred, or third preferred. In this event the first preferred is given preference in the payment of dividends before the second preferred is entitled to anything. Likewise the second preferred must be paid before the third preferred is entitled to receive a dividend.

The two rights usually given up by the preferred stockholders are the right to vote in stockholders' meetings and the right to participate in profits beyond the percentage fixed in the stock certificate. A few states prohibit any restriction upon any stockholder's right to vote.

When the stock is preferred as to dividends, this right may be cumulative or noncumulative. This fact is significant if the corporation operates at a loss about as often as it does at a profit. For example, a corporation that has $1,000,000 outstanding common stock and $1,000,000 outstanding 7 percent preferred stock operates at a loss for two years, and then earns 21 percent net profit the third year. If *noncumulative preferred stock* has been issued, it is entitled to only one dividend of 7 percent; and the common stock is entitled to the remaining 14 percent. If *cumulative preferred stock* has been issued, it is entitled to three preferences of 7 percent, or 21 percent in all, before the common stock is entitled to any dividend. Or if the company earns a net profit each year equal to only 7 percent on the preferred stock, the directors could, if the preferred stock is noncumulative, pass the dividend the first year and declare a 7 percent dividend on both the common and the preferred stock for the second year. Since the directors are elected by the common stockholders, the common stockholders could easily defraud the preferred stockholders. For that reason the law is that preferred stock is cumulative unless specifically stated to be noncumulative. This is true, however, only when the corporation earns a profit but fails to declare a dividend. Unless the stock certificate expressly states that it is cumulative, the preference does not cumulate in the years during which the corporation operated at a loss.

Preferred stock may also be participating or nonparticipating. Thus 7 percent *participating preferred stock* may pay considerably more than 7 percent annually; but if it is *nonparticipating preferred stock*, 7 percent annually would be the maximum to which the preferred stockholders would be entitled no matter how much the corporation earned. If the preferred stock is to participate in any profits beyond the rate fixed in the stock, this right must be expressly stated in the stock certificate or articles of incorporation. The law presumes it is nonparticipating in the absence of a contract to the contrary. If it does participate, it can do so only according to the terms of the contract. The contract may provide that the preferred stock shall participate equally with the common stock, or it may provide that the preferred stock is entitled to an additional 1 percent for each additional 5 percent the common stock receives.

THE PROSPECTUS

Every new corporation and every old corporation offering a new issue of stock to the public must provide every subscriber a prospectus. Before the stock is sold, a copy of the prospectus must be submitted to the Federal Securities and Exchange Commission and to appropriate state officials. The *prospectus* must set forth the nature of the corporation, the type or types of stock to be issued, the selling price, and other pertinent information. If the promoter of a new corporation is to receive any stock options or other compensation in stock, this information must be set forth in the prospectus.

- The following paragraph appeared in the prospectus of the Bankers Securities Corporation, a new company being organized in Georgia: "The Board of Directors has agreed to pay Ray Smythe one share of B voting stock for each share of A nonvoting stock sold, but not to exceed 20 percent of the authorized issue." The meaning of this paragraph is that when 20 percent of the authorized stock is sold for cash, the sale of stock will be stopped and Ray Smythe will have a majority of the voting stock. The Securities and Exchange Commission requires that this information be set forth in the prospectus, but the subscriber must interpret its significance.

SPLIT STOCK DEALS

In recent years a new type of stock arrangement has been quite common. Two classes of stock are issued, one voting common stock and one nonvoting common stock. The nonvoting common stock usually has most of the features of preferred stock. It is preferred as to dividends and is participating but usually not cumulative. The one feature that distinguishes nonvoting common stock from preferred stock is that the stock subscriber must purchase both classes, usually in units of 100 shares of A nonvoting stock, and then 80 shares of B voting stock are donated to the subscriber. For this reason the B voting stock must have a very low par value, usually one cent or even one-tenth of one cent a share. Ostensibly this arrangement overcomes the objection preferred stockholders have of giving up their voting rights. If one buys 100 shares of A nonvoting stock, he cannot vote this stock, but he receives a right to vote through the gift of 80 shares. The public is never permitted to buy just voting B stock; but unless the prospectus sets forth otherwise, there is nothing to keep the promoter or promoters from buying only voting stock. With an investment of $100 it would be possible to buy a majority of the voting stock in a $1,000,000 corporation.

PAR-VALUE STOCK AND NO-PAR-VALUE STOCK

Stock to which a face value, such as $25, $50, or $100, has been assigned is *par-value stock*. Stock to which no face value has been assigned is *no-par-value stock*. Preferred stock usually has a par value, but common stock may be either par-value or no-par-value stock. It is ordinarily assumed that par-value stock is issued at par value; but after the business is operating, the price at which the stock can be sold may be either more or less than the par value. No-par-value stock may be issued at any price, although some states do set a minimum price, such as $5, for which it can be issued.

If par-value stock is sold by the corporation at a discount, the purchaser is liable to subsequent creditors for the amount of the discount. No-par-value stock was intended to overcome this weakness of par-value stock.

TREASURY STOCK

If a corporation purchases stock that it has sold, this stock is referred to as *treasury stock*. When stock is first offered for sale, there may be less sales resistance encountered if the prospective purchaser can be assured that the corporation will repurchase the stock upon request. Treasury stock may also be reacquired by donation. The corporation then sells the stock and places the proceeds in a donated surplus account. This is generally done when the corporation is in financial difficulties and the stockholders agree to this plan of building up the working capital.

Treasury stock can be purchased only out of surplus. If the corporation resells it, the directors may fix any price which they deem feasible. Until it is resold, no dividends can be paid on it.

WATERED STOCK

When par-value stock is issued as fully paid up but the purchase price is paid with property of inflated values, it is said to be *watered stock*. If real estate actually worth $10,000 is paid for in stock having a par value of $100,000, it is watered to the extent of $90,000. In most instances, watering stock is not prohibited outright, but it cannot be used to defraud creditors. In the event of insolvency, the creditors may sue the owners of watered stock for the difference between the par value and the actual purchase price. This is not true, of course, if the creditors knew the stock was watered or if the holder of the stock purchased it from the one to whom it was originally issued. Except for creditors, most state statutes do not prohibit the watering of stock by corporations other than public utility companies.

If the payment for stock is in overvalued real estate, the extent of the watering can be determined with reasonable accuracy. If the payment is in the form of patents, trademarks, blueprints, or other similar assets, it may be difficult to fix the extent of the watering. The extent of the watering is not one of law, but one of fact, and is to be fixed by the jury based upon the evidence presented in each case.

TRANSFER OF STOCK

A stock certificate indicates the manner in which the stock may be transferred to another party. On the back of the certificate is a blank form which the owner may use in executing an assignment. The signature of the previous owner gives to the new holder full possession and the right to exchange the certificate for another made out to himself by the corporation. The new owner should have the certificate exchanged for a new one in his own name so that he will be registered as a stockholder on the books of the corporation. Unless he is so registered, he is not entitled to the rights and privileges of a stockholder, and he will not receive any dividends when they are declared.

STOCK OPTIONS

A *stock option* is a contract entered into between the board of directors of a corporation and an individual, giving the individual the option for a stated period of time to purchase a prescribed number of shares of stock in the corporation at a given price. If the stock in a new corporation is sold to the public at $2 a share, the individual having the option must also pay $2, but he may be given, two, five, or even ten years in which to exercise the option. If the corporation succeeds and the price of the stock goes up, the individual takes up his option. If the corporation fails, he does not have to buy stock. Existing corporations may give officials of the corporation in lieu of a salary increase an option to purchase a given number of shares of authorized but unissued common stock at a price substantially below the current market price. This type of option is usually for a short period of six to twelve months. If the market price of the stock does not fall, an official may make a capital gain by buying the stock, holding it six months, and selling it. The income tax on a capital gain is considerably less than that on a normal income. This type of compensation may be more attractive to top management officials than a straight increase in salary, enabling a corporation to retain their services at a lower cost than a salary increase.

DIVIDENDS

The profits of a corporation belong to the corporation until the directors set them aside for distribution as *dividends*. Dividends may be paid in cash, stock, or other property.

A cash dividend usually can be paid out of earned surplus only, but there are two exceptions. A cash dividend may be paid out of donated or paid-in surplus. Also, for corporations with depleting assets, such as coal mines, oil companies, lumber companies, and similar industries, cash dividends may be paid out of capital to the extent of the depletion.

Stock dividends are usually paid out of earned surplus, but they may usually be paid out of any surplus account. A stock dividend cannot be declared if there is no surplus of any kind, for this would result in stock watering. Dividends also may be paid in the form of property which the corporation manufactures, but this is seldom done.

The right to declare a dividend on either common or preferred stock depends entirely upon the discretion of the directors. The directors, however, must act reasonably and in good faith; otherwise the stockholders may invoke the aid of a court in compelling them to do so. There is no absolute rule as to when a dividend should be declared. If profits have accumulated but dividends have not been declared, the profits become part of the assets of the corporation and may be used in improving the property or in extending the business.

If a dividend is illegally declared and paid, either the stockholders or the directors may be sued by creditors for its return.

Once a cash dividend is declared, it cannot later be rescinded. It becomes a liability of the corporation the minute it is declared. A stock dividend on the other hand may be rescinded at any time prior to the issuance and delivery of the stock.

BLUE-SKY LAWS

The purpose of the so-called blue-sky laws is to regulate the sale of securities and to prevent fraud through the sale of worthless stocks and bonds.

These security laws usually stipulate that before a salesman may offer stocks or bonds for sale, a statement of the responsibility of the seller, the general financial condition of the corporation, and the nature of the stocks or the bonds that are for sale must be furnished to a designated state official or a commission. Criminal penalties are provided for violation of these laws, and there is a civil liability on the part of the seller to purchasers.

FEDERAL SECURITIES ACT, 1933

Because the state blue-sky laws apply only to intrastate sales of securities, in 1933 the federal Congress passed the Federal Securities Act to regulate the sale of securities in interstate commerce. Any corporation offering a new issue of securities for sale to the public must register them with the Securities and Exchange Commission. This act does not apply to the sales of securities under $100,000 by corporations, nor does the act regulate the sale or purchase of securities by individuals.

In addition to the registration and the information contained in it, the proposed prospectus must be filed and approved by the Securities and Exchange Commission before the securities can be offered for sale. Full information must be given relative to the financial structure of the corporation. Information filed must also include the types of securities outstanding, if any, the terms of the sale, bonus and profit-sharing arrangements, options to be created in regard to the securities, and any other data which the Securities and Exchange Commission may deem relevant.

The registration statement must be signed by the company, its principal officers, and a majority of the board of directors. If either the registration statement or the prospectus contains misstatements or omissions, the Commission will not permit the securities to be offered for sale. If they are sold before the false information is ascertained, an investor may rescind his contract and sue any individual who signed the registration statement for damages he has sustained. Any failure to comply with the law also subjects the responsible officials to criminal prosecution.

FEDERAL SECURITIES EXCHANGE ACT, 1934

The chief markets for the sale of securities are the security exchanges and over-the-counter markets. In 1934 Congress passed the

Securities Exchange Act to regulate such transactions. The act declares it unlawful for any broker, dealer, or exchange to use the mails for the purpose of using the exchange facilities in making a sale unless the exchange is registered with the Securities and Exchange Commission.

All the securities exchanges must declare definite rules for the regulation of members of the exchange. The bylaws of every security exchange must provide for the expulsion or disciplining of any member who violates the rules of the exchange or who engages in conduct contrary to the rules of the trade. No exchange can sell securities until it is registered with the Commission, and this registration may be withdrawn if the exchange violates the requirements of the statute. Individuals making misleading statements or contracts in violation of the Act may be punished by a fine and imprisonment.

QUESTIONS

1. Must all of the authorized stock of a corporation be sold before the corporation can begin business?

2. What evidence does one have that he owns stock in a corporation?

3. What are the two principal classes of stock?

4. How do the stockholders of a corporation manage the corporation?

5. Explain the difference between par-value stock and no-par-value stock.

6. What is meant by "split stock"?

7. What is a prospectus?

8. May dividends be paid in property of a corporation?

9. If one wishes to purchase stock in a new corporation, why is it important to know if there have been any stock options granted?

CASE PROBLEMS

1. Mrs. Dixon used the proceeds of her deceased husband's life insurance policies to purchase $50,000 worth of noncumulative 7 percent preferred stock in the belief that the $3,500 annual income from this investment would be adequate to support her. Over a ten-year period the corporation averaged 14 percent on its preferred stock, but during four years it earned no net profits and paid no dividends. Mrs. Dixon sued the corporation to compel it to pay these dividends. Was she entitled to dividends for the four years when the corporation operated at a loss?

2. Parrish, Mosteller, and Garrard operated a very profitable partnership in the wholesale meat business. Garrard died. Parrish and Mosteller persuaded Mrs. Garrard to enter the partnership as a general partner. She accepted their offer, and her share of the profits gave her a very nice income.

Parrish and Mosteller proposed that the partnership incorporate. Soon after the corporation was formed, Parrish and Mosteller decided not to pay any dividends and to use them instead to open up a new plant in another city. Mrs. Garrard protested so vehemently that they voted to discharge her as bookkeeper. She was then without any source of income. She brought suit to compel the directors to declare a dividend and also to restore her to her position as bookkeeper for the firm. Was she entitled to these remedies?

3. Smith was the promoter in forming the Life Insurance Stock Holding Company. The prospectus states the corporation has an authorized capital stock of 500,000 shares of nonvoting A stock, par value $5, and 500,000 shares of voting B stock, par value one cent. It further states the stock is to be sold in units of 100 shares of A and 40 shares of B stock at $5 a share for the A stock with the B stock as a bonus. Point out how Smith legally ends up owning a controlling interest in this corporation with an investment of only $3,000.

4. Malcolm, Blair, and Mattox are the three promoters for a new corporation to start a discount house. The authorized capital stock is 500,000 shares with a par value of $1. The prospectus states that 100,000 shares are reserved for options. The other 400,000 shares are sold for the par value, and the company begins operations and is very successful. After ten years, the book value of the stock is $5 a share. Malcolm, Blair, and Mattox then take up their options on the 100,000 shares at $1 a share. Show how this affects the book value of the 400,000 shares.

5. The capital stock outstanding of the Mattox Corporation is $1,000,000; the earned surplus is $800,000. No dividends have ever been paid. Grantham is a retired accountant for this firm. During his twenty years with the firm, he had been a member of an employee group who monthly purchased stock in the Mattox Corporation. When Grantham retired, he had 1,500 shares with a book value of $30,000. He had banked on his dividends from this stock to supplement his social security income. He brought suit to compel the board of directors to declare a dividend. Will he succeed?

6. Konter was the owner of 1,000 shares of stock for which he had paid only about 10 percent of their true value at the time the stock was issued. Later he sold 500 shares to Raul who paid full value for the stock. The corporation became insolvent, and the creditors sued Raul, claiming that since his stock was 90 percent watered, he was personally liable. Was this correct?

7. The profits and surplus of a corporation are equal to the capital stock. The corporation is ten years old and has never paid a dividend. The board of directors decide again this year not to pay a dividend but to use 80 percent of the accumulated profits to build an extension to the factory. A stockholder owning 20 percent of the stock brings suit to compel the directors to declare a dividend. Who will win the suit?

CHAPTER 37

MANAGEMENT AND
DISSOLUTION OF A
CORPORATION

NATURE OF CORPORATE MANAGEMENT

Since a corporation is an artificial being, existing only in contemplation of law, it can perform business transactions only through actual persons, acting as agents. The directors are both trustees and agents. To the corporation, they are trustees and are chargeable for breaches of trust. To third parties, directors are agents of the corporation.

The board of directors elects the chief agents of the corporation, such as the president, the vice-president, the treasurer, and other officers, who perform the managerial functions. The board of directors is primarily a policy-making body. The chief executives in turn appoint subagents for all the administrative functions of the corporation. These subagents are agents of the corporation, however, not of the appointing executives.

It is evident from this summary of the managerial scheme of a corporation that a stockholder cannot, merely by reason of his membership in the corporation, act as an agent or exercise any managerial function. His only control is in electing a board of directors.

Even if a stockholder owned 49 percent of the common stock of a corporation, he would have no more right to work or participate in the management of the corporation than a stranger would have. Under the partnership law, if a man owns even 1 percent of the partnership, he has just as much right to work for the partnership and to participate in its management as any other partner. In a corporation the only way one can be sure that he can have employment with his own company is to own 51 percent of the stock.

THE CINCINNATI SHOE COMPANY
Notice of Annual Meeting of Shareholders
MARCH 22

The annual meeting of the shareholders of The Cincinnati Shoe Company will be held at the Main Office of the Company, 170 East Main Street, Cincinnati, Ohio, on Thursday, March 22, at 10:00 o'clock A. M., Eastern Standard Time, for the purpose of electing directors, receiving reports of officers, and transacting such other business as may properly come before the meeting.

The Board of Directors has fixed the close of business, February 15, as the record date for determining shareholders entitled to notice of the meeting and to vote.

Proxy Statement accompanies this Notice.

T. L. LAWSON, Secretary.

By Order of the Board of Directors.
February 22.

You are requested to sign and return, as soon as possible, the attached Proxy.

A Notice of a Stockholders' Meeting

STOCKHOLDERS' MEETINGS

In order to make the will of the majority binding, the stockholders must act at a duly convened and properly conducted stockholders' meeting. These meetings must ordinarily take place in the state in which the corporation was organized, regardless of the number of states in which the corporation maintains branch offices or factories.

A regular meeting is usually held at the place and the time specified in the charter, and notice of the meeting is ordinarily not required. A special meeting may, however, be called by the directors of the corporation or in some instances by a particular officer or a specified number of stockholders. Notice is ordinarily required.

These meetings of the stockholders are theoretically a check upon the board of directors. If the directors do not carry out the will of the stockholders, a new board can be elected that will be amenable to the stockholders' wishes. This procedure is, in the absence of fraud or bad faith on the part of the directors, the only legal means by which the investors can exercise any control over their investment.

QUORUM

A stockholders' meeting, in order to be valid, requires the presence of a quorum. At common law a *quorum* consisted of the stockholders actually assembled at a properly convened meeting. A majority of the votes cast by those present expressed the will of the stockholders. It is now ordinarily required by statutes, bylaws, or charters that a majority of the outstanding stock be represented at the stockholders' meeting in order to constitute a quorum. This representation may be either in person or by proxy as described on page 368.

VOTING

The right of a stockholder to vote is his most important right because this is the only way in which he can exercise any control over his investment. The right to vote is limited to the bona fide stockholders, as evidenced by the stockholders' record book. An owner of stock purchased from an individual does not have the right to vote until he has the transfer made on the corporate books. Subscribers who have not fully paid for their stock are not as a rule permitted to vote.

The right to vote is controlled by the state corporation laws. There may be issued, if the law permits, voting and nonvoting common stock. The laws in all the states permit the charter of a corporation to restrict the right of preferred stockholders to vote. If the charter is silent in this regard, then the preferred stockholders have equal voting privileges with the common stockholders.

There are two major classes of elections in which the stockholders vote: the annual election of directors, and the elections to approve or disapprove some corporate policy which only the stockholders can authorize. Examples of some of these acts are consolidating with another corporation, dissolving, increasing the capital stock, and changing the number of directors.

METHODS OF VOTING

Each stockholder has one vote for each share of stock that he holds. In the election of a board of directors, the candidates receiving a majority of the stock actually voting win. In corporations with 500,000 stockholders, control of 10 percent of the stock is often sufficient to control the election. In all cases the owners of 51 percent of the stock can elect all the directors. This leaves the minority stockholders without any representation on the board of directors. To alleviate this situation, two legal devices are in existence which may give the minority stockholders a voice, but not a controlling voice, on the board of directors:

1. Cumulative voting
2. Voting trusts

(1) Cumulative Voting. In some states the statutes provide that in the election of directors a stockholder may cast as many votes in the aggregate as are equal to the number of shares held by him multiplied by the number of directors to be elected. This method of voting is called *cumulative voting*. Thus, if a stockholder owns ten shares and ten directors are to be elected, he can cast ten votes for each of the ten directors or one hundred votes for one director. As a result, under this plan of voting the minority stockholders may have some representation on the board of directors, although it is a minority.

(2) Voting Trusts. Under a voting trust stockholders give up their voting privileges entirely by transferring their stock to the trustee and receiving in return *voting trust certificates*. This is not primarily a device to give the minority stockholders a voice on the board of directors; but it does do that, and often in large corporations it gives them a controlling voice. Twenty percent of the stock always voted as a unit is more effective than individual voting. State laws severely restrict the use of voting trusts. Most of these laws require the trustee to be a stockholder and limit the trust to ten years.

PROXIES

Under the common law a stockholder was not permitted to vote unless he was present in person. Under the statutory law, the charter,

---

THE CINCINNATI SHOE COMPANY
PROXY
ANNUAL MEETING MARCH 22

KNOW ALL MEN BY THESE PRESENTS, That the undersigned shareholder of THE CINCINNATI SHOE COMPANY hereby constitutes and appoints O. W. PRESCOTT, A. B. BROWN, and GEORGE CONNARS, and each of them, the true and lawful proxies of the undersigned, with several power of substitution and revocation, for and in the name of the undersigned, to attend the annual meeting of shareholders of said Company, to be held at the Main Office of the Company, 170 East Main Street, Cincinnati, Ohio, on Thursday, March 22, at 10:00 o'clock A. M., Eastern Standard Time, and any and all adjournments of said meeting, receipt of the notice of which meeting, stating the purposes thereof, together with Proxy Statement, being hereby acknowledged by the undersigned, and to vote for the election of a Board of nine directors for the Company, and to vote as they or he may deem proper upon all other matters that may lawfully come before said meeting or any adjournment thereof.

Signed the ___ *10th* ___ day of March

___ *L. S. Simms* ___

A Proxy

or the bylaws, a member who does not wish to attend a meeting and vote in person may authorize another to vote his stock for him. This right is called *voting by proxy*; the person who is authorized to vote for another is known as a *proxy*.

If a stockholder should sign more than one proxy for the same stockholders' meeting, the proxy having the later date would be effective. A proxy is good in most states for no more than six months. If the stockholder attends the stockholders' meeting in person, this acts as a revocation of the proxy.

PROXY WARS

If the stockholders are dissatisfied with the policies of the present board of directors, a new board may be elected. To elect a new board is often a difficult or impossible task. If the corporation is a split-stock corporation in which one or even several men own a majority of the voting stock, there is no way the dissident stockholders can obtain a majority of the voting stock to insure success. If the voting stock is widely held and no group owns a majority of the voting stock, then the dissident stockholders at least have a numerical chance to elect a new board. To do this a majority of the stock represented at a stockholders' meeting must be controlled by this dissatisfied group. To insure success the leaders of the group must obtain proxies from stockholders who cannot attend the stockholders' meeting in person. The current board members will also attempt to secure proxies. This is known as a proxy war. The present board of directors is permitted in most instances to pay the cost of this solicitation from corporate funds. The "outsiders" must bear the cost of the proxy war out of their personal funds. If there are 1,000,000 shareholders, the cost of soliciting their proxies is enormous. For this reason proxy wars are seldom undertaken and seldom won when they are undertaken. The law protects stockholders against the wrongful acts of the board of directors. The stockholders must protect themselves against the poor judgment and the unprofitable policies of the directors. To do this proxy wars are sometimes necessary.

RIGHTS OF STOCKHOLDERS

The stockholders of a corporation enjoy several important rights and privileges. Three of these rights have been discussed. They are:

(1) A stockholder has the right to receive a properly executed certificate as evidence of his ownership of shares of stock.

(2) He has the right to attend corporate meetings and to vote unless this right is denied him by express agreement, the charter, or statutory provisions.

(3) He has the right to receive a proportionate share of the profits when profits are distributed as dividends.

In addition, each stockholder has the following rights:

(4) He has the right to sell and transfer his shares of stock.

(5) He has the right, when new stock is issued by the corporation, to subscribe for new shares in proportion to the shares that he owns. For example, if a stockholder owns 10 percent of the original capital stock, he has a right to buy 10 percent of the shares added to the stock. If this were not true, stockholders could be deprived of their proportionate share in the accumulated surplus of the company. Only stockholders have the right to vote to increase the capital stock.

(6) He has the right to inspect the corporate books in the absence of a statute to the contrary. He also has the right to have the corporate books inspected by an attorney or an accountant. This right is not absolute since most states have laws restricting the right. The tendency is for these laws to be drawn to protect the corporation from indiscriminate inspection, not to hamper a stockholder in his right.

There are two sets of corporate books, one called the *corporate books* and the other the *financial books*. The corporate books, which may be inspected by stockholders, contain a detailed record of all stock transactions and minute books for stockholders' meetings and directors' meetings. The other set, which in some states may not be inspected by stockholders, contains a record of the financial operations of the corporation.

(7) He has the right, when the corporation is dissolved, to share pro rata in the assets that remain after all the obligations of the company have been paid.

DIRECTORS

Every corporation is managed by a board of directors elected by the stockholders. The law requires every board to consist of at least three members; but if the number is in excess of three, the number, together with qualifications and manner of election, is fixed by the charter and the bylaws of the corporation.

The directors, unlike the stockholders, cannot vote by proxy. Nor can they make corporate decisions as individual directors. All decisions must be made collectively and in a called meeting of the board. The functions of the directors can be classified as:

1. Powers
2. Duties
3. Liabilities

(1) **Powers.** The powers of the board of directors are limited by law, by the charter, and by the bylaws. The directors have the power of general agents, and in this capacity may do any act reasonably necessary to achieve the purpose of the corporation so long as this power is not expressly limited. Unless authorized by statute, they do not have the power to divert corporate assets for charitable purposes. By law they are barred from using corporate funds directly for political purposes. As general agents they have the power to do only what they are expressly authorized to do or what may reasonably be implied as necessary to carry out their functions.

(2) **Duties.** The directors are charged with the duty of establishing policies that will achieve the function of the corporation, selecting executives to carry out these policies, and supervising these executives to see that the policies are efficiently executed. They must act in person, not by proxy, in exercising all discretionary power. The directors also must act as a group, not as individuals; and in the absence of authority to the contrary, a majority of the directors must be present before any binding discussions can be made. The directors may delegate ministerial and routine duties to subagents, but the duty of determining all major corporate policies, except those reserved to the stockholders, must be assumed by the board of directors.

(3) **Liabilities.** As trustees of the corporation, the directors are liable for bad faith and for gross negligence. They are not liable for losses when they act with due diligence and reasonably sound judgment. Countless errors of judgment are made annually by directors in operating a complex business organization. Only when these errors are due to a breach of good faith can a director be held personally liable.

- Gable was a director in the LeVisa State Bank. For five years he never attended a directors' meeting, and he never examined the company's books or records. The president and the cashier of the bank managed it in a careless and negligent manner, causing the bank to go into receivership. Gable was personally liable for the resulting losses to the stockholders.

The test of whether or not directors have acted in good faith and with reasonable skill and care in the discharge of their duties is: "Did they use the same degree of care and prudence that men prompted by self-interest generally exercise in their own affairs?" If the answer is in the affirmative, the directors are not personally liable for corporate losses. They are not insurers of the success of the business.

Directors may be held liable for some acts without evidence of negligence or bad faith either because the act is illegal or bad faith is presumed. Paying dividends out of capital and ultra vires acts are illustrations of acts that are illegal. Loaning corporate funds to officers and directors is an act to which the court will impute bad faith.

The board of directors may by majority vote approve some action which one or more directors feel is either unlawful or such bad faith that the directors can be held personally liable in damages. In some cases the directors may be deemed guilty of conspiracy, subjecting each director to criminal prosecution. Every director who is present at a board meeting is conclusively presumed to have assented to the wrongful acts unless he takes positive action to overcome this presumption. If the directors who are present and dissent have a record of their dissent entered in the minutes of the meeting, then they cannot be held liable for the acts of the majority.

DISSOLUTION

A corporation may terminate its existence by paying all its debts, distributing all remaining assets to the stockholders and surrendering its charter. The corporation then ceases to exist, and its dissolution is complete. This action may be voluntary on the part of the stockholders, or it may be involuntary by action of the court or state. The state may ask for a dissolution for any one of the following reasons: (1) forfeiture or abuse of the corporate charter, (2) violation of the state laws, (3) fraud in the procurement of the charter, and (4) failure to pay taxes for a continuous period of three or more years.

When a corporation dissolves, it is legally dead. It is then incapable of suing, owning property, or forming contracts except for the purpose of converting its assets into cash and distributing the cash to the creditors and stockholders. The distribution of the cash must be in this order:

(1) All taxes due all governmental units must be paid first.

(2) Secured liabilities must be paid next after taxes.

(3) All unsecured debts are paid after taxes and secured claims are met in full. Any payments out of this order subject the stockholders and the directors to personal liability for losses sustained by the state or by the creditors because of improper distribution.

(4) Stockholders that are preferred as to assets are paid.

(5) Any remaining cash is distributed to the common stockholders.

In the event that there are not enough assets to pay all creditors, the stockholders are not held personally liable. This is one of the chief advantages of a corporation over a sole proprietorship or partnership. It is an advantage from the stockholder's standpoint, but a disadvantage from the creditors' standpoint.

QUESTIONS

1. What is the only way that a corporation can perform business transactions?
2. What is the function of the board of directors?
3. How many stockholders must be present at a stockholders' meeting to constitute a quorum?
4. How does the corporation determine who is qualified to vote at a stockholders' meeting?
5. How many votes does each stockholder have?
6. What is cumulative voting?
7. If a stockholder cannot attend a stockholders' meeting, how may he vote?
8. (a) Does every stockholder have the right to vote?
    (b) If there are three members of a board of directors and all three agree to buy a certain piece of real estate, can they do so without formally calling a directors' meeting?
9. When are directors liable to the stockholders for errors of judgment that result in financial loss?
10. (a) Under what conditions may the state order a dissolution of a corporation against the stockholders' consent?
    (b) In the event of the dissolution of a corporation, how are the corporate assets distributed?

CASE PROBLEMS

1. The directors of the Lime Products Corporation declared a stock dividend of 10 per cent to all common stock. When the bookkeeper began calculating the size of each stockholder's dividend, he discovered there was not enough unissued common stock to pay the dividend in full. He realized

that it was illegal to issue stock that had not been authorized. He brought this to the attention of the board of directors, and they attempted to rescind the declaration of the dividend. A stockholder brought suit to compel the issuance of his dividend stock, alleging the board could not rescind its act of declaring a dividend. Is the allegation correct?

2. Rooney was the president of the Frozen Food Lockers, Inc. The three-man board of directors loaned Rooney $15,000 from the corporate funds. Later Rooney became bankrupt, and the corporation lost the entire loan. The stockholders brought suit against the board members personally for the loss. Were they liable?

3. Dawson, who owned 10 shares of common stock in a corporation, was very much dissatisfied with the management because of its failure to pay dividends. There was a movement to line up proxies to elect a new board of directors. Dawson received a letter from Carlton James who expressed great dissatisfaction also and asked Dawson to send him a proxy so that he could vote Dawson's shares. Dawson did this. After the election, he learned that James was the corporation's attorney and had used this ruse to inveigle Dawson to send a proxy actually to be voted in favor of the present board. Dawson brought suit to have the election of the board of directors nullified and a new election held. Was he entitled to this relief?

4. O'Malley was the bookkeeper for the Quitman Corporation, which had capital stock common outstanding of $100,000 and an earned surplus of $3,500. The board of directors declared a 2.5 percent dividend and instructed O'Malley to calculate the amount due and mail each stockholder a check. O'Malley, through an error, calculated the dividend at 25 percent instead of 2.5 percent. This resulted in a payment of dividend out of capital. Later the judgment creditors sued the directors personally for the amount of the dividend in excess of earned surplus. Were they liable?

5. Hanson, Dupree, and Rice are directors in a bank. The board votes to use a part of the bank's surplus to start an auto finance company under a trade name to conceal the bank's identity with the finance company. Rice dissented vehemently on the ground the act was clearly ultra vires. He was outvoted. To avoid future liability what might Rice do to protect himself?

6. Meeks was a stockholder in a corporation of 15,000 stockholders. The outstanding capital stock was $50,000,000; the earned surplus was $40,000,000. Meeks was dissatisfied with the operating policy of the corporation in retaining all profits for expansion instead of paying dividends. He started a proxy war to line up other stockholders who agreed with him. The board of directors retaliated by soliciting proxies at the corporation's expense. Meeks sought through legal action to enjoin the directors from spending corporate funds to solicit proxies. Will he succeed?

7. Henderson was a director on the board of directors of the Watson Corporation. Henderson also was a large stockholder in a competing firm. In a board of directors' meeting Henderson voted for a measure that was highly detrimental to the Watson Corporation but highly profitable for the competing firm. A stockholder in the Watson Corporation sought to make Henderson personally liable for the loss. Was he liable?

SUMMARY CASES

PART 8

1. Kirkup was one of the incorporators of the Anaconda Amusement Co. He had a contract with the other promoters whereby he was to sell the corporation's stock and receive a commission of ten percent for its sale. He sold 770 shares, but the corporation never assumed this contract either expressly or impliedly. He brought suit against the corporation to compel it to carry out the terms of his contract with the promoters. Is the corporation liable on this contract? (Kirkup v. Anaconda Amusement Company, 59 Mont. 469, 197 P. 1005)

2. The Kentucky State Bank loaned R. M. Jones $3,500 and received as collateral security 750 shares of stock in the Millner Construction Company, a corporation. The stockholders subsequently voted to liquidate the corporation. The assets of the corporation were converted into cash, and the cash was distributed to the stockholders without requiring the stockholders to surrender their shares of stock. The bank could not and did not register the 750 shares in its name. Consequently, when the cash was distributed, Jones, not the bank, received the cash represented by the 750 shares. Jones did not use the cash to liquidate his loan to the bank. The bank sued Bogardus, the officer of the corporation in charge of the liquidation for the loss sustained. (a) Was the bank entitled to any part of the cash distribution which represented a share of the profits? (b) Was the bank entitled to the cash that represented a return of capital? (Bogardus v. Kentucky State Bank, 281 S. W. 2d 904)

3. Harold Baker, Laura Baker, and Theodore Sweetland undertook to organize a corporation known as the Congress Square Men's Shop, Inc. The organizers failed to do two specific and important acts to become a corporation: (1) record the certificate of incorporation in the registry of deeds as required by law, and (2) file a copy thereof with the secretary of state. There were other minor failures to comply with the law. Stock was issued, bylaws were adopted, and a board of directors was elected. Harold Baker was the major stockholder and manager. Sweetland and Laura Baker held minor positions in the business but took no major part in management. Harold Baker incurred debts in the name of the corporation with the Bates-Street Shirt Co. and others. These creditors sued the three stockholders as partners, alleging there was never a de jure or a de facto corporation and that, therefore, it must be a partnership. Was this a partnership? (Baker et al. v. Bates-Street Shirt Co. et al., 6 F. 2d 854)

4. Margaret Morrison was a stockholder in the State Bank of Wheatland, a corporation. The corporation had never paid a dividend, although its reserves were about 600 percent of the capital stock. Morrison brought suit to compel the directors to declare at least $600 a share on the outstanding stock. She alleged but did not prove that the failure to pay a dividend was for a capricious purpose. Must the directors declare a dividend? (Morrison v. State Bank of Wheatland, et al., 58 Wyo. 138, 126 P. 2d 793)

5. The Tennessee and Kentucky Tobacco Co. was incorporated with R. T. Bohannon, H. T. Stratton, and R. F. Long, and R. F. Long, Trustee for E. B. Long, subscribing for $9,000 worth of stock each, the entire issue. The stock was issued but never paid for. The corporation borrowed money by the stockholders lending their credit, but none of them ever sustained any loss on these loans. The profits were substantial, but no dividends were ever paid. Due to a heavy fire loss, the corporation became insolvent, owing S. R. Russell and others $1,063.33. After the fire, there were no corporate assets with which to pay the debts. Russell and others brought suit against the four stockholders to collect their subscriptions. Is the lending of credit by the stockholders and the foregoing of dividends equivalent in value to the subscription price of the stock? (Russell et al. v. Tennessee and Kentucky Tobacco Company, 65 S.W. 2d 256, 16 Tenn. App. 561)

6. Charles Hammond owned $19\frac{2}{7}$ percent of the outstanding stock of the Edison Illuminating Company. The stockholders voted in a regular stockholders' meeting to increase the outstanding stock of the corporation. Since Hammond owned 140 shares of the stock before the increase, he contended that he was entitled to purchase additional 27 shares so as to keep his ownership at $19\frac{2}{7}$ percent of the outstanding stock. Is he entitled to purchase the 27 shares? (Hammond v. Edison Illuminating Company, 131 Mich. 79, 90 N. W. 1040)

7. The Zale Jewelry Company was a Kansas Corporation organized to engage in the jewelry business. It leased to Dr. Marks, a licensed optometrist, and to the Douglas Optical Company, owned by Carp, a portion of its premises. Both leases provided that the Zale Jewelry Company should handle the business and financial affairs of the lessees. All charges for services and optical supplies were carried on the Zale Jewelry Co.'s books. If Marks and Carp are employees, then the Zale Jewelry Company is practicing optometry, an ultra vires act. If they are true lessees, the company is not practicing optometry. Which are they? (State v. Zale Jewelry Co. of Wichita, Inc., 179 Kan. 628, 298 P. 2d 283)

8. The Mutual Bank and Trust Company, a corporation, entered into a unique savings plan with a life insurance company. The plan called for the depositors to undertake a systematic savings plan of $2,000 with the bank, the depositor to make monthly deposits to the account. If the depositor died before the savings account plus accrued interest reached $2,000, the life insurance company paid into his account enough to make it equal $2,000. The bank paid the premiums as a group rate. An action was brought to determine whether or not this was an ultra vires act. Was this an ultra vires act? (Mutual Bank and Trust Co. et al. v. Shaffner et al., 1952 [Mo.], 2485 S. W. 2d 585)

PART 9

RISK-BEARING DEVICES

Preview Cases for Part 9: Risk-Bearing Devices

- Thompson owned a fishing vessel. The ship and its crew left port on a ten-day fishing expedition. A day or two later a raging storm was reported in the area where the ship was supposed to be. Thompson could not contact the ship after the storm. He placed a marine hull policy on the ship and its rig but did not tell the agent about his concern for the safety of the ship. The ship and its crew were never heard from again, although there was no proof the ship had sunk when the policy was actually placed. The insurance company refused to pay. Is it obligated to pay?

- Crutchfield applies for a life insurance policy. On the application for insurance, the question was asked: "What is your occupation?" Crutchfield answered: "Airplane pilot." The insurance policy had a clause which stated that the company would not pay if the insured was an airplane pilot. The company issued the policy. One year later Crutchfield died of a heart attack, and the company refused to pay. Is the company obligated to pay?

- Ralston carried a $20,000 fire insurance policy on his house. He sold the house to Johnson for cash. Nothing was done about the insurance policy. Four months later Ralston repurchased the house from Johnson. Soon thereafter the house was totally destroyed by fire. The fire policy originally obtained by Ralston still had two months to go to the date of expiration when the fire destroyed the building. Is Ralston entitled to collect from the insurance company?

- Graham had a public liability policy covering both bodily injury and property damage to others. In a collision with another car, the driver of the other car was seriously injured and his car wrecked. Graham's policy provided for coverage up to $15,000 for bodily injury and $5,000 for property damage. The injured driver offered to settle the claim out of court for $14,000. The insurance company rejected the offer and defended the claim in court. The court gave judgment against Graham for $30,000. How much is Graham obligated to pay? How much is the insurance company obligated to pay?

These preview cases are designed to serve as a springboard for the study of this part. As you read through each chapter in this part, you will find the actual decisions for all these preview cases. Of course, there are many more such illustrative problems as well as case problems for decision at the end of each chapter. And there are also a number of even more challenging cases for review at the end of the part.

CHAPTER 38

NATURE OF INSURANCE

DEFINITION OF INSURANCE

It is the function of insurance to reduce uncertainty to a certainty. Life is full of unfavorable contingencies. The possibility of any one of these contingencies happening is ever present. A home owner is faced with the constant possibility that his home will burn with a large loss to him. By accepting an absolutely certain annual loss in the form of a fire insurance premium, he can shift the uncertainty, that is, the possibility of a large loss, to the insurance company. Not every peril in life can be shifted by insurance, but many of the most common perils can be shifted, or at least the burden can be shifted. *Insurance* is a contract whereby a party transfers a risk of financial loss for a fee to the risk bearer, the insurance company.

Every insurance contract clearly defines the specific risk being transferred. The insured should understand as well as the insurer what risk is being transferred. A particular contract may carry the name "Personal Accident Insurance Policy," but this name may not clearly indicate the risk being assumed by the insurance company. A reading of the contract may reveal that the company will pay only if the accident occurs while the insured is in actual attendance in a public school. The premium paid covers only this much protection against a financial loss due to an accident, not the loss due to any accident.

TERMS USED IN INSURANCE

The company agreeing to make good a certain loss is known as the *insurer,* or sometimes as the *underwriter;* the person protected against the loss is known as the *insured,* or the *policyholder.* In life insurance the person who is to receive the benefits or the proceeds thereof is known as the *beneficiary*.

Whenever a person takes any kind of insurance, he enters into a contract with the insurance company, just as in the case of other business agreements. The written contract is commonly called a *policy*. The amount that the insurer agrees to pay in case of a loss is known as the *face* of the policy, and the consideration the insured pays for the protection is called the *premium*. The danger of a loss of, or injury to, property, life, or anything else, is called a *risk* or *peril*; when that danger may be covered by insurance, it is known as the *insurable risk*.

Although the uncertainty is called the "risk," this term, by common usage, now also applies to the property itself. In this sense one speaks of a brick house as being a "good risk." The factors, such as fire, floods, and sleet, that contribute to the uncertainty are called *hazards*.

TYPES OF INSURANCE COMPANIES

There are two major types of insurance companies:

1. Stock companies
2. Mutual companies

(1) **Stock Companies.** A *stock insurance company* is a corporation organized for the purpose of making a profit. As in all other corporations, the stockholders elect the board of directors and receive the profits as dividends. The original capital is raised through the sale of stock, either common or common and preferred. Unlike other corporations, insurance companies must place a major portion of their original capital in a reserve account. As the volume of business increases, the reserve must be increased by setting aside a part of the premiums.

(2) **Mutual Companies.** In a *mutual insurance company* the policyholders are the members and owners and correspond to the stockholders in a stock company. In these companies the policyholders are both the insurer and the insured, but the corporation is a separate legal entity. If a person takes a $10,000 fire insurance policy in a mutual company that has $100,000,000 insurance in force, he owns 1/10,000 of the company and is entitled to share the profits in this ratio. He also may have to share losses in the same ratio if it is an assessment mutual. In a stock company he never shares the losses.

In a nonassessment mutual insurance company, the policyholder's liability is limited to the amount of premium which he contracts to pay. If his pro rata share of the losses for any year exceeds his premium, he cannot be assessed for the excess. In this case the insured is as fully protected as a stockholder in a stock company. In an assessment mutual insurance company, however, the insured is liable for his pro rata share of the losses of the corporation without reference to the premium he agrees to pay. If this premium is inadequate to pay all losses, the insured can be assessed for his pro rata share of the losses in excess of his premium.

WHO MAY BE INSURED

To become an insured, one must first of all have an insurable interest. The insurance contract is in its entirety an agreement to assume a specified risk. If the insured has no interest to protect, there can be no assumption of risk, and hence no insurance. The law covering an insurable interest is different for life insurance and for property insurance. Consequently, this law will be treated fully in the chapters dealing with these types of insurance.

To become an insured, one must also be competent to contract. Insurance is not a necessity; thus, a minor is not bound on his insurance contracts if he wishes to disaffirm them. A minor who disaffirms a contract may demand the return of his money, but he must return any goods which he still possesses. Since insurance contracts provide protection only, this cannot be returned. Some states hold that because of this a minor cannot demand a refund of his insurance premium except the unexpired portion. Most states, however, hold that he may demand a return of the entire premium.

SOME LEGAL ASPECTS OF THE INSURANCE CONTRACT

The laws applicable to contracts in general apply to insurance contracts. There are five principles, however, that have special significance for insurance contracts:

1. Concealment
2. Representation
3. Warranty
4. Subrogation
5. Estoppel

(1) **Concealment.** The nature of insurance is such that the insurer must rely upon the information supplied by the insured. This places upon the insured the responsibility of supplying all pertinent information. A willful failure to disclose this pertinent information is known as *concealment*. The concealed facts must be material; that is, they must materially increase the risk assumed by the insurer. Also, the concealment must be willful. The willful concealment of material facts renders the contract voidable.

The rule of concealment does not apply with equal stringency to all types of insurance contracts. In fire insurance where the agent has an opportunity to inspect the property, the court may consider the concealed hazard as waived. In ocean marine insurance the concealed hazard is never waived, and the concealment need not be willful.

> ▪ Thompson owned a fishing vessel. The ship and its crew left port on a ten-day fishing expedition. A day or two later a raging storm was reported in the area where the ship was supposed to be. Thompson could not contact the ship after the storm. He placed a marine hull policy on the ship and its rig but did not tell the agent about his concern for the safety of the ship. The ship and its crew were never heard from again although there was no proof the ship had sunk when the policy was actually placed. The insurance company refused to pay. It was justified. The owner concealed a material fact, a fact which he knew would cause the insurance company to refuse the coverage if he had revealed it.

Since all insurance contracts assume a narrow but well-defined risk or group of risks, the insured and the insurer are really not talking about the same risk when the insured conceals material facts. There is no meeting of the minds as described in Chapter 4. If the concealment is intentional, it is a fraud and makes the contract merely voidable. If it is innocent, then the contract is void because of a mistake as to the identity of the risk assumed, the subject matter of the contract. Concealment in insurance contracts, however, differs in one significant way from concealment in other types of contracts. For contracts in general, concealment consists of some overt act to cover up the fact concealed. In these contracts the rule is: "A mere failure to reveal is not to conceal." In insurance contracts there need be no overt act of concealment. A failure to reveal is to conceal.

(2) **Representation.** A statement of fact made by the insured as a basis for obtaining insurance is known as a *representation*. It must be substantially correct. The representation must be made as an

inducement to the insurer to enter into a contract. It is collateral to the contract, not a part of the contract. The significance of this distinction will be shown under warranties. A false representation, though innocently made, avoids the contract if the fact is material.

Misrepresentation is more easily established than concealment, which in a sense is a misrepresentation by silence. In concealment the insurance company must prove that the insured had an intent to defraud before it can avoid the contract. No intent to defraud need be shown in misrepresentation. An innocent misrepresentation of a material fact gives the insurance company the right to avoid the contract only. If the misrepresentation is both material and willful, it is a tort and gives the insurance company the right to avoid the contract and also to sue for damages if it cares to do so. The company must, of course, prove actual damages in order to hold the insured liable.

In life insurance contracts the application for insurance is always in writing, while the application for other types of insurance is usually oral. It is in the application that most misrepresentations appear. The life insurance application is attached to the policy, and a clause in the policy states that the application is made part and parcel of the policy. The purpose of this is to make all the statements in the application warranties, not mere representations. As will be seen below, a breach of warranty is far more fatal to an insurance policy than a mere misrepresentation.

- Gilmer owned a paper mill. He insured it against loss by fire in the amount of $100,000. At the time he took out the policy, Gilmer had installed some stone burrs and was using the mill to grind wheat and corn into flour and cornmeal on the shares for farmers. This use was temporary while the paper business was depressed. While the mill was being used as a grist mill, it was totally destroyed by fire. The company refused to pay on the ground of misrepresentation. The court held this was not misrepresentation since the mill was still a paper mill even though it was being used temporarily as a grist mill. Furthermore, the misrepresentation was not material since a grist mill is less likely to burn than a paper mill and is a superior risk.

(3) **Warranty.** A *warranty* is a part and parcel of the contract itself. Representations are made to induce the other party to contract, but a warranty is incorporated into the contract. If one states, in applying for fire insurance, that his house has fire stops in the framework, this is a representation. If the same statement is incorporated into the written contract itself, it is a warranty. The significance is this: A

warranty must be absolutely true whether material or not. A representation must be only substantially true and is not of significance unless it is material.

The rule that a breach of warranty avoids the contract even though the warranty was immaterial is often a harsh one. The insured in a life insurance contract stated he lived in Homer, Georgia. In reality he lived one mile beyond the city limits. The misstatement of the place of residence is wholly immaterial to the risk, but it avoided the policy anyway. Because of the harshness of this rule, many states have modified it by statute. The Illinois Insurance Code (1937) Section 154, is a good illustration of the content of these statutory changes: "No such misrepresentation or false warranty shall defeat or avoid the policy unless it shall have been made with the actual intent to deceive or materially affects either the acceptance of the risk or the hazard assumed by the company. This section shall not apply to policies of marine or transportation insurance."

A warranty is an affirmation of an existing fact or a commitment to future conduct on the part of the insured. This latter type is known as a continuing warranty. Sometimes these two types of warranties are called "affirmative" or "promissory." In automobile insurance the insured warrants that the car will not be used for hire. This is a promissory warranty. Some courts interpret this as a condition precedent to the continuation of the policy in force. If the promise is broken, the policy is void. Others hold that a breach of this warranty merely suspends the policy while the car is being used for hire.

(4) **Subrogation.** In insurance, *subrogation* is the right of the insurer under certain circumstances to "step into the shoes" of the insured. Subrogation is particularly applicable to some types of automobile insurance. If the insurer pays a claim to the insured, under the law of subrogation the insurer is entitled to any claims which the insured had because of the loss. For example, A has a collision insurance policy on his car. B negligently damages A's car. The insurance company will pay A but then has the right to sue B for reimbursement. If A commits any act after the accident which releases B, then the insurance company is released from liability to A. This is often referred to as the law of substitution. It is not applicable either to life insurance or to health and accident insurance.

(5) **Estoppel.** If one by word or act admits a fact, he is estopped to deny the truth of the fact. If the insurer, in order to induce the

insured to enter into the contract, waives some provision in the contract, the company is estopped to plead this fact as a defense to payment. *Waiver* is the abandonment of a right; when a right is lawfully waived, one cannot later insist on the right. Insurance agents are severely restricted as to their power to waive provisions of the contract, but the company itself may waive most provisions.

Estoppel arises when one by his acts leads another to believe that certain facts are true when they are untrue, thereby leading the other person to act to his detriment. Waiver, on the other hand, may be either an expressed or an implied abandonment of a right, usually the waiving of a provision in the written contract. The one doing the waiving must of course have the authority to waive. One cannot waive a provision in an insurance contract that is required by law to be in it. The insurance company cannot waive, for example, the legal requirement that the insured must have an insurable interest in the property insured.

- Crutchfield applied for a life insurance policy. On the application for insurance, the question was asked: "What is your occupation?" Crutchfield answered: "Airplane pilot." The insurance policy had a a clause which stated that the company would not pay if the insured was an airplane pilot. The company issued the policy. One year later Crutchfield died of a heart attack, and the company refused to pay. The court held the company had waived this provision regarding airplane pilots.

QUESTIONS

1. Define insurance.
2. May an application for insurance be oral?
3. Which is more fatal to an insurance policy, a breach of warranty or a misrepresentation?
4. What is the effect of the insured's concealing material facts in applying for insurance?
5. What is a continuing warranty in an insurance contract?
6. Does an insurance agent usually have the power to waive provisions in the policy?
7. What is estoppel as applied to insurance contracts?
8. Give an illustration of subrogation as applied to insurance contracts.
9. Does an "Accident Insurance Policy" cover loss due to all accidents?
10. How does a mutual fire insurance company differ from a stock fire insurance company?

CASE PROBLEMS

1. Thomas owned and operated a storage business and carried fire insurance to cover about 50 percent of its value. Someone called him and told him that smoke was coming from the gable end of the building and that he believed it was on fire. Before going to the building, Thomas saw his insurance agent and placed another $50,000 fire policy on it but made no mention of the smoke and possible fire. It developed that there was no fire. About two weeks later, however, the building was destroyed by fire, and the company refused to pay on the second policy because it had learned of the circumstances under which it was purchased. Was the insurance company liable on this policy?

2. A fire insurance policy contained a clause that no provision of the policy could be waived by the agent except in writing and attached to the policy. One provision in the policy stated that manuscripts were not covered unless specifically named in the policy. Mitchell, an author, had a manuscript almost completed for a novel which he felt would be a best seller. He called his agent and asked that the manuscript be named in his household effects policy. The agent said that was not necessary and that the company would insure it. A fire destroyed Mitchell's home and the manuscript was burned up. The company refused to pay for it. Was Mitchell entitled to collect for the value of the manuscript?

3. Hipps, the bookkeeper for the Concrete Block Corporation, was charged with the responsibility of keeping the insurable risks of the company fully covered. He placed a theft policy on the company's valuable papers. He was asked, "Where are the papers kept?" He replied, "In an iron safe in the office." The papers actually were seldom kept in the safe. About $5,000 worth of notes receivable were stolen from the drawer of a steel desk. Must the company pay for this loss?

4. In an application for comprehensive coverage of the Johnson Construction Company's equipment, it was stated the trucks were kept in "a garage at night at 1480 Stockbridge Road." The trucks were actually kept parked on an open parking lot next to the main building and were seldom placed in the garage. One truck caught fire while being driven on the highway and was destroyed. The company refused to pay. Must it?

5. Hendrix has a $20,000 fire insurance policy in an assessment mutual fire insurance company. The company has $200,000,000 worth of insurance in force. A fire results in a loss of $80,000. How much of this must Hendrix pay?

6. Savage applied for a disability income policy whereby the insurance company obligated itself to pay the insured $200 a month if he became so disabled that he could not continue his profession as a typesetter. At the time Savage took out the policy he knew he was going blind and would be totally blind within two or three years. He did not tell the insurance company about this condition. When the company refused to pay off on the policy, Savage claimed he did not reveal this fact because he did not think the company wanted the information. Must the company pay Savage disability compensation after he became blind?

7. Chandler had a fire insurance policy on his stock of merchandise and building for $20,000, approximately half of the actual value. A competitor set fire to the building and destroyed it and its contents. Chandler accidentally learned that the fire was set by his competitor. He made a secret deal with the arsonist that he would not reveal the information as to his guilt if he would agree to pay all the loss not covered by insurance. When the insurance company learned of this agreement, it refused to pay off on the fire policy. Must it do so?

8. Durwood's home was completely destroyed by fire caused by a spark from the smoke stack of an engine belonging to the Big Sandy and Cumberland Railroad. The law required all railroad companies to keep spark arresters on all smoke stacks. This was not done in this case. Durwood carried full fire insurance on his home, so he elected to collect from the insurance company. Can the insurance company compel him to sue the railroad?

9. Pennington carried fire insurance on his store building and merchandise. A clause in the policy stipulates that no act shall be committed that increases the hazard. The store was heated with a coal stove. The brick flue collapsed. Pennington, not wishing to build another, ran the stove pipe thru the window with the pipe jutting out about one foot from the outside wall. He asked the insurance company's agent if that would affect his policy and was assured it would not. A spark from the stove pipe ignited a wooden eave, and the building and contents were destroyed. Must the company pay for the loss?

10. Morrison, who owned three houses, asked his secretary to call the insurance agent and place a fire insurance policy on the one at 256 Cloverhurst. The agent asked her, "Is the house brick or frame?" She was not sure but thinking it made no difference, replied, "It is a brick building." It was in fact a frame building. The house was destroyed by fire, and the company refused to pay for the loss. Was Morrison entitled to collect?

11. A fire insurance policy on a sawmill contained this clause: "The insured warrants that a watchman will be on duty at all times while the mill is not operating." The mill caught fire during the day and was completely destroyed. The previous night the night watchman was ill and could not work. He called Brewer, the superintendent, and informed him that he could not report for work. Brewer did not get anyone to take the watchman's place and the mill was without a watchman for that one night only, but the fire was in no way remotely related to this fact. The insurance company refused to pay for the loss. Could the owner of the mill collect on this policy?

12. Schools, a minor, insured his house against loss by fire, and his automobile and jewelry against loss by either fire or theft. Eleven months later he demanded a return of his entire premium. Was he entitled to a refund?

CHAPTER 39

LIFE AND ANNUITY
INSURANCE

DEFINITION OF LIFE INSURANCE

Of all insurance contracts shifting a risk to the insurance company, the life insurance contract creates the most confusion and difficulty. The reason is that life insurance as an economic fact may be quite different to a life insurance contract. This is not true of other insurance contracts. The first requisite in understanding all insurance contracts is a clear definition of the risk assumed by the risk bearer. Life insurance has been defined in many ways, but perhaps the clearest is this: *Life insurance* is the transfer of the risk of the loss of income from services to one's dependents due to the premature death of the income producer. By this definition, one must have dependents and an income that will be cut off by death in order to have a need for life insurance. It may be defined in a shorter manner merely by calling it income protection insurance, although this would also define disability income insurance. Most life insurance contracts, however, have features in addition to life insurance in them.

TYPES OF LIFE INSURANCE CONTRACTS

There are many different types of life insurance policies and annuity contracts, but the following are the most important:

1. Term insurance
2. Endowment insurance
3. Whole life insurance
4. Combinations, and other types

(1) Term Insurance. As the name indicates, *term life insurance* contracts are those whereby the company assumes for a specified term the risk of the loss of income to the dependents by reason of the premature death of the insured. In this sense it is similar to a term fire insurance policy, or a term automobile insurance policy. This term may be for only one year; or it may be for five, ten, or even fifty years. The term must be stated in the policy. There are many variations of the term policies. In short-term policies, such as five years, the insured may, if the policy so provides, have the option of renewing it for another equal term without a physical examination. The cost is higher for each renewal period. This is called renewable term insurance. It is designed to enable young married people to buy a lot of life insurance when their needs are usually the greatest and their ability to pay low. In nonrenewable term insurance the insured does not have the legal right to renew it unless the company consents to the renewal.

Term policies also may be either level term or reducing term. In level term, the face of the policy is written in units of $1,000. The amount remains at this sum during the entire term of the policy. In reducing term contracts, the policy is generally written in multiples of $10 a month income. For example, a young man aged 20 could purchase a reducing term policy covering a period of 600 months or 50 years for ten units, that is $100 a month. If he dies the first month after purchasing the policy, his beneficiary would draw $100 a month for 600 months, or $60,000 ultimately. This is often called income protection insurance.

All term policies have one thing in common—they are pure life insurance. They shift the specific risk of premature death—and nothing more—just as a fire insurance policy shifts the risk of loss of property by fire, and nothing more.

(2) Endowment Insurance. An *endowment insurance policy* is reducing term insurance plus a savings account. The sum of the insurance plus the savings always equals the face of the policy. For example, a twenty-year endowment policy for $10,000 will cost a young man aged 20 about $450 a year. Approximately $60 of this compensates the insurance company for the risk of premature death during the term of twenty years. The other $390 is a savings account that with accrued interest equals $10,000 at the end of twenty years. If the insured dies during the twenty years, his beneficiary will collect the $10,000. If the insured is still living at the end of the term, he will collect the

$10,000 unless he has designated some beneficiary to receive the amount. All endowment policies then are really two contracts in one. One is a risk transfer; the other sets up a debtor-creditor relationship.

(3) **Whole Life Insurance.** In reality all life insurance contracts are either term insurance or endowment insurance. A whole life insurance policy is one that continues, assuming the premium is paid, until age 100 or death, whichever occurs first. If the insured is still living at age 100, he collects the face of the policy as an endowment. A whole life policy might correctly be defined as endowment insurance at age 100. As with all endowment policies, a whole life policy is reducing term insurance plus a savings account. Whole life policies consist of several classes. A straight life policy is a whole life policy calling for the payment of the premium till death or age 100, whichever occurs first. For a young man twenty years of age, this would be an eighty-pay eighty-year endowment. If he wants the same contract but wishes to limit the premiums to twenty years, the policy would be a twenty-pay whole life policy, or a twenty-pay eighty-year endowment. Either term accurately describes the contract.

(4) **Combination and Other Types of Policies.** The three basic life insurance contracts, term, endowment, and whole life, can be combined in almost an endless variety of combinations to create slightly different contracts. The Family Income Policy, for example, is merely a straight life policy with a twenty-year reducing term policy attached as a rider. A *rider* on an insurance policy is a clause or even a whole contract added to another contract to modify, extend, or limit the base contract. In addition to the reducing term insurance, there are several other riders frequently found in life insurance policies. The disability income rider may be attached to any policy and pays the insured an income if he becomes disabled. Life insurance pays for what is sometimes called a "casket" death. The disability income rider pays in the event of a "living" death. Other riders are waiver of premium rider, which waives the annual premiums if the insured becomes disabled, and the double indemnity rider, which doubles the face of the policy if death is by accidental means.

ANNUITY INSURANCE

An annuity insurance contract pays the insured a monthly income from named age, generally age 65, until death. It is a risk entirely unrelated to the risk assumed in a life insurance contract even though both contracts are sold by life insurance companies. Someone has defined life insurance as shifting the risk of dying too soon and annuity insurance as shifting the risk of living too long, that is, outliving one's savings. Annuity insurance provides for a systematic liquidation of one's savings and at the same time guarantees the insured an income for life even if he lives to be 110. If the annuity contract calls for the monthly payments to continue until the second of two insureds dies, it is called a *joint and survivor annuity*. This type of annuity is suitable for a man and wife who wish to extend their savings as long as either one is still living.

LIMITATION ON RISKS IN LIFE INSURANCE CONTRACTS

Either because of competition or by state laws life insurance companies place very few limitations upon the risk assumed. The two most common limitations are: (1) suicide, and (2) death from war activity.

Suicide. The typical suicide clause found in most life insurance contracts stipulates that the company will not pay if death occurs by suicide, whether sane or insane, within two years from the date of the policy. If death is caused by suicide after the two-year period lapses, the company must pay.

Death from War Activity. The so-called "war clause" provides that if the insured dies as a consequence of war activity the company will not pay. If a member of the armed forces dies a natural death, the company must pay.

> ▪ Raines was a bomber pilot. He had a $10,000 life insurance policy with a war clause. While over open water in the Pacific, he radioed his home base that he was being attacked by Japanese fighter planes. He was never heard from again, nor was any trace of his plane ever found. The court held that the insurance company had to pay since the company could not prove he died as a result of war activity. The court pointed out the pilot could have reached an island and died a normal death.

COMPARATIVE COSTS

The following table gives a comparison of the premiums on a $1,000 policy for a man thirty years of age:

Term insurance—twenty years .... $ 6.81
Straight life insurance 18.60
Limited payment life—twenty years 29.84
Endowment insurance—twenty years 46.38

If the insured should die within the twenty-year period, the beneficiary would collect the same amount under all four policies, that is,
$1,000.

PAYMENT OF PREMIUMS

The premiums must be paid within the time specified by the
policy. If they are not paid when due, the policy may lapse. The policy
or a statute of the state may provide that after a certain number of
premiums have been paid, the policy will be extended for a specified
time in case of the nonpayment of a premium. Under such a condition a paid-up policy is sometimes issued for the term of the insurance
but for a smaller amount. Sickness is no legal excuse for the nonpayment of premiums. In such a case the company may, if it so
elects, extend the time of payment or take a promissory note for the
amount of the premium.

GRACE PERIOD

All life insurance companies are required by law to provide a grace
period of 31 days in every life insurance policy. This grace period
gives the insured 31 days from the due date of the premium in which
to pay it without the policy's lapsing. This provision is extremely important in life insurance contracts. If the insured through an oversight
is one day late in paying his premium, the policy lapses. If he wants to
buy another policy, he must pass a physical examination and also pay
the higher rate for his then attained age.

INCONTESTABILITY

Life insurance policies are made incontestable, either by statutory
law or by the policies themselves, after a certain period of time,
usually two years. After the expiration of the period of contestability,
the insurance company usually cannot contest the validity of a claim
on any ground except nonpayment of premiums.

INSURABLE INTEREST

In most states every person can take out a life insurance policy on his own life and make any person he pleases the beneficiary. The beneficiary need not have an insurable interest in the insured's life.

When one person insures another's life, however, and makes himself or someone else whom he selects beneficiary, he must have an insurable interest in the life of the insured at the time the policy is taken out. This interest, however, need not be based upon a legal right as in the case of fire insurance. It is sufficient if it is based upon a reasonable expectation of benefit. For example, an employee cannot take out a fire insurance policy on the property of the business for which he works for he has no insurable interest.

A person has an insurable interest in the life of another when such a relationship exists between them that a direct pecuniary benefit will be derived from the continued existence of the other person. The relationships most frequently giving rise to an insurable interest are parents and children, husband and wife, employer and employee, principal and agent, partner and copartner, and a creditor in the life of the debtor to the extent of his debt. This list is not exhaustive, as there are numerous other relationships which give rise to an insurable interest. A sister may have such an interest in her brother if she has a reasonable expectation that he will support her.

A life insurance policy will remain enforceable after the insurable interest ceases to exist. In this respect life insurance differs from fire or other insurance. An insurable interest need not exist in fire insurance at the time the insurance is effected, but it must exist at the time the loss occurs; an insurable interest must exist in life insurance at the time the insurance is effected, but it need not exist at the time the policy is payable.

- A creditor insured the life of a debtor for the amount due him. Before the death of the insured, the debt was paid in full. The court held that the insurable interest which existed at the time the policy was taken out supported an action to recover against the insurance company after the death of the insured.

CHANGE OF BENEFICIARY

If a man takes out insurance on his own life and makes another his beneficiary, he cannot later change the beneficiary unless he reserved the right to do this. If the beneficiary pays the premiums, the insured does not have the right to change the beneficiary. There are both advantages and disadvantages in reserving the right to change the beneficiary, but most modern life insurance policies reserve this right to the insured. If a man takes out a life insurance policy on his life and makes his wife the beneficiary but later divorces her, he cannot change the beneficiary unless he reserved the right to do so. If he does reserve the right, his creditors can attach the surrender value of the policy for his debts. If he does not reserve the right, then the creditors of the beneficiary can attach the surrender value of the policy for her debts. Exemption statutes may limit the right of creditors to attach benefits of an insurance policy.

If the beneficiary dies before the insured, it frequently is highly desirable to change the beneficiary, which is impossible unless the right to change has been reserved. The rights of such a beneficiary are vested and, upon his death, pass to his personal representative. Since this rule may cause unintended results, some courts hold that if the beneficiary dies before the insured, the beneficiary's interest terminates and reverts to the insured.

ASSIGNMENT OF THE POLICY

Any claims under an insurance policy may be assigned unless the contract specifically prohibits an assignment. This prohibition is applicable only to the insured, not to the beneficiary. If the insured reserves the right to change the beneficiary, he has title to the cash surrender value or the loan value of the policy. He may assign this right as security for a loan. It is not necessary to notify the insurance company if there is no prohibition against assignment, but it is wise to give notice. The beneficiary may assign any of his rights under the policy freely. His chief right is the right to collect the face of the policy upon the death of the insured. Since this is merely a claim for money, there is no bar to its assignment.

OTHER TYPES OF INSURANCE

There are several other types of insurance closely related to life insurance. They are health and accident insurance, hospitalization insurance, and group medical insurance. These types of insurance differ from life insurance in a number of particulars. In the first place, the beneficiary is always the insured. The purpose is to protect the insured against cessation of earning power or burdensome expenses rather than to protect someone who depends upon the insured for support.

QUESTIONS

1. Define life insurance.
2. Define annuity insurance.
3. What is decreasing term life insurance? How does it differ from level-premium insurance?
4. Why is an endowment life insurance policy two contracts in one?
5. What is a rider on a life insurance contract?
6. What are some limitations on risks that a life insurance company may provide?
7. What is the nature of the incontestability clause in a life insurance contract?
8. When does a person have an insurable interest in the life of another?
9. Under what circumstances may the insured change the beneficiary of a policy?
10. Name other types of insurance closely related to life insurance.

CASE PROBLEMS

1. Stewart had carried a 40-year reducing term life insurance policy on himself for ten years. When the premium came due on March 21, he wrote the company he wanted to cancel the policy. Ten days later he died, and his wife immediately mailed the premium to the company and then demanded that she be paid the face amount due on the policy. This amounted to 300 monthly payments of $200 each. The company denied liability because Stewart had canceled the policy even though the grace period had twenty more days to run. Must the company pay?

2. Aunt Mary took out a life insurance policy on her five-year-old niece and made herself the beneficiary. About two years later, Aunt Mary poisoned her niece in order to collect on the policy. The insurance company, before it learned the child had been murdered, refused to pay on the ground Aunt Mary had no insurable interest. After the insurance company won, the body of the girl was exhumed and the death by poison detected. The father then sued the insurance company for selling his sister the policy when there was no insurable interest. Is the company liable to the father for damages?

3. Mason, age 26, has a wife and three children all under the age of six. He earns $450 a month. He has the choice of purchasing a twenty-pay life policy, face amount of $10,000, for an annual premium of $290 a year or a reducing term policy for $85,000 for $260 a year. The twenty-pay life policy will build a substantial cash value in a few years; the term policy has no cash value. Which would you recommend that he buy?

4. Goff was treated over a period of three years by Dr. Richardson for serious stomach ulcers. He applied for a life insurance policy and on the application was this question: "Have you been treated by a doctor for any illness during the past five years?" Goff answered "No." Three years after

the policy was issued, the insurance company learned of the false statement and brought suit to have the policy nullified. Will the insurance company succeed?

5. Donovan carried a $300-a-month reducing term policy on himself with his wife the beneficiary. The war clause in the policy stated, "The company will not be liable under this policy if the insured dies while engaged in military activities." Donovan was killed in an automobile accident on his way home on a furlough. Must the company pay?

6. Mrs. Watson had three adult children by her first husband and two children, ages two and five, by Mr. Watson, her second husband. Mr. Watson purchased a $30,000 life insurance policy and made Mrs. Watson his beneficiary. He did not reserve the right to change the beneficiary. Mrs. Watson predeceased her husband by two months just one year after the policy was taken out. Will Mrs. Watson's adult children by her first husband share in the $30,000?

7. Mr. Latture reached age 65 and retired. His only retirement income was $150 a month from Social Security plus $55 a month interest on their bank savings of $22,000. Mr. Latture feels he and Mrs. Latture must have at least $250 a month to live on so long as both of them are alive. He has two ways to obtain this sum. One is to withdraw a part of his principal each month so that the bank interest plus the withdrawn savings will always equal $100 a month. This, when added to his Social Security income, will provide the desired $250. The other way is to purchase a joint and last survivor annuity policy for $100 a month for a single premium of $18,000. Which method would you recommend?

8. Hawkins purchased a $10,000 Family Income Policy with a twenty-year reducing term rider for $100 a month. In addition he had a waiver of premium rider and a double indemnity rider. Three years after purchasing the policy he died in an automobile accident. How much will Mrs. Hawkins collect?

9. Matthew purchased a $200-a-month decreasing term life insurance policy for the protection of Mrs. Matthew and his four small children. He was 23 when he purchased it for an annual premium of $225.80. He carried this policy until age 35 but through an oversight forgot to pay the premium on the due date. Three weeks later he learned of the oversight. The rate for this same policy at age 35 was $497.20. May he still keep the $225.80 rate if he pays his premium immediately?

CHAPTER 40

PROPERTY INSURANCE

NATURE OF PROPERTY INSURANCE

Property insurance is a contract whereby the insurer, in return for a compensation, agrees to reimburse the insured for loss or damage to specified property that is caused by the hazard covered. A contract of property insurance is one of indemnity that protects the policyholder from actual loss.

If a building actually worth $10,000 is insured for $15,000, the extra premiums paid are to no avail since $10,000, the actual value, is the maximum that can be collected in case of total loss. On the other hand, if the building is insured for only $8,000 and it is totally destroyed, the insurance company must pay only $8,000. It will be seen from this that the maximum amount to be paid is fixed by the policy when the insurance is less than the value of the property. If the property is fully insured, the value of the property fixes the maximum.

FIRE INSURANCE

Fire is the greatest source of loss to property. Originally this was the only risk covered by insurance. For this reason all the early laws and court decisions dealing with property insurance covered loss by fire. As the additional types of property insurance developed, the same laws were applied to them that had been applied to fire insurance. Consequently, a thorough understanding of the laws of fire insurance will be adequate in the main in understanding the basic laws governing all types of property insurance.

LOSSES RELATED TO FIRE

Fire may cause much loss for which the fire policy alone will not pay. Smoke may cause enormous losses to merchandise even though none is burned. If the smoke is from a hostile fire, the fire policy will pay for the loss, but not if it is a friendly fire. A *hostile fire* is defined as one out of its normal place, while a *friendly fire* is one contained in the place where it is intended to be. Scorching, searing, singeing, and similar damages from a friendly fire are not covered under the fire policy. Furthermore, a hostile fire may cause many losses other than to the property insured; yet the fire policy on the building and contents alone will not cover these losses. An example is the loss of profits while the building is being restored. This loss is covered by a special policy called *business interruption insurance.* If one leases property on a long-term, favorable lease and the lease is canceled because of a fire damage to the building, the tenant may have to pay a higher rent in new quarters. This increased rent loss can be covered by a *leasehold interest insurance policy* but not by a fire policy. Then, too, there may be heat losses, but no flame or glow ever occurs. In one case several thousand bales of cotton were under water during a flood. After the flood receded, heat in the bales of cotton was so intense smoke poured forth for days, but no flame was ever detected. The court held there was no fire.

The whole institution of insurance is built on calculating a rate for each risk. The purchase of a suit does not entitle one to a hat and overcoat to go with it. One may purchase a whole wardrobe in one contract if he wishes to do so. In fire insurance one may purchase a group of risks in one contract, but each risk must be clearly named. The typical fire policy may also cover the risks of loss by windstorm, explosion, smoke damage from a friendly fire, falling aircraft, water damage, riot and civil commotion, and many others. Each one of these additional risks must be added to the fire policy by means of riders or extra clauses.

INSURABLE INTEREST

One must have an insurable interest in the property at the time of the loss to be able to collect on a fire insurance policy. Since fire insurance is fundamentally indemnity insurance, there must be some loss before there can be indemnity. Ownership is, of course, the clearest type of insurable interest; but there are many other types of insurable interest. The most common types of insurable interest other than ownership are:

(1) The mortgagee has an insurable interest in the property mortgaged to the extent of his mortgage.

(2) A lien creditor has an insurable interest in the property on which there is a lien. An unsecured creditor, however, does not have an insurable interest in the property of his debtor.

(3) When property is sold on the installment plan and title is retained as security for the unpaid purchase price, the seller has an insurable interest in the property.

(4) The bailee has an insurable interest in the property bailed to the extent of his possible loss. The bailee's loss is from two sources. He will lose his fees or commissions as provided for in the contract of bailment. Secondly, he may be held legally liable to the owner if the loss is due to the bailee's negligence or to the negligence of his employees.

(5) A partner has an insurable interest in his firm to the extent of his possible loss.

(6) An administrator or an executor as the personal representative for a deceased person's estate has an insurable interest, in his fiduciary capacity, in the property of the estate.

Any change of either title or possession of the insured property may render the contract void because the insurable interest ceases. This interest must exist at the time of the loss. If the change in the title or possession does not terminate the insurable interest, as when the insured executes a mortgage on the insured property, the insurance policy remains in effect. If the mortgagor insures the property for the benefit of the mortgagee, a sale of the property cancels the policy. If the mortgagee purchases a policy, a sale of the mortgaged property does not cancel the policy.

- Ralston carried a $20,000 fire insurance policy on his house. He sold the house to Johnson for cash. Nothing was done about the insurance policy. Four months later Ralston repurchased the house from Johnson. Soon thereafter the house was totally destroyed by fire. The fire policy originally obtained by Ralston still had two months to go to the date of expiration when the fire destroyed the building. Ralston could not collect because the sale to Johnson rendered the fire policy void, not merely voidable. A policy once rendered void cannot be revived.

THE FIRE INSURANCE POLICY

The type of fire insurance indicates the nature of the risk assumed. There are the valued policy and the open policy. On certain types of property, such as works of art and antiques, the face of the policy is its value. In the event of the destruction of such property, the insurer cannot raise the question of value. Seldom will an insurance company write a valued policy on homes, business, and personal property. The open policy merely sets the limit of the risk assumed. The insurer is liable only for the actual loss up to, but never exceeding, the face of the policy.

In an *open policy*, the face of the policy is merely the maximum the company will pay. In a *valued policy* the company will not question the value after the loss, and it will pay the face of the policy.

> ▪ Dudley owned the Anderson Antique Shop. The total value of his stock of antiques ran about $50,000. He carried the regular fire policy on his stock of antiques for $100,000. A fire destroyed about half the stock. After an extensive and expensive appraisal to ascertain the value of the items destroyed, he was able to collect only $25,000. Had he carried a valued policy, he could have collected $50,000 without an appraisal.

Insurance policies also may be specific, blanket, or floating. A *specific policy* applies to one item only, such as one house. A *blanket policy* covers many items of the same kind in different places or different kinds of property in the same place, such as a building, fixtures, and merchandise in a single location. *Floating policies* are used for trucks, theatrical costumes, circus paraphernalia, and similar items which are not kept in a fixed location. A floater policy is also desirable for items that may be sent out for cleaning, such as rugs or clothes. Articles of jewelry and clothes that may be worn while traveling are also covered in a floater policy. A fire insurance policy on household effects covers for loss only at the named location. The purpose of the floater policy is to cover the loss no matter where the property is located at the time of the loss.

Another type of fire insurance policy of particular interest to merchants is the Reporting Form for Merchandise inventory. This policy permits the merchant to report periodically, usually once a month, the amount of inventory on hand. This enables him to carry full coverage at all times and still not be grossly over-insured during periods when his inventory is low.

DESCRIPTION OF THE PROPERTY

Both personal and real property must be described with reasonable accuracy. This description applies both to the nature of the property and its location. A description of a house as brick when it is actually asphalt brick siding is a misrepresentation. Personal property should be so described that in the event of loss, its value can be determined. One "piano" does not indicate the value of the piano as does "one baby grand piano—new." Also, the general description "living room furniture" may make it difficult to establish the value and the number of items. A complete inventory should be kept and preferably one copy filed with the insurance company. In this event, such description as "household furniture" is adequate.

The location of the property is important because the location affects the risk. If personal property used in a brick house on a broad paved street is moved to a frame house on an out-of-the-way dirt road, the risk may be increased considerably. Express permission must always be obtained when property is moved except under a "floating" policy. Most fire policies sold today have a clause continuing the coverage at the new location for five days together with coverage during the moving trip. If a loss occurs during the five-day period, the company must pay even though no notice has been given of the changed location.

- Jordan carried fire insurance on his household effects at 1327 Ellis Street, a two-story frame building. He moved to 237 Beechwood Hills, a one-story stone building. He did not give notice of the move within the five days required. A fire damaged the furniture to the extent of $1,000. The company did not have to pay even though the new location carried a lower rate than the old.

RISK AND HAZARD

The insurance company assumes the risks caused by normal hazards. The insured must not commit any act which increases the risk. Negligence by the insured is a normal hazard unless so gross as to indicate a criminal intent. When a fire occurs, the insured must use all due diligence to minimize the loss. He is not held responsible for an increased risk over which he has no control or knowledge. The insured must remove household effects from the building if this can safely be done. Loss due to theft during or following the fire, however, is not covered.

- Mullin's house was on fire. Both the house and the furniture were insured. Part of the furniture was damaged while it was being removed; and while the furniture was piled in the street, a part of it was stolen and sparks damaged a part of it. The insurance company was liable for the breakage and the damage caused by sparks, but not for the loss due to theft. Yet, if the insured had not removed the property, he would have increased the risk to the company and thus rendered the policy voidable.

COINSURANCE

Under the principle of *coinsurance* the insured assumes a portion of the risk. Simply stated, coinsurance permits the insured to recover for a loss in the same ratio as his insurance bears to the amount of insurance which the company requires. Many policies contain an 80 percent clause. This clause means that the insured may carry any amount of insurance he wishes up to the value of the property, but that the company will not pay the full amount of a partial loss unless he carries insurance for at least 80 percent of the value of the property. If a building is worth $20,000 and the insured buys a policy for $8,000, the company under the 80 percent coinsurance clause will pay only half of the damage and never more than $8,000. The 80 percent clause requires the insured to carry $16,000, or 80 percent of $20,000, to be fully protected. Since he carries only half of this amount, he can collect only half of the damage.

The coinsurance clause may be some percentage other than 80 percent. In burglary insurance it may be as low as 5 percent or 10 percent and on rare occasions as high as 100 percent in fire insurance. Seldom is a coinsurance clause found in policies covering residential property.

REPAIRS AND REPLACEMENTS

Most insurance contracts give the insurer the option of paying the amount of loss or repairing or replacing the property. If the property is repaired or replaced, materials of like kind and quality must be used. The work must be completed within a reasonable time. A house thirty years old could not be replaced with materials of like kind since new material would have to be used. For this reason, the option to replace is seldom exercised by the insurer. He may also have the option of taking the property at an agreed valuation and then pay the insured the full value of the damaged property. Under no circumstances can the insured abandon damaged property to the insurer. The owner must do everything possible to minimize the loss by protecting the property from further damage from the elements. Any expense involved in doing this is recoverable as a part of the loss.

If the insurer pays a sum equal to the damage and the insured restores the property to its original status, new insurance must be obtained to cover the replaced part, unless there is an automatic restoration clause in the contract. Such a clause is frequently provided in insurance policies covering residential property where the loss is limited to a relatively small amount. Policies covering large industrial plants, motels, apartment buildings, and similar structures seldom contain a restoration clause.

CANCELLATION AND TERMINATION OF THE POLICY

Fire insurance policies permit each party to cancel by giving the other party notice. If a policy is canceled by the insured, a refund is made on the premium at the short-term rate. If at the end of six months the insured cancels a three-year policy costing $600, he is not entitled to a refund of $500. The short-term rate for six months is considerably higher than one-sixth of a thirty-six month policy.

QUESTIONS

1. What is meant by the statement that a property insurance contract is one of indemnity?

2. If one insures a fur coat for $2,000 against theft when its actual value is only $800, how much may the owner collect if the coat is stolen?

3. When must one have an insurable interest before he can collect under a fire insurance policy?

4. If A sells a house to B and at the time of the sale A has a $20,000 fire insurance policy on the house, what effect does the sale have on the insurance policy?

5. What is the difference between a valued fire insurance policy and an open policy?

6. What is the purpose of a floating insurance policy?

7. How must one identify his household furniture when he purchases household effects fire insurance?

8. When one insures property located at 256 Hope Street, what is the effect on the policy if the owner moves to a new location without notifying the insurance company?

CASE PROBLEMS

1. John, the bookkeeper for the Anderson Department Store, had the responsibility for placing all the needed insurance to protect the firm from the major hazards. The firm's merchandise inventory fluctuated from $40,000 during the dull season to $120,000 at the peak of the rush season. The average was about $70,000. In order to be fully covered, John carried a fire policy for $120,000 at the rate of 30 cents per hundred dollars. What insurance knowledge would enable John to reduce the cost of this policy?

2. In the above case the Anderson Department store sold several thousand dollars worth of television sets, suites of furniture, and other items on the installment plan with the seller retaining title until the merchandise was paid for. John placed no insurance on this merchandise. One customer owed the company $1,100 for furniture when his home was destroyed by fire. He carried no fire insurance on his household effects. How could the Anderson Department Store avoid similar losses in the future?

3. Anderson Department Store building was valued at $100,000. John calculated that the odds the building would be totally destroyed by fire were almost zero. To save money he placed a $50,000 fire and extended coverage policy on it. The policy contained an 80 percent coinsurance clause, but John did not understand what this clause meant. The building sustained a loss by fire amounting to $12,000. How much of this loss will be paid for by the insurance company?

4. The Anderson Department Store carries a line of moderately priced pianos. In an attempt to sell one to Halstead for $1,400, it permitted Halstead to buy on a "sale on approval" contract. Before Halstead indicated his approval or disapproval of the piano, his home and all its contents were destroyed by fire due to no negligence on Halstead's part. Did the company's merchandise inventory fire policy cover this loss?

5. Hunt owned a factory building. It was rented to Sevede Dressmakers, Inc. for $1,000 a month. A fire caused a $12,000 loss to one section of the building. This section was immediately restored, but soon thereafter the entire building was destroyed by fire. Hunt carried $100,000 fire insurance policy on the building, its full value. How much can he collect on this policy?

6. Donald purchased a home for $20,000, giving a mortgage to Tillman for $18,000. Tillman purchased an $18,000 fire policy on the house and paid the premium himself. The house was destroyed by fire. Since Tillman did not own the house, can he collect on the policy?

7. John gave his young bride, Josephine, a fur coat as an anniversary present. The cost of the coat was $2,500. John and Josephine had a fire insurance policy on their household effects in the amount of $2,000. Realizing that this amount was too low, especially since the value of their effects had been increased by $2,500, they increased the face of their policy to $5,000 and paid the additional premium. While visiting relatives, the relatives' home was destroyed by fire and the fur coat was burned up. Could Josephine collect for this loss on her insurance contract?

CHAPTER 41
AUTOMOBILE
INSURANCE

THE NATURE OF AUTOMOBILE INSURANCE

The laws dealing with automobile insurance can be understood best by discussing the major classes of insurance and their risks. These two classes of insurance are direct damage insurance, including fire, theft, and collision, and public liability, including bodily injury and property damage. To understand the law one must know what specific risk is assumed by the insurance carrier and the terms of the policy covering that specific risk.

DIRECT DAMAGE INSURANCE

As the name implies, *direct damage insurance* covers the risks of injury or damage to the car itself. It includes:

1. Fire insurance
2. Theft insurance
3. Collision insurance
4. Comprehensive coverage

(1) **Fire Insurance.** Much of the law of fire insurance discussed in the preceding chapter applies to automobile insurance. There are many differences, however, between automobile fire insurance and other types of fire insurance. If the car is damaged or destroyed by the collision, sinking, stranding, or burning of any conveyance upon which the car is being transported, such as a barge, boat, or train, the fire policy covers this loss.

There are many exclusions in this type of policy, the most important ones being:

(a) If the fire occurs while, with the permission of the owner, the car is being driven by one who is barred by law from driving, the loss is not collectible. Drivers without a driver's license, intoxicated people, and minors under a specified age (sixteen in most states for a regular driver's license) are prohibited either by law or by the policy from driving.

(b) If the fire occurs while passengers are being transported for hire, the company is not liable. Trips on which passengers share the cost do not constitute "passengers for hire" if such trips are only occasional and not done for the purpose of making a profit.

(c) If the car is driven in violation of law, such as with illegal license tags, the loss is not collectible.

(2) **Theft Insurance.** *Theft* is defined as taking another's property by stealth. Automobile theft insurance either by law or by contract covers a wider range of losses than those by stealth. If one pretends to be a prospective purchaser in order to obtain the keys to the car, he is not guilty of theft if he never returns the car. Obtaining possession of a car lawfully but converting it to one's own use is known as *conversion*. Taking another's car by force is known as robbery. In some states the automobile theft policy is required by law to cover all these losses. The policy itself may define theft broadly enough to cover theft, conversion, larceny after trust, and robbery. Unless the policy is broadened either by law or by the wording of the policy, a theft policy covers only the taking of the car by stealth.

Automobile theft insurance usually covers pilferage of any parts of the car but not articles or clothes left in the car. It also covers any damage done to the car either by theft or attempted theft. It does not cover loss of use of the car unless the policy specifically provides for this loss.

- Mrs. Snowden purchased a new car from Seagraves and paid for it by check. The check was not paid by the bank, for Mrs. Snowden had no money on deposit. The car was never recovered. Seagraves was able to collect on his theft insurance policy as it contained a "trick or device clause" designed specifically to cover this type of loss.

(3) **Collision Insurance.** The standard collision policy covers all damage to the car caused by a collision or upset. Just what constitutes collision is not always easy to define. The car need not be moving in order to have a collision. A rolling rock that crashed into the car while

it was parked was held to be a collision. A horse kicked and damaged a car door so that it had to be replaced. This was a collision. The Texas Supreme Court held that hail colliding with a car was not a collision.

Practically all collision policies provide that the policy is either void or suspended if a trailer is attached to the car unless insurance of the same kind carried on the car is placed on the trailer. There is some confusion as to what constitutes a trailer. A small boat trailer and a small two-wheel trailer generally are not considered trailers, but horse or cattle trailers must be covered if they are attached.

If collision insurance but not fire is carried on the car, the policy will not in most states pay both the fire loss and the collision loss, both occurring in the same wreck. If a fire ensues after the collision and as a direct cause of the collision, the collision policy pays only for the damage caused by the collision. A few states hold that since the collision is the direct and proximate cause of the fire, the collision policy covers both losses. This is a minority view, however.

Most collision insurance policies have a deductible clause. It is possible to buy policies without any deductible clause, but the rates are higher. It is cheaper for one to assume some of this risk.

If the insurance company pays the insured a claim for collision damage, under the law of subrogation the company has the right to sue the other party to the collision if he was at fault.

(4) **Comprehensive Coverage.** Insurance companies will write automobile insurance covering almost every conceivable risk to a car. A partial list will show the extent of the coverage: windstorm, earthquake, flood, strike, spray from trees, malicious mischief, submersion in water, acid from battery, riot, glass breakage, hail, and falling aircraft. Any one of these risks can be transferred to the insurance company for a fee. All companies today write what is called a *comprehensive policy* which may include all of these risks plus fire and theft. A comprehensive policy covers only the hazards enumerated in the policy.

PUBLIC LIABILITY INSURANCE

The second major division of automobile insurance law is the public liability for damage to the property and the life of other people. This type of insurance is logically divided into two basic classes:

1. Bodily injury insurance
2. Property damage insurance

(1) **Bodily Injury Insurance.** Insurance covering the risk of bodily injury to the insured's passengers, pedestrians, or the occupants of another car is correctly designated public liability insurance. The insurance company obligates itself to pay any sum not exceeding the limit fixed in the policy for which the insured may be personally liable. If he is not liable for damages, the insurance company has no liability except the liability for defending the suit in court. This type of insurance does not cover any injury to either the person or the property of the insured. Such loss is covered by other policies.

The coverage under the automobile liability policy is usually written as 5/10/1, 25/50/5, 100/300/10, or similar combinations. The first number indicates that the company will pay $5,000, $25,000, or $100,000, respectively, to any one person for bodily injury in any one accident. The middle number fixes the maximum amount the company will pay for bodily injury in any one accident. The third figure sets the limit the company will pay for property damage. This usually is the damage to the other person's car but may include damage to any property belonging to another not under control of the driver.

The driver of a car that is not his own is liable for injury to others even though he does not own the car he is driving. The owner of the car is liable for all injuries to the person and property of others if he is personally driving in a negligent manner, or if any member of his family is so driving, or if any other person is driving the car with the owner's permission.

Under the "defense clause" the insurer agrees to defend the insured against any claim for damages. The insurer reserves the right to accept or reject any proffered settlement out of court.

- Graham had a public liability policy covering both bodily injury and property injury to others. In a collision with another car, the driver of the other car was seriously injured and his car wrecked. Graham's policy provided for coverage up to $15,000 for bodily injury and $5,000 for property damage. The injured driver offered to settle the claim out of court for $14,000. The insurance company rejected the offer and defended the claim in court. The court gave judgment against Graham for $30,000. Graham had to pay all over and above his insurance. Had the insurance company settled out of court, Graham would not have had to pay anything. The insured has unlimited liability, but the insurer's liability is limited by the policy.

A bodily injury insurance policy does not cover accidents occurring while the car is being driven by a person who is under the age designated by state law. It does not cover accidents occurring while the car is rented or leased, while the car is used to carry passengers for a consideration, while the car is used for any purpose other than that named in the policy, or while it is used outside the United States and Canada. Some policies exclude accidents while the car is being used for towing a trailer or any other vehicle used as a trailer. These are the ordinary exclusions. Some policies may have additional exclusions of various kinds.

In the event of an accident resulting in bodily injury or death, the insured must give immediate written notice to the insurer. He must also furnish the fullest information obtainable at the time of the accident and must promptly forward any legal papers or summons served on the policyholder. It is also his duty to help secure information, evidence, and the presence of witnesses, and to cooperate to the fullest extent with the insurer. The insured is not permitted to settle claims or to incur expenses other than those for immediate surgical help. In the event that the insurance company pays a loss, it is entitled to be substituted to any rights that the insured may have against others because of such losses.

(2) **Property Damage Insurance.** In automobile property damage insurance the insurer agrees to pay, on behalf of the insured, all sums that the insured may be legally obligated to pay by reason of the liability imposed upon him by law for damages because of injury to or the destruction of property, caused by accident and arising out of the ownership, the maintenance, or the use of the automobile. The liability of the insurer, however, is limited to the amount stated in the policy.

In the event of an accident, it is the duty of the policyholder to give the insurer written notice regarding the damages resulting from the accident. The notice must identify the insured and give the name and the address of the owner of the damaged property and those of any available witnesses. It is also necessary to give information relative to the time, the place, and to the detailed circumstances of the accident.

If a claim is made or a suit is brought against the insured, he must immediately forward to the insurance company every demand, notice, or summons received in order that the insurer may be able to make the proper legal defense.

The policy usually provides that the insurer will not be liable in the event that the car is being operated, maintained, or used by any person in violation of any state or federal law as to age or occupation. The insurer is not liable for damage to property owned by, leased to, transported by, or in charge of the insured.

LAST CLEAR CHANCE RULE

In the public liability coverage of automobile insurance, the injured party must prove the driver of the car was at fault before the insured becomes liable. As often happens, both drivers are negligent. Formerly, the driver bringing suit had to come into court with clean hands. If his own negligence contributed even slightly to the accident, he could not recover. This harsh rule has been replaced in most states by the *last clear chance* rule. This rule simply states that if one driver is negligent but the other driver had one last clear chance to avoid hitting the negligent driver, but did not take it, then he is the one liable.

FINANCIAL RESPONSIBILITY LAWS

Two states have compulsory automobile liability insurance laws, and about thirty states have financial responsibility laws. These latter laws do not require one to have any insurance until he has his first accident. If he then cannot prove he is financially able to pay any claims against him up to the amount fixed by law, usually $11,000, then he must buy insurance for this amount, that is 5/10/1 coverage. If his net worth is $11,000 or more, he is not required to carry any insurance. If one is required to carry insurance in order to be permitted to drive but no insurance company will sell him a policy, then the state insurance commissioner will assign this driver to an insurance company. The company must issue the policy under the "assigned risk" rule.

QUESTIONS

1. What are the two main classes of automobile insurance?
2. If John, the owner of a car, and four other young men drive to Jacksonville to attend a football game and each is to pay one fifth of the cost of the trip, is the insurer liable if the car is destroyed by fire during the trip?

3. What is covered by theft automobile insurance?

4. What effect does attaching a trailer to an automobile have on collision insurance?

5. Why do most automobile collision insurance policies have a deductible clause?

6. Name several causes of damage that may be covered by comprehensive insurance.

7. What two kinds of losses are covered by public liability insurance?

8. Who is liable for property damage if the owner is not driving the car?

9. What must one do with reference to his insurance when he has an accident?

10. If A has in his possession a watch worth $100 belonging to B and as a direct result of an automobile accident the watch is destroyed, who must pay for the loss?

CASE PROBLEMS

1. A car owned and driven by John collided with a car owned and driven by Henry. The damage to John's car was $1,100 and that to Henry's car was $800. Henry carried collision and public liability insurance, but John carried no insurance. The collision was clearly the result of John's negligence. John and Henry were fraternity brothers, and Henry agreed to admit it was his fault. Miss Vaughn, secretary to the agent who serviced Henry's insurance policy, overheard the agreement between John and Henry and reported it to her employer. As a result, the insurance company refused to pay for the damage to either John's car or Henry's. Was the company within its rights?

2. John and Janet Kettle hooked their car to their house trailer and set out to tour the country. They carried full insurance on the car but none on the trailer. While crossing a mountain in West Virginia, John lost control of the car and it plunged over the mountainside, completely demolishing both the car and the trailer. The insurance company refused to pay the damage for either the car or the trailer. Must it pay for the car?

3. Bennett, a truck driver for the Beck Bakery, struck a child. The child was not hurt, and the police exonerated Bennett for the accident. Consequently Beck did not notify the insurance company of the accident. Six months later the boy's father sued the bakery for $10,000, alleging the boy suffered internal injuries. It cost Beck $800 to defend the suit even though he won it. Was the insurance company liable for the $800?

4. Kemp negligently ran into Benton's car causing Benton to lose control of his car and collide with a car owned and driven by Spooner. The damage to Benton's car was $1,400 and to Spooner's car, $900. In addition to this property damage, Benton received a bodily injury for which he was awarded damages of $8,000; Spooner was awarded $9,000 for bodily injury. Kemp carried 5/10/1 coverage on his car for any one accident. The question arose as to whether this was one accident or two accidents. How much will the insurance company pay?

5. Henderson came to a highway crossing at which there was a stop sign. Henderson did not stop. Fulcher approached from the right on the other highway at a speed of 60 miles an hour, the maximum speed limit. He struck Henderson's car on the rear fender and demolished it and injured Henderson. Fulcher had a clear view of the crossing and admitted he never applied his brakes. Had Fulcher slowed down so as to delay his arrival at the crossing one or two seconds, Henderson would have been in the clear. Who is liable for the loss in this case?

6. Seabolt carried a 5/10/1 liability policy on his car. He negligently injured a child who was playing in the street. The father of the child offered to settle the claim for $4,500. Seabolt insisted the insurance company accept the offer, but the company refused. The father sued Seabolt and obtained judgment for $16,000. How much will the insurance company pay?

7. Cullison carried full automobile coverage on his car. The policy contained this clause: "The policy shall be suspended while the car is being used to carry passengers for a consideration." On a trip Cullison took three riders who agreed to share the cost of the trip. They agreed to figure the cost at seven cents a mile and each one would pay one fourth the cost. On the trip Cullison collided with another car and suffered $420 damage to his car. Must his insurance company pay under the collision policy?

8. Colbert was accident prone. He had been in four serious car wrecks for which he had been held liable in each case. He was such a poor risk no company would sell him a policy. He did not have enough property to qualify for a driver's license under the state financial responsibility law. Is there any way he can be permitted to drive?

CHAPTER 42
GUARANTY AND
SURETYSHIP

NATURE OF THE CONTRACT

The peculiarity of the contract of guaranty or suretyship is that it is founded on another contract. Without a primary obligation there can be no occasion for a contract of guaranty or suretyship. It is from its very nature a contract to ensure or guarantee that someone else will perform his contract. It could not come into existence without this other contract since it is an agreement whereby one party promises that he will be responsible for the debt, default, or obligation of another. Such contracts generally arise when one person assumes responsibility for the extension of credit to another, as in buying merchandise on credit or in borrowing money from a bank.

A person who is entrusted with money of another, such as a cashier, a bank teller, or a county treasurer, may be required to have someone guarantee the faithful performance of his duties. This, too, is a contract of suretyship, although it is commonly referred to as a *fidelity bond*.

PARTIES

There are three parties to a contract of guaranty or of suretyship. The party who undertakes to be responsible for another is the *guarantor* or the *surety*; and the party to whom the guaranty is given is the *creditor*; and the party who is primarily liable is the *principal debtor*, or simply the *principal*.

DISTINCTIONS

The words "surety" and "guaranty" are often used interchangeably. Sometimes such usage is correct, and sometimes it is incorrect. In a contract of suretyship the liability of the insurer is coextensive with that of the principal debtor. The surety renders himself directly and primarily responsible for the debt or obligation as though he were the primary debtor himself. His obligation, then, is identical with the one for whom he assumes the responsibility.

A guarantor's obligation is collateral to that of the principal debtor. He promises to pay only in the event that the principal defaults. The guarantor's obligation does not arise simultaneously with the principal's. His obligation is contingent upon the happening of another event, namely, the failure of the principal to pay. The surety's obligation, on the other hand, arises the instant the contract is formed.

Charlotte, N. C., Jan. 10, 19--

Mr. Jack E. Smith
Blue Pine, North Carolina

Dear Sir:

      In consideration of the letting of the premises located at 861 South Street, this city, to Mr. William H. Prost for a period of two years from date, I hereby guarantee the punctual payment of the rent and the faithful performance of the covenants of the lease.

      Very truly yours,

      Herbert Hanason

A Letter of Guaranty

IMPORTANCE OF MAKING A DISTINCTION

Three reasons why it is important to distinguish between a contract of guaranty and a contract of suretyship pertain to:

1. Form
2. Remedy
3. Notice of default

(1) **Form.** Contracts of guaranty and suretyship have many similarities, but the dissimilarities particularly need to be recognized. All the essential elements of a contract must be present in both. If the nature of the contract is such that it falls within the description of a

contract of guaranty, it must be in writing; most contracts of surety-ship may be oral.

The Statute of Frauds provides: "The promise to answer for the debt, default, or obligation of another must be in writing and be signed by the party to be charged, or by his authorized agent." It is held, however, that this provision applies only to a promise that creates a secondary obligation, that is, an obligation of guaranty, not to a promise that creates a primary obligation, that is, suretyship. One must first classify the obligation as primary or secondary before he knows whether or not the contract must be in writing.

(2) **Remedy.** In the case of suretyship, the surety takes upon himself an original obligation. He binds himself to pay if the other party does not. The reason that the other party does not pay is immaterial. He is liable as fully and under the same conditions as if the debt were his from the beginning. The rule is different in many contracts of guaranty. If the guaranty is conditional, the guarantor is liable only if the other party cannot pay.

Arnold writes, "Let Brewer have a suit; if he is unable to pay you, I will." This guaranty depends upon Brewer's ability to pay. Therefore, the seller must make all reasonable efforts to collect from Brewer before he can look to Arnold. If Arnold had said, "Let Brewer have this suit, and I will pay you," he would have created an original obligation for which he would have been personally liable. Therefore, Arnold would be deemed a surety if the understanding was that Brewer was to pay for the suit, but the merchant could look to Arnold if Brewer merely did not pay, rather than if Brewer could not pay.

(3) **Notice of Default.** Since the surety is primarily liable for the debt, it is not necessary to notify him if the debt is defaulted. He is charged with a knowledge of the principal's default. The guarantor, on the other hand, must be notified by the creditor. Failure to give notice does not of itself discharge the guarantyship. If the guarantor is damaged by the failure to receive notice, he may offset the amount of the damage against the claim of the creditor.

- Hawkins was a surety on a debt for Crew for $150. When the debt came due, Crew was unable to pay. The creditor waited four months and then notified Hawkins of the default. Hawkins denied liability because of the delay in giving him notice of default. The court held he was not entitled to a notice of default since he was a surety and had a primary obligation to pay.

RIGHTS OF THE SURETY AND THE GUARANTOR

A guarantor and a surety have the following rights:

1. Indemnity
2. Subrogation
3. Contribution
4. Exoneration

(1) **Indemnity.** If the guarantor or the surety pays the debt or the obligation of the principal, he is entitled to be reimbursed for the amount paid. This right is known as the right of *indemnity*. The guarantor or the surety can collect only the amount he has paid; he cannot recover for damages suffered or sacrifices made because of the default of the principal. If he has paid part of the debt, he is a creditor for that amount and is entitled to reimbursement. The guarantor or the surety may be induced to pay the debt when it becomes due in order to avoid the accumulation of interest and other costs on the debt.

(2) **Subrogation.** When the guarantor or the surety pays the debt of his principal, he is entitled to all property, liens, or securities that were held by the creditor to secure the payment of the debt. This right of subrogation does not arise until the creditor has been paid in full, but it does arise if the surety or the guarantor has paid a part of the debt and the principal has paid the remainder.

■ Clayton wished to borrow $900 from the Bank of Elbert. The bank required Clayton to get a surety to go on the note with him. Reed agreed to become a surety for Clayton if he, Clayton, would give him a mortgage on his truck to secure him. This Clayton did. When Clayton defaulted, the bank attempted to foreclose on the mortgage on the truck to collect the debt. The court ruled the bank could do this under the rule of subrogation. The bank was subrogated to Reed's rights since Reed would have to pay the bank if he foreclosed.

(3) **Contribution.** When two or more persons are jointly held liable for the debt, default, or obligation of a certain person, they are known as *coguarantors* or *cosureties*. When one of two or more guarantors or sureties has paid more than his proportionate share of the debt, he is entitled to recover from the other guarantors or sureties the amount in excess of his pro rata share of the loss. This right is

known as the right of *contribution*. It does not arise until the surety or the guarantor has paid the debt in full or has otherwise settled the debt.

(4) Exoneration. If one becomes a surety for the benefit of another, he has a right to insist the debt be paid when due, that is, he has the right of *exoneration*. In suretyship the creditor may delay in pressing the debtor to pay because he has the security of the suretyship. The surety has the right to bring suit against the debtor to compel him to pay the creditor when the creditor refuses to bring such action. This is the only way the surety can be exonerated under these circumstances. Except for this right, the surety might have a potential liability hanging over him for years.

DISCHARGE OF A SURETY OR A GUARANTOR

Both a surety and a guarantor may be discharged from their obligation by the usual methods of discharging any obligation, including performance, impossibility, voluntary agreement, and bankruptcy. There are, however, some additional acts that will discharge the surety or the guarantor. These are:

1. Extension of time
2. Alteration of the terms of the contract
3. Loss or return of collateral by the creditor
4. Varying the surety's or guarantor's risk

(1) Extension of Time. If the creditor extends the time of the debt without the consent of the surety or the guarantor and for a consideration, the surety or the guarantor is discharged from further liability. This extension of time, however, must be such that the creditor waives his rights. So long as he reserves his right to sue at any time, his leniency is not penalized. Such an extension does not jeopardize the surety's or the guarantor's rights because he can pay the debt and then sue the principal immediately. It is only when the extension of time debars an immediate prosecution of the claim that the surety or the guarantor is released. The courts in a few states hold that a paid guarantor, such as a bonding company, is released by an extension of time only if it can be proved that the guarantor has been damaged by the extension.

- Russel owed a note for $2,231 at the Bank of Omar. Lamar was surety on this note. When the note came due, the bank promised Russel it would renew the note if he would get Slack as an additional surety. This Russell did. Lamar did not consent to the renewal—in fact, he was not even aware of it. This extension of time released Lamar even though an added surety was to his advantage. The new note paid off the one on which Lamar was surety.

(2) Alteration of the Terms of the Contract. Any material alteration of the contract by the creditor discharges the surety or the guarantor. The change must be prejudicial to the surety or the guarantor. A reduction in the interest rate has been held not to discharge the surety, while a change in the place of payment has been held to be an act justifying a discharge of the surety. Even though the change is made for the convenience or the benefit of the surety, his obligation is discharged if the change is material. A material change in a contract is in fact substituting a new contract for the old. The surety guaranteed the payment of the old contract, not the new one, even though the new one may be considered to be more onerous than the old one.

(3) Loss or Return of Collateral by the Creditor. If the creditor through negligence loses collateral security given to secure the debt, a surety or a guarantor is discharged. The same is true if the creditor returns to the debtor any collateral security. This collateral must be held for the benefit of the surety until the debtor pays the debt in full.

- Black loaned Hendon $7,200. The loan was partially secured with $3,000 of of bearer bonds deposited with Black by Hendon. Coe was a surety for the loan. Black used the bonds as collateral for a loan to buy stock for speculative purposes. He lost heavily on the stock market, and he lost the bonds as a result. Coe was released from his contract of suretyship by the amount of the bonds.

(4) Varying the Surety's or the Guarantor's Risk. If an act of the creditor varies the risk of the surety or the guarantor, the liability of the latter ceases. This variation need not necessarily increase the risk. The act might even be beneficial to the surety or the guarantor. The following acts have been held sufficient to discharge the surety or the guarantor:

(a) A tenant leased only a part of a building. He later leased all of it. This released the guarantor of the rent payments.

(b) The mortgagee accepted an additional guarantor in consideration of extending the time of payment. Since this altered the contract, the original guarantor was released.

(c) The creditor accepted a note for an open account. The guarantor of the open account was released even though the note was more collectible than the open account.

BONDING COMPANIES

In recent years *bonding companies* have taken over most of the business of guaranteeing the employer against losses due to the dishonesty of his employees. These bonding companies are known as paid sureties to distinguish them from accommodation or unpaid guarantors. In some instances the courts have held that paid sureties must prove damages before they are released from their contract by reason of some act of the creditor. If the bonding company's risk is not increased by the creditor's act, the guaranty will be enforced. For the most part, however, the law of suretyship and guaranty apply with equal force to both paid sureties and accommodation sureties. The bonding company's obligation arises from its written contract with the employer. This contract of indemnity sets out in detail the conditions under which the surety will be liable.

QUESTIONS

1. What is the nature of a contract of guaranty or suretyship?
2. Name the parties to a contract of guaranty or suretyship.
3. When does the obligation of a surety arise?
4. When does the obligation of a guarantor arise?
5. What must be the form of a contract of guaranty? Of suretyship?
6. If the guarantor or the surety pays the debt of the principal, what is his right to reimbursement called?
7. When does the right of subrogation of the guarantor or surety arise?
8. What is the right of contribution?
9. Explain the law of exoneration as applied to suretyship contracts.
10. If the creditor extends the time of payment without the consent of the guarantor, what effect does this have on the contract of guaranty?
11. If a creditor loses any collateral held as security for a debt on which there is a surety, what effect does this loss have on the surety's liability?
12. What is a bonding company?

CASE PROBLEMS

1. Chapman was bookkeeper and credit manager of the Rowe Lumber Company, from which Mason purchased building materials amounting to $750. Reece, Mason's brother-in-law, entered into an oral contract of suretyship whereby he promised to be fully responsible for the debt. The original credit period was for 90 days. When the account came due, Mason paid $150 and asked to be allowed to give his 60-day note in payment of the balance. Chapman accepted the note and about two weeks later notified Reece of the new arrangement. Mason never paid the note, and the Rowe Lumber Company sued Reece. Reece denied liability for four reasons: first, oral contract; second, an extension of time; third, improper notice of default; and fourth, discharge of the debt which he had guaranteed. Were any of these defenses valid?

2. Coulter leased the Parkview Apartment Hotel for $1,500 a month. Denton deposited with the owner stock valued at $18,000 to be held as collateral to guarantee the payment of the rent by Coulter. When the lease was renewed at the end of the first year, the rent was increased to $1,850 a month, but Denton was not notified of this increase. Coulter defaulted in the payment of the rent, and demand was made upon Denton as guarantor to pay the rent. Was Denton liable for the rent?

3. Flannagan entered into a contract with WGAU Radio Broadcasting Company to carry on an advertising campaign over a period of 60 days. The total cost was $6,000. The radio station required Flannagan to provide some guaranty of payment of the $6,000 before the advertising campaign could start. Gill, a wealthy friend of Flannagan, orally agreed "to be personally responsible for this debt if for any reason Flannagan fails to pay it." There were three witnesses to this oral contract. Flannagan failed to pay any part of the $6,000, and the radio corporation demanded that Gill pay. Was Gill liable for this debt?

4. Huntley was a guarantor on a debt of $700 which Bartlet owed to Whitley. The debt was long past due; and though Whitley had never legally extended the time of payment, he was in no hurry to sue Bartlet. Huntley was confident that Bartlet would pay and release him from the potential liability if suit were instituted. What right does Huntley have?

5. Riley and Baker were cosureties on a debt of $1,000 which Ferguson owed Smallwood. They paid the debt off and then demanded that Ferguson pay them. When Ferguson refused, Riley wanted to bring suit, but Baker wished to charge it off as a bad debt and forget it. Riley offered Baker fifty cents for his half, and Baker accepted. Riley then sued Ferguson for $1,000. How much is he entitled to collect?

6. Ross promised to pay Fludd $5,000 to burn down Remley's residence because he claimed Remley had defrauded him. Fludd agreed to do this if Ross would get Lane to guarantee the payment of the $5,000. Although Lane was unaware of the illegal nature of the debt, he promised to pay the $5,000 if Ross did not. When Ross refused to pay, Fludd sued Lane. Must Lane pay?

SUMMARY CASES

PART 9

1. Simpson, a minor, purchased a $500 twenty-year endowment life insurance policy from the Prudential Life Insurance Company of America. After Simpson had paid $54, she attempted to disaffirm the contract and demanded a return of her $54. Is an endowment life insurance policy a necessity? (Simpson v. Prudential Insurance Co. of America, 184 Mass. 348, 68 N. E. 673)

2. Dr. Charles F. Clayton was a doctor employed by the Southern Mining Company to treat all the company's workers. The doctor's pay was deducted from the miners' wages. Some of the miners became very much dissatisfied with the arrangement. The dissatisfied miners made several threats against Dr. Clayton. Because of these threats, he renewed his insurance policy on his home and personal property. He also applied for and received two additional policies on the same property. In none of these applications did he make any reference to these threats. The property was destroyed, and the insurance companies denied liability on the ground of concealment. (a) Were these threats material facts? (b) Was there a concealment? (Great American Insurance Company of New York v. Clayton, 247 Ky. 612, 571 S. W. 2d 467)

3. Mrs. Veit purchased a $25,000 policy and made her husband the beneficiary. She understated her age by 16 years. More than 17 years after the policy was purchased she died, and Mr. Veit collected the $25,000. Soon thereafter the insurance company learned of the misstatement of age and sued Mr. Veit for a return of a portion of the $25,000. Had Mrs. Veit given her correct age, the amount of the premium she paid would have purchased a policy for only $15,077. The insurance company admitted liability for this amount but demanded a return of $9,923. Was this suit barred by the incontestability clause? (New York Life Insurance Company v. Veit, et al., 249 N. Y. 222, 62 N. E. 2d 45)

4. Rohde purchased an automobile public liability policy with a 20/50/5 coverage for each accident. The insured while driving negligently struck three motorcycles simultaneously. The drivers of the motorcycles were injured and their vehicles damaged. The total damages assessed were in excess of the limits of the policy if this was one accident. If it was three separate accidents, then the policy limits were adequate to cover all damages. Was this one accident or three accidents? (Truck Insurance Company v. Rohde, 49 Wash. 2d 465, 303 P. 2d 659)

5. Bruener purchased a comprehensive automobile policy that specifically excluded collision damage. While driving on a wet pavement, Bruener lost control of his car when it skidded on the highway, finally coming to a violent stop when it hit the road embankment. The car was badly damaged. The question arose as to whether the direct and proximate cause of the damage was the skidding or whether the proximate cause was the collision with the road embankment. If it were the latter, then it came within the exclusion clause and the insurance company was not liable. Was the skidding the proximate cause of the damage? (Bruener v. Twin City Fire Insurance Company, 37 Wash. 2d 181, 222 P. 2d 833)

6. Charles Roehm negligently injured Roy T. Caldwell in an automobile accident. Roehm carried a public liability automobile policy, purchased through Goldsmith, an insurance broker. The policy contained the usual clause that in the event of an accident, immediate notice must be given to the insurance company. On the day following the accident, Roehm notified Goldsmith by telephone and was assured that Goldsmith would take care of things. By mistake Goldsmith reported an entirely different accident, and the error was not discovered until 26 days after the accident. The insurance company denied liability on the grounds that Goldsmith was the agent of Roehm and therefore notice of the accident was not given to the company immediately. There was considerable evidence that the insurance company had on many previous occasions accepted Goldsmith as its agent to receive notices of accidents. Was notice to Goldsmith notice to the insurance company? (General Accident Insurance Company v. Caldwell, 59 F. 2d 473)

7. C. E. Youse purchased a fire insurance policy on her household goods and personal property. She removed a valuable ring from her finger and laid it on the table with some cleansing tissue. By mistake the maid threw the tissue and the ring into the wastepaper basket and then threw the contents of the basket into a backyard incinerator. She lighted the contents of the incinerator intentionally, and the ensuing fire stayed within the incinerator. About one week later the ring was discovered in the ashes in the incinerator. It had been damaged about $900 by the fire. The insurance company refused to pay on the ground this was a friendly fire. Was this a friendly fire or a hostile fire? (Youse v. Employers Fire Insurance Company, 238 P. 2d 472 Kan.)

8. Short and Sinai dissolved their partnership and left several creditors unpaid. Sinai owed Short some money, so he and DeVincenzi jointly agreed that Sinai would pay these creditors and thus relieve Short of the liability. DeVincenzi's promise was merely an accommodation to Sinai. The debts were never paid by Sinai, but Short gave no notice of the default to De-Vincenzi. When suit was instituted, DeVincenzi denied liability on the ground he had received no notice of default before suit was filed. Is a surety entitled to notice of default? (Short v. Sinai, et al., 50 Nev. 346, 259 P. 417)

9. Cuesta, Rey & Company drew a check for $1,887.60 on the Citizen's Bank and Trust Company. The check was payable to the Collector of Internal Revenue for federal taxes. Before the check was delivered, the drawer had it certified. Before it was collected, the bank failed. The drawer then paid it from another fund. Since the federal government had a first lien on the deposits of the insolvent bank for the face of the check, the drawer upon payment from another fund petitioned the court to be subro-gated to the rights of the federal government and thus given a preferred lien against the bank's assets for this check. Was Cuesta, Rey & Company entitled to subrogation? (Cuesta, Rey & Company v. Newsom, 102 Fla. 583, 136 S. 551)

PART 10

PROPERTY

Preview Cases for Part 10: Property

■ Saul executed a general warranty deed conveying his home to his wife, Ilene. Since he did not want her to know of this act, he placed the deed in his safe deposit box. Only he had access to the box. Upon his death, the deed was discovered. John, Ilene's stepson, brought suit to have the deed nullified. Will the court declare the deed invalid?

■ Dince sold his home to Waller for $30,000 and received cash for it. The next day he sold the same property to Wright for $20,000 cash. Wright's deed was received by the county recorder on January 7 at 11 a.m. Waller's deed was received at 2 p.m. on January 7. Which party has the better right to the property?

■ Watson rented an apartment on the first floor of a three-story apartment building. The occupants on the second floor over Watson's apartment loved music and dancing. Every night they and some friends danced until midnight. Watson demanded that the landlord evict the tenants, but the landlord refused. Watson moved seven months before his lease expired. The landlord sued for the balance of the rent. May he recover?

■ In Georgia a man lay dying in a bed that was in the center of the room. When the witnesses to his will signed the will, they used a table six feet back of the head of the bed; as a result, the man did not see them sign the will. Will the court declare the will to be valid?

■ Graham provided in his will that his son, Henry, was to receive his lakeside home, Agua Vista, and the boat and boathouse. Before Graham died, he sold this property and purchased with the proceeds a beach home in Florida. He did not change his will. When he died, Henry demanded the beach home. Is he entitled to it?

These preview cases are designed to serve as a springboard for the study of this part. As you read through each chapter in this part, you will find the actual decisions for all these preview cases. Of course, there are many more such illustrative problems as well as case problems for decision at the end of each chapter. And there are also a number of even more challenging cases for review at the end of the part.

CHAPTER 43

NATURE OF PROPERTY

DEFINITION OF PROPERTY

Property is anything which may be owned, possessed, used, or disposed of for a price. Law is concerned with both property and property rights. After all, it is the use of property, not property itself, which has value. The right to use property is broader than ownership because one may enter into a contract with another to use property which does not belong to him. The law protects not only the right to own property but also the right to use it. In law property is defined in such a way as to include not only physical property but such things as money, notes, and bonds which give the right to acquire either physical property or the use of such property.

Property may be classified according to its movability. In this sense all property falls into one of two classes, real property and personal property.

REAL PROPERTY

Real property consists of land, timber, minerals under the soil, buildings, and all permanent attachments to the land, such as fences, walls, and other man-made property. Through court interpretations we have accumulated a definite set of rules to guide us in distinguishing real property from personal property. The most important of these rules pertain to:

1. Trees and perennial crops
2. Rivers and streams
3. Fixtures
4. Emblements

(1) Trees and Perennial Crops. Trees that are growing on the land, orchards, vineyards, and perennial crops, such as clovers, grasses, and others that are not planted annually and cultivated, are classed as real property. When land is sold, if there is any doubt as to whether or not a particular item belongs to the land, the parties should agree before the sale is completed just how the item is to be classed. If one sells land and does not mention the clover crop, for example, the buyer gets the clover.

Many disputes arise between neighbors over fruit trees growing on the boundary line. The fruit from the trees and plants belongs to the one on whose land the tree or plant stands. If the limb of an apple tree, for example, hangs across the line of an adjacent property owner, the fruit still belongs to the owner of the tree. If the fruit falls to the ground, the title to the fruit is not lost. If the adjacent property owner will not permit the owner to cross the line to harvest his fruit, the owner may obtain a warrant and have the sheriff get the crop. The adjacent property owner may, however, cut off all limbs or vines that extend over his property.

(2) Rivers and Streams. If a nonnavigable river flows through a man's land, he owns the river bed but not the water that flows over the bed, nor the fish that swim in the water. He cannot impound or divert the water to his own use in such a way as to deprive his neighbor of its use. If the river or the stream forms the boundary line, then each owner owns the land to the middle of the river bed.

Where navigable rivers form the boundary, the owner of the adjoining land owns the land to the low-water mark.

(3) Fixtures. Movable property attached to land is known as a *fixture*. Generally, a fixture remains personal property, but it can become real estate. To determine whether or not a fixture has become real estate, one or more of the following four rules may be applied:

1. How securely is it attached? If the fixture is so securely attached that it cannot be removed without damaging the real property to which it is attached, then it ceases to be personal property. A tenant cannot then remove these fixtures when the lease expires.
2. What was the intention of the one installing the fixture? No matter what one's intention, the fixture becomes real property if it cannot be removed without damaging the property. If it is

loosely attached but the person installing the fixture indicates his intention to make the fixture real property, then this intention is the controlling factor. Kitchen refrigerators were held to be real estate when the apartments were rented as unfurnished but contained refrigerators.

3. For what purpose was the fixture attached? If a tenant securely attaches machinery to the building, this machinery does not become real estate unless its removal would damage the property. The purpose for which the fixture is to be used shows the intention of the one annexing it. If a tenant installs expensive partitions between offices in rented floor space, the partitions have no use except as partitions for offices of these exact dimensions and are thus real estate. Machinery, on the other hand, may be moved readily when the lease expires.

4. Who installed the fixture? If the owner of a building installs a fixture, this usually indicates his intention to make it a permanent addition to the real property. If the tenant makes the same improvements, the presumption is that he intended to keep the fixture as personal property unless a contrary intention can be shown.

(4) **Emblements.** An *emblement* is an annual crop planted by a tenant and will not mature before the lease is terminated. Usually there can be no emblement in a fixed-period lease since the tenant should know when he plants a crop that it will not mature before the lease expires. If the lease is terminated before the crop matures, the tenant has a right to return and harvest it in tenancies at will or by sufferance, that is, when no definite time is fixed to terminate the lease.

PERSONAL PROPERTY

Personal property, often referred to as chattels, is any property or property right which is not classified as real property. Personal property includes movable physical property and notes, stocks, bonds, and all written evidences of debt. Personal property is divided into two classes:

1. Tangible
2. Intangible

(1) **Tangible Personal Property.** *Tangible personal property* consists of all physical items which are not real estate. The property itself

can be seen, touched, and possessed. Animals, merchandise, furniture, annual growing crops, clothing, jewelry, and similar items are all classified as tangible personal property.

(2) Intangible Personal Property. Many important property rights consist merely of evidences of ownership of personal property. Contracts, copyrights, checks, stocks, savings account certificates, and other evidences of rights give us the power to acquire tangible personal property or other intangible personal property.

ESTATES

An *estate*, strictly speaking, is an interest or a right in real estate. This interest may be classed as real property or personal property, depending upon the nature of the right. One's title to an estate not only indicates the extent of ownership but also its nature, that is, whether it is real or personal property.

REAL PROPERTY ESTATES

The following titles are classed as real estate:

1. Estate in fee simple
2. Life estate

(1) Estate in Fee Simple. A *fee simple estate* is the largest and most complete right which one may possess in real property. It gives the owner the right to the surface of the land, the air above the land "all the way to heaven," and the subsoil beneath the surface all the way to the center of the earth. The courts have held, however, that the right to the air above the land is not absolute. One cannot prevent an airplane from flying over his land unless it flies too low.

One can own the surface of the land only, but not the minerals, oil, gas, and other valuable property under the topsoil. One may also own the soil but not the timber.

(2) Life Estate. One may have the right to use land as long as he lives, but not the right to sell the land. This is known as a *life estate*. At the death of the owner, the title either reverts to the one who conveyed the life estate to the deceased, the interest of the grantor being called a *reversion*, or the property goes to someone other than the grantor, such interest being called a *remainder*.

- John Dotson conveyed to his wife, Minnie, a life estate in all his real estate. At her death the property was to go to his three sons in equal parts. This was a remainder. Had the property at Minnie's death returned to her husband or to his estate, it would have been a reversion. In either case, the property right is real property, not personal property.

PERSONAL PROPERTY ESTATES

The following interests in real property are classed as personal property: *estate for years,* such as leases for one month, one year, fifty years, or any other definite time; and *estates at will* or *by sufferance,* which are leases for no definite period of time. Although these estates give one the exclusive right to use real estate for the period fixed by the grant, the property right is classed as personal property.

METHODS OF ACQUIRING OWNERSHIP

The title to property may be acquired by (1) purchase, (2) will, (3) gift, (4) descent, (5) accession, (6) confusion, (7) creation, and (8) original possession.

Acquiring ownership of property through purchase is a common occurrence. The process of acquiring property through a will or a gift is also well known. Since the other methods are less common and in most cases less important, they are not so well known and understood.

One of these less common methods is *descent.* If a man dies *intestate,* that is, without leaving a will, his heirs acquire, as a matter of law, title to his personal property according to the law of descent existing in the decedent's state, and to his real property according to the law of descent in the state where the land is located.

One may get title to property by accretion or accession. *Accretion* takes place most commonly when property abuts streams, rivers, lakes, and oceans. If one's land extends to the low water mark of a navigable stream, he may get title to some land by the river's shifting its flow. This occurs slowly by the deposit of silt. Also the accretion may be the result of dredging or channeling of the river. If the silt and sand are thrown up on the river bank so as to increase the acreage of the upland contiguous to the river, the added acreage belongs to the owner of the upland.

If a nonnavigable stream is the dividing line between two property owners and the boundary follows the meandering of the stream, then one's line shifts with the river. One property owner, however, cannot take any action to encourage the river to change its course.

If one steals or finds the property of another and then adds considerably to its value, the owner gets title to the enhanced value by *accession.*

Confusion is the mixing of the goods of different owners so that the parts belonging to each owner cannot be identified and separated. Grain, lumber, oil, and coal are examples of the kinds of property that are susceptible to confusion. The property, belonging to different owners, may be mixed by common consent, by accident, or by the willful act of some wrongdoer.

When confusion of the property is brought about by common consent or by accident, each party will be deemed the owner of a proportionate part of the mass. If the confusion is willful, the title to the total mass passes to the innocent party, unless the one causing the confusion can clearly prove how much of his property was mingled with that of the other person; if he fails, the whole mass belongs to the other person.

One may acquire personal property by *creation.* This is particularly true of inventions, paintings, musical compositions, and other intellectual productions. Title to these is made secure by means of patents and copyrights.

The one who first applies for and obtains a patent gets title to the production. Creation alone does not give absolute title; it gives only the right to obtain absolute title by means of a patent. This is not true for songs, books, and other compositions that are copyrighted. This is a holdover from the common law which gave absolute title to one's mental creation but not to one who invented a new device. After one publishes a book, a song, or a painting, he must apply for and obtain a statutory copyright to replace his common-law right or he loses all right to his creation. A statutory copyright is superior to a common-law right because it fixes the date of the creation; thus it settles the question of priority when there are two or more contenders for the title.

LOST AND ABANDONED PROPERTY

A person who discovers and takes possession of property that has been abandoned and has never been reclaimed by the owner acquires a right thereto. The prior owner, however, must have completely relinquished his ownership.

FORM A

Application for Registration of a Claim to Copyright
in a published book manufactured in the United States of America

CLASS	REGISTRATION NO.
A	DO NOT WRITE HERE

Instructions: Make sure that all applicable spaces have been completed before you submit the form. The application must be **SIGNED** at line 10 and the *affidavit* (line 11) completed and notarized. The application should not be submitted until after the date of publication given in line 4, and should state the facts which existed on that date. For further information, see page 4.

Pages 1 and 2 should be typewritten or printed with pen and ink. Pages 3 and 4 should contain exactly the same information as pages 1 and 2, but may be carbon copies. Mail all pages of the application to the Register of Copyrights, Library of Congress, Washington 25, D. C., together with 2 copies of the best edition of the work and the registration fee of $4. Make your remittance payable to the Register of Copyrights.

1. Copyright Claimant(s) and Address(es): Give the name(s) and address(es) of the copyright owner(s). Ordinarily the name(s) should be the same as in the notice of copyright on the copies deposited.

Name ___South-Western Publishing Company___

Address ___5101 Madison Road, Cincinnati 27, Ohio___

Name _____

Address _____

2. TITLE: ___College Law, Sixth Edition___
(Give the title of the book as it appears on the title page)

3. Authors: Citizenship and domicile information must be given. Where a work was made for hire, the employer is the author. The citizenship of organizations formed under U. S. Federal or State law should be stated as U. S. A. Authors may be editors, compilers, translators, illustrators, etc., as well as authors of original text. If the copyright claim is based on new matter (see line 5) give requested information about the author of the new matter.

Name __A. Aldo Charles__
(Give legal name followed by pseudonym if latter appears on the copies)
Citizenship __U. S. A.__
(Name of country)

Domiciled in U. S. A. Yes __X__ No _____ Address __University of Georgia, Athens, Georgia__

Name _____
(Give legal name followed by pseudonym if latter appears on the copies)
Citizenship _____
(Name of country)

Domiciled in U. S. A. Yes _____ No _____ Address _____

Name _____
(Give legal name followed by pseudonym if latter appears on the copies)
Citizenship _____
(Name of country)

Domiciled in U. S. A. Yes _____ No _____ Address _____

4. Date of Publication of This Edition: Give the date when copies of this edition were first placed on sale, sold, or publicly distributed. (NOTE: The full date (month, day, and year) must be given.)

___June 15, 1963___

5. New Matter in This Version: (NOTE: Leave this line blank unless the following instructions apply to this work.) If any substantial part of this work has been previously published, give a brief general statement of the nature of the new matter in this version. New matter may consist of compilation, translation, abridgment, editorial revision, and the like, as well as additional text or pictorial matter.

___Additions and Revisions___

6. U. S. Edition of Book in English First Manufactured and Published Abroad: (NOTE: Leave this line blank unless the following instructions apply to this work.) If this is the U. S. edition of a book in English, and all or a substantial part of the English text of an earlier foreign edition was manufactured and first published abroad, complete the following spaces. *For further information, see page 4.*

Year date of first publication of foreign edition _____
(Year)

Was claim to ad interim copyright registered in the foreign edition? Yes ☐ No ☐

If claim to ad interim copyright was *not* registered, is U. S. copyright in the foreign edition claimed by virtue of the Universal Copyright Convention? Yes ☐ No ☐

Complete all applicable spaces on next page

An Application for a Copyright

Property is considered to be *abandoned* when the owner actually discards it with no intention of reclaiming it. Property is considered to be *lost* when the owner, through negligence or accident, unintentionally leaves it somewhere. The difference between abandoned and lost property lies in the intention of the owner to part with the property. If the relinquishment is intentional, the property is abandoned; if the relinquishment is unintentional, the property is lost.

The finder of lost property has a right of possession against all but the true owner; he does not have the right of possession against the true owner except in those instances when the owner cannot be found through reasonable diligence on the part of the finder and when certain statutory requirements are fulfilled. The finder of abandoned goods, however, has an absolute right to possession.

In a few cases the courts have held that if an employee finds property in the course of his employment, the property belongs to the employer. Also if property is mislaid, not lost, then the owner of the premises has first claim against all but the true owner. This is particularly true where property is left on trains, airplanes, in restaurants, and in hotels.

QUESTIONS

1. What is property?
2. What is real property?
3. What is a fixture?
4. What is an emblement? Give an illustration.
5. If a tenant who has installed trade fixtures on the property moves away without removing the fixtures, to whom do the fixtures belong?
6. Name three types of personal property that are intangible.
7. What is the name of the largest estate or title which one can have in land?
8. If a man dies intestate, how may his heirs obtain title to his property?
9. If Young willfully mixes 1,000 pounds of his low-grade rice with 3,000 pounds of high-grade rice belonging to Harris, who owns the mixture?

CASE PROBLEMS

1. The Hermitage consisted of ten apartments. Each apartment contained an electric stove and an apartment-size refrigerator. The owner of the apartment building became insolvent, and his creditors levied on the stoves and refrigerators. The mortgagee who held the mortgage on the building claimed that his mortgage attached also to the stoves and refrigerators. Did it?

2. A nonnavigable stream was the dividing line between O'Keefe's farm and Coppage's farm. The river at one spot ran along the edge of a rich bottom, the bottom all being on Coppage's side of the river. O'Keefe felled some trees across the river at the upper end of the bottom, inducing the river to swing to the opposite side of the bottom. O'Keefe claims this bottom under the law of accretion. Is he entitled to it?

3. Ivey leased a farm for one year from Barton. The lease ran from January 1 to December 31. In October, Ivey sowed 100 acres of winter wheat which would not be ready to harvest until June of the following year. Barton refused on December 31 to renew the lease. Ivey contends he has a right to return and harvest the wheat. Is his contention correct?

4. Stewart went to Dr. Thor's office to have his aching tooth treated. He left a roll of canvas in the waiting room and forgot to pick it up. De-Pellet, an artist, found the canvas, took it home and painted a portrait on the canvas. The painting proved to be excellent and was appraised at $5,000. Stewart learned that DePellet was the one who found his canvas and demanded the painting. Dr. Thor then claimed the painting because the canvas was found on his property. Who has title to the painting?

5. Holder was the only heir to his father's estate, consisting of tangible personal property and real estate. He signed a note that read: "90 days after I get title to my father's patents, etc." The question arose as to whether or not this note met the requirement that it must be payable at a due date absolutely certain to arrive. Is this note negotiable?

6. Eberhart owned a textile mill which manufactured cordage material from cotton. Brewer left with Eberhart 20 bales of cotton for storage. Eberhart used the 20 bales of cotton together with several hundred of his own and processed it into cordage. Brewer demanded all the finished cordage. Is he entitled to it?

7. Coe owned a life interest in 80 acres of land. His brother John was to get the land upon Coe's death. Coe constructed a $40,000 home on the land. Three years later he died. Coe's son, Roger, demanded that his uncle pay him $40,000 for the home. Must the uncle pay for it?

CHAPTER 44

TRANSFER OF REAL PROPERTY

TRANSFER OF REAL PROPERTY

The three common ways of transferring title to real estate are by:

1. Sale
2. Will or descent
3. Adverse possession

(1) **Sale of Real Estate.** The most common way of transferring title to real estate is by sale. If the entire interest in the estate is sold, the contract of sale is followed by delivery of a deed. One may transfer a leasehold title giving the rights to the use and possession of land for a limited period by means of a lease. The extent of the interest conveyed is determined by the provisions of the deed or the lease.

Even when title to real property is conveyed as a gift, the transfer must be evidenced by a deed. As soon as the gift is fully executed, that is, the deed is prepared, signed, acknowledged, and delivered, title vests fully in the donee. An executory promise to make a gift is unenforceable.

(2) **Transfer By Will or Descent.** The owner of real estate may convey title to another by will. Title to real estate is not absolute until the will is probated. Unlike personal property, one does not inherit real property. He inherits the right to obtain the deceased's real estate. An administrator, or an executor if the will names one, must transfer the title to the heirs; otherwise, there remains a cloud on the title that may cause difficulty later.

(3) **Adverse Possession.** One may obtain possession to real property by *adverse possession.* To do this one must occupy the land for the period fixed by statute. This statutory period varies from seven years in some states to twenty-one in others. Occupancy must be continuous, open, hostile, visible, and exclusive. If one has no color of title to justify his possession, then he can get title to only that land actually occupied. In colonial times this was known as "squatter's rights." To get title by adverse possession, one had to go one step further than the "squatter," that is, he had to have a color of title.

Possession for the statutory period then gave one clear title to all that land his color of title described. The color of title usually arises, but need not necessarily do so, from some defective document purporting to be a deed or a will, or even a gift.

DEEDS

A *deed* is a formal contract conveying title, other than a lease, to real property. The law sets forth the form which the deed must have, and this form must be observed lest one's title prove defective. The parties to the deed are the *grantor* or seller and the *grantee* or buyer. There are two principal types of deeds:

1. Quitclaim deeds
2. Warranty deeds

(1) **Quitclaim Deeds.** A *quitclaim deed* is just what the name implies. The grantor quits any claim which he may have to the real property. He makes no warranty that he has any claim, although a few states prohibit the use of a quitclaim deed unless the grantor has some interest in the property.

Unless it is prohibited by law, there is no reason why a quitclaim deed may not be used in making all conveyances of real property. The grantor's full and complete interest is as effectively transferred by a quitclaim deed as with a warranty deed. When one buys real property, however, he does not always want to buy merely the interest which the grantor has. He wants to buy a perfect and complete interest so that his title cannot be questioned by anyone. A quitclaim deed conveys only the interest of the grantor and no more. It contains no warranty that the grantor's title is good. The buyer in an ordinary sale is justified in refusing to accept this type of deed.

A quitclaim deed should be used only in making a sale of some minor right or claim to real property.

- Cross owned land adjoining that of Barrow. The deeds called for a small stream to be the boundary line. A fence, over sixty years old, ran along the banks of the stream on Barrow's side. Former owners of both farms had for over forty years considered the fence the boundary line. Barrow wished to sell his land and the buyer refused to buy, claiming Barrow's title to the land between the fence and the stream defective. To remove this cloud, Cross executed and delivered to Barrow a quitclaim deed. This was effective in removing the cloud from the title.

(2) **Warranty Deeds.** A *warranty deed* not only conveys the grantor's interest in the real property but in addition warrants that he has a right to sell. The two types of warranty deeds are general warranty deeds and special warranty deeds.

A *general warranty deed* not only warrants that the grantor has good title to the real property but further warrants that the grantee "shall have quiet and peaceable possession, free from all encumbrances, and that the grantor will defend the grantee against all claims and demands from whomsoever made." This warranty, then, warrants that all prior grantors had good title and that there are no defects in any prior grantor's title. The grantee is not asked to assume any risks as the new owner of the property.

A *special warranty deed* warrants that the grantor has the right to sell the real property. He does not warrant the genuineness of any prior grantor's title. This type of deed is used by trustees and sheriffs who sell land at a foreclosure sale. It is also used by executors and administrators. There is no reason why these officials should warrant anything other than that they have the legal right to sell whatever interest the owner has.

REQUIREMENTS OF A DEED

Since a deed is a contract, the requirements applicable to contracts in general apply to deeds. Unless statutes provide otherwise, a deed should fulfill the following requirements:

1. Parties
2. Consideration
3. Covenants
4. Description
5. Signature
6. Acknowledgment

Know All Men by These Presents:

That James L. Black and Louise A. Black, his wife

of Butler County, Ohio,

in consideration of twenty thousand ($20,000)

to them *in hand paid by* Willis B. Crunk, the grantee, the receipt of which is hereby acknowledged,

do hereby **Grant, Bargain, Sell and Convey**
to the said Willis B. Crunk

h is *heirs*

and assigns forever, the following described **Real Estate** *situate in the* City
of Hamilton *in the County of* Butler *and State of* Ohio
Lot No. 10, Section 14, Range 62, Randall Subdivision, being a
portion of the estate of Horace E. Cresswell and Alice B. Cresswell

and all the **Estate, Right, Title and Interest** *of the said grantor* s *in and to said premises;* **To have and to hold** *the same, with all the privileges and appurtenances thereunto belonging, to said grantee* , his *heirs and assigns forever. And the said* James L. Black and Louise A. Black

do hereby **Covenant and Warrant** *that the title so conveyed is* **Clear, Free and Unincumbered**, *and that* they *will* **Defend** *the same against all lawful claims of all persons whomsoever.*

In Witness Whereof, *the said grantor* s *ha* ve *hereunto set* their *hand* s *, this* first
day of December *in the year A. D. nineteen hundred and* --

Signed and acknowledged in presence of us:

Michael R. Wiser	*James L. Black*
Antonio C. Petricelle	*Louise A. Black.*

State of Ohio, Butler **County, ss.**

On this first *day of* December *A. D. 19* -- *, before me, a* Notary Public
in and for said County, personally came James L. Black and Louise A. Black
the grantor s *in the foregoing deed, and*
acknowledged the signing thereof to be their *voluntary act and deed.*

Witness *my official signature and seal on the day last above mentioned.*

Ronald R Stelzer

Notary Public

A Warranty Deed

(1) **Parties.** The contract must have proper parties, the grantor and the grantee, and they must be named in the deed. If the grantor is married, his name and that of his wife should be written in the deed. If the grantor is unmarried, this fact should be indicated by the term "bachelor" or "spinster," as the case may be; if he is divorced, this fact should be indicated by the terms "divorced and unmarried."

(2) **Consideration.** The amount paid to the grantor for the property is the consideration. The payment may be in money or in money's worth. A statement of the consideration must be made in the deed, although the amount specified need not be the actual price paid. In some localities the practice is to name a nominal amount, as one dollar, although a much larger sum was actually paid. The reason for stating a nominal amount as the consideration is to prevent a subsequent purchaser from learning the actual price paid for the property in the previous sale.

(3) **Covenants.** One of the most important parts of a deed includes the covenants. These include the assertions of the grantor that he has good title to the land and that the grantee and his heirs shall have quiet and peaceable possession. There may be as many additional covenants as the grantor and the grantee wish to include. Some of these are *affirmative covenants* whereby the grantee is obligated to do something, such as maintaining a driveway used in common with adjoining property. Others are *negative covenants* whereby the grantee agrees to refrain from doing some event. Such covenants are very common in urban residential developments. The more common ones prohibit the grantee from using the property for business purposes and setting forth the types of homes that can or cannot be built on the property.

Most covenants run with the land and are binding upon all future owners. The only exception is personal covenants. The grantor as a part of the consideration to be paid by the grantee may bind the grantee to perform some act not connected with the land conveyed. An example would be an instance where the grantee covenants with the grantor whereby the grantor may have free fishing rights for five years in a lake owned by the grantee.

(4) **Description.** The property to be conveyed must be correctly described. Any description that will identify the property will suffice.

Ordinarily, however, the description that was used in the deed by which the present owner acquired the title should be used if it is correct. The description may be by lots and blocks if the property is in a city; or it may be by metes and bounds, section, range, and township if the property is in a rural district.

(5) **Signature.** The deed should be signed by the grantor in the place provided for the signature. If the grantor is married, his wife also should sign for the purpose of giving up her dower right. Her signature should be written below that of her husband. In some states the signatures must be attested by a witness or witnesses. If the grantor is incapable of signing his name, he may execute the deed by making his mark, thus:

James Smith
Witness of the mark of   Henry $\left\{ \begin{array}{c} \text{His} \\ \text{X} \\ \text{Mark} \end{array} \right\}$ Hoe
Henry Hoe

(6) **Acknowledgment.** The statutes in practically all the states require that the deed be formally acknowledged before a notary public or other officer authorized to take acknowledgments. The purpose of the acknowledgment is to make it possible for the deed to be recorded. After a deed has been recorded, it may be used as evidence in a court without further proof of its authenticity being given. Recording is not essential to the validity of the deed, but it is invaluable as security of the title of the grantee.

The *acknowledgment* is a declaration made by the properly authorized officer, in the form provided for that purpose, that the grantor has signed and sealed the instrument in his presence; that the grantor has knowledge and understanding of its contents; and that the grantor is personally known to the officer. These facts are attested by the officer, who affixes his official seal, and are further evidenced by his certificate.

DELIVERY AND ACCEPTANCE

A deed is ineffective until it has been both delivered and accepted. *Delivery* consists of giving up possession and control over the deed. So long as the grantor maintains control over the deed and reserves the right to demand its return before the deed is delivered to the grantee, then there has been no legal delivery. If the grantor executes a deed and leaves it with his own attorney to deliver to the grantee, there has been no delivery until his attorney delivers the deed to the grantee. Since the attorney is the agent of the grantor, he, the grantor, has the right to demand that his own agent return the deed to the grantor. If the grantor, however, delivers the deed to the grantee's attorney, then there has been an effective delivery.

The mere delivery of the deed to the grantee or the grantee's agent does not pass title. The grantee must by word or act accept the deed. If, however, after reading it, the grantee is not satisfied with the provisions of the deed, the grantee may reject it.

- Saul executed a general warranty deed conveying his home to his wife, Ilene. Since he did not want her to know of this act, he placed the deed in his safety deposit box. Only he had access to the box. Upon his death, the deed was discovered. John, Ilene's stepson, brought suit to have the deed nullified. He succeeded. There was never a valid delivery of the deed prior to Saul's death. No one has the authority to deliver it after his death.

DOWER AND CURTESY

Dower is the common-law right of the wife to a life estate in one third of her husband's real estate. It is not an inheritable estate. The husband in most states cannot deprive his wife of her dower right by will or sale unless his wife consents in writing.

Curtesy is the husband's right to a life interest in all the wife's real estate. Unlike the dower right, the wife can deprive the husband of this right by sale without his consent. Also, the right of curtesy does not arise until a child is born.

Most states have modified the common-law right of dower and curtesy by providing that the spouse of the deceased shall inherit a percentage of the deceased's estate, usually a child's share.

TENANCIES IN COMMON AND JOINT TENANCIES

If two or more people own real property jointly, the tenancy is either common or joint. If it is a *tenancy in common,* each owns a pro rata part of the property and may sell it, mortgage it, or will it. In a *joint tenancy,* the survivor takes full title to all the property upon the death of the other joint tenant.

Joint tenancies can be created in most states only by a specific clause in the deed expressly stating the tenancy to be joint; otherwise, the court will interpret it to be a tenancy in common. In the community property states, real property owned by the husband or the wife is considered a joint tenancy. The survivor takes title automatically upon the death of the other.

RECORDING

A deed need not be recorded in order to complete one's title. Title is complete as soon as the deed is delivered and accepted. Recording the deed protects the grantee against a fraudulent second sale by the grantor, and against any liens which may accrue against the property while it is still recorded in the grantor's name.

- Dince sold his home to Waller for $30,000 and received cash for it. The next day he sold the same property to Wright for $20,000 cash. Wright's deed was received by the county recorder on January 7 at 11 a.m. Waller's deed was received at 2 p.m. on January 7. Wright has superior title since his deed was received for recording first. The date of the deed is irrelevant.

The recording official should stamp the deed immediately upon receipt to show the date, the hour, and the minute the deed was received for recording. The exact minute of receipt is important. A judgment recorded one minute before the deed is received becomes a lien against the real estate. The recording official may hold the deed several days before it is actually recorded. This is immaterial, since it is the date the deed is received to be recorded which determines the priority.

ABSTRACT OF TITLE

Before one buys real estate, it is advisable to have an abstract of title prepared. This may be done by a title abstract company or it may be done by an attorney. The *abstract of title* gives a complete history of the real estate, showing an unbroken line of transfers. It also shows whether or not there are any unpaid taxes and assessments, mortgages, or deeds of trust still outstanding, and any unpaid judgments or other unsatisfied liens of any type against the property. If an abstracting company makes the abstract, it is advisable to have an attorney read the abstract to see if it reveals any flaws in the title.

Many defects in the title to real estate cannot be detected by an abstract. Some of the most common of these defects are forgery of signatures in prior conveyances; claims by adverse possession; incompetency to contract by any prior party; fraud; duress; undue influence; defective wills; loss of real property by accretion; errors by title examiner, tax officials, surveyors, and many other public officials. A title insurance policy will cover most of these defects. The policy may expressly exclude any possible defects which the insurance company does not wish to be covered by the policy. With one premium, the insured is covered as long as he owns the property. The policy does not inure to the benefit of a subsequent purchaser or to a mortgagee. The policy does not insure a perfect title, but it does insure the individual named in the policy against suffering a financial loss because of a defective title.

QUESTIONS

1. If Hale wishes to transfer title to his land to his son by gift, what must he do?
2. If one obtains title to real estate by will, what must be done before the title is absolute?
3. How is it possible to obtain title to real estate by adverse possession?
4. What are the advantages and disadvantages of a quitclaim deed?
5. Define a warranty deed.
6. Who are the parties that must be named in a deed?
7. What is the difference between an affirmative covenant and a negative covenant?
8. When does a deed become effective?
9. (a) Is it necessary to record a deed in order to complete one's title to the land?
   (b) What does recording a deed do?
10. What is an abstract of title?

CASE PROBLEMS

1. Donaldson owned a home valued at $40,000 and personal property valued at $10,000. He desired that Mrs. Donaldson inherit all this property upon his death and wished to minimize the court costs and other expenses involved in transferring this property to her by will. Explain how he may do this and still retain full title until his death.

2. Donaldson purchased a house and lot. In a prior deed the grantor had inserted a covenant that the grantee would never use the property for commercial or business purposes. Such covenants were included by the original owner in the deeds for all the houses in that residential section. Donaldson wished to set up a dry-cleaning establishment in the basement of his house.

A neighbor brought an equity suit to enjoin him from doing so. This action was based upon the original restrictive covenant. Was Donaldson bound by this covenant?

3. Morris, as a notary public, was authorized to acknowledge deeds. A man brought Morris a deed to be acknowledged. He represented himself as Sullivan, the grantor named in the deed, whereby Sullivan conveyed to William Peyton a valuable tract of real estate. Morris did not know Sullivan, the grantor, but he acknowledged the deed and certified that Sullivan personally appeared before him and signed the deed of conveyance. The man who claimed to be Sullivan was actually not Sullivan but William Peyton, the grantee. Peyton immediately sold the land to Ashby for cash. When Sullivan, the true owner, learned of Ashby's claim to the land, he denied him access to it and notified him that he had never signed the deed of conveyance to Peyton. Ashby produced an abstract of title that had been prepared by an attorney. Point out the mistakes the various people made in these transactions, and show how they might have been avoided.

4. Tucker, who had two sons, owned two homes of about equal value. In an attempt to avoid the expense of a will or other costs incident to the transfer of this property to his two sons after his death, he executed two deeds, leaving each of the sons one of the houses. He gave the deeds to his sister and instructed her to "keep the deeds in a safe place and under no circumstances part with them during my life. After my death give each son his deed." This request was followed to the letter. One son, John, was dissatisfied with the house he received, claiming the other house was worth twice as much as his. He refused to record his deed and brought a suit to have both of them set aside. Were these deeds valid?

5. Riley sold to the Ruark Lumber Company "all the timber now on my farm." The timber was cut, and about ten years later Riley contracted to sell his farm to Greeley. Greeley refused to complete the purchase, claiming that Riley did not own the timber. Thereupon Riley obtained a letter from the Ruark Lumber Company stating that it did not claim to own the timber. Was this adequate to clear the title?

6. Stewart sold Stern a house and lot, executing a special warranty deed. About a year later Sprouse sued Stern to recover the property, claiming that the signature of the grantor of the property ten years earlier was forged. The man who sold the property to Stewart was not a party to the forgery. Must Stewart make good the loss to Stern? Would your answer be different if he had made a general warranty deed?

7. Holcomb executed a deed to his home, conveying all the property to his son, John. The deed was delivered to John, but before he had it recorded, a brother, Roger, found the deed and burned it up. Before Holcomb could make another deed, he died; and John sought to have the court declare him the rightful owner of the house and lot. Was John entitled to the property?

8. Henry owned 600 acres of land which he had purchased by general warranty deed from Bell. He purchased title insurance on the property. He sold the land to Dawson and gave him a special warranty deed. He

also agreed to assign the title insurance policy to Dawson. About two years after Dawson purchased the property, he learned an adjoining landowner claimed by adverse possession about 30 acres of the most valuable part of the land. In a court suit, the court awarded the 30 acres to the neighbor. What rights does Dawson have against Henry or the insurance company?

9. Walton in his young days lived with Margie for three years as man and wife under what is known as a common-law marriage. He left Margie and married Eva though he never divorced Margie. He lived with Eva for thirty years and acquired a sizeable estate. Margie never remarried. When Walton died, Margie demanded her dower right in Walton's real estate. Is she entitled to it?

10. Abney had three sons at the time of his death. They inherited jointly Abney's home. The three sons sold the property to Penker for $30,000. The three grantors were not individually named in the deed but simply stated, "We, the heirs of Howard Abney." Each one signed the deed, and each one separately had it notarized. Later the question arose as to whether or not this violated the rule that the grantor must be named in the deed. Would you be willing to accept a deed with the grantors thus designated?

11. Stillman purchased some land from Cope. He held the deed one week before having it recorded. In the meantime, Cope's creditors obtained judgments against Cope and had these recorded before Stillman's deed was recorded. Were these judgments a lien against Stillman's land?

12. Munson purchased lot "A" from Pepper. Through an error the deed actually conveyed title to lot "B." Munson built a house on lot "A" and lived on it for twenty-one years. Pepper's heirs attempted to dispossess Munson and take possession of lot "A" and the house on it. Were they entitled to the property?

CHAPTER 45

REAL ESTATE
MORTGAGES

DEFINITION

A *mortgage* is a lien given upon property to secure a debt. The mortgage is not the debt itself but only the security for the debt. Without a debt or potential obligation the mortgage would lack a consideration. Land or any interest in land may be mortgaged. Land may be mortgaged separately from the improvements, or the improvements may be mortgaged apart from the land. Growing crops may be mortgaged for the purpose of securing a loan. In fact, all kinds of property and property rights may be mortgaged.

Under the common law a real estate mortgage was an absolute transfer of both title and possession of real property to the mortgagee. The mortgagor received in substance an option to repurchase the real estate, that is, the right to regain both title and the possession upon the payment of the debt. Under the modern plan the mortgagor does not give up possession of the property, although he may contract to do so. The common law rule was rather harsh because one might lose a $10,000 piece of property because of his inability to repay a $1,000 loan. Since a modern mortgage does not give the mortgagee an absolute title, he must sell the mortgaged property at a foreclosure sale. If the property brings more than the debt and the costs, the mortgagor is entitled to receive the balance.

THE MORTGAGE CONTRACT

A mortgage that makes a contingent sale of the land, subject to reacquisition upon fulfilling the obligation secured, must be in writing. The contract, as a rule, must have the same form as a deed; that is,

445

it must be acknowledged and must be under seal. The mortgage, like all other contracts, sets forth the rights and the duties of the contracting parties. Over the years, however, courts have built up a body of court decisions interpreting these rights and duties. For this reason, one must look to these decisions as well as the contract for a full understanding of the nature of the mortgage contract.

A mortgage is usually given to raise money for the purchase price of real estate but may be given for other reasons. One may borrow money for any reason and secure the loan by a mortgage. One may assume a contingent liability for another, such as going on his bond, and receive a mortgage as security. The debt must be in existence at the time a mortgage is foreclosed, but not necessarily at the time the mortgage is given.

RECORDING

The mortgage gives the mortgagee a lien in a definite order of priority according to the time it is recorded. Recording the mortgage protects the mortgagee against subsequent creditors since the public record is notice to the whole world as to the mortgagee's rights. There may be both a first mortgage and a second mortgage. Since the second mortgage recites the fact that a first mortgage exists, the second mortgage does not achieve priority over the first even though it is recorded first. The mortgage is also recorded to notify subsequent purchasers that the purchase price, or as much as is necessary, must be paid to the mortgagee.

DUTIES OF THE MORTGAGOR

The mortgagor assumes three definite duties and liabilities when he places a mortgage upon his real estate. These pertain to:

1. Interest and principal
2. Taxes, assessments, and insurance premiums
3. Security of the mortgagee

(1) **Interest and Principal.** The mortgagor must make all payments of interest and principal as they become due. Most mortgages call for periodic payments, such as monthly, semiannual, or annual payments. These payments are used to pay all accrued interest to the date of payment, and the balance is applied on the principal. Other

mortgages call for periodic payment of interest and for the payment of the entire principal at one time. In either case, a failure to pay either the periodic payments of interest and principal, or of interest only, is a default and gives the mortgagee the right to foreclose.

If the mortgagor wishes to pay off the mortgage debt before the due date so as to save interest, he must reserve that right at the time the mortgage is given. He can pay off the debt at any time, but the interest must be paid till the due date in the absence of an agreement to the contrary.

(2) **Taxes, Assessments, and Insurance Premiums.** The mortgagor must pay taxes, assessments, and insurance premiums. The mortgagor is required by law to pay taxes and special assessments. If he does not do so, the mortgagee may pay them and compel a reimbursement from the mortgagor. If the mortgage contract requires the mortgagor to pay these charges, a failure to pay them becomes a default.

The law does not require the mortgagor to keep the property insured. This duty must be imposed on the mortgagor by contract. Both the mortgagor and the mortgagee have an insurable interest in the property to the extent of each one's equity or maximum loss.

(3) **Security of the Mortgagee.** The mortgagor must keep the security of the mortgagee unimpaired. The mortgagor must do no act that will materially impair the security of the mortgagee. Cutting timber, tearing down buildings, and all acts that waste the assets impair the security and give the mortgagee the right to seek legal protection. Some state statutes provide that any one of these acts is equivalent to a default. This gives the mortgagee the right to foreclose. Other statutes provide only that the mortgagee may obtain an injunction in a court of equity enjoining any further impairment. Many state laws also make it a criminal offense to impair willfully the security of mortgaged property.

RIGHTS OF THE MORTGAGOR

The mortgagor has four well-established rights:

1. Possession of the property
2. Rents and profits
3. Cancellation of lien
4. Redemption

(1) **Possession of the Property.** The mortgagor usually has the right to retain possession of the mortgaged property. In practically all states the mortgagor now has this right, either as a matter of law or by contract. A few states provide that in the event of default by the mortgagor, the mortgagee has the right to possession provided he is in possession at the time of the default or obtains such possession lawfully.

(2) **Rents and Profits.** The mortgagor is entitled to rents and profits. In the absence of an express agreement to the contrary, the mortgagor has the right to all rents and profits realized from the mortgaged property. If the mortgagor cuts timber from the mortgaged property, which can be done only with the consent of the mortgagee, the value of the timber must be applied on the mortgage lest the security be impaired. The mortgagor may retain the profits. This rule or any other rule may, of course, be superseded by a contract providing otherwise.

(3) **Cancellation of Lien.** The mortgagor has the right to have the lien canceled on final payment. As soon as the mortgage is delivered to the mortgagee, it becomes a lien upon the mortgaged real estate. As a practical matter, a mortgage must be recorded since an unrecorded mortgage is void as to subsequent purchasers, mortgagees, or judgment creditors who have no notice of the mortgage. A mortgage lien is canceled by having the clerk in the recorder's office enter a notation, usually on the margin, certifying that the debt has been paid and that the lien is canceled. The mortgagee, not the mortgagor, must have this done. If he fails or refuses to do so, the mortgagor may institute court action to have this cloud removed from his title so that he may have clear title.

If the mortgagee wishes to prepay the mortgage, he must have a prepayment clause in the mortgage. He may pay the principal in advance without this clause, but the interest must be paid for the full period of the mortgage. This clause is particularly important where mortgage life insurance is carried.

(4) **Redemption.** Most mortgages have an acceleration clause that calls for the entire balance of the mortgage to be due and payable at once if the mortgagor defaults on one payment. Were it not for the mortgagor's right of redemption, this could be a very burdensome

provision. The *law of redemption* provides that in the event the mortgagor does default on one or more payments, he may restore the mortgage to its original terms by making up all back installments. If foreclosure proceedings have been instituted by the mortgagee, then all court costs must also be paid. In most states the redemption must be made before the property is sold at a foreclosure sale. In a few states the property can be redeemed from the purchaser at a foreclosure sale if done within a fixed time limit of the sale. In this case, however, the purchaser must be reimbursed fully. If this is not enough to pay the balance of the mortgage and the court costs, the mortgagee must also pay these items.

A few states still adhere to the rule that considers a mortgage as a transfer of title to the real estate to the mortgagee. Redemption in these states simply means the right to get the title back when the mortgage is paid in full. In those states that consider a mortgage merely as a lien on the land, no redemption takes place upon payment since title was never transferred to the mortgagee.

FORECLOSURE

If the mortgagor fails to pay the debt secured by the mortgage when it becomes due, or fails to perform any of the other terms set forth in the mortgage, the mortgagee has the right to foreclose for the purpose of collecting the debt. *Foreclosure* usually consists in a sale of the mortgaged property made under an order of a court and generally by an officer of the court.

Foreclose literally means a legal proceeding to shut out all other claims. A first mortgage may not necessarily constitute a first claim on the proceeds of the sale. The cost of foreclosure and taxes always takes precedence over the first mortgage. People who furnish materials for the construction of a house and workers who work on it have a claim under what is known as a *mechanics' lien* that takes precedence over a first mortgage. The foreclosure proceedings establish the existence of all prior claims and the order of their priority. Foreclosure proceedings are fixed by statutory law and therefore vary in different states.

If the proceeds of the sale of mortgaged property are greater than the amount of the debt and the expenses of foreclosure, the surplus must be given to the mortgagor. If a deficiency results, however, the mortgagee may secure a deficiency judgment for this amount. In that case the unpaid balance of the debt will stand as a claim against the mortgagor until the debt is paid.

TRUST DEED

A trust deed is often used as a substitute for the ordinary form of mortgage for the purpose of securing a debt. A *trust deed* (sometimes called a *trust mortgage*) conveys the property to a disinterested third party, called a *trustee,* to be held in trust for the benefit of the creditor or creditors. If a default in payment occurs, the trustee must foreclose the property and apply the proceeds to the payment of the debt. The proceedings in the foreclosure of a trust deed are similar to those in the foreclosure of an ordinary mortgage. The right to redeem under a trust deed, when it exists, is similar to the right of redemption under a mortgage.

There are several advantages in the use of a trust deed as a method of securing an obligation. For instance, a trust deed can be used more conveniently than an ordinary mortgage to secure an indebtedness owed to a large number of persons. A bank or a loan agency that has made a large loan receives as evidence of the indebtedness bonds or notes usually for amounts that are multiples of $1,000. The bonds or notes are accompanied by a trust deed. They may then be sold to small investors. The purchaser of one of these bonds or notes becomes a mortgagee to the extent of his purchase.

In the event that the mortgagor defaults in his payments, the mortgagee who holds an ordinary mortgage can foreclose, that is, have the mortgaged property sold to satisfy the debt. In most states, however, he must go into court and have a judicial court foreclosure. In some states the trustee in a trust deed may sell the mortgaged property on the mortgagor's default outside of court without going through a time-consuming court foreclosure. Hence, the property can be more quickly sold at a trustee's sale.

BUYING MORTGAGED PROPERTY

It is a common practice to buy property on which there is a mortgage or a trust deed. The purchaser may agree to "assume the mortgage," that is, to be primarily liable for its payment. He should understand the difference between "assuming" the mortgage and buying the property "subject to the mortgage." In the first case he binds himself to be liable for the mortgage obligation as fully as if he had been the original mortgagor. If he takes the property "subject to the mortgage," he may lose the property, but no more. Observe how a knowledge of this point of law may prove to be worth several thousand dollars:

- Ratcliffe sold Hurley a farm for $20,000, Hurley agreeing to pay $5,000 down and "assume a $15,000 mortgage." He held the farm a few years during which time the value of farm land declined considerably. The mortgagee foreclosed on the mortgage and sold the farm for $9,000. This left an unpaid balance of $3,000 which Hurley was compelled to pay. Had he purchased the property "subject to the mortgage," he would not have had to pay the balance of $3,000.

The original mortgagor is not automatically released when he sells mortgaged property whether the purchaser assumed the mortgage or bought it subject to the mortgage. He remains fully liable in both cases. He may be released by the mortgage by novation, that is, the mortgagee agrees to release the mortgage by extending the time of payment without the mortgagor's consent. Courts have held that the acceptance of interest payment after the principal of the mortgage has become due constitutes an extension of the mortgage. If this is done without the mortgagor's consent, he is fully released from all liability under the mortgage.

ASSIGNMENT OF THE MORTGAGE

The mortgagee may assign his rights under the mortgage agreement. The assignee, that is, the purchaser, obtains no greater rights than the assignor had. To protect himself, the assignee should require the assignor to produce an estoppel certificate signed by the mortgagor. This certificate should acknowledge that the mortgagor has no claims of any kind in connection with the mortgage. This would bar him from subsequently claiming the right of offset.

The assignee of a mortgage should have his assignment recorded. In the event the mortgagee assigns the mortgage to more than one party, the one who records his assignment first has preference in case the proceeds are not adequate to pay both assignees.

QUESTIONS

1. (a) Define mortgage.
   (b) Does the mortgagor lose possession of the mortgaged property at the time the mortgage is executed?

2. If two mortgages are executed on the same land, which mortgagee has priority?

3. When one executes a twenty-year mortgage on his home, what must he do if he wishes to prepay the mortgage at some future date?

4. If there is a street assessment against mortgaged property for $1,000, who must pay this, the mortgagor or the mortgagee?

5. If the mortgagor tears down a garage worth $800, does this give the mortgagee the right to foreclose?

6. When the mortgage is paid in full, how is this fact indicated in the record books in the county clerk's office?

7. How may the mortgagor redeem his property after it has been sold under a foreclosure sale?

8. If the proceeds of a foreclosure sale of property are not enough to pay off the mortgage, how is the balance of the debt canceled?

9. Name two characteristics that distinguish a trust deed from a mortgage.

10. What is the difference in the liability of the purchaser when he buys mortgaged property "subject to the mortgage" and "assuming the mortgage"?

CASE PROBLEMS

1. Johnson owned a farm, which included 10 acres of growing cotton. He borrowed $5,000 from Dupree and executed a real estate mortgage on his farm to secure the debt. The mortgage contained the usual clause that the mortgagor must not commit any act that would decrease the mortgagee's risk. It also provided that if the mortgagor sold any timber, pulpwood, or any other part of the real property, the net proceeds must be applied on the $5,000 note. Johnson later sold the cotton for $1,500 but spent the money for living expenses. Dupree brought suit to foreclose on the mortgage, claiming that Johnson had violated his contract. Was Dupree entitled to foreclose?

2. Jensen, who had some extra money to invest, agreed to lend Bowen on a first mortgage $15,000 with which Bowen was to build a house on a lot he owned. Jensen agreed to let Bowen have $3,000 to start, and $3,000 a month as the construction progressed, the balance of the $15,000 to be loaned when the building was completed. About 30 days after the home was completed, Jensen and Bowen learned that the contractor had purchased on credit about $3,500 of materials for the house and had not paid for these materials out of the money Bowen paid him for building the house. In addition he owed $1,200 for labor that he had not paid. The materials supplier and the workers demanded that Bowen pay them. He had no money and could not pay. They threatened to sell the house unless Jensen paid them. Jensen contended his first mortgage took precedence over these items. Was this correct?

3. Dennison owned the timber on 1,000 acres of land but did not own the land or any other interest in the land. He borrowed $10,000 from Swanson and executed a first mortgage to Swanson on the timber as security for the loan. He sold about half of the timber to the Logan Lumber Company for $12,000 but did not pay any part of the proceeds on the $10,000 mortgage. Swanson indicted Dennison for willfully impairing the security

of his loan, and he brought an action to foreclose the mortgage. Was he legally justified in taking these actions?

4. Barbara and Donald Shea brought a home for $20,000 and financed it by paying $4,000 down and giving a 20-year first mortgage for $16,000 at 5 percent. Donald wished that in the event of his premature death, Barbara have the home free of debt. Consequently he purchased a mortgage life insurance policy whereby the insurance company agreed in event of Donald's death to pay off the balance of the principal of the mortgage plus accrued interest. Donald died one year later. At that time there was a balance of $15,860 principal and accrued interest on the loan. The life insurance company paid this. The mortgagee refused, however, to cancel the mortgage, claiming an additional $7,200 for interest for the next 19 years since the mortgage did not contain a prepayment clause. Must Barbara pay this $7,200?

5. Billy and Yvonne Rogers owned 80 acres of land with a modern dwelling. There was a first mortgage on the property for $12,000. The entire property was worth about $14,000. Yvonne's father was retired on a pension of $80 a month. Billy and Yvonne deeded him and his wife two acres of land so that he could take what cash he had and build himself a modest house for $6,000. Soon after the father-in-law completed his house, the country experienced a rather serious recession. Real estate values declined about 25 percent. Billy lost his job and was unable to keep up his payments on the mortgage. The mortgagee foreclosed on the 78 acres and sold it at public auction. It brought only $9,000, leaving a balance on the mortgage of $3,000. The mortgagee threatened to sell the father-in-law's two acres and house if the father-in-law did not pay the $3,000. Was Billy's mortgage also a lien on the father-in-law's property?

6. Holleran borrowed $10,000 from Carswell and executed a first mortgage on his home as a security for the loan. Carswell later purchased a restaurant from Holcomb for $20,000 and, as part payment, assigned to Holcomb the first mortgage which he held on Holleran's home. At the time of the assignment Holleran had a claim against Carswell for $3,000 as a result of an automobile accident caused by Carswell's negligence. Holcomb did not know of this claim at the time he sold his restaurant to Carswell. When the mortgage came due and Holcomb demanded payment, Holleran contended he did not owe $10,000, but only $7,000 after taking credit for the $3,000 damage claim. May Holleran offset his claim of $3,000 against Holcomb's claim for $10,000?

7. Carlson placed a mortgage on his home for $12,000. He paid the mortgage in full. About one year later, he contracted to sell the property to Rowe. An abstract of title showed that the mortgage was still a lien on the house. The mortgagee refused to release the mortgage unless Carlson paid him $1,000. Rowe would not purchase the property until the title was cleared. What are Carlson's rights?

8. Mr. and Mrs. North purchased a home and agreed to pay $18,000 for it. They paid $3,000 down and assumed a $15,000 mortgage, which was to be paid off at the rate of $100 a month. The company for which Mr. North worked moved away, and Mr. North therefore lost his job. As a result he was unable to keep up the payments on the mortgage. The property was foreclosed and sold. The purchaser paid $10,000. This left an unpaid balance of $2,000. Were Mr. and Mrs. North liable for the payment of this $2,000?

9. Rankell had a ten-year mortgage on his home, to be paid at the rate of $75 a month. He was discharged from his job and defaulted on two monthly payments before he obtained another job. The mortgagee foreclosed immediately upon the first default. What were Rankell's rights?

10. Cook wished to borrow his neighbor Fleeman's truck to haul cotton to the gin. Fleeman, fearing that Cook might have a wreck which would subject Fleeman to a suit for damages, had Cook execute and deliver to him a mortgage on Cook's farm for $5,000. Was this a valid mortgage?

11. Poe was the mortgagor and Corkrell the mortgagee to the extent of $2,500 upon certain real estate. Poe, before the mortgage was paid, sold the mortgaged property to a corporation, and the corporation in turn conveyed the property to Burke who assumed the mortgage. When Burke defaulted on the mortgage, Corkrell brought suit to foreclose and also secure a deficiency judgment against both Poe and Burke. Was Burke liable for the deficiency?

CHAPTER 46

LANDLORD AND TENANT

RELATION OF LANDLORD AND TENANT

The relation of landlord and tenant is created by a contract, written or implied, whereby one person agrees to lease land or a building to another. No special words or acts are necessary to create such an agreement. The possession of the premises and the payment of rent for its use are the chief characteristics that determine the relation of landlord and tenant.

The owner or the holder of the property is known as the *landlord* or *lessor*. The person who is given possession of the property is the *tenant* or *lessee*. The contract between the two parties is called a *lease*. The amount the landlord is to receive for the use of the property is the *rent*.

A tenant is distinguished from a lodger or roomer in that the former has the exclusive legal possession of the property, while the latter has merely the right to use the premises subject to the control and supervision of the owner.

THE LEASE

A lease is a contract creating the relation of landlord and tenant. The lease may be oral or written, express or implied, formal or simple, subject, however, to statutory requirements in some states that a lease of land for a term longer than one year must be in writing. Regardless of the form of the lease, the parties are bound by the terms of the contract. If a dispute arises between the tenant and the landlord over their rights and duties, the court will look to the contract to determine the correct decision. If, as so often happens, the contract is silent on the point in dispute, then the court falls back on the vast accumulation of

455

House Lease

THIS INDENTURE, made the _____6th_____ day of _____April_____, 19 63

BETWEEN   Daniel J. Slade   , Lessor *(whether one or more);*
           Cincinnati, Ohio

AND   Jerry E. and Betty L. Sargent   , Lessee *(whether one or more);*
           Cincinnati, Ohio

WITNESSETH: *That for and in consideration of the payments of the rents, and the performance of the covenants contained herein, on the part of the said Lessee, and in the manner hereinafter specified, said Lessor does hereby lease, demise and let, unto the said Lessee, that certain ___single-family___ dwelling house and its appurtenances situated at* 3780 Goodson Drive, Cincinnati 43, Ohio

for the term of ___one (1) year___, commencing on the ___1st___ day of ___May___, 19 63, and ending on the ___30th___ day of ___April___, 19 64, at the total rent or sum of ___Eighteen hundred (1800)___ Dollars, payable ___monthly___ in advance on the ___1st___ day of each and every calendar month of said term in equal ___monthly___ payments of ___One hundred fifty (150)___ Dollars,

AND *the said Lessee does hereby promise and agree to pay to the said Lessor the said rent, herein reserved in the manner herein specified.*

AND *not to let or sublet the whole or any part of said premises, nor to assign this lease, and not to make or suffer any alteration to be made therein without the written consent of the said Lessor. And it is further agreed, that the said Lessor shall not be called upon to make any improvements or repairs whatsoever upon the said premises, or any part thereof, but the said Lessee agrees to keep the same in good order and condition at___their___ own expense.*

AND *it is agreed, that if any rent shall be due and unpaid or if default shall be made in any of the covenants herein contained, then it shall be lawful for the said Lessor to re-enter the said premises and to move all persons therefrom.*

AND THAT *at the expiration of the said term or any sooner determination of this lease the said Lessee will quit and surrender the premises hereby demised, in as good order and condition as reasonable use and wear thereof will permit, damage by the elements excepted. And if the Lessee shall hold over the said term with the consent, expressed or implied, of the Lessor, such holding shall be construed to be a tenancy only from month to month, and said Lessee will pay the rent as above stated for such term as ___they___ hold___ the same. ___Lessee___ agrees to pay the water rate during the continuance of this lease.*

IN WITNESS WHEREOF: *the said parties have hereunto set their hands and seals the day and year first above written.*

_____Daniel J. Slade_____ (Seal)_____

_____Jerry E. Sargent_____ (Seal)_____

_____Betty L. Sargent_____ (Seal)_____

A Lease

judicial precedents covering the point. The judicial precedents may be supplemented by state statutes.

For the above reasons a lease should preferably be in writing and should be complete and cover all the terms of the contract. Such items as the time and place of payment of rent, the notice required to vacate, the duration or the nature of the tenancy, and any specific provision desired by either party, such as the right of the landlord to show the property to prospective purchasers or agreement requiring the landlord to redecorate, should be included.

TYPES OF TENANCIES

One becomes a tenant by contract, either express or implied. The nature of the contract determines the class of tenancy created. There are four separate and distinct classes of tenancies, each having some rule of law governing it that does not apply to any other type of tenancy. The four classes of tenancies are:

1. Tenancy for years
2. Tenancy from year to year
3. Tenancy at will
4. Tenancy by sufferance

(1) **Tenancy for Years.** A *tenancy for years* is any tenancy for a definite period of time, whether it be one month, one year, or ninety-nine years. The termination date is fixed by the lease. The payment of the rent may be by the month even when the tenancy is for ten years. Some states hold that no notice to terminate the tenancy is required when the termination date is fixed by the lease. Other states fix by statute the number of days' notice which must be given.

(2) **Tenancy from Year to Year.** When the tenancy is for an indefinite period of time with rent due at stated intervals, it is known as a *tenancy from year to year*. Under such a tenancy, a tenant merely pays the rent periodically and the lease lasts until the end of the period after proper notice of termination has been given. A tenancy of this kind may be by the week, by the month, by the year, or any other period agreed upon.

Notice to terminate this type of tenancy must follow exactly the state law governing it. In a tenancy from month to month, notice is usually required thirty days before the rent due date. In a tenancy from year to year, one group of states requires a ninety-day notice to terminate. Failure to give this notice at least ninety days before the end of the year automatically renews the lease for one more year on the same terms as those of the preceding year. Other states hold that failure to give notice of intention to terminate the lease merely creates a tenancy at will.

(3) **Tenancy at Will.** A *tenancy at will* exists when the tenant has possession of the property for an uncertain period. Either the tenant or the landlord can terminate the tenancy at will, although a reasonable notice to that effect is required, usually thirty days. Of all the types of tenancies, this is the only one that is automatically terminated upon the death of the tenant.

(4) **Tenancy by Sufferance.** When a tenant holds over his tenancy after the expiration of the lease without permission of the landlord, a *tenancy by sufferance* exists until the landlord elects to treat the tenant as a trespasser or as a tenant. The landlord may treat the tenant as a trespasser, sue him for damages, and have him removed by legal proceedings; or, if the landlord prefers, he may accept payment of the rent due for another period and thus recognize the tenant's possession as rightful.

RIGHTS OF THE TENANT

A lease gives the tenant certain rights, as follows:

1. Right to possession
2. Right to use the premises
3. Right to sublease

(1) **Right to Possession.** When the landlord signs the lease, he warrants that he has the right to lease the premises and that the tenant shall have quiet possession during the period of the lease. During the term of the lease, the tenant has the same right to exclusive possession of the premises as if he owned the property. If someone questions the owner's right to lease the property, the landlord must defend the tenant's right to exclusive possession. Failure of the landlord to give possession on time or to protect the tenant's rights subjects the landlord to liability for damages.

A particular cause of dispute between landlord and tenant is the existence of a nuisance that disturbs the tenant's quiet enjoyment of the property. If the nuisance existed at the time the tenant leased the property and he was aware of its existence, he will be deemed to have waived his right to complain. Also if the nuisance is one over which the landlord has no control, the tenant cannot avoid his contract even though the nuisance arose subsequent to the signing of the lease. If the landlord fails or refuses to abate a nuisance over which he has control, the tenant not only may terminate the lease but may sue for damages also. In other cases he may seek an injunction compelling the landlord to abate a nuisance. Failure to remove dead rats from the wall, failure to stop disorderly conduct on the part of other tenants, and frequent and unnecessary entrances upon the property by the landlord or his agents are examples of acts which the courts have held destroy the tenant's right to quiet enjoyment and constitute a breach of warranty on the part of the landlord. For such a breach the landlord may be held liable.

- Watson rented an apartment on the first floor of a three-story apartment building. The occupants on the second floor over Watson's apartment loved music and dancing. Every night they and some friends danced until midnight. Watson demanded that the landlord evict the tenants, but the landlord refused. Watson moved seven months before his lease expired. The court held he was liable for the rent since moderate dancing to soft music was not a nuisance. The court indicated that had the music been loud and the dancing rowdy, Watson would have been justified in terminating the lease.

(2) **Right to Use the Premises.** Unless this right is expressly restricted in the lease, the tenant has the right to use the premises in any way consistent with the nature of the property. He cannot convert a dwelling into a machine shop nor a clothing store into a restaurant. Damage to leased property other than that which results from ordinary wear and tear is not permissible. The tenant may cut wood for his own use but not to sell.

(3) **Right to Assign or Sublease.** If the tenant assigns his entire lease to another party who agrees to comply with its terms, including the payment of the rent to the landlord, this is an *assignment*. Unless the lease expressly prohibits both assignment and subleasing, either may be done. If only subleasing is prohibited, then the lease may be assigned. In *subleasing*, the tenant usually collects the rent from the

subtenant; in assignment the rent is paid by the assignee directly to the landlord. Assignment must include the entire premises, although one may sublease to another person only a part of the property and retain the rest.

Closely related to subleasing is joint occupancy. A provision in the lease prohibiting subleasing does not debar a contract for a joint occupancy. In joint occupancy the tenant does not give up exclusive control of any part of the premises. He merely permits another party to occupy all or a part of the premises jointly with him.

DUTIES OF THE TENANT

Duties of the tenant are:

1. To pay rent
2. To protect and preserve the premises

(1) **To Pay Rent.** The tenant's main duty is to pay the rent. This payment must be made in money unless the contract provides otherwise, such as a share of the crops. The rent is not due until the end of the term, but leases almost universally provide for rent in advance.

It is a common practice for the landlord to appoint an agent for the purpose of collecting the rent. The death of the principal automatically terminates the principal-agent relationship. If rent is paid to the agent after this termination and the agent does not remit to the proper party, the rent must be paid again.

If the rent is not paid on time, the landlord may terminate the lease and order the tenant to vacate, or he may permit the tenant to continue occupancy and sue for the rent. Under the common law the landlord could seize and hold any personal property found on the premises. This right has been either curtailed or abolished by statute. Most states permit the landlord to obtain a *distress warrant* and have the sheriff sell the property to pay the rent.

(2) **To Protect and Preserve the Premises.** The tenant must make all repairs necessary to prevent damage to or deterioration of the premises. He is not required to make repairs of a structural nature, however. If the roof blows off, the tenant need not put on a new roof unless he wishes to keep out the snow and rain. The landlord is under no obligation to put on a new roof, either, unless a state law requires the landlord to keep the property habitable.

RIGHTS OF THE LANDLORD

The landlord has three definite rights under the lease:

1. To regain possession
2. To enter upon the property to preserve it
3. To assign his rights

(1) To Regain Possession. Upon the termination of the lease, the landlord has the right to regain peaceable possession of the premises. If this possession is refused, the most common remedy is to bring an *action of ejectment* in a court of law. Upon the successful completion of this suit, the sheriff will forcibly remove the tenant and his property.

When the landlord repossesses the property, he may also retain all permanent improvements and fixtures securely fastened to the property. The test is whether or not the improvements have become a part of the real estate. If they have, they cannot be removed.

(2) To Enter Upon the Property to Preserve It. The landlord has a right to enter upon the property to preserve it. He cannot make extensive renovations that interfere with the tenant's peaceable occupancy. If the roof blows off or becomes leaky, the landlord may repair it or put on a new roof. He cannot use this occasion to add another story. If the landlord comes upon the property without permission, he may be treated as a stranger. He has no right to show the property to prospective purchasers or tenants. He may, of course, reserve this right in the lease itself.

(3) To Assign His Rights. The landlord has the right to assign his rights under the lease to a third party. The tenant cannot avoid any of his duties and obligations by reason of the assignment of the lease. Like all other assignments, the assignment does not release the assignor from the contract without the consent of the tenant. If, for example, the tenant was injured because of a concealed but defective water main cover, and the landlord knew of this condition, the landlord would be liable even though he assigned his rights before the injury.

DUTIES OF THE LANDLORD

The lease imposes certain duties upon the landlord:

1. To pay taxes
2. To protect the tenant from latent defects

(1) To Pay Taxes. Although the tenant occupies and uses the premises, the landlord must pay all taxes and special assessments. Sometimes the lease provides that the tenant shall pay the taxes. In such event, he is not liable for special assessments for sidewalks, street paving, and other improvements.

(2) To Protect the Tenant from Latent Defects. If the tenant is damaged because of latent defects, the landlord is liable. Such defects might be contamination from contagious germs, unfilled wells that are concealed, and rotten timbers in the dwelling. Defects which can be seen by inspection are the tenant's responsibility. Most cities and many states have tenement laws that require the landlord to keep all rental property habitable and provided with adequate fire escapes. Any damage due to a failure to observe these laws may subject the landlord to liability for damages.

TERMINATION OF THE LEASE

A lease that is to exist for a fixed time automatically terminates upon the expiration of that period. The death of either party does not ordinarily affect the lease. If the leased property consists of rooms or apartments in a building and they are destroyed by fire or any other accidental cause, the lease is terminated without liability on the part

---

NOTICE TO LEAVE THE PREMISES

To Mr. C. Harold Whitmore

You will please take notice that I want you to leave the premises you now occupy, and which you have rented of me, situated and described as follows:

Suite 4

Lakeview Apartment

Lake Shore Drive at Overview Street

in Cleveland, County of Cuyahoga and State of Ohio

Your compliance with this Notice by July 31

will prevent legal measures being taken by me to obtain possession of the same, agreeably to law.

Yours respectfully, H. L. Simpson

May 1 19

A Landlord's Notice to Leave the Premises

of the tenant. The landlord may agree to the voluntary surrender of the possession of the premises before the lease expires. An abandonment of the premises without the consent of the landlord is not a surrender, however, but a breach of contract.

If the lease is to run from year to year or from month to month, the party wishing to terminate it must give the other party a written notice of his intention. Statutes prescribe the time and the manner of giving notice; they may also specify other particulars, such as the grounds for a termination of the tenancy.

If either party fails to give proper notice, the other party may continue the tenancy for another period.

A tenant refusing to surrender possession of the property after the expiration of his lease may be liable in a summary action brought by the landlord to regain possession. This is called a *forcible entry and detainer action.* In this matter the statutes of the different states have provided for the quick recovery of real property by the one legally entitled to it.

In long-term leases for business purposes, serious problems arise if the property is destroyed by fire, tornado, or other causes. Under the common law the tenant had to continue to pay rent even though the property was destroyed. Many states retain this rule while other states have modified it. If the landlord has a ten-year lease on a $100,000 building and it is destroyed by fire one year after the lease is signed, he would not be inclined to rebuild it if he has full fire insurance coverage. He would find it more profitable to invest his $100,000 and continue to collect the rent. To prevent this, the Georgia law, for example, provides that if the landlord refuses to restore the property, the lease is canceled. The lease itself may contain a can-

---

To _____ Mr. George A. Hardwick _____

_____ 1719 Glenview Road, St. Louis, Missouri _____

Take notice that I shall on the __31st_____ day of __March_____, 19___,

quit the possession and remove from the premises located at_____

_____ 1292 Clarendon Road, St. Louis, Missouri _____

_____

which I now hold as your tenant. This __2nd_____ day of __January_____, 19___.

John N. Richter

A Tenant's Notice That He Is Leaving the Premises

cellation clause. If it does not, the tenant can carry fire insurance for the amount of his possible loss.

IMPROVEMENTS

Tenants frequently make improvements during the life of the lease. Many disputes arise as to the tenant's right to take these improvements with him. The test is whether an improvement is temporary or permanent. If a farm tenant builds a fence in the normal way, the fence is a permanent improvement, and he has no right to remove it when he leaves. If the fence is loosely attached to temporary posts in such a manner as to indicate temporary usefulness, it is removable. In one case it was held that a poultry house built in the usual way was a permanent improvement and could not be removed. In a similar case the tenant built the poultry house on sled-like runners. When he was ready to leave, he hitched his team to the poultry house and hauled it away. The court held that he was within his rights because it was a temporary improvement.

It is well to remember that one may freely contract away his rights or he may waive them. In one case a tenant built a permanent frame house on leased property with the landlord's assurance that he could remove the house at the end of the lease. The landlord was bound by this contract.

EASEMENTS AND LICENSES

An *easement* is an interest in land, such as a right-of-way across another's land or the use of another's driveway. Strictly speaking, an easement is not a tenancy, but it is in the nature of an estate. Being an interest in land, the right must be created by a written contract or acquired by adverse possession by continued and uninterrupted use of the land.

A *license* is not an interest in land but a right to use in some minor way the real property of another. It may be acquired by an oral contract if the license is to run for one year or less.

QUESTIONS

1. Distinguish between a tenant and a lodger.
2. Explain the difference between subleasing and assigning.

3. Does a tenant have exclusive control of the leased premises?
4. May a tenant refuse to let the landlord enter upon the premises during the period of the lease?
5. What rights does the tenant have when he leases property?
6. (a) If a hurricane breaks all the windows in a dwelling, must the tenant replace these windows at his own expense?
   (b) If leased property is destroyed by fire, must the tenant continue to pay rent?
7. Who must pay the taxes on leased property, the landlord or the tenant?
8. Name three rights that a landlord has.
9. If a tenant builds a garage on the property, may he take the garage with him when he moves? Explain.
10. What is an easement?

CASE PROBLEMS

1. A storm blew off the roof of a farm house. At his own expense the tenant immediately put on a new roof. The contract was silent about repairs. The tenant refused to pay any more rent until the rent equaled the cost of the roof. The landlord brought suit to evict the tenant for nonpayment of rent. Who was entitled to win the suit?

2. Ellis leased a house from Hunt. About one month after moving in, Mrs. Ellis fell through the wooden floor of a back porch and was seriously injured. The floor was badly infested with termites, but this fact could not be detected by a casual inspection. Ellis sued Hunt for damages. Is he entitled to them?

3. Arnold rented a building in a new shopping center for a dress shop. The lease was for five years with an option for renewal. One year later Arnold sold the business in bulk to Redwine who agreed to take over the lease and make all rent payments to the landlord. The lease contained a clause prohibiting subleasing. The landlord demanded that Redwine vacate the premises. Must Redwine do so?

4. West leased a building for ten years to be used for a men's clothing store. The rent was $1,000 a month. There was no cancellation clause in the lease, and the state law followed the common law. Due to the rapid growth of the city, five years later similar property would rent for $1,500 a month. The building was damaged by fire so badly it could not be used until restored. (a) Must the landlord restore the property? (b) Must the tenant restore the property? (c) Could West protect himself for the monthly rent by carrying a fire insurance policy? (d) If there had been a cancellation clause in the lease, what would your answer be to (c)? (e) Under (d) would the landlord be inclined to cancel the lease? (f) If the landlord does cancel the lease, does West have an insurable interest to protect him against having to pay $1,500 a month for the restored building?

5. Harrel rented an apartment for one year starting September 1. The rent was $150 a month. The state law stipulated that if either party did not wish to renew the lease, he must give notice to that effect ninety days before the lease expires. The following June 1 Harrel thought he wanted to keep the apartment for another year and did not give notice of intent to terminate it. On July 1, he was told by his employer he was being transferred to another state on August 1. What might Harrel do to minimize his loss in this case?

6. On May 15 Pauly rented a house by oral agreement for one year; the occupancy was to begin on June 1. In the state where this property was located, when property is rented from month to month, a thirty-day notice of intention to vacate is required. If the rental contract is for one year or more, a ninety-day notice must be given. A failure to give the required notice renews the contract. On April 28 of the following year, Pauly gave written notice that he intended to vacate the house on June 1. The landlord contended that the lease ran for one more year. Was this correct?

7. Rex purchased the timber on Howington's farm. He could save considerable time and expense by crossing Brown's land. Brown agreed orally to let Rex cross his land upon the payment of $10. When the job was half completed, Brown attempted to prevent Rex from crossing his land. Did he have the right to stop him?

CHAPTER 47

WILLS AND
INHERITANCES

WILLS

Title to all property, both real and personal, may be transferred by a will. A *will* is an instrument, prepared in the form prescribed by law, which provides for the disposition of a person's property to take effect after death. A will is not a contract, but it has the effect and force of a contract after the one who makes the will dies.

Although a will is not a contract, practically the same rules that determine competency to contract apply to wills. Any person, other than a minor, of sound mind ordinarily is competent to make a will. In a few states minors can, under limited circumstances, make a will.

LIMITATIONS ON FREEDOM TO DISPOSE OF PROPERTY BY WILL

The right to dispose of property by will is a highly prized right and but few restrictions are placed upon it. These restrictions are:

(1) One cannot deprive a spouse of his common-law right in the property unless this right has been abolished by statute. Under the common law, and the statutory law in many states, the wife is entitled to a life interest in one third of any real property that her husband owned at the time of his death. This right is termed *dower*. It does not extend to personal property. Dower is sometimes called the "widow's third." If the husband made a provision for his wife in his will, the wife may usually elect either to take the right of dower or to take under the will.

Curtesy is the right that a husband has in the real property of his wife after her death. The right of curtesy does not exist unless a lawful

467

marriage was entered into and a child capable of inheriting was born. The fact that the child may have died immediately after birth does not affect the right. Many states have abolished the right of curtesy. In those states the husband takes a one-third interest in the property in the same manner as a widow.

Some states have changed or abolished both dower and curtesy. In such a case the surviving wife or husband inherits according to the statutory provision of the particular state.

(2) Confidential data cannot be bequeathed. A public official, such as the Secretary of State, cannot leave confidential data to a legatee.

(3) One cannot control by will the distribution of his property in perpetuity. The maximum time for the vesting of a devised estate under the rule against perpetuities is fixed as the duration of lives now in being, such as A and B, and until a third party, such as C, reaches twenty-one.

(4) In a few states, one cannot, through the provisions of a will, deprive a spouse, a child, or a parent of more than half his estate by leaving it to charity.

TERMS COMMON TO WILLS

The person making the will is called a *testator*, if a man, and a *testatrix*, if a woman. If the gift is real estate, the one receiving the gift (the beneficiary) is called the *devisee;* if it is personal property, he is called the *legatee.* A *bequest* is a gift of personal property in general. A *legacy* is a gift of a sum of money. The person named in a will as the one to administer the estate is an *executor* (man) or an *executrix* (woman). One who dies without having made a will is said to die *intestate.* The person appointed by a court to settle the affairs of an intestate is an *administrator* (man) or an *administratrix* (woman).

DISTINGUISHING CHARACTERISTICS OF A WILL

A will has the following outstanding characteristics that distinguish it from many other legal instruments:

(1) A will is construed by the courts with less technical strictness than a deed or any other kind of written document.

(2) A will devising real property must be executed in conformity with the law of the state in which the property is situated. A will

bequeathing personal property is governed by the law of the state in which the testator was domiciled at the time of his death.

(3) A will may be revoked at any time during the life of the testator, and at his pleasure.

FORMALITIES

All states, either by legislative enactment or judicial decision, have prescribed the formalities for wills. These formalities vary from extreme simplicity to absurd complexity, but, simple or complex, the form must be strictly adhered to.

When property is left by will, title does not vest in the devisee until the will is probated, that is, until the court directs that the terms of the will be carried out. Naturally this division of property could not be accomplished if the will were not in writing. If a will is written in the testator's own handwriting and is dated, it need not be witnessed in more than a third of the states. In all other states the will must be witnessed by at least two, and in some states three, witnesses regardless of how it is written. The same rule applies in the other states if the will is typed or printed. Probably it is this requirement which has resulted in more wills being broken than any other requirement. The usual requirement is for the witnesses and the testator to sign in the presence of each other.

- In Georgia a man lay dying in a bed that was in the center of the room. When the witnesses to his will signed the will, they used a table six feet in back of the head of the bed; as a result, the testator did not see them sign the will. The court would not probate the will because the witnesses did not sign in the presence of the testator.

Usually the witnesses must testify when the will is probated that they signed the will as indicated by their signatures. Some typical pieces of testimony which have destroyed wills are: "He didn't say, 'This is my last will and testament' "; "After I signed it, the lawyer took it into another room for the boss to sign it"; "He told me he was making me his executor, but I didn't know this disqualified me as a witness"; "I didn't know a beneficiary couldn't be a witness."

These and many other instances testify to the extreme urgency of seeing that every technical requirement of the law is complied with. If a person's will is not drawn according to the legal requirements, the court may disregard it and the property may be disposed of in a manner entirely foreign to the testator's wishes.

LAST WILL AND TESTAMENT OF F. J. ROSE

I, F. J. Rose, of the City of Chicago and State of Illinois, do make, publish, and declare this to be my last Will and Testament in manner following:

FIRST: I direct that all my just debts, funeral expenses, and the cost of administering my estate be paid by my executrix hereinafter named.

SECOND: I give, devise, and bequeath to my beloved daughter, Anna Rose Scott, now residing in Englewood, New Jersey, that certain piece of real estate, with all improvements thereon, situated in the same city and at the corner of Hudson Avenue and Tenafly Road.

THIRD: All the remainder and residue of my property, real, personal, and mixed, I give to my beloved wife, Mary Ellen Rose, for her use and forever.

FOURTH: I hereby nominate and appoint my wife, Mary Ellen Rose, executrix of this, my last Will and Testament, and I direct that she not be required to give bond or security for the performance of her duties as such.

LASTLY: I hereby revoke any and all former wills by me made.

In witness whereof I have hereunto set my hand this tenth day of October, in the year nineteen hundred .

F. J. Rose

Signed, published, and declared by the above-named F. J. Rose as and for his last Will and Testament, in the presence of us and each of us, who, in his presence, and at his request, and in the presence of one another, have hereunto subscribed our names as witnesses on the day and in the year above written.

C. O. Moore   4316 Cottage Grove Avenue, Chicago, Ill.

Sarah J. King   1313 East 63 Street, Chicago, Ill.

J. J. Samuels   2611 Elm Street, Joliet, Ill.

A Will

SPECIAL TYPES OF WILLS

There are at least three special types of wills to meet special circumstances. First, there are *holographic wills*, which are written entirely in longhand by the testator. Many states will permit such wills to be probated even if there are no witnesses to the will. If its validity is questioned, a handwriting expert can prove whether or not the handwriting in the will is that of the testator. Second, there are *nuncupative wills*, which are oral wills. An emergency, such as a serious injury in an automobile accident, may make it necessary to make an oral will. The testator, who may be conscious of imminent death, may summon two or more people and orally make his will. These witnesses must then reduce the will to writing within a specified number of days. Some states limit the use of nuncupative wills to members of the armed forces in time of war and mariners at sea. Third, most states make special provision for blind people. The reason for these laws is to excuse blind people from the requirement to see all witnesses sign.

THE WORDING OF A WILL

Any words that convey the intention of the testator are sufficient. No matter how inelegant and ungrammatical the language may be, if the intention of the testator can be ascertained, the court will order that the provisions of the will be carried out. Poor wording in wills, however, is not confined to the illiterate. Since the court will order the terms of a will to be carried out exactly, the wording of the will should express the exact wishes of the testator.

- A well-to-do man, who had provided for his children previously, inserted into his will this provision: "To my brother, Kirby, I leave $8,000." By the time the testator died, his estate had shrunk from $80,000 to $10,000. He had intended to leave his brother one tenth of his estate; but, because of the wording used in the will, his brother received almost the entire estate after the expenses were paid. The testator should have written, "To my brother, Kirby, I leave one tenth of my estate, which sum in no event is to exceed $8,000."

- Two sisters drew wills, each leaving the other all her property. It was their intention that the survivor was to use the estate until her death, at which time she would devise it so that a worthless brother would not get any part of it. They both died at the same time in an automobile accident, and the brother inherited the entire estate. Their prime purpose in making a will had been to keep their property from going to "laughing heirs," those who are delighted when the testator dies. They could have prevented this by including a "common disaster" clause, stipulating how their estate should be distributed in the event both died simultaneously or even within thirty days of each other. Had they done this, the brother would not have gained the entire estates of his sisters.

The flaws in the wills described in the preceding paragraphs indicate clearly the danger of relying on "homemade" wills. The task of preparing a will which will meet all legal technicalities is clearly a job for an expert. This does not relieve the testator from all responsibility, however. A will may be expertly drawn, but later events may demand a modification.

- Another man left by his will everything he possessed to his wife. The language was clear and explicit. Soon after the will was drawn, a child was born; but no change was made in the will. In most states a man cannot entirely disinherit his children. He must at least recognize them in his will, or the document will be void. In this particular case after the man died, the will was disqualified; one third of the estate went to the wife, and two thirds to the child. The child's part could not be spent except under court order. Before the child became self-supporting, court costs and lawyer's fees consumed 60 percent of the estate. The father's intentions were to enable his wife to use the money as she saw fit to provide for the child. He should have altered the will as soon as the child was born and left a nominal sum to the child and the bulk of the estate to his wife.

ABATEMENT AND ADEMPTION

If a testator leaves $20,000 to his son John, $10,000 to his sister Mary, and a painting to his brother Adam, it is possible there will be both an abatement and an ademption in the will. When the will is probated, there may not be enough money after all debts are paid to comply with the terms of the will. If there is only $15,000 in cash left, then the cash gifts to John and Mary will *abate*. This means each will receive a proportionate share, in this case fifty percent, or $10,000 and $5,000 respectively. If the painting was sold, stolen, or destroyed before the death of the testator, then Adam would get nothing. The gift to him is *adeemed* since the property is not in existence at the time of the testator's death. He is not entitled to its cash value or any other substitute item of property.

- Graham provided in his will that his son, Henry, was to receive his lakeside home, Agua Vista, and the boat and boathouse. Before Graham died, he sold this property and purchased with the proceeds a beach home in Florida. He did not change his will. When he died, Henry demanded the beach home. He was not entitled to it since his devise adempted.

PROBATION OF A WILL

When the testator dies leaving a will, the will must be probated. Probation is a very simple process if there is no contest of the will. If the will does not name an executor, then upon petition of one of the beneficiaries the court will appoint an administrator. The executor or the administrator will proceed to carry out his duties as described in the succeeding paragraph. After proper notice has been given to the public and all interested parties, the executor will ask the court to order the terms of the will to be carried out. If specific pieces of property have been devised and have not adempted, then the devisees will receive this property. If the property is real estate, the devisees will receive an administrator's deed. If the property is personal property, carrying out the will consists merely of delivering the property to the proper parties. After all administrative expenses have been paid, all cash will then be paid to the parties determined by the court to be entitled to it. As the final act in the probation, the executor will be discharged from his duties and his bondsmen released.

If the will is contested, the procedure is the same as in an uncontested will except the court must hear the contest to determine if it is valid. If the will is held to be valid, then the court will order the executor to proceed with the probation. As a rule, the will is either valid or invalid in its entirety. The suit contesting the will may not attempt to invalidate the entire will but merely to clarify or modify certain provisions because of ambiguity or mathematical errors. If the contest alleges and proves fraud, undue influence, improper witnessing, mental incapacity of the testator, revocation of the will, or any other infirmity in the will affecting its legality, the entire will is nullified and the property of the testator distributed according to the law of descent described later in this chapter.

REVOCATION

A will may be revoked at any time prior to the death of the testator. The revocation may take any one of several forms.

(1) Destruction or Alteration. If the testator deliberately destroys a will, this constitutes a revocation. If the testator merely alters the will, this may or may not revoke it depending upon the nature and the extent of the alteration. If he merely obliterates a part of the will, this in most states does not revoke the will. If, however, he interlines additional bequests in the will then the will is revoked unless it is rewitnessed.

(2) Marriage and Divorce. If a single man makes a will and later marries, this automatically revokes the will on the grounds that new moral obligations have been created by the marriage. A man cannot deprive by will his wife of her dower right. If he made the will before he was married and bequeathed the entire estate, the terms of the will could not be carried out without depriving the wife of her dower right. A divorce automatically revokes a will if there is a property settlement; otherwise, a divorce in no way affects the will.

(3) Execution of a Later Will. The execution of a later will automatically revokes a prior will if the terms of the second will are inconsistent with the first will. If the second will merely changes a few provisions in the first will and leaves the bulk of it intact, then a second will does not revoke the first. Most lawyers prefer to incorporate the terms of the first will in the second and insert a clause that all prior will are expressly revoked. This will often avoid a contest.

(4) After-Born Child. If a child is born after the will is made, and no codicil is added to provide for the after-born child, then this will revoke the will. If the will provides that the entire estate shall go to the testator's three children, share and share alike, then the court will merely order the executor to distribute the property in four parts instead of three. In this case the will is not revoked.

CODICIL

A *codicil* is an addition that is written below the main portion of the will, after the signature. It is considered a supplement to the will. The word "codicil" literally means a "little will." A codicil must be executed with all the formalities of the original will and must be signed and witnessed in like manner.

TITLE BY DESCENT

When a person dies intestate, his property is distributed in accordance with the state law of descent. Every state in the union has such a law. Although these laws vary slightly, on the whole they provide as follows: The property of the intestate, especially his real estate, goes to his children subject to the dower (or curtesy) right of the surviving spouse. If there are no surviving children or grandchildren, the father and the mother, as the next of kin, receive the property. If they are not living, the brothers and sisters become the next of kin; and they are followed by grandparents, aunts and uncles, and so on. Some laws trace the kinship as far as third cousins; others let nieces and nephews precede grandparents. If there are no relatives in the range set out in the statute, the property belongs to the state.

If the owner of property makes no will but leaves his property to be distributed according to the law of descent in force in his state, he has no assurance that his property will be distributed in the manner he desires.

- A man gave his wife a $50,000 home which he had bought with money he had inherited from his parents. Shortly afterward, his wife died without leaving a will. A $20,000 share in the home thereupon went to the dead wife's brother.

PER CAPITA AND PER STIRPES DISTRIBUTION

The lineal descendants of a testator are his children and his grandchildren. If all his children are living at the time of the father's death, and his wife has predeceased him, his property will be distributed *per capita*. If one child predeceased the father and left three surviving children, then the property would be divided into three equal parts and one third would then be divided into three equal parts with one of these parts going to each of the grandchildren. When this is done, the property is said to be divided *per stirpes*. If the deceased child left no children and no wife, then the surviving children would take its share.

EXECUTORS AND ADMINISTRATORS

For the most part the duties and responsibilities of executors and administrators are similar, but there are three significant differences. (1) With but few exceptions anyone may be appointed an executor; but in the appointment of an administrator, there is a clear order of priority in most states. The surviving spouse has first priority, followed by children, grandchildren, parents, and brothers or sisters. One's right to be an administrator is not absolute; certain minimum qualifications as to age, education, and residence are required. (2) An executor looks to the will to ascertain his duties and authority, while the administrator must look to the law governing administrators. (3) The executor may be excused by the testator from furnishing a bond, but an administrator must in all cases execute a bond guaranteeing his faithful performance of his duties. In rare cases the court may require a bond of an executor even when the will expressly exempts him.

The prime duty of an executor or an administrator is to preserve the estate and distribute it to the rightful parties. Any loss due to negligence, bad faith, or breach of trust subjects him to liability. He is required to act in good faith, with prudence, and within the powers conferred on him by will or by law. If any part of the estate is a going business, with but few exceptions the business must be dissolved. All existing contracts must be carried out, but no new commitments may be made except those necessary to preserve the estate or fulfill a contract. If a manufacturer, for example, has $10,000 worth of "goods in process," these may be carried on to finished goods so as to make them salable. A contract to purchase new raw materials to accomplish this purpose is binding on the estate. A will may expressly provide that the executor continue the business. But since neither an executor nor an administrator is an agent of the deceased, nor of the estate, he cannot bind the estate on contracts except those expressly authorized by will or those necessary for a proper administration of an estate. Third parties are charged with knowing these limitations upon the administrator's authority.

A will does not become effective until the death of the testator. If part of the property devised is sold before the will is in effect, the will is inoperative in regard to that particular piece of property.

In addition to an executor, many wills appoint a guardian for the minor children. If this is not done in a will, the court will do so. It is a question of which is the wiser course. Probably the safest plan is for the testator to appoint some close relative in whom he has confidence for the care of the surviving children.

QUESTIONS

1. What is a will?
2. What restrictions are there upon one's right to leave his property by will to anyone he chooses?
3. If one receives $5,000 by will, is this a bequest or a legacy?
4. How does one get actual title to property left to him by will?
5. (a) Do all states require all wills to be witnessed?
   (b) How many witnesses are required to validate a will when witnesses are required?
6. What is the difference between ademption and abatement?
7. What is the difference between distributing property per capita and per stirpes?
8. Does a second will automatically revoke a first will?
9. Do the devisees under a will inherit the real property or the right to get the real property? Explain.

10. If a testator has real estate in California and personal property in Georgia, the laws of which state apply to the will if he was living in Georgia at the time of his death?

11. Must the testator obtain the consent of the beneficiaries of the will before he can revoke it?

12. Must a codicil be witnessed in the same way as a will?

CASE PROBLEMS

1. Kirkland, sales manager for the Langford Furniture Company, received an order for furniture amounting to $10,285 from the John Quarles Furniture Mart. The order was signed by John Knowles, executor for John Quarles. Kirkland shipped the merchandise promptly. When the account was long past due, it was found upon investigation that Quarles' will had never authorized Knowles to continue the business. The heirs of Quarles demanded that the bill not be paid. Kirkland sued both the estate and John Knowles, executor. There were no bondsmen. Knowles was insolvent. Could Kirkland look to the estate for this debt?

2. Tom Middlebrooks, age twenty-nine and unmarried, made a will and left all of his property, both personal and real, to his church since he had not planned to get married. Later he married Cynthia, but he failed to revoke his will. Over a period of twenty years he accumulated a considerable estate. After his death, the church pastor found the will and presented it to the court for probate since Tom had left his wife and children ample property by gift for their needs. Will the court order the property to be transferred to the church?

3. Joseph made a will and left his son, Johnathon, 1,000 shares of stock in the United States Steel Corporation. Before Joseph died, he sold the stock and purchased with the proceeds stock in the Atlantic Steel Corporation. When the will was offered for probate after Joseph's death, Johnathon petitioned the court to have the stock in the Atlantic Steel Corporation transferred to him. Is he entitled to this stock?

4. Bunting died intestate, leaving an estate of $300,000. He had two children, John and Harold, who survived him. One child, Bentley, had predeceased him, leaving three minor children. In addition, Bunting had raised his brother's son James but had never formally adopted him. How will this property be distributed?

5. Henry's father died leaving an estate of $200,000. Henry was named as the executor in the will. When the fire insurance policies on two of the houses belonging to the estate expired, Henry failed to have them renewed. Several months later one of the houses was totally destroyed by fire. The beneficiaries of the estate demanded that this loss be borne by Henry. Are they correct in their demand?

6. Welch, a single man, sold a patent for $50,000. He then married Evaline and gave her $25,000 in government E bonds as a wedding present.

Shortly after their marriage Evaline died. They had no children, and Evaline left no will. Welch's mother-in-law demanded one half of the E bonds. Was she entitled to them?

7. Over the years Harvey and his wife, Lydia, accumulated an estate of $200,000. Harvey made a will leaving all his property, both personal and real, to Lydia. Two or three years later they were divorced, but no property settlement was made. Harvey remarried. Soon after his remarriage, he died without having changed or revoked his will. Sally, his second wife, demanded all his estate since there were no children. Lydia claimed that all the estate belonged to her. Who was entitled to the estate, Sally or Lydia?

8. McKay, who was seriously injured in an automobile accident, was convinced that he would die. He told two of his friends how he wanted his property distributed. The next day these two men wrote down what McKay told them and both signed it. McKay recovered in about three weeks but then died of a heart attack about two weeks later. There was no connection between his heart attack and his injury in the automobile accident. McKay did nothing before he died to change his oral will. One son, Todd, was dissatisfied with his share of the estate and took legal action to bar a probation of the oral will. Was the will valid?

9. At the time of his death Cohen lived in Georgia. He owned personal property worth over $1,000,000, most of which was kept in Virginia. The Georgia law requires three witnesses to a will, while the Virginia law requires only two witnesses. Cohen made a will just one month before his death and obtained two witnesses to his signature. He left $500,000 to a charitable organization. His two sons brought an action to invalidate the will because it did not meet the requirements of the Georgia law. Was this a valid will?

CHAPTER 48

BANKRUPTCY

PURPOSES OF BANKRUPTCY

Bankruptcy is a legal, not a financial status. No matter what the status of one's finances may be, he is not bankrupt until the court in a bankruptcy proceeding declares him a bankrupt. Insolvency is purely a financial status, that is, inability to pay one's debts. It may warrant a petition asking the court to declare the insolvent person a bankrupt; but mere insolvency is not bankruptcy. The Bankruptcy Act defines *insolvency* as insufficient assets to pay all debts outstanding, or an inability to pay one's debts when they come due.

The bankruptcy law has two very definite purposes:

1. To give the debtor a new start
2. To give creditors an equal chance in the collection of their claims

(1) **To Give Debtor a New Start.** If an honest debtor is hopelessly insolvent, he may be tempted to cease trying even to earn a living. Hope is the great stimulant to enterprise and honest endeavor. If hope vanishes, effort diminishes or may even vanish. By permitting an insolvent debtor to give up all his assets with a few minor exceptions and thereby get forgiveness of his debts, he can at least start anew with the hope of success. Frequently a debtor has assets considerably in excess of his debts, but the assets are "frozen" so that he cannot obtain enough cash to pay his current claims. The present Bankruptcy Act allows one to go into receivership without actually being declared a bankrupt. The court prescribes an equitable settlement under the circumstances; and when these conditions are fully met, the debtor may resume full control of his business.

(2) To Give Creditors an Equal Chance. If one is bankrupt, it is unfair to permit some unsecured creditors to get paid in full while others receive nothing. By appointing a trustee to take over the bankrupt's property and to pay each creditor in proportion to his claim, a more equitable settlement is achieved. Not only is this arrangement more equitable, but it is also less wasteful and less expensive than for each creditor to sue the debtor in separate suits.

WHO MAY FILE A PETITION FOR BANKRUPTCY

Originally only traders were permitted to become bankrupt since bankruptcy was only for those who suffered losses due to no fault of their own. Today any business or person may become a bankrupt, either voluntarily or involuntarily, except banks, insurance companies, savings and loan associations, railroads, and municipalities. All of these exempted institutions except municipalities may be thrown into receivership but cannot formally be declared bankrupt. A receiver is appointed to take charge of the assets and if possible to restore the firm to financial solvency.

KINDS OF BANKRUPTCY

There are two kinds of bankruptcy:

1. Voluntary
2. Involuntary

(1) Voluntary Bankruptcy. Anyone, except a city, a railroad, an insurance company, or a bank, may file a voluntary petition to be adjudicated a bankrupt. It is not necessary that the petitioner be insolvent, but in practice only insolvent debtors ask to be declared bankrupt.

(2) Involuntary Bankruptcy. Under certain conditions one may be forced into involuntary bankruptcy. Three or more creditors, whose aggregate claims amount to $500 in excess of any collateral held as security, are necessary to file a petition to have an insolvent debtor declared a bankrupt if there are twelve or more creditors.

If the debtor is declared a bankrupt, the procedure in liquidating his estate is the same whether it is a voluntary bankruptcy proceeding or an involuntary one.

ACTS OF BANKRUPTCY

Before one may be declared an involuntary bankrupt, he must have committed an act of bankruptcy. Any one of the following six acts is considered sufficient to warrant the court in declaring the debtor an involuntary bankrupt:

1. A fraudulent transfer
2. Giving preference to creditors
3. Permitting a lien to be obtained
4. Assignment of claims for the benefit of creditors
5. Appointing a receiver for assets
6. Admitting insolvency in writing

(1) Fraudulent Transfers. As a rule, insolvency is not a sudden catastrophe but a creeping malady. When a debtor realizes he is in financial difficulty, he may attempt to transfer some of his property beyond the reach of his creditors. If these transfers are made without an adequate consideration with the intent that he will later get the property back, the transfer is fraudulent. If the transfer is made within four months immediately preceding the filing of a petition in bankruptcy, the court may presume intent to defraud existing creditors. If the transfer is made within twelve months preceding the filing of the petition, the creditors may have the transfers declared null and void if they can prove intent to defraud.

(2) Giving Preferences to Creditors. If within four months immediately preceding the filing of the petition in bankruptcy the debtor transfers property to a creditor with the intent to prefer one creditor over another creditor, this is an act of bankruptcy. Not only is it an act of bankruptcy, but the trustees in bankruptcy may petition the court to have the transfer avoided and the property restored to the debtor's estate. Before the transfer can be avoided, the trustee must prove not only that the debtor had the intent to prefer one creditor over another but also that the creditor at the time of the transfer had reasonable cause to believe that the debtor was insolvent. Every transfer during insolvency cannot be avoided. If this were not true, then no business firm could pay any of its debts during a period of financial stringency without committing an act of bankruptcy.

(3) Permitting a Lien to Be Obtained. If an insolvent debtor permits a lien to be obtained against him through a legal proceeding, he has committed an act of bankruptcy. The debtor may redeem himself, however, by paying the lien within thirty days, or at least five days before the enforcement of the lien.

> ▪ Spivak owed ten various creditors $75,000. He had assets of $30,000 in real property and $10,000 in personal property. One of the creditors obtained judgment for $5,000 and had the judgment recorded. He also attached two trucks worth $3,000. Both these liens are acts of bankruptcy. To avoid being declared an involuntary bankrupt, Spivak must pay them within thirty days or sooner if the property is to be sold at a sheriff's sale.

(4) **Assignment of Claims for the Benefit of Creditors.** If an insolvent debtor makes an assignment of claims due him for the benefit of some of his creditors, he commits an act of bankruptcy.

(5) **Appointing a Receiver for Assets.** An insolvent debtor may have the court appoint a receiver for his estate. Also, under most state laws the creditors may have a receiver appointed. For either this voluntary or involuntary appointment of a receiver to be an act of bankruptcy, the debtor must be insolvent. Insolvency in this sense does not necessarily mean an excess of liabilities over assets. It means a mere inability to pay one's debts as they mature. The receiver, with the permission of the court, may permit the debtor to continue to operate his business under strict supervision of the trustee. If the operation of the business proves successful and all debts are paid, then the debtor is restored to full control.

(6) **Admitting Insolvency in Writing.** The debtor may admit his insolvency in writing and express his willingness to be declared a bankrupt. In this event, none of the preceding acts need be committed in order for the creditors to have him declared a bankrupt. The chief difference between this type and a voluntary petition is that the creditors must employ the counsel and advance the necessary costs for bringing the action.

PROCEDURE IN A BANKRUPTCY CASE

After the court declares a debtor bankrupt, the first step is to call a meeting of all creditors. These creditors then, with the approval of the referee in bankruptcy, elect a trustee to take over all the assets of the bankrupt. The trustee steps into the shoes of the bankrupt. He collects all debts due the bankrupt, preserves all physical assets, sues all delinquent creditors of the estate, and finally distributes all money realized according to a definite priority which will be discussed later in this chapter.

EXEMPT PROPERTY

Each state has laws exempting certain property from seizure for the payment of debts. The most common types of property that are excluded are household effects, tools of the trade, such as a carpenter's tools, a dentist's equipment, and similar items within reasonable limits. Life insurance creates a problem because of the diversity of state laws on this subject. If the bankrupt is the insured and if he reserved the right to change the beneficiary, the general rule is that he owns the cash surrender value; and this asset must be included in his assets which he turns over to the trustee. If he did not reserve the right to change the beneficiary, the cash surrender value does not belong to him. If the policy were bought, however, in contemplation of bankruptcy and for the purpose of defrauding creditors, the trustee may order the cash surrender value included.

Most states specifically exempt all necessary wearing apparel for the bankrupt and members of his family, and such items as the family Bible, and all pictures of the members of the family even though some of these may be portraits of some value.

CORPORATE REORGANIZATION

In 1938 Congress passed a bankruptcy act designed especially for corporations. The usual result in a bankruptcy case is for the bankrupt to turn over to a trustee in bankruptcy his entire business for the purpose of having it liquidated. Under this act, the corporate business is turned over in most cases to a trustee, not to liquidate it but to operate it in the hope that the business can be restored to solvency. When solvency is restored, the business is turned back to the absolute control of the stockholders. During the time the trustee in bankruptcy operates the business, he may and usually does employ the executives of the corporation to help him operate the business. They are the employees of the trustee, not of the corporation during this period. He fixes their salaries, defines their duties, and may discharge them at his discretion.

During this interval of operation, a reorganization plan is worked out. This plan is developed in cooperation with the creditors, the stockholders, and the Securities and Exchange Commission. The federal court in which the reorganization petition is filed must approve the reorganization plan before it becomes official. If all parties concerned are satisfied with the new plan, the trustee puts it into operation by relinquishing his authority and turning over control to the new directors. In the event no acceptable plan of reorganization can be worked out, the corporation is adjudged bankrupt; and the business is liquidated like all other bankrupt firms.

ARRANGEMENTS

If the insolvent debtor is not a corporation but a person, partnership, sole proprietorship, real property owner, or wage earner, he may work out an arrangement or composition of creditors that attempts to achieve for him the same advantages the corporate reorganization act gives to corporations. Under the common law, one recalcitrant creditor could prevent a composition among creditors of an insolvent debtor. Under the present law a majority of creditors can impose a settlement upon the rebellious minority. The debtor is as fully released from his debts as if he had been formally declared a bankrupt. The purpose of these arrangements or compositions is to reduce the expense and to enable the debtor to avoid the stigma of bankruptcy. The creditors receive as much or more than they would under a full bankruptcy procedure.

DUTIES OF THE BANKRUPT

The bankrupt must cooperate fully with the trustee. He must attend all creditors' meetings when requested and furnish all relevant evidence about debts due him. He must file with the trustee a schedule of all his assets and all his liabilities. This schedule must be in sufficient detail so that the trustee can list the secured creditors, the partially secured creditors, and the unsecured creditors. Failure of the bankrupt to cooperate with the trustee and to obey all orders of the referee not only may prevent his being discharged from bankruptcy, but may also subject him to criminal prosecution for contempt of court.

PROOF OF CLAIMS

All creditors of the bankrupt must present proof of their claims to the trustee. A maximum of six months is allowed for presenting proof of claims, after which time all right to the claim is lost. This is true even though the creditor had no knowledge of the bankruptcy proceedings.

RECLAMATIONS

Frequently the bankrupt has in his possession at the time he is adjudicated a bankrupt property that does not belong to him. This property takes the form of bailed goods, or property held in trust for another, or as security for a loan. The true owner of the property is not technically a creditor of the bankrupt. He should file a reclamation claim for the specific property. If he files a proof of claim along with the other creditors, he forfeits his right to the specific property and assumes a position as a creditor.

If one is in possession of a check drawn by the bankrupt, he may or may not lose depending on the circumstances. If the check is an uncertified check, the holder is a mere creditor of the bankrupt and is not entitled to have it cashed. This is the rule because of the fact that a check is not a true assignment of the funds in the bank. If the check is certified, however, the certification constitutes an assignment of funds sufficient to pay the check no longer belong to the bankrupt. The holder can apply for a specific claim upon the fund represented by the check.

PRIORITY OF CLAIMS

All claims of a bankrupt may be classified as fully secured claims, partially secured claims, and unsecured claims. Bankruptcy does not disturb this order of priority, although the expenses of the bankruptcy proceedings take precedence even over claims that are classed as fully secured claims.

Fully secured creditors may have their claims satisfied in full from the proceeds of the assets used for security. If these assets sell for more than enough to satisfy the secured debts, the remainder becomes available to general creditors.

Partially secured creditors are those with a first lien on some assets but not enough to satisfy the debts in full. The proceeds of the assets on which there are liens are used, with the exceptions set out below, to pay the partially secured creditors, and these creditors become general creditors for the balance of their claims.

The priority of claims is as follows:

(1) The expenses of preserving and administering the estate

(2) Wage claims not exceeding $600 for any one wage earner provided the wages were earned not more than three months prior to bankruptcy proceedings

(3) Tax claims

(4) Rent due and owing at the time the bankruptcy proceedings were instituted but not to exceed three months' rent

(5) Fully secured creditors

(6) Partially secured creditors

(7) Unsecured creditors

DEBTS NOT DISCHARGED

Certain obligations cannot be avoided by bankruptcy. The most important of these claims are:

(1) Claims for alimony and child support

(2) All taxes—federal, state, and local

(3) Debts owed by reason of embezzlement or larceny

(4) Debts due on a judgment for malicious injury to others, such as a judgment obtained for assault and battery

(5) Wages earned within three months of the bankruptcy proceedings

(6) Deposits left with the bankrupt in a fiduciary capacity or as an employer who accepted a cash deposit from an employee as a fidelity bond

There are many circumstances under which certain debts are not discharged by bankruptcy, but the list above includes the most common ones.

DISCHARGE FROM BANKRUPTCY

Before the bankrupt can engage in any type of business activity, he must be discharged from bankruptcy. When the court adjudicates one a bankrupt, this operates as an application for a discharge in bankruptcy. If the bankrupt cooperates fully with the court and the trustee in bankruptcy and meets all other requirements for discharge, the application will be granted. The bankrupt is then free to engage in all types of business transactions, and his contracts are fully binding upon him. If the bankrupt is a corporation, it must wait at least six months after it is declared bankrupt before it can file an application for discharge.

QUESTIONS

1. Is bankruptcy a legal or a financial status?
2. State two purposes of the law permitting one to go bankrupt.
3. Who may be adjudicated a bankrupt?
4. What is the difference between a voluntary and an involuntary bankrupt?
5. Give an illustration of a fraudulent transfer that will be considered null and void.
6. If a business firm is insolvent, is every payment on its liabilities a preference to creditors that renders the payment an act of bankruptcy?
7. What is the purpose of listing as an act of bankruptcy the bankrupt's admitting in writing that he is insolvent and agreeing to be declared a bankrupt?
8. John, a bankrupt, had a portrait of his wife done by an artist of some note. At the time of the application for bankruptcy, the portrait had a sale value of $500. May he keep this portrait?
9. What is a reclamation?
10. What is the purpose of an arrangement?

CASE PROBLEMS

1. Henderson held a check drawn by Sellers for $700. He held this check two weeks before presenting it to the bank for payment. When he did present it, he was told that Sellers had been declared a bankrupt two days before, and for that reason the check could not be paid although Sellers had ample funds in the bank to pay it. Henderson contended Sellers had assigned $700 to him before he became bankrupt and therefore this $700 did not belong to Sellers. Was this contention correct?

2. Rachels conducted a jewelry business. He put on a big sale and took in $25,000 in cash. About thirty days later he asked the court to declare him a voluntary bankrupt. He refused to tell the trustee what he did with the $25,000. Did he have to reveal this information?

3. The three Hill brothers were laborers for Mayberry, a bankrupt. Mayberry owed each of them $300 earned in the last two months. Mayberry's assets amounted to only $1,100 after all costs of the bankruptcy proceedings were paid. His debts amounted to $11,000. How much were the Hill brothers able to collect?

4. O'Hara was in extreme financial difficulties and realized he could not avoid eventual bankruptcy. He accumulated $50,000 in cash by selling much of his property at a large discount. He then purchased a ten-year endowment insurance policy on himself and made his wife the beneficiary. He did not reserve the right to change the beneficiary. He paid for the policy with a single premium payment of $50,000. The state law provided that the cash surrender value of a life insurance policy could not be levied

on by creditors when the insured did not reserve the right to change the beneficiary. The creditors contended the cash value belonged to them since the policy was purchased while insolvent and for the purpose of defrauding the creditors. Could the trustee demand that the cash surrender value of this policy be included in the bankrupt's assets?

5. Henderson was the payee of a certified check for $2,000 given to him by Donaldson. Before the check was cashed, Donaldson was adjudicated a bankrupt. Henderson claimed that he was entitled to be paid the full $2,000 from Donaldson's bank balance before the creditors should receive anything. Is this contention correct? Why?

6. Davis borrowed $5,000 from Harrell and deposited with him 125 shares of U. S. Steel common stock as collateral security. Before Davis paid the debt, Harrell was declared bankrupt. Should Davis file a reclamation or a proof of claim? Why?

7. Middlebrooks was the accountant for the Three Minute Wash Corporation. The company owed Middlebrooks $3,000 for his salary for the past six months. After all assets were converted into cash and the cost of administration paid, there remained only $4,000 in cash. How much of this, if any, is Middlebrooks entitled to, assuming there are $30,000 in total debts, unsecured?

8. Presley had assets valued at $18,000 and liabilities of $12,000. Most of his assets were "frozen" so that he could not meet his current liabilities. To persuade one creditor not to sue him, Presley gave the creditor a deed of trust on his stock of merchandise. The other creditors sought to have Presley declared a bankrupt. Was this an act of bankruptcy?

9. Short's wife divorced him, and the court ordered Short to pay his wife $200 a month indefinitely as alimony. Short sought to avoid this claim by admitting bankruptcy. Could he do this?

10. Dr. McAlpin was declared an involuntary bankrupt. His offices were equipped with the most modern X-ray machines and other equipment, valued at $30,000. The state law stipulated that the tools of one's trade could not be attached by creditors, but the law was not specific as to what constituted tools of trade. Dr. McAlpin contended that none of his equipment need be turned over to the trustee in bankruptcy. The creditors contended that all but the bare minimum needed for general practice of medicine should be turned over. How much of this equipment could Dr. McAlpin keep?

SUMMARY CASES

PART 10

1. Jacobson by oral contract sold some standing timber to Sorenson. Sorenson started immediately to cut and haul the timber. Since there was no time limit set on when the timber was to be removed, two years later much timber remained to be cut. Jacobson then served written notice on Sorenson that he had only ten days more to complete the contract. When the ten days expired, there were about 70,000 board feet of logs on the ground that had not been removed. Jacobson refused to let him haul these away even though Sorenson was willing to pay for them. The question was raised to what extent an oral contract for the sale of interest in land can be enforced. Was this oral contract enforceable? (Sorensen et al. v. Jacobson, 125 Mont. 148, 232 P. 2d 332)

2. A 1947 Plymouth Sedan was stolen from the owner, Skellinger. The thief installed in the 1947 Plymouth a motor from a 1946 Plymouth to which he had legal title. The insurance company paid Skellinger for the theft of his 1947 Plymouth and was subrogated to his rights. Merlin Motors later purchased the 1947 Plymouth containing the 1946 motor from the thief and later sold it to Gambino, an innocent purchaser. Gambino admits he does not have good title to the entire 1947 Plymouth but contends he has title to the 1946 motor. The insurance company contended that the accession in value made by the thief to the car owned by Skellinger became the property of Skellinger and thus to the insurance company by subrogation. Is the insurance company entitled to the entire 1947 Plymouth sedan? (National Retailers Mutual Insurance Company v. Gambino, 1948, 1 N. J. Sup. 627, 64 A. 2d 927)

3. Over a period of several years, Jessie Gordon sent money to Joseph Bryan for safekeeping. In her last letter just before her death, she wrote Bryan: ". . . and at my death the money I have down there you take it and divide it among your sisters, your brother, and yourself." Gordon had made a will devising her estate to several parties, including Bryan, his sisters, and his brother. Bryan contended the $5,000 was not a part of her estate but that he, his brother, and sisters had acquired title to it by gift before Gordon's death. Was this a gift? (In re Gordon's Will, 27 N. W. 2d 900)

4. Moretti received a very painful injury from an electric fan blade projecting from the outside of the wall of the building. The building was occupied by a tenant who installed the fan. The lease was on a month-to-month basis so that the landlord could have re-entered the premises for the purpose of removing the fan by giving the tenant 30 days' notice to vacate. He did not do this, nor did he order the tenant to remove the fan. Moretti sued the landlord for damages for his injury. Is the landlord liable in this case for the injury to Moretti? (Moretti v. C. S. Realty Co., 78 R. I. 341, 82 A. 2d 608)

5. Arthur H. Kelley executed a deed to his home to his son. The deed was complete in every detail. When Kelly handed it to his son, he said, "Here is the deed to the home property. . . . The only request I want to make is that you do not record the deed until after my death." The father made many statements after this to the effect he had not given his son the property except on the condition that he die from a serious operation he was to undergo. The son's acts corroborated these statements by his failure to assume possession of the property, pay tax on it, or in anyway assert ownership during his father's lifetime. Since a deed cannot serve as a will, this deed was not effective unless there was a delivery and an acceptance for the purpose of passing title. Was there a valid delivery and acceptance? (Kelley v. Bank of America, National Trust and Savings Association, 112 Col. App. 2d 388, 246 P. 2d 92)

6. Halliday constructed an apartment building of several stories on his lot. On one side were windows to admit light and air. Hibbard, who owned the adjoining lot, constructed a building up against Halliday's lot with a solid brick wall facing the windows of Halliday's apartment building, thereby greatly reducing the value of his property. The evidence showed that Hibbard did this out of malice toward Halliday. Hibbard contended he could use his property any way he wished. Is Halliday entitled to damages for the reduced value of his property? (Hibbard v. Halliday, 58 Okla. 244, 158 P. 1158)

7. The People's Savings and Trust Company held a first mortgage on a building. Munsert sold and installed, subsequent to the mortgage, an expensive sprinkler system. The owner of the building defaulted in his payments, and the mortgagee brought suit to foreclose on the mortgage. The question arose as to whether or not the real estate mortgage attached to the sprinkler system. Did the sprinkler system become a part of the real estate? (People's Savings and Trust Company v. Munsert, 212 Wis. 449, 249 N. W. 527)

8. The Whellkin Coat Co. sent an expensive fur coat to Silberstein to be treated. While in Silberstein's possession, it was badly damaged due to a leaky roof which permitted water to enter the room where the coat was stored. Silberstein had rented only a portion of the building, so he had no control over the roof, hallways, and other parts of the building. The Whellkin Coat Company sued the landlord for the damage to the coat. The landlord denied liability, claiming the tenant if anyone should be held liable. Who is liable in this case? (Whellkin Coat Co. v. Long Branch Trust Co., 1-21 N. J. L. 106, 1 A. 2d 394)

9. Stevens and Co. leased warehouses, wharves, and docks to Pratt. The lease provided that the lessor would keep the premises in a good state of repair. He failed to do this even though several demands were made upon him to do so. The lessee then abandoned the property and refused to pay any more rent. Must the tenant pay rent? (John B. Stevens & Co. v. Pratt, 119 Wash. 232, 205 Pac. 10)

GLOSSARY OF LEGAL TERMS

(Other legal terms are defined elsewhere in the text. Refer to the Index for them.)

Abrogate: recall or repeal; abolish entirely.

Absolute liability: liability for an act that causes harm even though the doer was not at fault.

Acceleration clause: provision in a contract or any legal instrument that upon a certain event the time for the performance of specified obligations shall be advanced.

Acceptance: an accepted draft; the assent by the person on whom a draft is drawn to pay it when due.

Acceptor: one who assents to an order or a draft.

Accession: acquisition of title to property by virtue of the fact that it has been attached to property already owned.

Accommodation party: a person who signs a negotiable instrument as a favor to another.

Accord and satisfaction: an agreement made and executed in satisfaction of the rights one has acquired under a former contract.

Accretion: acquisition of title to additional land when the owner's land is built up by gradual deposits made by the natural action of water.

Accused: a person charged with a criminal offense.

Acknowledgment: the admission of the execution of a writing made before a competent officer; the formal certificate made by an officer.

Acquittal: the action of a jury in a finding of not guilty.

Act of God: an act of nature that is not reasonably foreseeable.

Action: proceedings at law.

Adjudication: a judicial determination.

Administrator—administratrix: the person (man—woman) appointed by a court to take charge of the estate of a deceased person.

Adult: one who has reached full legal age.

Adverse possession: the hostile possession of real estate, which when actual, visible, notorious, exclusive, and continued for the required number of years, will place title to the land in the person in possession.

Affidavit: a voluntary sworn statement in writing.

Affirm: to declare to tell the truth under a penalty of perjury; to confirm.

Agency: the relationship that exists between a person identified as a principal and another by virtue of which the latter may make contracts with third persons on behalf of the principal.

Agent: one who is authorized by the principal to make contracts with third persons on behalf of the principal.

Alias: Latin word meaning "another name"; an assumed name.

Alibi: a plea of having been in another place when a wrongful act was committed.

Alien: a citizen of one country residing in another.

Alienate: to transfer voluntarily the title to real property.

Alimony: an allowance made to a woman living apart from her husband.

Allegation: a statement of a fact in a legal proceeding.

Alteration: a change or a substitution of one thing for another.

Ambiguity: doubtfulness; the state of having two or more possible meanings.

Annuity: a sum payable yearly for a certain or an uncertain period.

Annulment: the act of making void.

Answer: a written statement of the defendant's claim, as to the facts in a suit in equity; response; reply.

Antedate: a date prior to the true one; an earlier date.

Appeal: taking the case to a reviewing court to determine whether the judgment of the lower court was correct.

Arbitration: the trial and determination of a controversy by persons chosen by the parties to the dispute.

Arraign: to accuse; to impeach; to read the charge of an indictment.

Assault: to attempt to do harm to another by physical violence.

Assent: to consent; to concur.

Assets: property available for the payment of debts.

Assign: to transfer property or a right to another.

Assignee: one to whom property has been assigned.

Assignment: transfer of a right. Used in connection with personal property rights, as rights under a contract, a negotiable instrument, an insurance policy, or a mortgage.

Attachment: the legal process by which property is seized in process of a debt settlement.

Attest: to bear witness.

Attorney: one legally appointed to act for another.

Avoid: to make void; to annul.

Award: the decision of arbitrators.

Bad check laws: laws making it a crime to issue a bad check with intent to defraud.

Baggage: articles of necessity or personal convenience usually carried for personal use by passengers of common carriers.

Bail: security given for the appearance of a person in court.

Bailment: the relation that exists when personal property is delivered into the possession of another under an agreement, express or implied, that the identical property will be returned or will be disposed of in accordance with the agreement.

Bankrupt: one who has been judicially discharged from the obligations of certain past claims.

Battery: the unlawful touching of another.

Bearer: the person in physical possession of a negotiable instrument payable to bearer.

Beneficiary: the person named in an insurance policy as the one who is to receive the proceeds or benefits accruing thereunder.

Bequest: a gift of personal property by will.

Bilateral: a contract executory on both sides.

Bill of lading: a document issued by a carrier showing the receipt of goods and the terms of the contract of transportation.

Bill of sale: a writing signed by the seller showing that he has sold to the buyer the personal property described.

Blue-sky laws: statutes designed to protect the public from the sale of worthless stocks and bonds.

Bona fide: in good faith; without deceit or fraud; genuine.

Bond: an instrument under seal, in which a person binds himself to pay to another a sum of money.

Breach: in contracts, the violation of an agreement or obligation.

Brief: written or printed arguments or authorities furnished by a lawyer to a court.

Burglary: the breaking open and entering of a dwelling with the intent to commit a felony.

Capital: net assets of a corporation.

Capital stock: the declared money value of the outstanding stock of the corporation.

Case: an occurrence upon which an action in court is based.

Caveat emptor: let the buyer beware.

Charter: the grant of authority from a government to exist as a corporation.

Chattel: any article of personal property.

Chattel mortgage: a security device by which the owner of personal property transfers the title to a creditor as security for the debt owed by the owner to the creditor.

Client: one who employs a lawyer to represent him in legal matters.

Closed shop: a place of employment in which only union members may be employed. Now generally prohibited by statutes.

Code: a compilation of laws by public authority.

Codicil: an addition of supplement to a will.

Collusion: a secret agreement between two or more persons, designed to obtain an object forbidden by law or to defraud another.

Commission merchant: a bailee to whom goods are consigned for sale.

Common carrier: a carrier that holds out its facilities to serve the general public for compensation without discrimination.

Competency: legal power, adequacy, or ability.

Composition of creditors: an agreement among creditors that each shall accept a part payment as full payment in consideration of the other creditors doing the same.

Compromise: a settlement reached by mutual concessions.

Conditional sale: a credit transaction by which the buyer purchases on credit and promises to pay the purchase price in installments, while the seller retains the title to the goods, together with the right of repossession upon default, until the condition of payment in full has been satisfied.

Consanguinity: relationship by blood.

Consignee: one to whom goods are shipped.

Contract of record: name sometimes given to a judgment of a court.

Conveyance: an act by which the title to real property is transferred.

Cooperative: a group of two or more persons or enterprises that act through a common agent with respect to a common objective, as buying or selling.

Corporation: an artificial legal person or being created by law, which for many purposes is treated as a natural person.

Corporeal: material; tangible; substantial.

Counterclaim: a claim that the defendant in an action may make against the plaintiff.

Covenant: a promise contained in a sealed instrument; a solemn compact.

Coverture: the status or condition of a woman during marriage.

Crime: a violation of the law that is punished as an offense against the state or government.

Curator: a legally appointed custodian of property.

Custody: care, possession, or keeping of property.

Damages: compensation that the law awards for a wrong or an injury done.

Deceit: a device of false representation by which one person misleads another to the latter's injury.

Decree: the decision of a court of equity or admiralty.

Default: the nonperformance of a duty or an obligation.

Defendant: a person against whom a suit is brought.

Defense: that which is relied upon by a defendant to defeat an action; the resistance to an attack.

Del credere agent: an agent who sells goods for the principal and guarantees that the buyer will pay for the goods.

Demur: to raise an objection as to legal sufficiency.

Deposition: testimony taken down in writing under oath.

Descent: the hereditary succession to an estate.

Disability: incapacity for the performance of a legal act.

Disaffirm: to repudiate; to refuse to confirm.

Divorce: the dissolution of the marriage ties.

Domicile: the place where a person has his permanent home.

Duress: constraint or compulsion.

Easement: the right that one person has to use the land of another for a special purpose.

Embezzlement: the fraudulent appropriation of property by a person to whom it has been entrusted.

Emblements: growing crops that have been sown or planted.

Enact: to make into a law.

Equitable: just; fair; right; reasonable.

Escrow: a written document held by a third person until the happening of a prescribed condition.

Estate: an interest in property.

Estoppel: that which precludes a man from denying or affirming certain facts in consequence of his previous conduct or admissions.

Eviction: the expulsion of an occupant of real property.

Evidence: documents, exhibits, and other facts introduced in a trial.

Ex parte: upon or from one side only.

Execution: a writ which authorizes an officer to carry into effect the judgment of the court.

Executor: the person named by the maker of a will to carry out its provisions.

Extradition: the surrender by one government to another of a person charged with a crime.

Extraordinary bailment: a bailment in which the bailee is subject to unusual duties and liabilities, as a hotelkeeper or common carrier.

Factor: an agent appointed to sell goods on commission.

Felony: a criminal offense that is punishable by confinement in prison or by death, or that is expressly stated by statute to be a felony.

Fiduciary: involving a relation of trust or confidence.

Forbearance: refraining from doing an act.

Foreclosure: a proceeding by which the right of the mortgagor to redeem his property is extinguished.

Forfeiture: the loss of some right or privilege.

Franchise: a right or privilege conferred by law.

Garnishment: a process whereby property is attached.

Guardian: one who has the care of a person or property.

Heir: one who inherits property by right of relationship.

Hotelkeeper: one regularly engaged in the business of offering living accommodations to all transients.

Incidental authority: authority of an agent that is reasonably necessary to execute his express authority.

Indemnity: compensation for loss sustained.

Indenture: a writing in two parts containing a seal.

Independent contractor: a contractor who undertakes to perform a specified task according to the terms of a contract but over whom the other contracting party has no control except as provided for by the contract.

Indictment: a formal charge preferred by a grand jury.

Infant: any person not of full legal age.

Injunction: a judicial order or decree forbidding the doing of a certain act.

Insolvency: the state of being unable to pay one's debts.

Instrument: a written document.

International law: law observed by independent nations in their intercourse with one another.

Intestate: one who dies without having made a valid will.

Invalid: void; of no legal effect.

Joint and several contract: a contract in which two or more persons are jointly and severally obligated or are jointly and severally entitled to recover.

Joint contract: a contract in which two or more persons are jointly liable or jointly entitled to performance under the contract.

Joint tenancy: the estate held by two or more jointly with the right of survivorship as between them.

Judgment: a decision of a court.

Legacy: a gift of personal property by will.

Legal: authorized or prescribed by law.

Legal tender: such form of money as the law recognizes as lawful and declares that a tender thereof in the proper amount is a proper tender which the creditor cannot refuse.

Legatee: one to whom a legacy is given.

Levy: to take possession of property to satisfy a judgment.

Libel: defamation of another without legal justification.

License: a permit to do an act which would otherwise be unlawful.

Lien: a right to control, hold, and retain, or enforce a charge against another's property as security for a debt or claim.

Limited liability: loss of contributed capital as maximum liability.

Liquidated damages: the amount agreed upon in advance by the parties to a contract, to be paid in case of a breach.

Litigation: a suit at law, a judicial contest.

Malfeasance: the doing of some wrongful act.

Malice: ill will towards some person.

Mandamus: a writ issued by a court directing the performance of certain acts.

Merger: an absorption, union, or extinguishment of one contract or interest in another.

Minor: any person not of full legal age.

Misrepresentation: a false statement of fact.

Negligence: the omission to do what a reasonable, prudent person would do, or doing what such a person would not have done.

Negotiation: the transfer of a negotiable instrument by indorsement and delivery by the person to whom then payable in the case of order paper, and by physical transfer in the case of bearer paper.

Nominal damages: a trifling sum given for the violation of a right where no actual loss has resulted.

Nuisance: something which wrongfully disturbs, annoys, or injures another.

Obligation: a duty.

Ordinance: a rule of law passed by the legislative body of a city.

Ouster: ejection; dispossession.

Parole: the promise of a prisoner that in return for conditional freedom he will follow certain requirements.

Pawn: a pledge of tangible personal property.

Per se: in itself.

Perjury: willful false testimony under oath in a judicial proceeding.

Plaintiff: one who brings an action in a court.

Postdate: to insert or place a later date on an instrument than the actual date on which it was executed.

Price: the consideration for a sale of goods.

Prima facie: at first view; apparently true; on the first appearance.

Probate: a court having jurisdiction over estates.

Property: the rights and interests one has in anything subject to ownership.

Prosecute: to proceed against by legal means.

Protest: formal certification that proper presentment of a negotiable instrument was made to the primary party and that he defaulted.

Proxy: a substitute; a person authorized to act for another.

Ratification: confirming an act which was executed without authority or an act which was voidable.

Realty: real property.

Reasonable care: that degree of care that a reasonable man would take under all the circumstances then known.

Receiver: a person appointed by a court to take charge of property pending litigation.

Redemption: the buying back of one's property which has been sold because of a default.

Release: the surrender or relinquishment to another of a right, claim, interest, or estate.

Remedy: means employed to enforce a duty or redress a wrong.

Replevin: an action to recover possession of property unlawfully detained.

Rescission: cancelling, annulling, avoiding.

Revocation: the annulment or cancellation of an instrument, act, or promise by one doing or making it.

Sentence: the penalty pronounced upon a person convicted of a crime.

Several contracts: separate or independent contracts made by different persons undertaking to perform the same obligation.

Slander: defamation of character by spoken words or gestures.

SS. or ss.: abbreviation for the Latin word scilicet, meaning, to wit; namely; that is to say.

Stare decisis: the principle that the decision of a court should serve as a guide or precedent and control the decision of a similar case in the future.

Subpoena: a writ commanding a person to appear as a witness.

Suit: the prosecution of some claim in a court of justice.

Summons: a notice to a person to appear in court.

Syndicate: an association of individuals formed to conduct a particular business transaction, generally of a financial nature.

Testimony: statements of witnesses.

Third-party beneficiary: a third person whom the parties to a contract intend to benefit by the making of the contract.

Tort: a private injury or wrong arising from a breach of a duty created by law.

Trespass: an unwarranted invasion of another's right.

Trustee: one who holds property for the benefit of another.

Ultra vires: beyond the power, exceeding authority.

Unilateral: one-sided, applied to contracts where only one promise is still unperformed.

Usury: the taking of more than the legal rate of interest.

Valid: legal.

Venue: the place where the trial is held.

Verdict: a decision rendered by a jury.

Versus: against (abbreviated vs. and v.).

Void: no legal effect and not binding on anyone.

Voidable: a transaction that may be set aside by one party because of fraud or similar reason but which is binding on the other party until the injured party elects to set the contract aside.

Voting trust: the transfer by two or more persons of their shares of stock of a corporation to a trustee who is to vote the shares and act for such shareholders.

Waiver: the voluntary surrender or relinquishment of a right or privilege.

Waste: damage or destruction to property done or permitted by a tenant.

Will: an instrument executed with the formality required by law, by which a person makes a disposition of his property to take effect upon his death.

Witness: a person who gives testimony in court; one who sees a document executed and signs his name thereto.

Works of charity: in connection with Sunday laws, acts involved in religious worship or aiding persons in distress.

Works of necessity: in connection with Sunday laws, acts that must be done at the particular time in order to save life, health, or property.

Writ: a formal written command issued by a court of law.

INDEX

497